THE SATIRES OF HORACE

THE SATIRES OF HORACE

A STUDY BY

NIALL RUDD

Associate Professor of Classics at
University College, Toronto

CAMBRIDGE
AT THE UNIVERSITY PRESS
1966

PUBLISHED BY

THE SYNDICS OF THE CAMBRIDGE UNIVERSITY PRESS

Bentley House, 200 Euston Road, London, N.W. 1
American Branch: 32 East 57th Street, New York, N.Y. 10022
West African Office: P.M.B. 5181, Ibadan, Nigeria

©

CAMBRIDGE UNIVERSITY PRESS

1966

Printed in Great Britain at the University Printing House, Cambridge
(Brooke Crutchley, University Printer)

LIBRARY OF CONGRESS CATALOGUE
CARD NUMBER: 66–11031

To my wife Nancy

CONTENTS

Preface   *page* ix

Abbreviations   xi

   I   The Diatribes of Book 1 (1.1, 1.2, 1.3)   1

  II Poet and Patron (1) (1.6)   36

 III Entertainments (1.5, 1.7, 1.8, 1.9)   54

 IV Horace and Lucilius (1.4, 1.10, 2.1)   86

   V The Names   132

 VI The Diatribes of Book 2 (2.2, 2.3, 2.7)   160

 VII Food and Drink (2.4, 2.8)   202

VIII A Consultation (2.5)   224

 IX Poet and Patron (2) (2.6)   243

Appendix: Dryden on Horace and Juvenal   258

Notes   274

Bibliographical Note   308

Indexes

   1 Horatian Passages Quoted or Referred to   309

   2 Names and Topics   312

PREFACE

In spite of their intrinsic quality and their immense influence on eighteenth-century literature, there has never been a full-length study of the *Satires* in English. Such neglect might seem to indicate a prejudice against Horatian satire, until one recalls that there was no comprehensive book on Ovid before 1945 or on Juvenal before 1954 or on Livy before 1961, and that there is still no such work on Propertius, Persius, Petronius, Lucan or Pliny. There are many reasons for this—not all of them discreditable. But to discuss them fully would be too complex a task and anyhow this would be no place to attempt it. Instead it will perhaps be enough to state the facts as above, bringing them to the attention of those who assume that Roman literature is 'worked out'.

The present book is intended mainly for university students and for teachers of Latin who are not Horatian specialists. But I hope it may also be of interest to non-Latinists and may help in some small way to bridge the alarming gap which has opened in the last fifty years between ancient and modern literary studies. As most people will probably wish to read the book without having to refer to a text, I have made fairly extensive use of translation and paraphrase. I have also tried to bring out the main lines of interpretation by consigning certain types of argument and comment to the notes. It is hoped that as a result it may be possible to read each chapter through without distraction and, in general, to use the book as a book instead of as a work of reference.

My thanks are due to the editors of the *Classical Quarterly*, *Hermathena*, *Phoenix* and the *University of Toronto Quarterly* for allowing me to reproduce in a revised form material which had previously appeared in those journals, and also to the Dial Press, New York, for permission to quote a stanza from a poem by Morris Bishop printed in *A Bowl of Bishop* (Dial Press Inc. 1954).

Grants from the President's Travel Fund enabled me to work in Oxford and Tübingen during two vacations, and a subvention from the Humanities Research Council of Canada helped to reduce the cost of printing. My colleagues in University College, Toronto—especially Professors Bagnani, Goold, Rist and Sumner—all gave help on points of detail. Mr R. G. M. Nisbet read certain chapters in draft form; Professor A. Dalzell read the whole work in typescript; and both scholars made perceptive criticisms. I would also thank those who, at different stages, read the book for the Cambridge University Press. Their vigilance has removed many errors. My chief debt, however, is to those who have worked on the *Satires* in the past. The commentaries of Palmer, Lejay and Heinze—'men whom one cannot hope to emulate'—have been on my desk for over ten years. I have often consulted the translations of Wickham and Fairclough; and one must not forget the small, but compact and independent edition of James Gow. Like so many scholars in other branches of classical philology I owe a great deal to the work of Professor Eduard Fraenkel. The chapters on the *Satires* in his *Horace* represent a major contribution to the subject, and where I have taken a different line I have done so with hesitation.

In writing a book of general interpretation it was necessary to touch on a number of matters about which I had little first-hand knowledge. What these matters are will be apparent soon enough, and I can only hope that the various experts will not be too grossly affronted. As the manuscript was finished at the end of 1964 I was unable to take account of anything which appeared after that date. Various other kinds of apology and justification come crowding in, but the moment has arrived when instead of prolonging his excuses the writer must finally grit his teeth and say *i, libelle!*

N. R.

University College, Toronto
January 1966

ABBREVIATIONS

AJP	*American Journal of Philology.*
Aristippus M.	*Aristippi et Cyrenaicorum Fragmenta*, ed. E. Mannebach (Leiden, 1961).
Cichorius	C. Cichorius, *Untersuchungen zu Lucilius* (Berlin, 1908).
CJ	*Classical Journal.*
CP	*Classical Philology.*
CQ	*Classical Quarterly.*
CR	*Classical Review.*
CW	*Classical World.*
Democritus D.	Diels' numeration of Democritus' fragments as found in Kathleen Freeman, *Ancilla to the Pre-Socratic Philosophers* (Oxford, 1956).
D.L.	Diogenes Laertius.
Edmonds	J. M. Edmonds, *The Fragments of Attic Comedy* (Leiden, 1961).
Fiske	G. C. Fiske, *Lucilius and Horace* (Madison, 1920).
Fraenkel	Eduard Fraenkel, *Horace* (Oxford, 1957).
JRS	*Journal of Roman Studies.*
Lucilius W.	*Remains of Old Latin*, III, Lucilius, edited and translated by E. H. Warmington (Loeb Classical Library, 1957).
Menander K.	Kock's numeration of Menander's fragments as found in the Loeb translation of Menander by F. G. Allinson.
Mnem.	*Mnemosyne.*
Phil.	*Philologus.*
P–W	Pauly–Wissowa–Kroll, *Real-Encyclopädie der Classischen Altertumswissenschaft.*
Rh. Mus.	*Rheinisches Museum.*
TAPA	*Transactions of the American Philological Association.*
Teles	*Teletis Reliquiae*, ed. O. Hense (Tübingen, 1909).
Varro B.	*Varronis Menippearum Reliquiae*, ed. Bücheler–Heraeus, reprinted with F. Bücheler's edition of Petronius (Berlin, 1958).
Wien. Stud.	*Wiener Studien.*

Note

The notes are to be found on pp. 274–307.

CHAPTER I

THE DIATRIBES OF BOOK 1

I.1, I.2, I.3

In the mid-twentieth century sermons are out of fashion. We submit with varying degrees of apathy to being told what to eat, how to dress, and where to spend our holidays, but if anyone presumes to lecture us on our moral character we regard it as the height of impertinence. This might seem to tell against any effort to revive interest in Horace's *Satires*, for although the collection contains several entertainment-pieces and some literary criticism its reputation must stand or fall by the diatribes, and the diatribes are essentially sermons.

They are sermons, however, of a rather special kind. They do not call for allegiance to any divine power or any sacred writings, nor do they urge us to repent and seek salvation. Their only appeal is to common sense. What is it, they ask, that makes man unhappy? Horace's age, like our own, was one of exceptional strain and anxiety. Under the threat of war men wore themselves out in competitive money-making, in romantic attachments which had no future, and in the endless struggle for power and prestige. Was all this striving really necessary? Why not, in our own phrase, withdraw from the rat-race and live quietly with one's friends? The suggestion was not meant, of course, to convert the Roman intelligentsia into a society of non-attached saints. Horace was no Gandhi. But he did see that a great many people who were, by his own standards, sufficiently well off never quite managed to enjoy what they had. And he made bold to point this out in poems which for good humour, lightness of touch, and absence of priggishness have never been surpassed.

The first three diatribes are broadly similar in structure. I shall begin with the third, because it is the most straightforward and

I   I   RSH

also the most neglected. Here is a translation based mainly on the Oxford text:

Singers are all the same. When asked to perform for their friends they never will; when *not* asked they never stop. Tigellius, that typical Sardinian, had the same kink. If Caesar (who could have ordered a recital) had requested one on the strength of Tigellius' friendship with his father and himself, he would have wasted his time. Yet when he felt in the mood the fellow would keep breaking into 'Ho, ye Bacchanals!' throughout an entire meal, one moment singing in a high tenor and the next in a deep bass in tune with the lowest note of the
8 tetrachord.

The fellow was a bundle of inconsistencies; often he would dash along as if someone were after his blood, more often you would think he was carrying the sacred vessels of Juno. Sometimes he would keep a couple of hundred servants, sometimes only a dozen. One day he would talk in a high and mighty way about kings and princes he had known, the next he'd say 'I ask for nothing but a three-legged table, a shell of pure salt, and a cloak, no matter how coarse, to keep out the cold'. If you'd given a thousand pounds to that model of thrift and simplicity it would have burnt a hole in his pocket in less than a week. He never went to bed until dawn, and then spent the whole day snoring. He was
19 the most contradictory creature that ever lived.

Now someone may say to me 'What about yourself? Have *you* no faults?' Indeed I have, but they are different and perhaps less serious. Once when Maenius was pulling Novius to pieces behind his back, somebody said 'Just a minute. Are you blind to your own character, or do you think you can blind us?' 'Oh, where *I'm* concerned I just turn a blind eye', said Maenius. That kind
24 of egotism is stupid and brazen, and ought to be roundly condemned.

How is it that before you examine your own faults you smear your sore eyes with ointment, but when it comes to the failings of your friends your sight is as sharp as an eagle's or an Epidaurian snake's? The result is, however, that they in their turn also scrutinize *your* failings. So-and-so's a bit hot-tempered and not quite up to the fastidious standards of modern society; he may cause amusement by his countrified haircut, the sloppy fit of his toga, and by shoes a size too large which only just stay on his feet. Nevertheless, he's a good man— none better, *and* he's your friend, *and* there's a prodigious talent lurking behind that uncouth exterior. So just give yourself a thorough shaking in case the seeds of wickedness have already been planted in you, whether by nature her- self or through some bad habit. For if you once neglect a field, bracken appears
37 and eventually has to be burnt out.

Let's consider instead how a young man blindly in love fails to notice his sweetheart's unsightly blemishes, or is even charmed by them as Balbinus was by Hagna's wen. I only wish we made the same sort of mistake when judging our friends and that this delusion had an honourable name in the language of decent

2

people. At any rate if a friend happens to have some defect we shouldn't view it with disgust, but should follow the example of a father with his son. If the boy has a squint his father calls him 'Boss-eye', if he is miserably undersized as the dwarfish Sisyphus used to be he is called 'Chick', if his knees knock together he is called 'Hen-toe', if he is so bandy that he can hardly stand then his father's pet name for him is 'Splay-foot'. So if one of our friends is rather close-fisted let's say he is thrifty; if another is inclined to be tactless and loud-mouthed, well, he wants his friends to think him sociable; or suppose he's rather ill-mannered, and outspoken to the point of rudeness, then let's call him forthright and fearless. Is he something of a hot-head? Then put him down as a keen type. In my view this habit both joins and cements friendships.   54

But in practice we turn the *good* qualities upside down, and we love to sling mud at a white fence. If one of our acquaintances is a decent, genuinely un-assuming fellow, we nickname him 'Slowcoach' or 'Fathead'. Another escapes every trap and never leaves himself open to malicious attack, for we are engaged in a life where envy is sharp and slander active. Instead of saying he's a wise fellow and no fool, we call him insincere and crafty. If a man has rather an open manner (and is the sort of fellow that I would often be glad to have you think me, Maecenas) so that he breaks in with some chatty remarks when his friend is perhaps reading or in silent thought, we say 'What a nuisance! He's got absolutely no *savoir faire*'.

How thoughtless of us to endorse a law which works against ourselves! For no one on earth is free from faults. The best is he who has to cope with the smallest. My kindly friend should, as is only fair, weigh my virtues against my failings, and if he wants my affection he should come down on the side of my virtues as being more numerous (provided of course they *are* more numerous!). On that principle he will be weighed in the same scales. If you expect your friend not to be put off by your boils, you will overlook his warts. It is fair that anyone who asks indulgence for *his* faults should grant the same in return.   75

Since, then, anger and the other failings which are ingrained in foolish mortals cannot be wholly cut out, why does Reason not use weights and measures of her own and suppress each type of offence with appropriate punish-ments? Suppose a servant who has been told to clear away a dish takes a lick at the half-eaten fish and the lukewarm sauce; if his master had him crucified, sane people would swear he was more insane than Labeo. How much madder and more serious a fault is this: a friend is guilty of some trivial offence which it would be churlish not to forgive, yet you hate him bitterly and avoid his company like some poor devil who owes Ruso money and just *has* to scrape up the interest or principal from somewhere before the grim first of the month or else put up his hands like a prisoner of war and listen to Ruso's histories with teeth on edge. What if a friend in a tipsy moment wets the couch or knocks off the table an old bowl worn down by the fingers of Evander? Or say he is feeling hungry and snatches up a pullet which has been served in my side of the dish, shall I like him any the less for that? What would I do if he stole something or betrayed a trust or broke his word of honour? Those who hold that all sins are much the same are in a quandary when faced with actual situations. Common sense and tradition say no, and so does Expediency herself who is 98 virtually the mother of what is right and fair.

When living things crawled forth from the earth, which was still young, they were inarticulate, brutish creatures. They fought over their acorns and lairs with nails and fists, then with clubs, and so on, step by step, with the weapons shaped by experience. Eventually they discovered verbs and nouns which enabled them to give meaning to their cries and feelings. From that point they began to give up war, to build towns, and to pass laws against theft, brigandage and adultery. For Helen was not the first bitch to cause a war by her foul behaviour; but men in those days died in obscurity, making love hurriedly and promiscuously like animals and being done to death in the act by someone physically stronger, as in a herd one bull is destroyed by his rival. If you turn the pages of world history you will have to admit that justice arose from the fear of injustice. Nature cannot distinguish right from wrong as she distinguishes desirable from undesirable and the beneficial from its opposite. Nor will Reason ever prove that the man who breaks off a juicy cabbage in someone else's garden and the man who makes off at night with the holy emblems of the gods are committing one and the same offence. Let's have a scale to fix fair penalties for offences, otherwise you may flay with the terrible cat something which deserves no more than the strap. You might, of course, give a caning for some crime which deserved the lash, but that's not what I'm afraid of when you say larceny is on a par with armed robbery and threaten to use the same hook for pruning all crimes great and small if you were given the 124 crown.

But if the wise man alone is rich and handsome and a good cobbler and a king, why ask for something you already have? 'You don't understand', he says, 'what our father Chrysippus means. The wise man has never made himself shoes or sandals; nevertheless the wise man is a cobbler.' How's that? 'Well, even when he's silent Hermogenes is still a first-rate singer and musician; that clever fellow Alfenus even after throwing away all the tools of his trade and shutting up shop was still a cobbler; so too the wise man is the sole master of every craft, hence he is a king.'

Cheeky youngsters tug at your beard, and if you don't keep them at bay with your stick they swarm round and hem you in, while you, poor devil, roar till you burst your lungs—O highest of Royal Highnesses! In short, as you tread your kingly way to a sixpenny bath, with no one in attendance except that ass Crispinus, my friends will be kind enough to forgive me if I, a mere fool, do something wrong; I in turn will gladly forget their lapses, and (though only a commoner) I shall live a happier life than Your Majesty.

4

On studying the poem we find that the argument is presented in the following sequence:

Opening passage (1–19). The perversity of singers in general is illustrated by the case of Tigellius, but it soon becomes clear that Tigellius' vocal habits were but one example of his unbalanced behaviour—*nil aequale homini fuit illi* (9). Other examples follow, which are then rounded off by *nil fuit umquam | sic impar sibi* (18–19). Three cases (his spasmodic singing, his unpredictable gait, and the varying number of his slaves) have to do with in-consistent behaviour. The fourth is rather different: one day he would brag about kings and princes, the next affirm his devotion to the simple life. This points to inconsistent talk. We then hear that these professions of frugality were completely bogus—'If you'd given a thousand pounds to that model of thrift and simpli-city it would have burnt a hole in his pocket in less than a week.' So here the inconsistency is between words and deeds. Finally, in staying up until dawn and then spending the day snoring Tigellius was not so much inconsistent as abnormal. This method of establishing and then varying a pattern is typically Horatian.

Transitional passage (19–24). A listener now intervenes, saying 'What about you? Have you no faults?' 'Why yes,' says Horace, 'but they are different and perhaps less serious.' A man like Maenius who backbites his friends is often blind or indifferent to his own defects. Such complacency is reprehensible: *stultus et improbus hic amor est dignusque notari*. This leads us into the first main section of the poem, which is a plea for tolerance amongst friends.

But if that is Horace's real concern, what is the function of the opening passage? We can see that the epigram on singers and the comic description of Tigellius are meant to provide an arresting introduction which, by leading casually to the main topic, will prevent the treatment from appearing too formal and precise. The poem, after all, is a conversation-piece, not a dissertation. We still wonder, however, whether there is any connexion of theme. Fraenkel says there is none.[1] Others believe that by his own ridicule of Tigellius Horace has given a specimen of the behaviour which he is about to attack. This idea contains a germ of truth, in that both passages have to do with personal criticism. But Horace does not really fall under his own censure. Tigellius was now dead, and there is no suggestion that Horace was ever his friend. Also, unlike the scoffers mentioned in the main section, the poet was well aware of his own shortcomings. I believe, however, that the two parts are connected, and I hope the nature of the connexion will become clear in what follows.

First main section (25-75). If you are harsh in judging your friends, they will be harsh towards you. If a man is a little too hot-tempered (*iracundior*) or if he is a bit slovenly in appearance (*rusticius*) we should remember that he has other, admirable, qualities and that we ourselves are not perfect. Lovers are blind to each other's blemishes. 'I wish we made the same sort of mistake when judging our friends and that this delusion had an honourable name in the language of decent people' (38-42). Fathers give charitable names to their children's physical defects. (Notice how the idea of naming acts as a link between the two thoughts.) The same kindliness should be extended to our friends. If, for instance, a man is inclined to be boorish and too outspoken (*truculentior atque | plus aequo liber*), we should regard him as open and forthright. But in fact we do the very opposite (55). If a man is a bit too open in his manner (*simplicior*) we say 'He has absolutely no *savoir faire*'. Then, reverting to the idea with which the section opened, Horace observes how quick we are to pass an unfair law (*legem iniquam*) against ourselves. For no one is faultless. A kindly friend will, as is only fair (*aequum*), weigh one's virtues against one's shortcomings. In such matters it is fair (*aequum*) to give and take.

The comparatives, some of which are quoted above, indicate the sort of excess that constitutes a moral fault. In the case of a friend, however, we should minimize such faults by interpreting them in the kindliest possible way. This indulgence is not strict justice, but it is humane (*aequum*). Yet in another sense the *aequitas*

6

required is quite objective and forbids any feelings of moral superiority; for we are also told to weigh the man's virtues against his faults. (Since the man is our friend it is assumed that the good will preponderate.) And finally we are to weigh his faults against our own. The first main section, therefore, is about *aequitas* or fairness. It will now be recalled that the opening passage dealt with the related concept of *aequabilitas* or consistency. Here the connexion lies in the fact that men like Maenius (21–3) and the person described in vv. 25–7—men who pounce on other people's faults while ignoring their own—are not only inconsistent but also unfair.

Second main section (76–118). Denique ('moreover') points forward, but instead of a sharp break we get a recapitulation. The progress of thought has been 'Everyone has his faults, so let us be fair in our judgements'. Moving from friendship to society as a whole, Horace now says 'Everyone is prone to do wrong, so let us be fair in our punishments'. He has been talking of *vitia* (68 and 70); therefore instead of saying *ira* he says *vitium irae* (76). He has just mentioned boils and warts (73–4); with these still half in mind he says 'Since the vice of anger cannot be wholly *cut out*'. He has spoken of weighing virtues against defects (70–2), so he now calls on Reason to use her own *weights and measures* (78) in determining punishments. The new element, namely crime and punishment, is left to the very end of the sentence, and thus the transition is accomplished. There follow in vv. 80–95 various examples of cruel retribution, which correspond to the examples of harsh judgement in the previous section. Then, at v. 96, the target comes into full view. It is the orthodox Stoic, who believes that all sins are equal (*paria esse...peccata*). As Horace has already indicated, such a belief is simply inapplicable to the realities of social life. He now goes on to show that it is also mistaken in principle, for it affronts Self-Interest or Expediency (*Utilitas*), which is 'virtually the mother of justice and fairness' (98).

The word *Utilitas*, especially when combined with *sensus* and *mores*, has strong Epicurean associations which prepare us for the account of man's social evolution. A similar function is performed by the phrase *iusti prope mater et aequi*. Though apparently no more than a flourish to round off the paragraph, it introduces the idea of maternity, which is taken up by the image of mother earth in v. 99. More important, it points to the birth of laws. Like other features of civilization, laws are the product of need. They were worked out by man for his own protection, and since they are in essence social agreements rather than scientific discoveries they do not allow categorical judgements. Nature, as Horace says, cannot distinguish just from unjust (*iusto secernere iniquum*) as she distinguishes the beneficial from its opposite. That is, nature tells us it is wrong to eat deadly nightshade, but she says nothing about stealing a cabbage. This brings us back to the Stoics and their attempt to turn moral judgements into mathematical equations. For them stealing a cabbage would be no less serious than robbing a temple. *Peccet* (115) looks back to *peccata* (96), and the cases of theft in vv. 116–17 recall the theft in v. 94. The section is then summed up in the plea *adsit / regula, peccatis quae poenas irroget aequas* (117–18)—'Let us have a scale to fix fair penalties for offences'. There is nothing less equitable than the equality of sins.

Transitional passage (119–24). This opens, as often, with a subordinate clause tacked on to the end of the previous section—'lest you flay with the terrible cat something which calls for the strap'. This is taken up in v. 120: 'As for the chance of your giving too *light* a punishment, that's not what I'm afraid of when I hear you assert that larceny is on a par with armed robbery (*pares res*) and that you would use the same hook (*falce simili*) to prune all crimes great and small, if you were given charge of the kingdom.' Up to the last conditional clause we are still in touch with the equality of sins. But the mention of kingship leads into the final section, which is concerned with another Stoic tenet, namely that the true sage is a king. The whole sequence might be condensed as follows: Stoic social theory is impossible, since it flouts expediency, and social relations *function* by expediency; so do political relations, hence Stoic political theory is also impossible.

Final section (124–42). By calling the sage a king the Stoics meant that in virtue of his control over passion, his indifference to circumstances, and his willing acceptance of divine fate, he was superior to other men and hence was the only person fitted for kingship.[2] Horace understood this reasoning perfectly well, but the pretentiousness of the whole attitude annoyed him, and so he first reduces it to absurdity by making his Stoic adversary compare the potential king to a silent singer and a one-time cobbler; then he presents the sage as he really is—an object of derision.

So ends the most humane of all the diatribes. The picture of the royal sage forms a companion piece to the opening picture of Tigellius. At the same time it recalls the theme of forbearance by showing how the Stoic's harsh perfectionism has cut him off from the friendship of ordinary men. To the Stoic such ordinary men are fools (cf. the ironical *stultis* in v. 77 and *stultus* in v. 140); but to Horace the really foolish (*stultus* v. 24) are those who are so devoid of self-awareness that they condemn others while congratulating themselves.

The second satire begins with a brief obituary of Tigellius, observing how sadly his extravagance will be missed by all his raffish friends. Fufidius, however, is so afraid of extravagance that he never spends money; he only lends it—at ruinous interest. These and other unbalanced characters illustrate the text *nil medium est* (28)—'there is no middle course'. This theme continues for another eight lines, but from v. 28 all the examples of imbalance have been sexual. One man persists in adultery with society ladies, another confines his attention to the stews. After v. 36 the rest of the poem (four-fifths of the whole) is concerned with the folly of adultery and is therefore omitted from our English editions.

The game, it seems, is not worth the candle. One poor fellow when trapped throws himself off a roof, another is flogged, another raped by the husband's kitchen-boys, and another castrated (37–46). It is much wiser to choose freedwomen, for they represent a happy medium between married ladies and the lowest type of whore. But even here common sense is required; some fools have become so infatuated with these freedwomen that they've thrown away their money and reputation. Reverting to the hazards of adultery, Horace proceeds to give some sound tap-room advice: look here, the thing's simply an urge which has to be satisfied; why insist on social status? Anyhow, these high-class women are greatly over-rated; often you don't know what you're getting with those long dresses. And just think of the crowd they always have hanging round them. Now take my type of girl—she's lively and pretty, and everything's in the open without any nonsense. To go chasing after the other sort is sheer idiocy (47–110). Then (moving into the lounge): why not ascertain your minimum needs and distinguish what matters from what doesn't? When your throat's parched do you insist on a silver tankard? It's the same with women; that's why I go for the sort that's easy to get.

The closing lines recall some of the livelier scenes from *Tom Jones*:

When she slips her left side under my right she is Lady Ilia and the Countess Egeria—I call her what name I like. And when I'm hard at it I'm not afraid that her husband will come rushing back from the country, the hall door crash open, the dog bark, and the whole house reverberate with a terrible din; that the woman, deathly white, will jump out of bed, her maid (who is in the secret) will shriek and yell, and we'll all be in an agony of fear—the maid for her legs, the guilty mistress for her dowry, and I for myself. I have to flee barefoot with my clothes in disarray, otherwise it's all up with my cash or my backside or at least my good name. It's a grim business to be caught—I could prove that in court even before Fabius.[3]

The bawdy theme and treatment, the plentiful and aggressive use of names, and the absence of any reference to Maecenas all point to an early date. So does the rather uncertain structure. Up to v. 36, as we saw, the theme is *nil medium est*. The rest of the poem deals with the disadvantages of adultery compared with casual affairs. Now this would be quite consistent if Horace had kept a firm Aristotelian framework, rejecting the extremes of high and low society and recommending relations with an intermediate class. It would also be clear, though less consistent, if he had abandoned the idea of the mean and developed a simple two-term argument on the advantages of the 'call-girl' over married ladies. Unfortunately he appears to do now one, now the other, and the result is confusing.

A hint of the difficulty already occurs in vv. 31–6. Seeing a young man emerging from a brothel Cato congratulates him for sparing other men's wives. Cupiennius the adulterer comments 'I shouldn't care for such praise'. Probably Horace meant to censure both Cato and Cupiennius; for the foulness of *olenti in fornice* (30) carries over into *fornice* (31), and the lofty phrase *sententia dia Catonis* (32) is clearly ironical.[4] Nevertheless, the weight of Horace's attack falls so heavily on the adulterer that the brothel, which is represented as an *escape* from adultery, seems to be half condoned.

After expounding the tribulations of adulterers (37–46) Horace now recommends freedwomen as a happy medium between society wives and the lowest prostitutes. But he immediately adds that even this type of woman can ruin you if you fail to keep your head; there is no use in pleading that you've avoided adultery; your money and reputation are gone; what difference whether the cause is a *matrona* or an *ancilla togata* (63)? The position of the freedwoman as a desirable mean is therefore obscured, and Fraenkel goes so far as to say that 'dealings with an *ancilla togata* seem to be just as harmful as those with a *matrona*'.[5] Yet that is not quite the case, for it seems that a *matrona* invariably involves risk, whereas the other does not.

In vv. 64–79 Horace reverts to the hazards of adultery, and by now one may be wondering why he has let the other extreme (that is, the foul brothel) drop out of sight. Possibly it was because the only 'disadvantage' of the lowest whore as compared with the freedwoman was aesthetic, and this did not seem worth elaborating in a discussion whose primary aim was to distinguish amours which involved fear, trouble, deception and expense from those which did not. At any rate after v. 63 the *togata* no longer appears as an intermediate figure. When she returns in vv. 82 ff. she is treated as the simple antithesis of the *matrona*, and thus she comes to stand in a general way for cheap, available satisfaction 'with no strings attached'. The irrelevance of her intermediate position as a freedwoman is further underlined by the fact that in v. 117 her place is momentarily taken by two household servants, a girl and a boy.

While the structural uncertainties of 1. 2 are plain enough, there is much disagreement over 1. 1.[6] The extent of its unity may perhaps be seen if we set out the argument as follows. Men are discontented with their lot and envy those in other occupations. Why? *Answer*: because they want a change. But that can't *really* be the reason, for if offered a change they would not take it (1–22). If they don't like what they're doing, then why not give up? *Answer*: they want to save enough for a secure retirement. But that can't *really* be the reason, for even when they've saved enough they still go on making more (23–40). By now discontent is seen to proceed in some way from greed. Why, then, should a man be perpetually hoarding wealth? *Answer A*: because once you start to spend, the whole lot disappears. But use is money's only *raison d'être*. *Answer B*: it's *nice* to have a big pile. But enough is all you need. *Answer C*: money brings prestige. But this kind of prestige is purchased at the price of happiness. *Answer D*: money ensures attention when you're ill. In fact it does nothing of the kind. Such attention springs from love (41–91). After some further argument the opening topic is reintroduced in a modified form (108–9) and then developed in the next few lines. As a result of such envious greed, says Horace, few people can say they've had a happy life.

This summary, however, makes the poem appear more systematic than it is. Like 1. 3, it opens with an arresting generalization:

> qui fit, Maecenas, ut nemo, quam sibi sortem
> seu ratio dederit seu fors obiecerit, illa
> contentus vivat, laudet diversa sequentis?

How is it, Maecenas, that no one is content with his own way of life
—whether he has chosen it deliberately or taken it up by chance—
but envies those in other occupations?

Two pairs of examples follow: the soldier envies the merchant,
and the merchant envies the soldier; the lawyer envies the farmer,
but now the pattern varies, for the farmer envies not the lawyer
in particular but those who live in the city (12). Yet a connexion
with law is retained by bringing the farmer up to town for a
court case (*datis vadibus*). These types all grumble about their
jobs, and such grumbling, as we know, is often unrealistic. The
lawyer, for example, who complains about early clients, seems to
think that if he had been a farmer he could have lain in bed.
This lack of real seriousness is exposed by Horace, who points
out that if a god offered the grumblers a change of job they would
refuse. The chief point to note, however, is that this restless discontent, which the Greeks called μεμψιμοιρία, is here based on a
desire for easier work, not more money. When the types reappear
in vv. 28 ff., however, their yearning is said to be inspired by greed
(φιλαργυρία), a vice which occupies the central section of the
poem. We also note that the lawyer has been replaced by a crooked
innkeeper, presumably because the latter was thought to be a more
suitable example of avarice. The satire, therefore, is presented in
such a way as to suggest that the fundamental role of φιλαργυρία
only occurred to Horace in the course of writing. That is part of
the poem's informal aspect.
   We are faced with a rather similar situation at the end:

> illuc unde abii redeo: nemon, ut avarus,   108
> se probet ac potius laudet diversa sequentis?
> quodque aliena capella gerat distentius uber
> tabescat? neque se maiori pauperiorum
> turbae comparet? hunc atque hunc superare laboret?[7]

I return to my starting-point: is no one, because of his greed, to be
content with his own situation, and is every man to envy, instead,
those pursuing other ways of life? Because his neighbour's goat

carries a more bulging udder is he to be consumed with jealousy, instead of comparing himself with the thousands who are worse off? Is he to struggle to surpass first this man, then the other?

Horace clearly intends to conclude the poem by relating his main theme of φιλαργυρία to his opening remarks on μεμψιμοιρία. We can see that most of v. 108 and all of v. 109 refer back to the start, while the central theme is recalled by *ut avarus* (108) and by vv. 110–12, in so far as they describe greed. In combining the two subjects Horace alleges, as he has already done in vv. 28 ff., that the discontent of the grumblers is ultimately based on greed, and that they envy people in other occupations because the latter make more money. Secondly, he now suggests that the greedy man is eager to surpass all competitors. This is something of a new development, because, except for a strong hint in v. 40, such hostile emulation has played no part in the picture of the *avarus*. As a result of these modifications μεμψιμοιρία and φιλαργυρία both converge towards the larger concept of πλεονεξία. This vice had two complementary aims—more money for oneself and more money than other people.[8] And so within this idea, for which there is no Latin word, *avaritia* and *invidia* are as inseparable as concave and convex.

Structurally, then, these poems are alike in having an opening theme of about twenty verses introduced by some striking hyperbole or comic effect, and then illustrated in a series of antithetical pairs. A second, related theme then emerges and receives a much more extended treatment, though here too Horace avoids the appearance of a systematic arrangement by gliding casually from one topic to another.[9] In two cases there is a short final section recalling earlier motifs, and in all three the end is enlivened by a gibe at the expense of a living person. This subtle control can hardly be ascribed to Lucilius or to any other satirist before Horace. It is a personal achievement of a very high order, and it is one of the factors which caused Roman *satura*, in spite of its modest pretensions, to be reckoned as a serious poetic form.

Certain features of this poetry are already clear. First of all, it is concerned entirely with the behaviour of the individual in society. Institutions, whether political, religious or professional, are ignored, and when reference is made to a group of friends or relatives what matters is not the group as such but the private relations of its members. Moreover, this concern with the individual is largely a moral concern. Eccentricities of fashion, social *faux-pas*, odd habits of speech and dress, failures of taste, all the vanities and blunders which so enrich the eighteenth-century scene—these have but a small place in the Horatian diatribe. Instead the reader is laughed and argued out of his subjection to money (I. I), sex (I. 2), and power (I. 6)—the three most magnetic forces in his life and the most dangerous to his peace of mind. The rejection of malice and cruelty in social relations (I. 3) is scarcely less fundamental. These wide issues are handled in a suitably general way. The figures who come under attack (one cannot call them characters in the full sense) are etched with a few quick strokes—just enough to provide a neat illustration; then they vanish in the wake of the argument. One does not, of course, look for rounded characters in satire, but two-dimensional figures (like MacFlecknoe, for example) can be presented in such detail as to dominate a satiric poem. This never happens in Horace. Even Tigellius, the most elaborate of his cartoons, is confined to a couple of introductory passages and has no part in the major themes.

The modern reader, who expects to have his moral judgements evoked by more devious means, may find this straightforward preaching rather naïve. Without assuming that such a response is entirely to our credit, we *can* maintain that Horace often argues his case at a very superficial level. If, for instance, a man has taken a job because it happened to be available (I. I. 2), must he resign himself to it for the rest of his life? It may not suit his talents; it may cut him off from his friends; it may not pay even a decent minimum wage. Such criticisms, however, are really beside the point. Horace is not writing a philosophical disquisition. His argument is not intended to be comprehensive and unassailable.

It is quite enough if what he says is *often* true; and one does not need great insight to recognize that now, as in his day, a great deal of discontent *is* painful and unnecessary. As for Horace's phrasing, he does admittedly start off with a sweeping generalization, but anyone who holds that categorical *nemo* against him should give up reading satire altogether.

Finally, in its attitude to social conformity, the Horatian diatribe stands in contrast to two modern types of popular satire. One type, represented by magazines like *Punch* and the *New Yorker*, laughs at familiar forms of bourgeois behaviour. But the humour is usually so bland that it nourishes what it pretends to attack (like firing a water-pistol at a vegetable marrow). The victims, if they recognize themselves at all, are not in the least offended. They may be secretly grateful to the satirist for giving them some kind of identity in a featureless world. The other type, though purveyed in recent years on the professional stage, is essentially undergraduate in spirit. Its trademark is an exuberant mockery of everyone who forms or perpetuates an influential pattern; it is not concerned to establish any positive position of its own. This anarchic laughter can, of course, be highly entertaining, but we have to remember that it is only feasible in certain historical conditions. At other periods, like the eighteenth century and the end of the Roman Republic, satire will be seen as a social corrective. Its targets will be those who *deviate* from an acceptable norm, and it will use its traditional weapons in defence of balance and restraint.

Horace's satire is of this conservative kind, and to understand why, we must consider the intellectual climate in which he was writing. As so often, we have to start by going back to Athens. One of the most impressive features of the Athenian *polis* was its extraordinary integration. Religion and drama, art and sport were all associated with public worship, and the young were educated for a life in which they might become admirals, financial officials, and cabinet ministers, all within a few years. Such an organization gave the citizen an unusual *esprit de corps*, and with it a very high degree of participation and control. After the *polis* lost its independence in the latter half of the fourth century the authority of the Olympians, who had formerly guaranteed its safety, began to fade, and other strands which had held the unit in dynamic tension gradually went slack. The change can be seen most clearly in the New Comedy of Menander, which for all its charm lacks the political courage, the exuberant imagination, and the sheer rude energy of Aristophanes. So too, the post-Aristotelian philosophies reflect a world in which man has somehow lost the initiative in his struggle with life. Stoicism, Epicureanism, and Cynicism all teach that happiness can only be achieved by rendering oneself immune to shock. This immunity demands a careful discipline of the passions and a constant awareness that wealth, power, and sensual delight have no bearing on true contentment.

How, it may be asked, did these withdrawn, inward-looking systems exert such an influence on the Roman mind? First of all there is the simple fact that in the period after 200 B.C., when Rome's conquests brought her into close touch with Greek culture, these were the systems she encountered. Moreover, some of the extreme positions which had been adopted by the founders were modified in the course of time. This happened quite early in the case of Cynicism. The respect which people paid Diogenes for his independence and singlemindedness had always been tinged with horror at his rude unsociability. Crates of Thebes, however (who lived till about 290 B.C.), was an altogether more civilized figure. He spent less time denouncing his fellow-citizens and more in giving practical help. We are told that he would visit people's houses, reconciling enemies and cheering those in misfortune. He also took the very un-Cynical step of getting married, though admittedly our sources give the impression that Hipparchia made all the running and that Crates only said yes for the sake of peace.[10] Cynicism was further modified by Bion, the son of a fishmonger from the Black Sea port of Borysthenes.[11] After an unsuccessful attempt at tax evasion the father, with his whole family, was sold into slavery. Bion was lucky enough to be bought by a rhetorician who gave him an education and eventually left him enough money to move to Athens. Arriving there about 315 B.C. he seems to have spent some time in the Academy. Later he studied under Theodorus (an atheistic hedonist) and finally under Theophrastus the Peripatetic. Whereas Diogenes had practised an austere and often ill-tempered asceticism, Bion (influenced, no doubt, by Theodorus and Aristippus) said a man should enjoy any pleasure that came his way but should preserve a certain detachment so as to be ready for a change of fortune. Bion's other contribution lay in the field of homiletics (and here we can discern the influence of Theophrastus). Many of the techniques found in the Horatian diatribes, such as the fictitious adversary, character sketches, animal similes, allegorical personification, and verbal wit, had already been employed by Bion, and it is no wonder that in *Epist.* 2. 2. 60 Horace should have referred to his own poems as *Bionei sermones.*

Greek culture flowed into Rome through many channels. Officers who had campaigned in Greece brought back works of art to their Italian villas and then sent their sons to study in Athens. Greek poets and teachers (many of them prisoners of war) were employed as tutors in the houses of the Roman aristocracy. The most important focus of Hellenism was the circle of Scipio Aemilianus, in which men like Polybius and Panaetius were invited to expound their ideas.[12] Nor was the influence all in one direction. Polybius' Roman history was a monument to the new Mediterranean power; and if we consider the teaching of Panaetius, who rejected orthodox beliefs in survival, divination, and world cycles, and who concentrated less on theoretical perfection than on man's practical duties in society, we can see how the Stoic system became adapted to the pragmatic Roman mind.[13] Fifty years later the same kind of process was taking place in the Academy. Philo of Larissa, who came to Rome in 88 B.C., became dissatisfied with the rigid scepticism of Carneades regarding the possibility of knowledge, and this desire for surer foundations was reflected in the thought of his onetime pupil,

Antiochus of Ascalon.[14] Asserting that truth must be attainable, Antiochus developed a loose eclectic philosophy with a strong Stoic colouring, and these unsystematic ideas were disseminated in Rome by Cicero, who had studied under Antiochus in Athens. Even Epicureanism, the most conservative of all the schools, showed signs of development in the last century B.C. Arguments from sources later than Epicurus were used against post-Epicurean opponents, as when Velleius and Lucretius borrowed arguments from the New Academy to attack the Stoic belief in a benevolent Providence.[15] Moreover, instead of remaining a quasi-esoteric system, Epicureanism was now made known in popular writings like the *De Rerum Natura* of Lucretius and, more especially, the tracts of Philodemus. The latter, who may have been personally known to Horace, also wrote a work of literary theory in which he rejected the rhetoricians' distinction between style and content, and asserted that 'the moral effect of poetry, if it had one, was not an essential outcome of its aesthetic nature'.[16] Philodemus showed further evidence of his heretical interest in culture by shaping sophisticated epigrams, some of which are preserved in the *Greek Anthology*. Finally, in the last years of Caesar's dictatorship many Epicureans (Cassius among them) became so indignant at his acceptance of divine honours and at the general suppression of free speech that they felt justified in supporting violent political action.[17]

These few remarks will be enough to indicate that by the time when Horace was writing his *Satires*, i.e. from about 39 B.C. on, the distinctions between the main philosophical schools had become blurred at a number of points. There was also disagreement within particular schools—Posidonius, for example, reimported into Stoicism much of the nonsense which Panaetius had discarded. Such an atmosphere of freedom suited Horace well, for he was the least doctrinaire of men. This does not mean that his philosophical equipment was a mere rag-bag of multi-coloured scraps, but it does mean that he would never commit himself to any orthodoxy, whether Cynic or Academic, Epicurean or Stoic. The famous

2-2

phrase in *Epist.* 1. 1. 14 *nullius addictus iurare in verba magistri*
—a phrase from which the Royal Society takes its motto—was
valid for the whole of his career. So within the *Satires* themselves
there is no hope of tracing any development in the poet's philosophy. The final quip of 1. 1 shows that this poem, like 2. 3,
contained much that would have been acceptable to the Stoics;
1. 2 has a Cynic flavour—so has 2. 5; Epicureans would have
endorsed most of 1. 3, and the same is true of 2. 6. But it is time to
look more closely at the detail.

We shall start with passages illustrating the kind of material
which lay behind the opening of the first satire. Maximus of
Tyre, a sophist of the second century A.D., speaks about discontent as follows (I give a short paraphrase of the text, which can
be consulted in Heinze's note on *Sat.* 1. 1. 16): 'You could see
the farmer envying the townsman, and public figures complain-
ing of their own situation and envying the peasant. You could
hear the civilian expressing his envy of the soldier and vice versa.
And if a god, as in a play, made each actor exchange roles with
his fellow, the very same people would yearn for their former
ways of life. So hard a creature to please is man.'[18] Differences of
scope and detail make it unlikely that Maximus copied Horace,
and it is generally agreed that both writers were drawing on a
common fund of Hellenistic material. Another reflexion on
discontent, also later than Horace, is found in one of the pseudo-
Hippocratic letters: 'Men continually seek things which they
dislike. After refusing to sail, they put to sea; after refusing to
farm, they farm; they divorce their wives and then take others;
they hope for old age and then complain when it is upon them.
Leaders and kings envy private citizens, and vice versa. Statesmen
and artisans envy one another.'[19] A third passage, which goes
back at least as far as the first century B.C., occurs in the pseudo-
Platonic *Axiochus*: 'Is there anyone who, after choosing an occupation, does not find fault with it and complain about present
circumstances?'[20] Various illustrations then follow. Similar sentiments are found in Varro and Cicero,[21] and also in Lucretius:

> nunc plerumque videmus
> quid sibi quisque velit nescire et quaerere semper
> commutare locum quasi onus deponere possit
> . . . . . .
> sed dum abest quod avemus, id exsuperare videtur
> cetera; post aliud, cum contigit illud, avemus.[22]

As it is, we usually see people failing to realize what they want and continually seeking a change of scene, as if that would relieve them of their burden...But as long as we lack what we crave, that seems to overshadow everything else; then, when we've got it, we crave for something further.

Finally we have the remarks of Bion as preserved in Teles' essay *On Self-Sufficiency* (περὶ αὐταρκείας): 'When old do not yearn for youth...when poor do not seek riches.' Later Teles speaks of one who 'as a little boy wants to be a youth, as a youth wants to be a man, as a man is eager to reach old age...Then, when old, he desires to be young once more...As a slave he wants to be free, and when free he wants to be a slave.'[23] Discontent was therefore one of the commonplaces of popular philosophy.

The same sources indicate that discontent was often closely associated with greed. The pseudo-Hippocrates, after describing various forms of discontent, says: 'And the cause of all these things is φιλαργυρίη—love of money.'[24] Bion says the same: 'But we are unable to remain satisfied with what we have, since we spend a lot on luxuries.'[25] And he makes the same point more fully later on, when he depicts the discontented man as insatiable.[26] Finally, Maximus' sermon on discontent begins as follows: 'The wholly adequate life is hard to find, as is the wholly adequate man. Everyone feels within himself a certain lack in regard to perfection, and one person strives to outdo (πλεονεκτεῖ) the other whose deficiencies are fewer.'

Another reason for citing these passages is to stress the variety of their provenance. For the tendency to label all such material as Cynic can only be justified if the term is given an extremely broad sense. Behind the words of Lucretius lies the thought

21

THE DIATRIBES OF BOOK I

expressed by Epicurus in *Sent. Vat.* 35: 'We shouldn't spoil what we have by desiring what we lack; we should rather remember that what we have was also something desirable.' The speaker in the *Axiochus* is Socrates, and he attributes the ideas in question to Prodicus, the fifth-century sophist.[27] The words quoted from the pseudo-Hippocratic letter are there assigned to Democritus.[28] Horace himself reverts to the same theme in his first ode:

> luctantem Icariis fluctibus Africum
> mercator metuens otium et oppidi
> laudat rura sui; mox reficit ratis
> quassas, indocilis pauperiem pati.   (15-18)

The merchant in his dread of the African wind as it struggles with the waves of the Icarian sea longs for ease and the farms of his home town. In due course he repairs his battered craft, for he cannot learn to endure poverty.

This, in turn, recalls Euripides, *Philoctetes* (Frag. 793 Nauck):

> 'μακάριος ὅστις εὐτυχῶν οἴκοι μένει.'
> ἐν γῇ δ' ὁ φόρτος· καὶ πάλιν ναυτίλλεται.

(At sea the merchant says) 'Happy the man who in his prosperity remains at home.' But no sooner is his cargo ashore than he puts to sea again.[29]

As another example of Horace's easy eclecticism we shall take I. I. 92-107. In v. 92, towards the end of his lecture to the miser, Horace says *denique sit finis quaerendi*, 'so set a limit to your money-making'. Then in vv. 106-7 the idea of limit is brought in again to round off the section:

> est modus in rebus, sunt certi denique fines,
> quos ultra citraque nequit consistere rectum.

There is a certain proportion in everything. There are, in short, definite limits, and if you step outside them on this side or on that you cannot possibly be right.

Within this framework we hear the tale of Ummidius (the Roman counterpart of the Athenian miser in v. 64), who only attained a knowledge of the middle way when he was split down the centre by a freedwoman's axe. The opposite extreme is represented by two spendthrifts, and then the mean is affirmed once again in v. 105:

est inter Tanain quiddam socerumque Viselli.

There is a state between Tanais and the father-in-law of Visellius.

Tanais, according to the scholiast, was a eunuch; the other extreme was typified by Visellius' father-in-law. The line has a gnomic sound and is supposed to have been adapted from the Greek proverb ἢ σπάδων ἢ κηλήτης, which is the equivalent of our more decorous 'feast or famine'.

Behind these seemingly frivolous lines, with their dialogue, anecdote, and vulgar humour, lie two sets of serious ideas. The first is the division of desires or pleasures into those which are both natural and necessary, those which are natural but unnecessary, and those which are neither natural nor necessary. This scheme was taken over from Plato[30] and Aristotle[31] by Epicurus, who sets it out in his *Letter to Menoeceus* 127 ff. It is also implied in other passages of Epicurus of which the most apposite is perhaps no. 21 of the Κύριαι Δόξαι:

The man who knows the limits of life realizes that what removes the pain due to want and renders the whole of life complete is easy to obtain; so there is no need for actions which involve competition.[32]

Within these natural limits Horace locates the happy medium—his second main idea. The fullest and most sophisticated treatment of the happy medium is found, of course, in Aristotle's *Nicomachean Ethics*,[33] but it goes back through Plato[34] to Pythagorean and Sicilian researches into music and medicine.[35] And even this is being over-precise, for the ideal of moderation was deeply embedded in the religion of early Greece. The precept 'Nothing too much' (μηδὲν ἄγαν) was inscribed above the portals of Apollo's temple at Delphi, where its primacy as a rule of moral wisdom was disputed only by 'Know thyself' and 'Give a guarantee at thy peril!'

23

In 1. 2. 111–13 the idea of nature's limit is applied to sexual gratification:

> nonne cupidinibus statuat natura modum quem,
> quid latura sibi, quid sit dolitura negatum,
> quaerere plus prodest et inane abscindere soldo?[36]

Is it not more useful to ask what limit nature sets to one's desires, what gain she will derive and what she will sorely miss if it is denied her, and so to mark off the solid from the void?

In his physics Epicurus postulated only two basic features, namely solid atoms and void; so in his ethics he used to speak of solid and empty desires. In *KD* 29, for instance, he states that desires which are neither natural nor necessary are due to κενὴ δόξα—'empty fancy'. Cicero, describing the system, says *inanium autem cupiditatum nec modus ullus nec finis inveniri potest* (*De Fin.* 1. 45)—'in the case of empty desires no limit or boundary can be discovered'. So Horace here contends that the desire for an affair with a Roman matron is *inane*—'empty'. Up to this point he has been working within a strictly Epicurean framework, but the questions which follow reflect a much more general outlook:

When your throat is parched with thirst do you insist on drinking from a silver tankard? When hungry do you wave away everything but peacock and turbot? When you are tense with passion and when a maid-servant or a slave-boy is at hand to gratify it, would you sooner be racked with desire? Not me. I like the sort of girl that's easy to get.

On the desirability of *Venus parabilis* there seems to have been some uncertainty in the teaching of Epicurus himself. In *Sent. Vat.* 51, which is written in answer to the queries of an over-ardent young man, Epicurus says:

Provided you don't break the laws or good customs and do not cause annoyance to any of your neighbours or do yourself physical harm or waste your money, you may indulge yourself as you please. But you are bound to encounter one of these obstacles, for sexual pleasure never did a man any good, and he is lucky if it doesn't do him harm.

On the other hand we have the doctrine reported by Diogenes Laertius (10. 118) that 'the wise man will not have intercourse

with any woman with whom the law forbids it',[37] which implies
that relations with *meretrices* were permissible. This is put more
positively by Lucretius, who says that one way of avoiding the
emotional disturbance of love is by having casual intercourse
(*DRN* 4. 1065, 1071, 1073). And the same sentiment occurs in
the epigram of Philodemus referred to by Horace in 1. 2. 120 ff.
Casual liaisons of this kind were also advocated by the Cynics, as
may be seen from a papyrus fragment of Cercidas which bears
a notable resemblance to 1. 2. 125–7:

> ἁ δ' ἐξ ἀγορᾶς 'Αφροδίτα...
> οὐ φόβος οὐ ταραχά.
> ταύταν ὀβολῶ κατακλίνας
> Τυνδαρέοιο δόκει
> γαμβρός...[38]

As for Aphrodite of the market-place...there is no fear, no disturbance. Lay her for a shilling and fancy yourself son-in-law to
Tyndareus. [That is, imagine she is Helen of Troy.]

The theme occurred in comedies by Philemon and Eubulus,[39]
and it also played some part in one of Lucilius' satires.[40] It is
sometimes suggested that in defending this widely held attitude
Horace was asserting his opposition to the Stoics who maintained
that fornication, though less injurious than adultery, was just as
great a sin.[41] I should think, however, that if Horace had wished
to draw our attention to the Stoics he would have mentioned them
quite explicitly.

It is now time to show how Horace often gives an individual
twist to the commonplaces of popular philosophy. In 1. 3 a large
section is devoted to the misuse of complimentary and pejorative
terms (38–66). The connexion between linguistic and moral
behaviour was observed at least as early as the fifth century.
Thucydides has a famous description of how in a period of civil
strife ethical standards become perverted and words lose their
proper meaning.[42] Plato (*Rep.* 560 DE) shows the same corrupting process at work within the soul of a democratic man. And

Aristotle, in a rather different vein, treats the misuse of terms as a conscious rhetorical technique (*Rhet.* 1367 A, 28 ff.). It is Lucretius, however, who provides the most illuminating parallel with Horace. In *DRN* 4. 1160 ff. he describes the lover's blindness as follows:

> nigra melichrus est, immunda et fetida acosmos,
> caesia Palladium, nervosa et lignea dorcas,
> parvula, pumilio, chariton mia, tota merum sal,
> magna atque immanis cataplexis plenaque honoris.

The black-skinned is *café au lait*, the dirty and stale is *savamment désordonnée*, the cat-eyed is the image of Athena, the wiry and desiccated is *une gazelle*, the puny mite is *une des trois Graces*—just the cutest thing—the large and ungainly is *une merveille* and every inch a lady.

In Horace (44–8) we have:

> strabonem
> appellat paetum pater, et pullum, male parvus
> si cui filius est, ut abortivus fuit olim
> Sisyphus; hunc varum distortis cruribus, illum
> balbutit scaurum pravis fultum male talis.

If the boy has a squint the father calls him 'Boss-eye'; if he is miserably undersized as the dwarfish Sisyphus used to be, he is called 'Chick'; if his knees knock together he is called 'Hen-toe'; if he is so bandy that he can hardly stand, his father's pet name for him is 'Splay-foot'.

The first thing we notice is that, in the interests of pure Latinity, Horace has got rid of the Greek, which was the language of love.[43] In substituting parents for lovers he comes closer to his theme of friendship, and at the same time achieves a totally new effect, which cannot be translated; for all those names—Paetus, Pullus, Varus, and Scaurus—belonged to aristocratic families and were borne by some of the poet's most distinguished contemporaries. Finally, whereas Lucretius says 'Lovers are deluded, and what fools they are!', Horace says 'Lovers and parents are deluded—yes, and it's a pity there aren't more like them!' Thus by a deft surprise the scorn of the great Epicurean evangelist is transformed into Horatian benevolence.[44]

The second and third satires (and to a lesser extent the first) open with passages on inconsistency. This again was a common-place, and was recognized as such by Plato, who quotes the saying 'Bad men are never the same and never consistent' (*Lysis* 214 C). The proverb suited the philosopher's teaching, for an inconsistent man lacked that steady, rational control which unified the personality and fitted it for the good life. This ideal of steadiness, passing down through Aristotle[45] and the Stoics,[46] gave men a centre of gravity; it told them not to be unsettled by adversity or prosperity, to show themselves reliable in dealing with others, and to preserve a decent restraint in their social habits. Such principles were not, of course, adopted by the Roman aristocracy merely as an exotic import. They were already firmly rooted in the Italian tradition. The *imperium Romanum*, after all, was not the work of bohemians.

Perhaps the easiest way to see how Horace handles this idea is to compare his method with Cicero's. In *De Off.* I. 130, which is based on Panaetius, Cicero says:

adhibenda praeterea munditia est non odiosa neque exquisita nimis, tantum quae fugiat agrestem et inhumanam neglegentiam. eadem ratio est habenda vestitus, in quo, sicut in plerisque rebus, mediocritas optima est.

> In the matter of personal appearance one ought not to put people off by being over-fastidious. It should be enough to avoid a boorish and uncivilized carelessness. The same principle applies to dress, where, as in most things, the middle course is best.

In *Sat.* I. 2. 28 Horace shows his familiarity with the philosophical tradition of *mediocritas* by the sentence *nil medium est*, but instead of theorizing he gives a personal illustration taken from the streets of Rome:

Maltinus tunicis demissis ambulat; est qui
inguen ad obscenum subductis usque, facetus
pastillos Rufillus olet, Gargonius hircum.[47]

> Maltinus walks with his tunic trailing, another with his hoisted up to the point of indecency. The exquisite Rufillus smells of tablets, Gargonius stinks like a goat.

27

(Notice the liquids and gutturals in that last verse.) In *De Off.*
1. 131 Cicero has

cavendum autem est ne aut tarditatibus utamur in ingressu mol-
lioribus, ut pomparum ferculis similes esse videamur, aut in
festinationibus suscipiamus nimias celeritates.

> Care must be taken to avoid an unmanly slowness of walk which
> would make us look like figures carried in a procession; nor must
> we use excessive haste in hurrying.

In *Sat.* 1. 3. 9–11 Horace, specific as ever, attributes both these
habits to Tigellius, and by eliminating the long abstract nouns he
gains a lighter effect:

saepe velut qui
currebat fugiens hostem, persaepe velut qui
Iunonis sacra ferret.

> Often he would dash along as if someone were after his blood; more
> often he would move like an attendant bearing the sacred vessels of
> Juno.

But again the description is given a philosophical framework by
the comments *nil aequale homini fuit illi* (9) and *nil fuit umquam |
sic impar sibi* (18–19)—the man lacked *aequabilitas*; he had no
steadiness or consistency.

Horace shows the same individual flair in his handling of other,
less philosophical, material. In 1. 1. 23–6 he compares his method
of mixing serious and gay to the practice of giving children
cakes as a reward for learning their ABC. Most scholars quote
Lucretius 1. 936, where the poet compares himself to a doctor
who smears the rim of a medicine-cup with honey. One or two
go on to point out that the medical analogy is also attributed to
Diogenes by Antonius Melissa.[48] And with all this *Wissenschaft*
it is easy to overlook the fact that Horace's simile is without
parallel.

Or suppose we take the comparison of busy men to ants. In
vv. 28 ff. Horace says:

That fellow who turns the heavy soil with his hard plough, this crooked barman, the soldier and the sailors who dash so bravely across the seven seas, claim

28

that their only purpose in enduring this toil is to enjoy a secure retirement in old age, when they have made their pile; just as the tiny ant (for he is their model) with immense toil hauls along in his mouth whatever he can and adds it to the heap he is building, thus making conscious and careful provision for the future.

The ant is an ambiguous creature. It may represent mere acquisitiveness, as in Crates, Aeschrion, and Theocritus.[49] But here Horace gives a kinder picture—one suggestive of thrift rather than greed. As a result he seems to accept the busy men's account of their motives, and we tend to forget the irony that plays over those early lines with their heavy toil, crooked barman and so on. In this unsuspecting mood we move on to v. 36:

[The ant] who (*quae*), as soon as the year wheels round into dismal Aquarius, never sets foot outside and very sensibly makes use of what he has laid in,

Then suddenly the trap closes:

whereas in *your* case neither scorching heat nor the cold of winter can interrupt your money-grubbing. Hail, rain, or snow—nothing can stop you; no one must ever be richer than you!

So the innocent *quae* in v. 36 has actually the force of *at ea*. It represents the very thin end of the wedge which Horace is about to drive between the ant and the greedy man. This, like the mock-epic description of winter in the same line, is a characteristically Horatian touch. It is not to be found in Lucilius, though he probably used the same simile (W. 586–7).

The image of life as a stage is, again, entirely conventional.[50] Even the special form employed by Horace in I. I. 15–22 (i.e. a *deus ex machina* who offers a change of roles) had numerous antecedents—in Plato, Herodotus, Heraclitus, and ultimately in the world of fairy tales.[51] Yet we shall appreciate what Horace has done if we recall the bare outline of the idea as sketched by Cicero (*De Sen.* 83), *si quis deus mihi largiatur ut ex hac aetate repuerascam et in cunis vagiam, valde recusem*—'if at this time of life a god gave me the opportunity of becoming a child again and screaming in my cradle, I should certainly refuse'. So too, Crato in Menander's Θεοφορουμένη or *The Woman Possessed* (K. 223) says:

29

If one of the gods came up and said to me 'Crato, when you die, you shall live all over again. And you shall be whatever you wish—a dog, a sheep, a goat, a man, or a horse; for you have to live twice. This is decreed by fate. Choose what you want', I think I should immediately say 'Make me anything rather than a human being'.

Here even Menander is less dramatic than Horace, whose god uses a mixture of interjections and brisk, peremptory commands:

If some god said 'Behold! Here am I, ready to grant your wishes. You who a moment ago were a soldier shall be a merchant; and you who were a lawyer shall become a farmer. Right! Exchange parts and away you go...Well? Why are you standing there?', they would refuse; and yet they could have their heart's desire.

It will be noted that the last few examples have all been drawn from the first satire. That is because the poem owes much of its character to the age-old similes of life as a stage, life as a race-course,[52] and life as a banquet.[53] The antiquity of these similes, along with the conventional nature of the characters and the scarcity of Italian names, prevents the satire from having any firm roots in Roman life. In its matter it is essentially a Hellenistic poem, though no one but Horace could have written it.

The distinctive character of 1.2 is derived partly from its names, which will be discussed in chapter v, and partly from its use of literary material. In concluding his description of the miserly Fufidius, Horace says:

>   ita ut pater ille, Terenti
> fabula quem miserum gnato vixisse fugato
> inducit, non se peius cruciaverit atque hic.   (20–2)

So that the father who is represented in Terence's play as living in misery as a result of banishing his son never tortured himself worse than he.

The play referred to is, of course, the *Heauton Timorumenos* or *The Man Who Punished Himself*. But if the reader happened to be a little forgetful, or even downright ignorant, he did not suffer for it, because Horace provided him with a translation of the title (*se cruciaverit*) and a summary of the opening scene; verbal quotation plays no part in the effect.[54]

In vv. 31–5 we have an allusion of a different kind, namely a free rendering in verse of a saying ascribed to Cato. On seeing a young man come out of a brothel Cato exclaimed 'Good for you! Better to appease your lust here than with other men's wives.' The original form of the anecdote or *chria* is lost, so we cannot tell how much, if any, of the quotation is authentic, but we do know of a sequel which Horace has passed over. For, according to the pseudo-Acron, after meeting the man several times in the same place Cato said 'I commended you, young man, for paying an occasional visit, not for becoming an *habitué*'. Clearly the weight of the story falls on the second half, yet Horace did not hesitate to suppress it, presumably because adultery was his chief concern and it did not suit his argument to have the brothel associated with a virtuous moderation.

Like many satirists of note, Horace was an accomplished literary mimic. And he uses this gift to introduce the main theme of the poem. Thus the noble lines of Ennius:

> audire est operae pretium procedere recte
> qui rem Romanam Latiumque augescere voltis[55]

It is worth your while to give ear, you who wish all success to the Roman state and increase to Latium

reappear in vv. 37–8 as:

> audire est operae pretium procedere recte
> qui moechis non voltis.

It is worth your while to give ear, you who wish ill success to adulterers.

There are two allusions to the epigrams of Philodemus. In one case (120 ff.) Philodemus is mentioned by name and his poem is summarized in a masterpiece of vivid compression, in which syntax is almost squeezed out:

> illam 'post paulo', 'sed pluris', 'si exierit vir',
> Gallis, hanc Philodemus ait sibi, quae neque magno
> stet pretio neque cunctetur cum est iussa venire.

The 'later on'—'yes, but more money'—'if my man goes out' sort of woman is, according to Philodemus, for the Galli; his own choice is the one who doesn't cost much and comes at once when called.

The pun on *Galli*, 'Gauls', and *Galli*, 'eunuch priests of Cybele', must have been in the original, which unfortunately is lost. The attempt to identify the epigram with no. 126 in the fifth book of the *Greek Anthology* is no more than a bad guess.[56]

The other allusion to Philodemus comes at v. 92. Lovers, we are told, are often so infatuated with one or two features of the beloved that they fail to notice all the concomitant defects:

> o crus! o bracchia! verum
> depugis, nasuta, brevi latere ac pede longo est.

O legs! O arms! But she has too small a bottom, too big a nose, a short waist and huge feet.

In this case the poem in question is extant:

> ὢ ποδός, ὢ κνήμης, ὢ τῶν ἀπόλωλα δικαίως
> μηρῶν, ὢ γλουτῶν, ὢ κτενός, ὢ λαγόνων,
> ὢ ὤμοιν, ὢ μαστῶν, ὢ τοῦ ῥαδινοῖο τραχήλου,
> ὢ χειρῶν, ὢ τῶν μαίνομαι ὀμματίων,
> ὢ κατατεχνοτάτου κινήματος, ὢ περιάλλων
> γλωττισμῶν, ὢ τῶν θῦ' ἐμὲ φωναρίων.
> εἰ δ' Ὀπικὴ καὶ Φλῶρα καὶ οὐκ ᾄδουσα τὰ Σαπφοῦς,
> καὶ Περσεὺς Ἰνδῆς ἠράσατ' Ἀνδρομέδης.[57]

O feet! O legs! O thighs for which I died (and with good reason)! O buttocks, O fringe, O flanks, O shoulders, O breasts, O slender neck, O arms, O eyes that fill me with madness, O clever movement, O superlative kisses, O little cries of 'love me!' If she's Italian and her name is Flora and she does not sing Sappho—well, Perseus loved the Indian Andromeda.

Here again Horace has been rather less than fair; for, whatever shortcomings Philodemus' poem may have, the vision of his lover is nothing if not comprehensive.

The fullest rendering is of an epigram by Callimachus, which runs as follows:

The huntsman, [Epicydes, on the hills] tracks [every] hare [and the trail of every hind] through the [frost and] snow. [And if anyone says 'Look, here is an animal] lying [wounded'] he does not take it. My love is [also] like this. It [constantly] pursues that which flies, but flies past what is ready to hand.[58]

As well as reducing the poem from six to three and a half lines by the omissions indicated, Horace moves from indirect to direct speech and reverses the final sequence so as to give a neat chiasmus. He also leaves out the author's name—perhaps as a tactful gesture, since he quotes the poem only to reject its sentiment.

These few examples show that even at this early stage Horace commanded various techniques of literary allusion and that he used them with an independence sometimes amounting to ruthlessness.

The third satire, unlike the first, has none of the universal similes of popular philosophy, nor, except for the Lucretian section in vv. 99 ff.,[59] does it make any use of literary material. It proves, however, to be richer in metaphor than either of the other pieces. I do not mean that we are startled by novel perceptions or daring feats of language; such effects are rare even in Horace's lyrics, and he seems to have felt that brilliance of that kind was inappropriate to his conception of satire. (And no doubt if satire is thought of as moral discourse delivered in an unpretentious, conversational style, this is a perfectly defensible opinion.) Nevertheless, I. 3 does contain several quietly successful metaphors, which are not restricted to one expression but are elaborated over a number of lines. A straightforward example occurs in vv. 58–61:

> hic fugit omnis
> insidias nullique malo latus obdit apertum
> cum genus hoc inter vitae versemur ubi acris
> invidia atque vigent ubi crimina.

This fellow escapes every trap and never leaves his flank open to malicious attack; for we are engaged in a life in which envy is sharp and slander active.

Sometimes we can watch the metaphor develop from a single word:

33

> amicus dulcis ut aequum est
> cum mea compenset vitiis bona, pluribus hisce,
> si modo plura mihi bona sunt, inclinet, amari
> si volet: hac lege in trutina ponetur eadem.   (69-72)

My kindly friend should, as is only fair, weigh my virtues against my faults, and if he wants me to like him he should come down on the side of my virtues as being more numerous—provided they *are* more numerous. On that principle he will be weighed in the same scales.

Here the idea implicit in *compenset* and *inclinet* emerges finally in *trutina*. At the same time the form of the image is constantly shifting. The friend first holds the balance, then appears to be identified with the balance, and finally ends up *in* the balance. The same kind of movement is encountered in vv. 34-7:

> denique te ipsum
> concute, num qua tibi vitiorum inseverit olim
> natura aut etiam consuetudo mala; namque
> neglectis urenda filix innascitur agris.

So give yourself a good shaking in case the seeds of evil have already been sown in you, whether by nature or through some bad habit. For if you once neglect a field, bracken springs up which eventually has to be burnt out.

The personality begins as a garment in which the seeds of evil have lodged, and it ends as an overgrown field.

This last example shows how Horace often combines a metaphor with a piece of proverbial wisdom. So too in vv. 55-6 we have:

> at nos virtutes ipsas invertimus atque
> sincerum cupimus vas incrustare.

But we turn virtues themselves upside down and do all we can to dirty a clean jar.

Finally, after the figure of the balance quoted above, Horace adds:

> qui ne tuberibus propriis offendat amicum
> postulat, ignoscat verrucis illius.

The man who expects a friend to overlook his boils will forget the other's warts.[60]

Boils and warts—a typically Roman version of beams and motes.

In spite of their stylistic variety, which includes a free use of dialogue and reported speech, these satires are all straightforward diatribes in the sense that the poet speaks directly to his audience and takes responsibility for what he says. But while his manner is direct and unequivocal, his material is so general that we learn practically nothing about himself. That is the main point of contrast between these satires and 1. 6—a remarkable poem, in which the diatribe has been made the medium of a personal declaration.

CHAPTER II

POET AND PATRON (1)[1]

I. 6

It is hard for an Englishman, with his long history of civic order, to imagine the almost continuous violence which Rome endured in the last sixty years of the Republic. Sulla, who played a large part in crushing the Italian rebels in 88 B.C., had only just left to take command in the east when Marius and Cinna seized power in Rome. The slaughter of their opponents went on for five days. Sulla's return brought a new outbreak of fighting which culminated at the Colline Gate in 82 B.C. Thousands fell in battle, thousands were killed after surrendering, and thousands more died in the proscriptions which followed. Savagery, even on this scale, failed to bring peace, and within four years the army of Lepidus was marching on Rome. After Lepidus' defeat many of his soldiers fled to Sertorius, the Marian general, who had been conducting successful operations in Spain. These operations, which included victories over Pompey, were brought to an end when Sertorius was assassinated in 72 B.C. Pompey returned to Italy in time to help Crassus stamp out the revolt of Spartacus. Six thousand slaves were crucified along the Appian Way. In less than ten years another revolt had broken out, this time under Catiline, and the senatorial armies were on the march again. Under the first triumvirate there was an uneasy peace (interrupted by gang warfare in Rome), until Caesar crossed the Rubicon in 49 B.C. The battles which ensued at Pharsalus, Thapsus and Munda took a terrible toll of Roman life. After Caesar's murder war flared up again. In 43 B.C. Antony was twice defeated at Mutina, but he found reinforcements in Gaul and returned to Italy, where along with Octavian and Lepidus he set up the second triumvirate. More proscriptions followed. Appian puts the number of those murdered as high as two thousand knights and three hundred senators. After the carnage at Philippi Octavian came back to Italy and within a year had to suppress a rebellion led by Antony's brother. And even now there was no peace. For Pompey's son, Sextus, was still carrying on a naval war from Sicily and Sardinia. He inflicted more than one defeat on Octavian before he was overcome in 36 B.C. When, after Actium, Octavian finally turned to the task of rebuilding the Roman state, the wonder is that there was anything left to rebuild.

Of all these calamities there is scarcely a trace in the *Satires*. The few political references are mostly confined to the later poems of Book 2, by which time the struggle was over. In fact it may be said that Horatian satire as a whole implies a conscious rejection of public life. Nevertheless, the violent social changes which took place in these years are reflected in the career of the poet, who was a freedman's son, a knight,[2] a military tribune, a treasury official, a friend of republican nobles, and an *amicus* of Octavian's first minister. The stresses imposed by this career are most apparent in 1. 6, and the way they are handled makes this a poem of unusual interest.

7–18: You say, Maecenas, that a man's parentage doesn't matter provided he is *ingenuus*. In taking this view you recognize that before the régime of Tullius and his far-from-noble kingship many men of no pedigree often lived good lives and were honoured with high offices, whereas Laevinus, a descendant of that Valerius who drove Tarquin the Proud from his throne into exile, was never rated higher than a brass farthing, even in the opinion of the people (that judge whom you know so well), who foolishly give positions of distinction to the undeserving, who are stupidly enthralled by family fame, and who gape in fascination at inscriptions and busts. *quid oportet | nos facere a vulgo longe longeque remotos?*

In view of the preceding clause (*quali sit quisque parente | natus*) the word *ingenuus* is naturally taken to mean 'freeborn', and in spite of his comparatively liberal outlook Maecenas may well have believed that no one of servile birth should be admitted to political office. We note, however, that Horace goes on to endorse

Maecenas' opinion by citing the case of Servius Tullius, who was *not* freeborn. He was *patre nullo, matre serva* (Livy 4. 3); and there were many good men before him, says Horace, who rose high without having a pedigree. Now this may be simply an oversight, but the effect of these lines, whether intentional or not, is to cast doubt on Maecenas' reservation and to remind us of the broader sense of *ingenuus*, which is 'noble in nature'.

Maecenas' main principle, though based on morality, is presented in political terms in such a way as to suggest that low birth should not be an obstacle to high office and that high birth should not be a guarantee of high office. We cannot say how deeply Maecenas believed in this principle, but it would be unrealistic to expect a man of Horace's status and temperament to make it the nucleus of a diatribe. Lucilius, Persius and Juvenal are all equally conservative in this respect, and indeed Roman satire is no place in which to look for a reformer's manifesto. So we are not wholly surprised when, after this opening passage, a new theme emerges in vv. 23–44. This is just what happened in the first three diatribes. The trouble here, however, is that the new theme runs counter to what has already been said: Commoners, no less than nobles, are the slaves of ambition. This is foolish, because when a man thrusts himself into prominence he at once arouses malicious curiosity. 'Who *is* this fellow? What was his father?' A man like the effeminate Barrus annoys the girls by his exhibitionism. They dislike the competition and make jealous inquiries about him. So a commoner who has become tribune provokes hostility, and such hostility is bound to cause unhappiness.

Now since these two ideas (the irrelevance of birth and the folly of ambition) pull in different directions—the first towards a dynamic society with a *carrière ouverte aux talents*, the second towards political quietism—there is a danger that between them they may dislocate the structure of the poem. The strain falls most heavily on vv. 19–22, and one must admit that the joint is perilously weak. To examine it we must return to the question in vv. 17–18, *quid oportet | nos facere a vulgo longe longeque*

38

remotos? From ancient times this has been interpreted in two different ways. Some commentators think it means 'How much more should we, who stand apart from the mob, assess a man at his true worth?'[3] This makes excellent sense and provides a logical conclusion to the opening passage. But it does not lead smoothly to what follows. In vv. 19 ff. we have this: 'For, granted, the people would have preferred to give office to a Laevinus rather than to an unknown Decius, and Appius the censor would have struck me off the roll for not being the son of a freeborn father.' We now expect something like 'But men of our kind take a different view'. Instead, Horace says '—and it would have served me right for not resting contentedly in my own skin. Yet [i.e. in spite of prejudice from above and below] Glory drags behind her dazzling car the obscure no less than the noble.'

The other interpretation of vv. 17–18 is somewhat as follows: 'What am I to do, who am so far removed from the public's gaze?'[4] The implied answer, i.e. 'stay out of politics altogether', leads directly to the next section. Unfortunately the link with the opening passage is now very much weaker, for one has to assume that the question has no connexion with Maecenas' liberal principle and arises solely from the behaviour of the people, as described in vv. 15–17. Whichever solution one adopts (I myself favour the first), it is clear that Horace's usual dexterity has deserted him. He might, after all, have taken the line that although birth *ought* not to matter, in fact it did, and therefore anyone who tried to force his way to the top should reckon with the consequences. Or he might have argued on a purely personal level by introducing a hypothetical opponent saying 'What? Do you mean that you, with your tastes and outlook, are eager to enter on the *cursus honorum*?' Horace could then have disclaimed any such ambitions in his own characteristic way. However, even if the transition is poorly managed, it does not follow that the two themes cancel each other out. We shall find presently that when one is subtracted from the other we are left with a highly significant remainder. In the meantime, lest we become too engrossed in general ideas, we should remember that the satire was written as a protest against something distressingly personal, namely the resentment which people felt at the poet's good fortune.

1–6: Though you, Maecenas, are noble (*nemo generosior*) and have distinguished generals amongst your ancestors, you don't despise me, as most people do, because I'm a freedman's son. This introduction is deliberately recalled in vv. 45–8. Thus

> nunc ad me redeo libertino patre natum,
> quem rodunt omnes libertino patre natum

Now I revert to myself, a freedman's son, carped at by everyone because I'm a freedman's son

recalls *libertino patre natum* (6). Also *nunc quia...Maecenas* (47) echoes *non quia, Maecenas* (1), and *quod mihi pareret legio Romana tribuno* (48) harks back to *qui magnis legionibus imperitarent* (4). Therefore a new structural unit begins at v. 45. In this new section Horace points out that he is disliked not, strictly speaking, because he is a freedman's son, but because he has achieved fame in spite of being a freedman's son. Now in view of what has just been said about the hazards of ambition, surely this dislike was only to be expected. Why should Horace complain when he has broken his own rules? In answer the poet distinguishes between the two types of eminence he has known. The first, his commission in the republican army, was a position of military and potentially political power. As such it was perhaps bound to excite envy. But all that is over. His new distinction, i.e. his friendship with Maecenas, is something quite different. Being non-political it gives him no power over his fellow-citizens, and therefore it ought not to cause resentment.

Horace's aversion to politics, however, is not developed until the last section of the poem. In the meantime he deals with the social aspect of his position. This posed a more delicate problem. His prestige as a friend of Maecenas was undeniable, and he could not pretend it was unwelcome. What he could do was to ignore his position as a celebrity, thus implying that the relationship was a purely private affair. He could also contend that his privilege had been fairly won. With this in view he gives an account of his first interview with Maecenas:

> The excellent Virgil previously told you what I was; then Varius did the same. When I came before you I gulped out a few words—for shyness struck me dumb and prevented me from saying more. I didn't make out that I had a distinguished father or that I rode round my estates on a Tarentine nag. I told you the facts about myself. Your reply was characteristically brief, and I left. Nine months later you sent for me again and invited me to join your circle of friends.
>
> (54–62)

The meeting, then, was no haphazard affair (*non . . . casu, nulla . . . fors*, 52–4)—an important point to make, for as we learn from 2. 6. 49 there were many who called Horace *Fortunae filius*, 'Luck's pet'. Lady Luck in the Elder Pliny's words (*NH* 2. 22) was 'blind, fickle, inconstant, unreliable, shifting, and a patroness of the unworthy (*indignorumque fautrix*)'. Maecenas, however, was not a patron of the unworthy. Immediately before the passage just quoted he is said to be *cautum dignos adsumere, prava / ambitione procul*, 'careful to admit only the worthy, above all sordid ambition'.[5] And immediately after the same passage Horace says:

> magnum hoc ego duco
> quod placui tibi, qui turpi secernis honestum,
> non patre praeclaro sed vita et pectore puro.

> I consider it a great thing to have pleased you, who distinguish the honourable from the base, not by my father's glory but by my blameless life and heart.[6]

By focusing attention on Maecenas Horace has reminded his enemies that in criticizing him they were also criticizing his friend and patron. We notice, however, that he says nothing at all about the decisive factor in the whole business, namely his poetry. (Maecenas, after all, did not keep open house for every upright citizen.) No doubt Horace knew very well that, although he might possibly reduce people's resentment a little by protesting his decency, he would only inflame it if he mentioned his talent.

If we abstracted the argument in Hegelian terms we should find that it had now reached a final synthesis: humble birth ought not to be an obstacle to success, at least when the success is of a non-political kind and when the man in question deserves the honour. That is the degree to which the opening themes have been reconciled.

Although there is a pause at v. 64, it is a mistake to think of the poem as falling into two halves. Lines 65–88 are linked much more closely with what goes before than with 89–131. The satire in fact consists of three groups of pairs. The first group (1–22 and 23–44) presents opposite aspects of glory, the second is concerned with merit (45–64 and 65–88), and the third with freedom (89–111 and 111–31). From now on this division will form the basis of our discussion.

In vv. 65–71 tone and structure are again complementary. By resuming the topic of merit these verses connect the two parts of the second group; at the same time they diminish our uneasiness at the poet's self-praise:

If my faults are not too serious or too many; and if my nature, apart from these blemishes, is otherwise sound—just as on a handsome body you might find a mole here and there; if no one can justly accuse me of greed or meanness or licentiousness; if (to indulge in a little self-esteem) my life is clean and above reproach; and if my friends are fond of me; the credit is due to my father.

Now comes the famous account of how Horace's father took him to school in Rome, accompanying him to and fro each day, providing him with the proper clothes and equipment, and watching over his moral welfare. It was an unusual step to take, but apart from recognizing his son's promise the father may well have decided that the local school was an undesirable place. It is likely that as a penalty for its defection in the Italian war (90–88 B.C.) Venusia had to relinquish some of its land to Sulla's veterans. If so, the centurions and their families must have formed an unpopular 'ascendancy' in the district.[7] This is supported by Horace's satirical phrase *magni...pueri magnis e centurionibus orti*, 'great sons descended from great sergeant-majors'. We can imagine these children jeering at the freedman's son as they

swaggered to school with satchel and tablet swinging from the
left arm (74).

The father's concern for the boy's purity (81–4) may seem rather
exaggerated until we recall what other writers say about Roman
education. 'Insist', says Juvenal, 'that the teacher himself be a
father to the class, in case they play dirty games' (7. 239 f.). To
encounter the same warning in Quintilian is rather like hearing
the ghoulish fantasies of Ronald Searle confirmed by the head-
mistress of a public school. Yet that is what happens. 'I do not
approve of young boys sitting beside adolescents', writes Quintilian. Then in words strikingly similar to Horace's he adds 'Not
only should the charge of indecency be avoided, but also the very
suspicion of it'.[8] The famous rhetorician also agrees with Horace
in the stress he lays on purity. 'If anyone chooses a teacher for his
son without taking care to avoid the most obvious kind of im-
morality, he may be sure that all the other precepts which I am
trying to compile for young people's good are utterly useless...'[9]
The same kind of sentiment is also found in Cicero and Pliny.[10]
Now we may be sure that Orbilius, that stern old knight, saw to
it that his school had a healthy atmosphere, but Orbilius was not
Horace's only teacher and anyway he was an exception. Many
teachers were slaves, all of them were wretchedly paid (even
Orbilius was a poor man), and as a group they were treated with
condescension or indifference. Nothing illustrates better the
dilemma of the Roman social system. Fathers were anxious for
their sons to be trained by reliable and dignified teachers; at the
same time they were determined to retain the privilege of despising
the profession.

What bearing does all this have on Horace's argument? He is
contending that people should not grudge him his position,
because he deserves it. And why does he deserve it? The first
argument is *a posteriori*: 'Maecenas invited me to join his circle,
and he chooses only those who are worthy of the honour.' The
second is *a priori*: 'I am worthy of the honour because of the moral
discipline I received from my father.' Such is the connexion of the

two parts, but their power is not derived from their logical cogency so much as from the fact that they have been placed side by side at the very centre of the poem, to pay a debt of gratitude and affection to the two chief influences on the poet's life— Maecenas who recognized and accepted him for what he was, and his father who made him what he was.

The theme of merit ends, properly speaking, at v. 88, but the transition to the final section has already begun with the idea expressed in vv. 85 ff., 'I should have been quite content to follow my father's footsteps'. The notion of contentment is carried over into the following passage by *nil me paeniteat sanum patris huius*, 'never in my right mind would I be dissatisfied with such a father'. But the continuity is only apparent, because the story of Horace's education and the part played in it by his father is over. In its new context the poet's contentment with his parents is contrasted with the embarrassment of those who feel handicapped by their low birth. Such embarrassment, says Horace, is useless and misconceived. If he had the choice he would pick the same parents again. Then seemingly as an afterthought he adds:

> demens
> iudicio vulgi, sanus fortasse tuo quod
> nollem onus haud umquam solitus portare molestum.
>
> (97–9)

> Mad in the opinion of the mob, but sane perhaps in yours for refusing to shoulder a tiresome and unaccustomed burden.

But this is no afterthought. It is the beginning of the final theme. In this last section Horace returns to the folly of ambition,[11] emphasizing now not the unpopularity of a public career but rather its burdens. Making money, greeting callers, acquiring more servants and horses and wagons—these are the duties from which the poet is free. In the middle of the list we catch a glimpse of his *positive* freedom:

> If I like I can go right to Tarentum on a gelded mule whose flanks are chafed by the weight of the saddle-bag and whose withers are chafed by the rider

44

—a vivid Lucilian cameo.[12] Passing through vv. 110–11, where *hoc* refers back and *milibus atque aliis* points forward, we find ourselves in the second part of the final section, which describes a typical, lazy day in the poet's life. The description starts in the afternoon, as Horace strolls through the markets comparing the prices of vegetables; later he explores the stalls round the Circus Maximus, an area which had all the seedy excitement of old Soho. Back in his house dinner is served, and as Horace looks at the table the various objects form themselves into an exquisite still life:[13]

> lapis albus
> pocula cum cyatho duo sustinet; adstat echinus
> vilis, cum patera gutus, Campana supellex.

On a slab of white marble stand two cups and a ladle, beside them a cheap jug, an oil flask and saucer—all of Campanian ware.

We join the poet again next morning about ten o'clock and remain in his company until the afternoon. The whole description reflects his positive freedom—*quacumque libido est | incedo solus* (111–12), 'I go wherever I like on my own'. But again he gives variety, this time by inserting a negative expression in the middle—he is not worried about having to rise early (119–20).

This final section on freedom is an integral part of the poem, for it presupposes everything that has gone before. Without the father's moral training such a life would not have seemed worthwhile; without the generosity of Maecenas it would have been impossible. It is a life free from ambition, and it reminds us that the things most worth having do not depend on birth. The last two links are carefully provided in the closing lines:

> haec est
> vita solutorum misera ambitione gravique;
> his me consolor victurum suavius ac si
> quaestor avus pater atque meus patruusque fuissent.

Such is the life of those who are free from the cruel pressure of ambition. I comfort myself with the thought that I shall enjoy life more fully in this way than if my grandfather, father and uncle had all been quaestors.

Horace himself could probably have had a quaestorship if he had wanted it, but there is no need to assume that Maecenas was pressing him to take the job. To understand the defensive tone it is enough to remember the picture which Horace presented to his enemies. In their eyes he was nothing but a small-town upstart with privileges beyond his deserts. His father, an absurdly ambitious man for one of servile birth, had pushed him into a respectable Roman school, and not content with that had sent him to study at Athens in the company of his social superiors. After Philippi, instead of being grateful for his pardon and working quietly in the civil service, the fellow had taken advantage of a slender poetic talent to ingratiate himself with Maecenas. Perhaps he had his eye on higher things. Had he not already shown a taste for power by acquiring a commission in Brutus' army? Many better men had changed sides after defeat and were now embarked on successful careers. Horace, with his extraordinary mixture of impudence and good luck, might well do the same.

Looking more closely at the poem we detect certain features of a conventional kind. The themes of high birth, foolish ambition and the quiet life need no illustration, but it is worth recalling that the autobiographical material (parentage, education, friends, habits) can easily be paralleled from ancient lives.[14] Another parallel can be found in ancient invectives, which were often a kind of 'anti-biography'. One started with the victim's parents, who came from some outlandish area and who, if not actually slaves, were invariably soiled by some menial occupation. From there one proceeded to his squalid upbringing, his schooldays which were already tainted with vice, his comic and bestial appearance, his grotesque dress and so on.[15] The prevalence of indecent abuse in lampoons of this kind may also help to explain the emphasis with which Horace asserts his purity.

Precedents can also be found for Horace's boasting. In Roman eyes self-praise was always justified in self-defence. Cicero, for instance, says:

dicendum igitur est id quod non dicerem nisi coactus—nihil enim umquam de me dixi sublatius adsciscendae laudis causa potius quam criminis depellendi.[16]

> I must therefore say what I would not say except under compulsion—
> for if I have ever sounded a little conceited it has always been for the
> purpose of rebutting a charge, not for eliciting praise.

Another excuse for boasting was the danger that one's proudest achievements might be put down to luck. Cicero took some trouble to prevent such a vulgar error:

ego committam ut ea quae pro salute omnium gessi casu magis et felicitate a me quam virtute et consilio gesta esse videantur?[17]

> Shall I allow all that I did for the safety of the state to be ascribed to
> chance and good luck instead of to my character and policy?

When massaging the ego in this way it was prudent, however, to keep in touch with one's listeners. Plutarch, writing a century after Horace's death, advises the speaker to congratulate his audience as well as himself, and to put them in a receptive mood by admitting some minor foibles.[18] As we have seen, both precautions are taken by Horace in the present satire.

Such techniques, of course, were conventional only because they had proved reliable in practice, and therefore the question here is not whether they are new but whether they are effectively employed. This question brings out the satire's true freshness. I am not thinking so much of the smaller touches—how envy is caught in a snatch of conversation at the theatre, how ambition is illuminated by Gloria in her triumphal chariot and by Tillius travelling east, complete with portable lavatory. I am thinking rather of the way in which the themes of glory, merit, and freedom are built into a unique artistic structure. This brings us back to the poet's ambiguous position in society. His dilemma was in many ways similar to those faced in 1. 4 and 1. 10. In 1. 4 he had to maintain that wicked people deserved to be attacked while at the same time indicating his reluctance to attack them. In 1. 10 the problem was to justify his divergence from Lucilius without repudiating the satiric genre. As he wrote 1. 6 Horace was well aware that high birth did not automatically confer the qualities of statesmanship. No doubt he felt equal in ability to many of the young aristocrats whom he had known at school and university. Therefore his pride demanded the *right* to attain eminence, and he was stung to indignation by taunts against his humble background. Yet he knew he was temperamentally unsuited to public life, and when he observed the type of person who *was* gaining power as a result of the civil wars he turned away in disgust:

> quid attinet tot ora navium gravi
>   rostrata duci pondere
> contra latrones atque servilem manum
>   hoc, hoc tribuno militum?   (*Epod.* 4. 17–20)

What is the point of sending so many ships with heavy beaks against a gang of pirates and slaves when he, yes he, is a military tribune?

'I have a perfect right to stand for office.' 'The whole thing is so sordid that I wouldn't dream of standing for office.' These two attitudes pull against each other, particularly in the first section of the poem. And even at the very end, after describing the joys of the quiet life, Horace cannot refrain from that sarcastic *consolor*—a word which betrays that his wounds were still smarting.

The relation of poet to patron was also a delicate affair. Horace realized that he owed some respect to Maecenas in virtue of his superior position, and that in winning his patronage he had contracted certain obligations in return. On the other hand he was not the sort of man to accept charity. Until the debacle at Philippi his career had been highly successful, and even now he had no intention of sacrificing his independence in order to become an official lackey. The result was a series of mutually qualifying assertions:

My father was a freedman, but I ought not to be penalized for that. That doesn't mean I have any political aims; such aims are foolish since they cause resentment. But my friendship with Maecenas should not cause resentment, for it was he who offered it; but he only offered because I deserved it; but I only deserved it because of my father. Anyhow the friendship involves no official duties; which suits me well, since I value my independence.

The poem however, like 1. 4, is more than just a personal defence. This can best be appreciated by asking whether there is any concept which will include and unify the themes of glory, merit, and freedom. I believe there is such a concept and that it is developed in a series of antitheses which are sometimes so sharp as to seem paradoxical. Let us start with the *ignobile regnum* of Tullius (9). His reign was *ignobile* because of his low birth, but in comparison with the noble Tarquin who was *regno pulsus*, or with the worthless aristocrat Laevinus, he was clearly a distinguished ruler. In Horace's time, to be 'somebody' one had to point to freeborn ancestors; yet in former days many a good man who was by nature *ingenuus* had no ancestors at all (10). Of the *generosi* and *ignoti* who follow Gloria (24) the former are noble by birth and the latter hope to become so by their own efforts (27–8). Such efforts are hazardous, for even at the level of the tribunate people inquire whether a man is *honestus* or *inhonestus* (36), meaning 'Is he well-born or low-born?' Now to Horace's mind there was something wrong about applying the words 'noble' and 'honourable' to a tyrant or a reprobate or a man obsessed by ambition, while reserving 'disgraceful' and 'disreputable' for those whose parents happened to have been slaves. It was part of Maecenas' excellence that in spite of his high birth and his familiarity with power he distinguished the base from the honourable by purely moral criteria. So far Horace has isolated himself from his parents. Like Bion before him he has said in effect σκόπει με ἐξ ἐμαυτοῦ—'judge me on my own merits'.[19] But at v. 71 it now appears that when the right standards are applied his father was honourable too, though not made honourable by the appurtenances of office (97). And it was because he was a gentleman by nature that he was able to teach his son *virtus*. So Horace can be proud of his father after all.

Closely related to parentage was the question of *dignitas*. Cicero tells us that status had once been the prize of excellence (*Mur.* 17) and that after the expulsion of the kings it was agreed that access to the highest rank should be available to men of diligence and character (*Sest.* 137). Sallust says that in the old days one's status was based on noble deeds (*Cat.* 7); in fact nobility itself was once achieved by valour (*Jug.* 85. 17). According to Horace this was true even before the expulsion of Tarquin (9–11). But as the government passed into the control of a self-perpetuating oligarchy *dignitas* began to change its meaning. It was still attainable through public offices (*honores*), but since such offices were monopolized by an aristocratic clique the word acquired a class connotation, and status itself became something which could be claimed as an inheritance. As Marius fiercely declared, *nobilitas* ...*omnis honores non ex merito sed quasi debitos a vobis repetit* (*Jug.* 85. 37), 'the nobility command you to give them every high office not on their merits but as their due'. Hence a candidate of non-senatorial rank was almost bound to fail (however virtuous and diligent) on account of being *indignus*. If he succeeded, his enemies still regarded him as unworthy. Catiline says he was driven to revolution because he saw unworthy men elevated to high office—*quod non dignos homines honore honestatos videbam* (*Cat.* 35. 3)—the most unworthy of all being, of course, Cicero. This is the perversion of values that Horace is attacking. It is a perversion compounded by the stupidity of the people, who have often given office to the undeserving—*honores / saepe dat indignis* (15–16). And even now, when the old senatorial patronage is in decay, the men gaining power are no better; they are certainly no more popular. The only place where merit is still given its due is in certain areas of private life, such as the circle of Maecenas. The great patron was careful to accept only those who were worthy (*dignos* in v. 51), and with him worth was a question of character.

Our final concept is that of freedom. A manumitted slave ceased to be another man's property and acquired rights guaranteed by Roman law. But as a *libertinus* he could not record the name of his tribe or father; he was identifiable by his servile cognomen, and on certain formal occasions he wore the freedman's conical hat.[20] Again, though accepted by plebeians and often by knights as well, he could never hope to win political distinction.

Nor, unless he was a man of learning like some of the Greek professors,[21] was he admitted to aristocratic society. The stigma of slavery became fainter in the second generation, but although a freedman's son might occasionally reach the senate his position was always precarious. P. Popilius was ejected from the house in 70 B.C. (Cic. *Cluent.* 132). Others were expelled by Appius Claudius twenty years later (Dio 40. 63). More reappeared under Caesar (47–45 B.C.)[22] and more again under the Triumvirs in 39 B.C. (Dio 48. 34), but their presence was fiercely resented.[23] Furthermore, in senses other than the strictly legal one, *liber* and its cognates could indicate distinctions within the citizen body. What was *libertas* for the well-born was *licentia* for the lower orders.[24]

As a freedman's son, therefore, Horace knew what discrimination was like. But was *libertas*, he wondered, simply a question of birth? Were not the free men who competed in the scramble for office really the slaves of Gloria? And when they had climbed to one stage of the *cursus honorum* would they not have to acquire even more influence and more clients in order to reach the next? It was obvious that to win and maintain *gloria, dignitas* and *clientelae*,[25] which were the prerequisites of power, a man had to organize his day on a rigid plan, attending all kinds of tiresome functions and 'cultivating' people who in themselves were boring and disagreeable. That was not the kind of freedom which appealed to Horace. He preferred to live a quiet, relaxed life, enjoying his friends and realizing his creative talents. Such freedom was possible only for those who were *ambitione soluti* (129), and this detachment required moral discipline. It therefore turns out that Horace is more free than those who despise him, thanks to the guidance of a man who was once a slave.

It is clear, then, that this satire implies a thoroughgoing critique of the aristocratic-republican system. According to Horace the concepts of *nobilitas, dignitas,* and *libertas* have been perverted and misunderstood. They have lost their moral significance and have become identified with *gloria, honores, clientelae* and all the other prizes of ambitious self-interest. As a man with strong Epicurean sympathies Horace attempts to uphold the true meaning of these ideas, using all the resources of his satiric art. Some of these resources have already been noted, but two features are especially striking and both contribute to the same rhetorical effect. The first is the unusual number of comparative expressions: *non...ut plerique* (1–5), *contra* (12), *non...pluris licuisse* (14), *quid oportet / nos facere*, etc. (17–18), *mallet...quam* (19–20), *non minus* (24), *minor* (26), *dissimile* (49), *non ut honorem...ita te* (49–50), *maior* (88), *longe discrepat* (92), *demens...sanus* (97–8), *maior* (100), *plures* (101), *plures* (103), *nemo sordes mihi quas tibi* (107), *commodius quam tu* (110), *suavius* (130). The function of these expressions is to endorse some kind of choice—'this rather than that'. And the choice in its most general aspect is that between wisdom and folly. The second feature, already perceived by Hendrickson,[26] is the figure known as ἀναίρεσις, which takes the form 'not this (nor this) but that'. Thus, indicating the positive element with a capital letter, we have *non quia...nec quod...Referre negas* (1–7), *non hoc...nulla fors...Vergilius...Varius dixere* (52–5), *non ego me claro...non ego circum...Sed quod eram narro* (58–60), *non patre praeclaro Sed vita et pectore puro* (64), *neque avaritiam, neque sordis nec mala lustra...Purus et insons* (68–9), *noluit...Sed est ausus* (72–6), *nec timuit...neque essem questus...At hoc* (85–7), *non ut magna...pars...sic me defendam...Nam nollem* (90–7), *non avide, Quantum interpellet* (127). The figure can have various functions, but here it clearly represents an attempt to re-educate the moral judgement.

As well as defending himself against malicious detractors Horace is therefore trying to put across a persuasive definition, that is 'one which gives a new conceptual meaning to a familiar word without substantially changing its emotive meaning, and which is used with the conscious or unconscious purpose of changing, by this means, the direction of people's interests'.[27] Juvenal had a similar purpose in mind when he said *nobilitas sola est atque unica virtus* (8. 20), 'the one and only nobility is virtue', and indeed if titles were appropriate this satire might well be headed 'Of True Nobility'.

One last qualification is necessary. I have cited familiar passages from Livy, Sallust, and Cicero to illustrate the discontent which at one time or another was felt towards the ruling class. But it would be quite wrong to imagine that Horace was echoing the sentiments of Canuleius, Marius, or Cicero. Those men and others like them were passionately involved in political life, and their primary concern was to broaden the base of the governing class by securing the admission of new magistrates and senators. But Horace had seen too many new magistrates and senators. He knew what they were like and he saw the contempt in which they were held. To him, and to many thinking men, the whole constitutional system seemed to have gone rotten; honours and offices were no longer worth having. Disillusion with all kinds of political endeavour was reflected in a widespread longing for peace and security. And when it became clear that only one man could provide such blessings, the days of the Republic were over.

CHAPTER III

ENTERTAINMENTS

I. 5

In the spring of 38 B.C. Antony agreed to meet Octavian in Brundisium to discuss the threat presented by Sextus Pompeius. Octavian, who was in Etruria at the time (Dio 48. 46), failed to keep the appointment, but by sending ships, men and equipment he gave the impression that he intended to come, and he remonstrated with Antony for not waiting (Appian 5. 80). In due course, against Antony's advice Octavian attacked Sextus on his own, with such disastrous results that he was forced to send Maecenas to Athens, where Antony had his headquarters, asking for another conference in Italy the following spring. Since Antony was prepared to let Octavian have ships in exchange for infantry and was anxious to settle affairs in Italy before starting on his eastern campaigns, he agreed, and eventually in 37 B.C. a meeting took place at Tarentum which postponed the final clash for another six years.

The present satire, usually known as The Journey to Brundisium, relates what happened to Maecenas' party on the way to one of these conferences. We do not know for certain which,[1] but that does not oblige us to accept the view held by Musurillo and others that 'the poem itself is *a poetic fiction*, a composite picture perhaps of journeys made at different times and bound together as a *jeu d'esprit* in imitation of Lucilius'.[2]

About eighty years earlier Lucilius had travelled south to visit his estates in southern Italy and Sicily[3] and had sent an account of his experiences to a friend who was due to follow later. The forty-odd fragments (W. 94–148) suggest that it was a lively, intimate piece of work, typically Roman in character. It appealed to Horace in both conception and tone, and without it his own poem would have been very different, if indeed it had been written at all.[4] Yet I do not believe that Horace invented any episode in 1. 5 either to provide a literary allusion or to invite stylistic comparisons. Since this is an unfashionable view at the moment, I had better say a few words in its defence. In 1. 5. 82–5 we are told that at Trivicum, after waiting till midnight for a girl who never turned up, Horace went to sleep and had an erotic dream. Now there is an unplaced fragment of Lucilius (W. 1183) which has been convincingly emended so as to read *perminxi lectum, imposui pede pellibus labes* ('I wet the bed and with my member made a mess on the skins').[5] This is often taken as the 'model' of the Horatian passage, and is therefore assigned to Lucilius' Sicilian Journey. Then, since it is rather unlikely that both poets should have had the same experience on their respective travels, the next step is to allege that Horace is writing fiction. But this is bad methodology, for there is no evidence at all that W. 1183 does come from the *Iter Siculum*. Lucilius, after all, wrote quite extensively about his erotic escapades. To treat an isolated fragment in this way is like finding an unidentified anecdote of Boswell's about some olive-skinned girl and assigning it at once to his Corsican diary—a work which is in fact devoid of gallantry.[6]

If we rule out W. 1183, we can also rule out W. 136–7— verses which are supposed to describe Lucilius' sexual frustration:

> Tantalus qui poenas ob facta nefantia poenas
> pendit.[7]

Tantalus who pays a penalty, yea a penalty, for his unspeakable deeds.

If we must seek a clue in Horace I should prefer to quote 1. 5. 7–9:

> hic ego propter aquam, quod erat deterrima, ventri
> indico bellum, cenantis haud animo aequo
> exspectans comites.

Here, on account of the water (for it was appalling), I declared war on my stomach and waited impatiently for my friends as they had their dinner.

Horace was not the first or the last traveller to have trouble with his stomach. Suppose Lucilius had the same complaint and was forced to watch his companions dealing with a well-cooked meal, might he not have suffered the torments of Tantalus?[8] To sum up: while Lucilian influence may well account for the *mention* of the erotic episode we have no right to infer that the episode itself is fictitious.

Another fragment which Horace is said to have copied is W. 109–10, where the speaker says of his opponent *dente adverso eminulo hic est | rinoceros*—'this fellow with his tooth sticking out in front is a rhinoceros'. In Horace's poem (56 f.) an altercation begins when one buffoon says to another 'I declare you're the image of a wild horse' (*equi te | esse feri similem dico*). He then calls attention to a scar on the other man's forehead, suggesting that he once had a horn. More will be said about these lines later; here it is enough to point out that if Lucilius speaks of a tooth and a rhinoceros and Horace of a scarred forehead and a wild horse that is no proof that Horace borrowed the whole incident from his predecessor. Animal similes, after all, are one of the most basic elements in peasant abuse.

Finally, Horace has some descriptive touches of a general kind where it is merely silly to insist on literary dependence. As Tenney Frank has said, 'Critics point out that . . . there are muddy roads and a boat trip in Horace as in Lucilius—as though Horace ought to have trudged the wagon route and left the barge for originality's sake, or sent a commission to pave the road so as to avoid Lucilian mud'.[9] Unlike love elegy, the journey poem had not developed a set of conventions which allowed fact and fiction to exist side by side. Maecenas, Virgil and other members of Horace's audience were actually involved in the incidents described—indeed the poem was written largely for their sake. At least two possible dates can be found for the journey itself, and there is nothing in Lucilius to show that Horace was drawing on literature rather than life. And so we need not hesitate to join those readers who for two thousand years have accepted the poem as a piece of authentic narrative.

We now turn to the poem itself. Gibbon thought little of it. 'The maxim that every thing in great men is interesting applies only to their minds and ought not to be extended to their bodies.'[10] Clearly what bored Gibbon was the trivial nature of the episodes. In order to excuse Horace he felt obliged to suggest that the satire was written 'to convince his enemies that his thoughts and occupations on the road were far from being of a serious or political nature'. Other readers have not given up so easily. We are told that when Horace puts ointment on his sore eyes (30) it indicates his scepticism about the forthcoming conference;[11] that the slanging match in Cocceius' villa is a symbol of the diplomatic exchanges at Tarentum;[12] and that when Sarmentus compares Cicirrus to the Cyclops he is really poking fun at Sextus Pompeius.[13] What these critics overlook is that without the aid of fantasy the satire in question is an extremely neat and skilful poem. Anyone who doubts this should start from the article by H. Düntzer in *Phil.* LV (1896), where he will find the whole journey recounted stage by stage in about four and a half thousand words. Horace took six hundred.

His powers of compression are evident in the opening lines:

> egressum magna me accepit Aricia Roma
> hospitio modico.

On leaving mighty Rome I was received by Aricia in a modest inn.

The departure is contained in *egressum*, the arrival in *accepit*, and Aricia, as well as being contrasted with mighty Rome, is defined by the type and quality of its accommodation. All in eight words.
    A more elaborate example occurs in vv. 77–80:

> incipit ex illo montis Apulia notos
> ostentare mihi, quos torret Atabulus et quos
> numquam erepsemus, nisi nos vicina Trivici
> villa recepisset.

From that point Apulia began to show me her familiar hills, which are scorched by the Altino, and over which we should never have crawled had not a villa near Trivicum taken us in.

As the hills of Apulia come into view we are told three quite different things about them. The first is a matter of sentiment—they hold memories of the poet's boyhood; the second is descriptive—they are parched by the Sirocco (here called by its local name) and are therefore exhausting to the traveller; the third is both descriptive and structural, for as well as indicating the long steep climb the subjunctive *erepsemus* points forward to the villa at Trivicum with its smoky dining-room and deceitful maid. Lightness and speed are achieved by ellipse, asyndeton, historic infinitives, and especially by clever variations in the use of the participle, e.g.

milia tum pransi tria repimus atque subimus
impositum saxis late candentibus Anxur.
huc venturus erat Maecenas optimus atque
Cocceius, missi magnis de rebus uterque
legati, aversos soliti componere amicos.   (25–9)

After breakfast we crawl three miles uphill to Anxur, standing on its white rocks which can be seen from far and wide. The admirable Maecenas was due to come here with Cocceius; both of them were envoys on an important mission, with experience in settling differences between friends.

These lines will show how useful the participle was for the terse, casual, and yet disciplined style of the poet's notebook.

The most obvious danger in writing a diary of this kind is that it may become a mere list of places visited. 'We started from *A*, then we went to *B*, and finally reached *C*.' A few examples will show how Horace deals with the problem. At v. 9 he begins the account of his embarkation at Forum Appii. But instead of saying 'We went aboard the barge', he lets the voices of the servants and bargees come drifting out of the dusk. 'Bring her in here!' 'You're packing them in like sardines!'[14] 'Hey there, that's enough!' Arrivals and departures are sometimes passed over altogether, and notice how rarely we meet a colourless travel-word like *pervenimus* (94). Instead we are shown pictures of the group 'crawling up' the Apulian hills (*erepsemus*) and 'bowling down' to the plain in their wagons (*rapimur raedis*), until the arrival at Brundisium, which is itself made part of a neat zeugma:

> Brundisium longae finis chartaeque viaeque est.
>
> Brundisium is the end of a long tale and journey.

The same ease and variety are discernible in his handling of time, which may be indicated by the sun (20), by the hour (23), by a meal (70), or by the weather (96). And it is worth remarking how careful Horace is to avoid concluding every entry at the end of a line. In nearly a quarter of the cases a new entry begins within the verse—and not always after the caesura either. All this gives the narrative a continuous flow, and so while it is possible to make a fair attempt at reconstructing the travellers' route and speed, the satire never reads like a log-book.

The details selected for comment throw an interesting light on the poet's sensibility. Forum Appii, where the Decennovium canal begins, is 'crammed with boatmen and stingy landlords', Canusium earns mention by its gritty bread, Gnatia by its local superstition. In other words the interest of a place lies in the comfort or entertainment which it affords the travellers. Horace is not concerned with natural beauty. Thus while 'fishy Barium' is a phrase worthy of Dylan Thomas, including as it does the site of the town, its occupation, its market, and to a modern reader perhaps even its smell, it does not present a precise visual image. Commenting on the journey through the Pomptine Marshes, Fraenkel says 'Horace has caught the true character of that melancholy stretch of marshland'.[15] Perhaps, but he has caught it by enduring it, not by painting it. For he is so distracted by croaking frogs, biting mosquitoes, and singing boatmen that he never looks beyond the towpath. To this general observation there is one striking exception:

> impositum saxis late candentibus Anxur.
>
> Anxur, standing on its white rocks which can be seen from far and wide.

But that is the only picture of its kind in the book. Moreover, in view of Lucilius W. 498:

> Carpathium Rhodus in pelagus se inclinat apertum,
> Rhodes slopes down into the open Carpathian sea,

and Catullus 67. 32–3:

> Brixia Cycneae supposita speculae,
> flavus quam molli praecurrit flumine Mella,
> Brixia set under the Cycnean height, with the gentle stream of the
> yellow Mella running by,

it is hazardous to suggest, as Fraenkel does,[16] that landscape photography was invented by the generation of Horace and Virgil.

Early in this century Dr Dorsch was following Horace's route when he chanced to meet a peasant above Terracina (Horace's Anxur). After listening to Dorsch rhapsodizing about the beauty of the mountain view, the peasant turned towards the plain, and pointing to the carefully cultivated land below exclaimed, not without some guile, 'Che bel panorama!'[17] Our romantic heritage makes it hard for us to grasp that Horace is no more interested in natural beauty than in the progress of agriculture or the details of local government. 'Wir ergötzen uns', says Fritzsche, 'an der jugendlichen wahren Reiselust, welche sich durch das Ganze ergiesst.'[18] Here we catch a glimpse of Horace the happy wanderer, striding over the mountains with knapsack and *Lederhosen*. Yet if Fritzsche had read the sections where the travellers are *en route* he would have found not a word to prove that the poet's foot ever touched the ground.

We may be fairly sure, then, that the pleasure Horace felt at receiving Maecenas' invitation was mainly due to the prospect of spending a fortnight with his friends in rather novel surroundings. This in turn explains the nature of the poem; for it is not a private reverie, but rather an evening with slides. The selection is drawn from scenes in which the audience has taken part—an almost infallible formula—and on inspection they fall into two alternating types. One is the happy scene—Horace and Heliodorus wash in the spring at Feronia's temple; Maecenas joins the party from Octavian's headquarters; the arrival of Virgil, Varius, and Tucca; Cocceius entertains the travellers in his villa at Caudium. The other type ought to be the miserable scene, but it isn't. Why it isn't is something of a mystery. When someone back from the continent tells how he has been sea-sick in the Channel, fleeced in a French restaurant, and despoiled of his girl-friend by some smooth Italian, we laugh unreservedly—for is not comedy the tragedy which happens to other people? But the strange thing is that the victim himself enjoys reliving his woes. In the same way, as Horace's fellow-sufferers recall that sleepless night in the middle of a swamp, the foul drinking-water, the gritty bread, and the roads reduced to a quagmire by torrential rain, the whole experience begins to seem quite gay. Horace himself had a particularly bad time. He had a bout of diarrhoea at Forum Appii; after that his eyes became inflamed by the marsh gases— a condition which the smoke-filled room at Trivicum did little to relieve; and then there was that girl—all of which gave Horace a special claim on the others' amused sympathy.

Rueful memories of this kind demand two qualities which Horace possessed and Juvenal clearly did not. The first is detachment—the author must be able to see his own situation with the eyes of a spectator. And the second is assurance—the assurance which comes from feeling at ease with one's audience. The last point will be developed in connexion with 1.9; here it need only be observed that the Journey to Brundisium both reflected and consolidated Horace's position within Maecenas' circle.

There is also another aspect of the satire's spirit, and that is its delightful combination of Roman *urbanitas* with the humour of rustic Italy.

iam nox inducere terris
umbras et caelo diffundere signa parabat.　　(9–10)

Night is coming on, 'the night of cloudless climes and starry skies'. It is a perfect setting for high romance. But the air is filled, not with music, but with raucous backchat. This is followed by a popular song—antiphonal, affectionate, and very drunken. Then the boatman moors his barge and settles on his back, and soon his snores are punctuating the frogs' chorus. Next morning a choleric eye peers out of the barge; it registers no progress. In a second its owner is on the bank with a branch of willow in his hand, walloping the boatman, who no doubt kept 'God's time'. Singing, snoring, walloping—it is all pure Plautus, or rather pure Italy, for these were elements in popular entertainment long before New Comedy was ever thought of. At Beneventum

> sedulus hospes
> paene macros arsit dum turdos versat in igni. (71–2)

> The fussy host nearly burnt his house down while turning some skinny thrushes over the fire.

Pure farce. But it is developed in two lines which in spite of the *vetus culina* foreshadow Virgil's burning of Troy:

> nam vaga per veterem dilapso flamma culinam
> Volcano summum properabat lambere tectum.

> For as Vulcan slipped out through the old stove the darting flame quickly rose to lick the ceiling.

The alliteration of v's (often a violent sound), the stately metonymy of Vulcan for *ignis*, and the serpentine fire-imagery all anticipate Book 2 of the *Aeneid*. Then the action reverts to farce as the guests scramble frantically to save their dinner.

At Gnatia, amid a lot of banter, some locals try to convince the party that frankincense will melt if placed on the temple steps. Horace enjoys the fun but at the same time waves their superstition aside with a fine parody of Lucretius:

> namque deos didici securum agere aevum,
> nec, si quid miri faciat natura, deos id
> tristis ex alto caeli demittere tecto. (101–3)

For I have learned that the gods live a carefree life, and that, if
nature does anything abnormal, it is not the gods who send it down in
anger from their high home in the sky.

This blend of simplicity and sophistication is also evident in the
exchange of abuse which takes place in the centre of the poem and
provides a diversion from the travelogue:

> nunc mihi paucis
> Sarmenti scurrae pugnam Messique Cicirri,
> Musa velim memores.   (51–3)

Now O Muse recount in brief, I pray thee, the fight between Sarmentus the clown and Messius Cicirrus.

This solemn formula would be recited in a deep resonant tone.
But the names have already destroyed any hope of grandeur.
Sarmentus suggests *sarmentum* 'a faggot' and obviously suits its
owner's physique, while Cicirrus recalls the 'cock-man' who was
a standard figure in local farces. Nevertheless, the poet continues
as though he were singing of Aeneas and Turnus: 'And tell from
what lineage each entered the fray of words. Messius comes from
glorious stock—Oscans.' (Oscans were proverbially oafish and,
according to some, supplied the origin of the word 'obscene'.)
'Sarmentus' mistress is still alive. Such was their ancestry as they
joined battle.' In other words, Sarmentus was of servile birth and
had no ancestors at all.

Sarmentus strikes first. 'I declare you're the image of a wild horse!' 'Right!'
says Messius amid laughter, and tosses his head. 'Hey! If you can threaten us
like that when your horn's been cut off, what would you do if it was still on
your head?' (The left side of his hairy brow was in fact disfigured by an ugly
scar.) After a string of jokes about the other's face and his Campanian disease
he begged him to do the dance of the shepherd Cyclops—he would need neither
mask nor tragic buskins.[19]
   Cicirrus was not lost for a reply. Had Sarmentus dedicated, as promised, his
chain to the household gods? The fact that he was a civil servant in no way
diminished his mistress's claim upon him. And why had he ever run away
when one pound of meal would have been ample for such a tiny puny fellow?

This immemorial peasant humour with its quick repartee and
earthy similes is the germ of all popular drama. It is true that

Livy (7. 2) sees the first phase of Roman drama in the stately movements of some Etruscan dancers who visited Rome in 364 B.C. But the young men who parodied their dance and exchanged scurrilous abuse among themselves had enjoyed the same kind of fun long before that date; and when official performances became tainted with professionalism and art, they reverted to their old practice. Livy expressly connects this badinage with the Oscan farces, and Cicirrus, we recall, was an Oscan. Nor was such humour confined to the proletariat. Here is an example from Cicero (*De Orat.* 2. 266). The speaker is Julius Caesar Strabo:

'Caricatures are also exceedingly funny. They are usually directed at ugliness or some physical defect and involve a comparison with something rather discreditable—like my joke at the expense of Helvius Mancia. "Now I'll show what sort of a man you are." "Go on, then", he said. So I pointed at a Gaul portrayed on Marius' Cimbrian shield, which was hanging on one of the New Shops. His body was twisted, his cheeks were baggy, and his tongue was hanging out. There was loud laughter, for it was the very image of Mancia.'

So too Horace and his friends were amused—*ridemus* (57), *prorsus iucunde* (70). Clearly this boisterous humour appealed to something very deep in the Roman character, something which the imperial *gravitas* overlaid but never wholly effaced.

I. 7

A rather similar altercation comprises the seventh satire of Book I. The situation, in brief, is this: on being proscribed by the Triumvirs in 43 B.C., Rupilius Rex, a man of pungent wit, took refuge in Asia. There he became involved in a lawsuit with a tough businessman from Clazomenae called Persius. The case, which came before Brutus, soon developed into an exchange of invective, culminating in a sally by Persius. Turning to Brutus, whose ancestor had expelled King Tarquin from Rome and who himself had killed that uncrowned monarch Julius Caesar, he cried 'In heaven's name, Brutus! You are used to getting rid of kings. Why don't you cut this King's throat? Believe me, this is just the job for you!'

In itself the pun is not too bad. Cicero (*Att.* 1. 16. 10) tells how he used it in reply to Clodius. 'Quousque,' inquit, 'hunc regem feremus?' 'Regem appellas', inquam, 'cum Rex tui mentionem nullam fecit?'—'How long are we going to stand for this king?' he said. 'Do you speak of King,' said I, 'when King made no mention of you?' (Clodius had hoped for a legacy from Rex, who was his brother-in-law.) A few weeks before his death Caesar had evaded the title *rex* by shouting to the crowd that he was not Rex but Caesar—a remark which was subtly analysed by Francis Bacon.[20] Modern instances would not be hard to find. The late Mackenzie King, prime minister of Canada, used to be called Rex as an undergraduate. Today British journalists sometimes comment on the regal power of Mr Cecil King. Such considerations, however, would not have impressed Dryden. 'I am sorry to say it for the sake of Horace, but certain it is, he has no fine palate who can feed so heartily on garbage.'[21] Even if we grant that the joke falls short of the up-roarious, Dryden's disgust is still out of place; for it is not really Horace's garbage. Here, as in 1. 5, he is playing a double game. He is amused by the characters and their repartee, but he also finds them rather crude and silly. So he introduces the contest in elaborate mock-heroic language:

inter

Hectora Priamiden animosum atque inter Achillem
ira fuit capitalis ut ultima divideret mors.   (11–13)

Between Hector, son of Priam, and the valiant Achilles the wrath was
so murderous that in the end only death could part them.

The gigantic shadows of Hector and Achilles are thus projected behind the squabbling litigants. Perhaps we may go further and suggest that it is Achilles' shadow which looms over the half-breed Greekling Persius, while Hector's falls on his Roman descendant Rex. In any case the function of the irony is un-mistakable. It dissociates Horace from the buffoonery which follows. And so in its full perspective the poet's position is that of a man at a party who stands on the fringe of a rather boisterous and drunken group. He stays close enough to enjoy what is being said, but for the benefit of the other guests he wears a satirical smile.

The poem's dramatic date is 43 or 42 B.C. When it was written is another question. The third line, which implies that the story is well known in Rome, points to a date after Horace's return from Philippi. Some critics have tried to fix a *terminus ante quem* on the assumption that the references to Caesar's murder and the subsequent proscriptions would have been unthinkable after the poet's introduction to Maecenas in 39 B.C. But then why was the poem ever published? Again, Heinze remarked that a short piece of this kind would have been preceded by a few longer works in the manner of Lucilius. Perhaps, but this doesn't help, because there may have been two or three other poems like 1. 2 which were not preserved in the collection. We are therefore left with a date some time between 40 and 35 B.C. I doubt if any greater precision is either possible or necessary.

What does matter is our estimate of the poem. I myself think it is a failure, and since Fraenkel (p. 118) admires 'its perfect neatness and easy poise' I had better give my reasons. First of all it is tiresome merely to be told that X is a brilliant raconteur and Y an incomparable wit. We must have evidence. Here we are offered only two specimens of Persius' talent and none at all of Rex's. It may be answered that the satire is simply a *chria* (or clever retort) inflated into a mock-heroic incident, and that therefore everything must be subordinated to the one climactic joke. This only proves that the basic idea was unworkable. By way of contrast consider Ovid's lament for Corinna's parrot (*Am.* 2. 6). The germ of this poem is provided by the dirge for Lesbia's sparrow (Catullus 3), but Ovid expands the idea into a successful burlesque 'by following the set form of a funeral elegy: the bidding to mourners (1–16); the regrets "Ah, what avails—" (17–24); the outburst against the powers responsible—σχετλιασμός— with a list of those who could have been better spared (25–42); the deathbed scene (43–8); the hopes of a suitable future life

(49–58); the committal (59–62)'.[22] But whereas the death of a bird has many aspects and lends itself to comic decoration, a retort can only be simple and momentary. The difficulty is reflected in the satire's structure. After an effective opening, which prepares us for the clash of wits, Horace goes on to describe Persius and his rough tongue. Then comes a deliberately ponderous transition *ad Regem redeo*. And what do we hear of Rex? Nothing at all. Instead we have a lengthy and highly wrought parenthesis designed to build up atmosphere. At v. 18 the construction is resumed without any sign of the story getting under way, and in fact the poem is three-fifths over before the first blow is struck. After all the fanfare and skirmishing the knock-out punch comes as an anticlimax, and having paid for a ringside seat we feel like demanding our money back.

1. 8

Though it resembles 1. 7 in being a tale of comic revenge, 1. 8 is a much superior work. One reason for this can be inferred from the position of the revenge motif. Whereas in 1. 7 it is presented in the second line, thus creating expectations which are never properly fulfilled, in 1. 8 it does not appear until v. 44 (*non... inultus*), where it heralds a surprising climax. The first part of 1. 8 is therefore more than prefatory material; the incidents and observations exist in their own right. The opening is beautifully concise:

> olim truncus eram ficulnus, inutile lignum,
> cum faber, incertus scamnum faceretne Priapum,
> maluit esse deum. deus inde ego...

Once I was the trunk of a fig-tree—a useless lump of wood. Then the carpenter, in two minds whether to make me into a stool or a Priapus, decided that I should be a god; so a god I am.

After recounting his rather fortuitous birth Priapus goes on to describe his distinguishing characteristic (a large vermilion member), his regalia (the sickle in his right hand and the split reed on his head), his function (to frighten away thieves and birds) and his precinct (the gardens of Maecenas). This is the kind of information that might be given in a comic prologue—one thinks of Arcturus in Plautus' *Rudens*. And in fact Macrobius tells us (*Sat.* 6. 5. 6) that Priapus spoke the prologue in one of Afranius' comedies.

The opening lines also owe something to epigram. The *Greek Anthology* has several pieces in which an artifact speaks of its former mode of existence. Thus a bow remembers when it was a pair of horns (6. 113), a boat was once a pine-tree (9. 131), and a pen was once a reed (9. 162). Other relevant epigrams belong to the so-called *Priapea*.[23] This was originally a Hellenistic genre, but surviving specimens date from the beginning of the imperial age. Written mainly in elegiacs or hendecasyllables, they deal with various aspects of Priapus' worship, and they contain numerous references to his appearance and to his task, which was something between that of a head gardener and a scarecrow. Naturally enough, the personality which emerges is many-sided. Sometimes the god sounds like Catullus in splenetic mood; sometimes, like an elegant rake—perhaps one of Ovid's more disreputable friends; sometimes, as in no. 86, he becomes a kindly pastoral figure telling of the offerings he receives. But most often he is a clown who brags continually of the obscene outrage which he will visit upon thieves. The habit is most succinctly illustrated by no. 22, which is very much in the style of Martial:

> femina si furtum faciet mihi virve puerve,
> haec cunnum, caput hic praebeat, ille nates,

which may be timidly paraphrased as 'If a woman or man or boy commits a theft, I shall punish each in the appropriate way'. From time to time, like all clowns, he is humiliated, and then his bluster subsides into querulous impotence, as in no. 55 where his sickle has been stolen and he is apprehensive of more serious losses.

But Priapus had not always been a buffoon. In Lampsacus, his place of origin, he was worshipped as the son of Dionysus and Aphrodite; he received the sacrifice of asses; his image appeared on the city's coins; and according to Pausanias (9. 31. 2) he was honoured above all other gods. From there his cult spread through the coastal towns of Asia Minor, where as well as promoting the fertility of crops and herds he also watched over fishing and navigation. In Greece Priapus blended with aspects of Hermes and Pan, and his adaptability is further proved by his admission to certain Orphic rites in which he was regarded as a symbol of regeneration. Perhaps the oddest episode in his history was the attempt of the gnostic Justinus to have him recognized as the first person of the Trinity. 'But the Good One is Priapus, who created before anything existed; whence he is called Priapus, because he first made all things.'[24] In spite of its absurd etymology the passage does bear witness to the resourcefulness of the old phallic god. For the most part, however, Priapus and his Italic forerunner Mutinus (Titinus) received a more primitive kind of respect. Their images were carried through the streets at public festivals; and Lactantius, Arnobius, and Augustine all speak of the custom whereby married women sat astride the god's member in the hope of joyful issue.[25]

After the official adoption of Christianity constant attempts were made to eradicate the older religion, but it continued to reappear with all the vigour and persistence of a weed. An eighth-century tract *Judicia Sacerdotalia De Criminibus* ordained bread and water for 'anyone who has chanted prayers to the phallus', and from then until the Synod of Tours in the fourteenth century the practice was regularly proscribed in ecclesiastical edicts. In certain areas the Church quietly compromised, and then history saw the emergence of that odd phenomenon, the phallic saint. The best known of several examples is Saint Foutin, whose name is apparently a corruption of Photinus, first bishop of Lyons. When the Protestants entered the church at Embrun in 1585 they found an object, alleged to be the saint's phallus, which had received numerous libations from women in need of help. His worship in the early seventeenth century is described by Pierre de L'Estoile as follows: 'Témoin Saint Foutin de Varailles en Provence, auquel sont dédiées les parties honteuses de l'un et de l'autre sexe, formées en cire: le plancher de la chapelle en est fort garni, et, quand le vent les fait entrebattre, cela débauche un peu les dévotions à l'honneur de ce Saint.' An even more recent priapic survival was the festival of Saint Cosmo and Saint Damian, described by Sir William Hamilton in a letter dated 30 December 1781. At this ceremony, which was held at Isernia in the Abruzzi, a brisk trade was done in votive offerings of the kind just described, and the healing oil of St Cosmo was either sold for private use or else applied by the priest. 'No less than 1400 flasks of that oil were either expended at the altar in unctions or charitably distributed...and as it is usual for everyone who either makes use of the oil at the altar, or carries off a flask of it, to leave an alms for St Cosmo, the ceremony of the oil becomes likewise a very lucrative one to the canons of the church.' On 26 July 1805 Isernia was destroyed by an earthquake.[26]

To revert to Horace's poem, Priapus tells us he is made of fig-wood—not unnaturally, since the fig was an emblem of fecundity, and the wood was cheap and easy to work.[27] His business is to protect the gardens which Maecenas is constructing outside the *agger* of Servius Tullius on the Esquiline Hill. As a result of the new landscaping 'the Esquiline is now a healthy place to live in, and one can stroll along the sunny Rampart'. Priapus' garden had not always been such a lovesome thing. Not long ago it had been the site of a paupers' cemetery, where corpses were carried out in cheap coffins and dumped into communal graves. Even now, when the transformation is almost complete, at night the macabre past takes over, and the place becomes a haunt of thieves, witches, and scavenging animals. Though worried at his inability to deal with the situation Priapus comforts himself with the memory of one glorious occasion on which he put the witches to rout and asserted his ancient power over sorcerers.[28]

The moon has just risen, when suddenly the air is filled with shrieking, a sound which exerts a magic control over the spirits of the dead.[29] Soon Canidia enters, along with her companion Sagana. Since one who binds another must not be bound,[30] she wears no shoes, and her hair is undone. Taking a lamb (black in colour, because destined for the powers of darkness) they tear it apart with their teeth and let the blood drip into a trench which they have scraped with their fingernails.[31] Their purpose in summoning the dead becomes more apparent at v. 30 with the mention of two dolls. The larger represents Canidia herself. It is made of wool (a powerful apotropaic material)[32] and is in the act of punishing a smaller figure of wax, which stands for the errant lover.[33] Sympathetic magic of this kind, where the victim's image is bound, pierced, and burnt, is familiar from all periods, but the best-known example in classical literature is the mime of Theocritus (*Id.* 2), where Simaetha's incantations are quoted at length, e.g.

ὡς τοῦτον τὸν κηρὸν ἐγὼ σὺν δαίμονι τάκω,
ὡς τάκοιθ' ὑπ' ἔρωτος ὁ Μύνδιος αὐτίκα Δέλφις.

As with the goddess's aid I melt this wax, so may Delphis the Mindian melt at once with love.[34]

The aim of Simaetha's spell is not to destroy Delphis, but to cause him unbearable anguish until he returns her love. Only if all else fails will she consign him to Hades. No doubt Canidia's purpose is much the same. Like Simaetha she invokes the aid of Hecate, while Sagana calls on the avenging Fury Tisiphone. The approach of these divinities is revealed by hell-hounds and serpents—a sight so dreadful that the moon hides her face behind the gravestones. All this is vouched for by Priapus in a suitably ordurous oath (37–9).

And now the ritual is reaching its climax. A wolf's beard and the tooth of a spotted snake are buried as a precaution against counter-spells, and finally the wax image is plunged into the fire. But at the very moment when the flame leaps up, Priapus is overcome with terror and breaks wind with a deafening explosion. The effect is immediate and shattering. The witches drop everything, and as they flee back to town in wild panic, herbs, love-knots, a chignon, and false teeth lie strewn in their wake.

Their discomfiture represents a dramatic reversal of roles. Instead of two fearsome witches with all hell at their command they are suddenly revealed as a pair of silly old hags. And as they scurry away they leave the god serenely in control, no longer a terrified spectator. It is in keeping, however, with Priapus' character that the catastrophe should be due not to any majestic assertion of *numen* but simply to muscular weakness. And this in turn may give us a clue to the origin of the poem; for when he was walking in Maecenas' gardens Horace may possibly have seen a wooden Priapus with an oddly warped posterior.[35] If so, the satire, as well as owing something to epigram and mime, will be in conception an aetiological poem.

Where official ceremonies were concerned, the Roman authorities were quite prepared to encourage a belief in magic. But they were less indulgent to witchcraft and astrology, which had an undesirable effect on the popular mind. Disapproval, however, was one thing, suppression another. In 33 B.C. magicians and astrologers were expelled from Rome on the orders of Agrippa (Dio 49. 43. 5). In A.D. 16 they had to be ejected once again.[36]

Among the upper classes many people professedly sceptical retained private superstitions. Julius Caesar, though 'never deterred or delayed from any enterprise by fear of the supernatural' (Suet. *Jul.* 59), used to repeat a certain charm three times after climbing into his carriage (Pliny, *NH* 28. 21). A deeper inconsistency is apparent in the work of the Elder Pliny, who can inveigh against *magicas vanitates* (*NH* 30. 1) and yet talk quite seriously about the marvellous virtue of Pyrrhus' big toe (*NH* 7. 20). However, it is safe to say that even if some of Horace's readers, like Maecenas himself, were not wholly free from superstition none of them would have had anything but contempt for a creature like Canidia. So too, in a more sceptical age, it is possible for a man who has read the evidence for psychic phenomena collected by G. N. M. Tyrell to feel that 'there may well be something in it', and yet to smile sarcastically at the gipsy palmist in the local fair.

On his evening stroll Horace himself would sometimes listen with amusement to the fortune-tellers outside the Circus (1. 6. 113–14). And on a later occasion he used the language of astrology in an effort to lift Maecenas from a bout of depression (*Carm.* 2. 17). But this does not mean that he ever paid serious attention to any kind of magic. I put it deliberately in this way, because (as with most of us) Horace's outlook is more a matter of pre-occupation than of doctrine. Instead of denying dogmatically that diseases could be cured by spells or that the future could be foretold, he preferred to convey his view of such beliefs by ignoring them. This healthy aversion to superstition was shared, as we might expect, by all the ancient satirists from Lucilius to Lucian. But in case we take such an attitude too much for granted we might consider the following extract, written by one of the most civilized men of the eighteenth century:

Three young ladies of our Town were on Saturday last indicted for Witchcraft. The witnesses against the First deposed upon Oath before Justice Bindover that she kept Spirits locked up in Vessels, which sometimes appeared in flames of blue Fire; that she used Magical Herbs, with some of which she drew in Hundreds of Men daily to her, who went out of her presence all inflamed, their mouths parched, and a hot Steam issuing from them, attended with a grievous Stench; that many of the said men were by force of that Herb metamorphos'd into Swine...It was proved against the second that she cut off by Night the Limbs from dead Bodies that were hang'd, and was seen to dig Holes in the Ground, to mutter some conjuring Words, and bury Pieces of the Flesh, after the usual Manner of Witches. The Third was accus'd for a notorious Piece of Sorcery...of moulding up Pieces of Dough into the Shapes of Men, Women, and Children; then heating them at a gentle Fire, which had a sympathetic Power to torment the Bowels of those in the Neighbourhood...But the Parson of our Parish, a strange refractory Man, will believe none of this...He goes about very oddly to solve the Matter. He supposes that, the First of these Ladies keeping a Brandy and Tobacco Shop, the Fellows went out smoking, and got drunk towards Evening, and made themselves Beasts. He says the Second is a Butcher's Daughter, and sometimes brings a Quarter of Mutton from the Slaughter-house over Night against a Market-Day, and once buried a Bit of Beef in the Ground as a known Receipt to cure Warts on her hands.

The Parson affirms that the Third sells Gingerbread, which to please the Children she is forced to stamp with Images before 'tis baked, and if it burns their Guts, 'tis because they eat too much, or do not drink after it.

(*The Tatler*, 1, no. 21, 1709.)

A gay conceit; but Horace would not have asked his readers' indulgence for that bit of beef.

I. 9

This is an amusing account of how Horace, on his morning walk, fell into the clutches of one who has been variously described as 'an impertinent fellow', 'a forward coxcomb', and (more recently) 'a bore'. There is in fact no word which will include the garrulity, the conceit, the persistence, and the crass insensitivity of this social climber. Since, however, in the poem he is of equal importance with Horace himself, it is convenient to have some name for him; and so I shall call him 'the pest'.

Unlike Jonson's Crispinus, who with his red beard, little legs, and feathered cap was obviously Marston,[37] the pest has no individual features. His behaviour recalls certain characters of Theophrastus, such as The Chatterbox (ὁ ἀδολέσχης) and The Windbag (ὁ λάλος),[38] and also other Horatian figures like the *captator* of 2. 5. 32–7 who says:

Publius (susceptible gentlemen like the sound of their own first names), I admire your character and wish to be your friend. I know the ins and outs of the law and am a capable defence counsel. I'd lose a leg before I'd see you insulted or robbed of a nut-shell. I'll take care that no one swindles or makes a fool of you.

The pest, therefore, cannot be identified with any real person—least of all with Propertius, who was only in his teens at the time and whose mother was still alive.[39] Nevertheless, the poem was not simply the product of Horace's imagination. We know that he was envied for his intimacy with Maecenas and that he was sometimes accosted on the street by people in search of inside information. No doubt there were many who would have been

74

glad to share his success, and it may well be that a genuine incident, in which the humorous Aristius Fuscus was involved,[40] provided the germ of the present poem. But having undertaken the work Horace immediately thought of the general type of person he was going to portray, and this led him to literature as well as life. His mind drew naturally from both sources and in the final product the ingredients cannot be distinguished.

The action of the piece may be described as a miniature drama. In each of the first three scenes Horace's attempts to escape end in frustration and despair. Early on he quickens his pace, stops, talks to his servant, and then starts off again. He even speaks of visiting a sick friend who lives two miles away on the other side of the river. But it is no good. The pest is a man of relentless energy and is prepared to go the whole way with him. Scene 1 ends with Horace's resistance broken (20). Scene 2 at once reveals that the pest is not really interested in exercise and casual conversation. He has a more sinister purpose in mind, namely friendship. Apart from one rather feeble interruption in vv. 26–7[41] Horace can only brood on the awfulness of this discovery. Hope flickers for a moment at the mention of a lawsuit which was due to be heard that morning,[42] but the pest decides to let the case go by default, and the pair walk on (43). So ends scene 2. As Heinze points out, the motif of the lawsuit which eventually leads to Horace's escape is introduced exactly half way through the poem; but here it only makes his plight seem worse, because it shows that the pest is willing to make serious sacrifices in order to achieve his purpose. The ultimate nature of this purpose, when revealed in scene 3, represents a further humiliation for the poet. Up to this he could console himself with the illusion that he himself was the coveted prize. It now becomes clear that he is merely a pawn and that Maecenas is the fellow's real objective. Thus after first intruding on Horace's privacy the man has now wounded his *amour propre*. Nor does the new discovery in any way improve Horace's position. The final objective may lie farther back, but he himself is still in the front line. It is therefore with immense relief that he sights reinforcements in the person of his friend Aristius Fuscus. But Fuscus turns traitor. Horace's hopes are again dashed, and the scene closes leaving him a helpless and deserted victim (74). But if the poet is beyond all human aid he has not been forsaken by his patron deity. From the beginning Apollo has watched the encounter, and he now intervenes by bringing the pest face to face with his accuser. The drama which began with one act of seizure (*arrepta manu*) ends with another (*rapit in ius*). Deliverance has come.

The satire's variety of incident is reflected in its means of communication. On the most simple level we have Horace himself relating the event to his friends. This narrative mode is of course implied throughout the poem, but it never exists for long by itself. Half way through the fourth line it becomes overlaid with dialogue. I say overlaid rather than supplanted, because although *suaviter, ut nunc est* in v. 5 is spoken to the pest, it is overheard by Horace's audience. A further degree of complexity is introduced in vv. 11 and 12. The words *o te, Bolane, cerebri | felicem!* are provoked by the pest, but they are not spoken to him. They are a private exclamation of the poet's; and yet they are not entirely private, for in a sense they are addressed to Bolanus. At v. 28 we find the same situation. *Felices! nunc ego resto. | confice* is a silent prayer occasioned by the pest's reply in the previous line. But again it cannot be called wholly private, since in form it is a command directed to the pest. Then, still further within this inner context, we have the words of the fortune-teller (31–4). And so the old gipsy is inside a private thought of Horace's which was caused by the pest and was intended ultimately for the poet's audience. When we add to these complexities the power of Apollo who can impose his will without words at all, we realize how many modes of discourse are included in the poem.

These modes are related to another aspect of the satire's variety, namely its variety of language. We know from Lucilius that *ibam forte*—'I happened to be going'—was quite a normal way of introducing a story. He has *ibat forte aries* (W. 559) and *ibat forte domum* (W. 258). The phrase strikes the right casual note, and here it is continued by *nescioquid nugarum*—'some trifle or other'. So the reader is prepared for a piece of light-hearted narrative. If it is to be light it must also be rapid, an effect achieved by asyndeton and ellipse, and by using the historic infinitive and the historic present. Rhythm also plays its part. In v. 9 we can hear Horace accelerating in the dactyls *ire modo ocius*, slowing down in the molossus *interdum*, and coming to a halt with *consistere*. The language is enlivened by colloquialisms like *misere* (8)—'desperately'—a usage common in Plautus and Terence,[43] *cerebri* (11) which has the sense of 'temper' only in Plautus and Petronius,[44] and *garrio* (13)—'I chatter'—which, apart from half a dozen passages of comedy, is mostly limited to Cicero's letters. Still confining ourselves to the narrative, let us look at *ventum erat* in v. 35. Now there is nothing peculiar in this form being preferred to *venimus*,[45] but can it be pure chance that the actual encounter is never once described in the first person plural? Does it not look as if the poet is avoiding even a grammatical association with his adversary? True, the satire does contain two cases of the first person plural, but notice where they come. In v. 48 Horace says *non isto vivimus illic/quo tu rere modo*; here *vivimus* refers to Maecenas and his friends and *tu* only confirms the pest's exclusion. In v. 62 we find *consistimus*, but, as the subsequent dialogue shows, this means Fuscus and Horace. There is still no *rapport* between the poet and his tormentor.

Instead of analysing the dialogue in the same way I would simply point to certain colloquial expressions which can be readily paralleled from the comic writers and Cicero's letters: v. 5—*suaviter* (nicely), *ut nunc est* (at the moment), *cupio omnia quae vis* (all the best); v. 6—*numquid vis?* (nothing else, is there?); v. 38—*interteam* (confound me); v. 41—*sodes* (please); v. 53—*sic habet* (that's the way it is). These phrases are all spoken by Horace. The pest's language is on the same stylistic level, but its familiarity is more abrasive in view of his position: v. 4—*quid agis dulcissime rerum?* (how are things, my dear fellow?); v. 38—*si me amas*

(be a pal); v. 43—*quomodo tecum?* (how do you find him?);
v. 47—*hunc hominem* (yours truly), *dispeream* (damn me); v. 52—
magnum narras (a tall story). Such phrases delineate character like
the strokes of a cartoonist's pencil. Rhythm also has its contribution to make, as when in v. 42 we are told that the pest walked on
in front—*et praecedere coepit.* This hexameter ending, coming as it
does in the first half of the line, has an air of finality and marks the
second phase of the pest's victory. Or again, consider the two
rhyming molossi in the middle of vv. 57 and 58—*corrumpam* and
desistam. Here we have a statement of the pest's determination—a
statement reiterated by the following *quaeram, occurram, deducam,*
and completed by the old maxim 'if at first you don't succeed,
try, try again'.

The *sermo cotidianus* represents one element in the poem's
stylistic structure. But this only attains full significance when set
beside another element which exists, as it were, on a higher emotional plane. In v. 26 Horace asks whether the pest has any next
of kin. 'Not one,' he answers, 'I have buried them all.' *Felices!
nunc ego resto,* cries Horace. 'Happy for them! Now I remain.'
With the word *felices* we are at once transported to the realm of
epic suffering. In *Odyssey* 5. 306 the storm-tossed hero exclaims:

> τρισμάκαρες Δαναοὶ καὶ τετράκις οἳ τότ' ὄλοντο.

> Thrice blessed, yea four times blessed are the Danaans who perished at
> that time.

And Aeneas has a similar cry (*Aen.* 1. 94). From the epic we pass
easily to the oracular. Horace's doom is closing in, a doom pre-
dicted by an old fortune-teller many years before. The lines have
a stately ring and should not be reduced to Christmas-card
doggerel:

> hunc neque dira venena nec hosticus auferet ensis,
> nec laterum dolor aut tussis, nec tarda podagra;
> garrulus hunc quando consumet cumque: loquaces,
> si sapiat, vitet, simul atque adoleverit aetas.   (31–4)

Not deadly poison, no, nor foeman's hand,
nor pleurisy nor cough nor slow-foot gout
shall slay him; at some moment heaven has planned
a chatterbox will surely wear him out.
On reaching manhood let him keep this rule:
never to wait and hear a babbling fool.

Dirus perhaps never lost that aura of dread which made it such
a natural epithet for Hannibal. *Hosticus* is an archaic word used by
Plautus in a passage of urgent entreaty,[46] and by the tragedian
Accius.[47] Varro (*LL* 5. 33) says that the phrase *hosticus ager* belonged to the official language of augurs. The one other Horatian
instance occurs in *Carm.* 3. 2. 6—a passage of decidedly epic tone.
Of *ensis* it is enough to say that Virgil uses it sixty times more often
than *gladius*, whereas Livy uses *gladius* ninety times more often
than *ensis*. We are struck by the semi-active sense of *tarda* and by
its application to *podagra*. The phrase may derive comic overtones
from a disreputable passage of Catullus (71. 2). The unusual use of
consumo in the active with a personal subject seems to imply that
the pest is a kind of wasting disease. 'Sooner or later' is not the
normal sense of *quando cumque*, and Fraenkel calls attention to
'the archaizing tmesis' and 'the oracular mystery of the date'.[48]
The same scholar has also illustrated the ominous significance of
vitet.

In v. 54 the style rises again with the aid of a military metaphor.
'Such is your valour', says Horace with heavy sarcasm, 'that you
will take Maecenas by storm. He is open to conquest; that is
why he makes the outer approaches so difficult.' It is not the
first time that the metaphor has appeared. It previously emerged
in vv. 42–3, and before that it was implicit in such words as
occupo (6), *consistere* (9), and *persequar* (16). Moreover, it does not
fade out at v. 56; it continues in words like *eriperet* (65) and
fugit (73), and it winds up the whole piece in v. 78, for *sic me
servavit Apollo* ('thus did Apollo save me') is an imitation of
Homer's τὸν δ' ἐξήρπαξεν Ἀπόλλων, which describes how Apollo
rescued Hector from the onslaught of Achilles (*Il.* 20. 443). Thus

the entire action may be seen as a running fight between Horace and his assailant.[49]

Between the worlds of conversation and heroic action lies a third which has affinities with both—I mean the world of civil law. Immediately after the gipsy's warning (35) the scene changes to the temple of Vesta and the law-courts, where proceedings have already been in progress for an hour. The pest must answer bail (*respondere vadato*) or else lose his case (*perdere litem*); he asks Horace to accompany him (*ades*), but Horace is unqualified to appear as a party (*stare*) and is ignorant of civil law (*civilia iura*). So the pest fails to present himself at the hearing (*relinquere rem*). Later in the poem, again after a moment of crisis (74), the law appears and takes charge of proceedings. The *adversarius* calls Horace as a witness (*licet antestari?*). Horace allows his ear to be touched as a sign of consent, and the pest is hustled off to court (*rapit in ius*). Civil law, as we all know, is a very mundane affair. Its material is depressingly human, its methods patient, prosaic, and exasperatingly tedious. But it has also another aspect, one which is attested by its formal ritual and its solemn, archaic language. I mean law as the preserver of civilized traditions and the guarantee of moral principles; law as Dike daughter of Zeus. This dual aspect of civil law becomes plain in the satire's conclusion. For although the *adversarius* is acting in his own interests, he is also the agent of a higher power. If he comes on the scene *casu* (74), it is the sort of chance that brought Oedipus to the cross-roads. But this time Apollo is bent on salvation, not on ruin; and so the drama turns out to be a comedy after all.

This poem, with its amusing tension between the appalling and the trivial, will always be a general favourite. As a condemnation of sycophancy and bad manners it also implies a moral judgement of universal validity. But to the Roman reader it must have given an additional pleasure, moving as it does among the familiar streets and buildings of the capital. The Sacra Via, Vesta's temple, Caesar's Gardens, and the Trastevere all receive special mention. Other sites are included by implication in *vicos* (13). Very little is known of the Sacra Via's topography at this period, but if the satire belongs to the year 36 or 35 B.C. then on coming through the Fornix Fabianus the two men could have seen the restored Regia with its white marble gleaming in the morning sunshine.[50] They might also have seen work in progress on the Basilica Aemilia,[51] and since the pest extended his praise so as to include the whole city we may imagine him becoming enthusiastic about other buildings under construction at the time, such as the temple of Apollo Palatinus, and possibly the Villa Publica.[52]

After noting the poem's universal appeal and the particular charm which it held for the Roman reader, we must take one step closer and discuss what it meant to Horace's friends, for in a sense this poem, like 1. 5, is the document of a coterie. We do not have to review the whole course of Horace's friendship with Maecenas, but it is important to remember that in its early years at least it was by no means a simple spontaneous relationship. As their temperamental sympathy asserted itself the tension caused by class consciousness relaxed, and instead of being merely a member of his patron's retinue Horace gradually became an *amicus* in the fullest sense of the word. But it was not an easy process; it required tact on both sides, and it put Horace in a delicate position not only as a man but also as a writer. How was he to address his patron and his other distinguished friends without sounding either rude or obsequious? One answer was to tackle the problem boldly as in 1. 6. That poem, with its series of qualified statements, is a skilful piece of balancing, and like all good balancing it looks effortless from a distance. But the feat was difficult to sustain, and it could not easily be varied or repeated.

There was, however, a more oblique method, which allowed many variations and was well suited to Horace's genius. As an illustration we may take 1. 9. 48–50, where the circle of Maecenas is said to be free from internal rivalries:

> non isto vivimus illic
> quo tu rere modo; domus hac nec purior ulla est
> nec magis his aliena malis.

> We do not live there in the fashion which you have in mind. No
> household is cleaner than his and more free from such low intrigues.

This compliment is not addressed to Maecenas, and we are made
to feel that it might never have been uttered had it not been for
the vulgar insinuations of the pest (45–8). One is reminded of the
close of I. 10, where by naming his opponents and revealing
their malicious attitude Horace is enabled to affirm his respect for
Maecenas, Messalla, Pollio, and the rest.

Or consider vv. 22–3:

> si bene me novi, non Viscum pluris amicum,
> non Varium facies.

> If I'm any judge, you will not think more highly of Viscus or of
> Varius as a friend.

This shows the very high place held by Viscus and Varius in the
poet's affections, and it must have given pleasure to the men concerned; the words, however, are spoken not by Horace but by
the pest, and so their testimony is strengthened by appearing to
come from an outside witness.

Again, the affirmation may be masked by ironic banter, as in
the episode of Aristius Fuscus (60–74). 'Ah,' says Horace, 'here
comes dear old Fuscus (*carus*). He'll help me to get rid of this
nuisance.' But Fuscus does nothing of the sort. With a mad-
dening smile he turns a deaf ear to Horace's appeals, and runs
away leaving the poet at the point of death. *Fugit improbus*—the
'dear friend' has suddenly become a scoundrel. Fuscus would
have taken this abuse very happily, because it confirmed the
effectiveness of his joke. In fact I should imagine that with the
possible exception of Maecenas no one enjoyed the poem more
than Fuscus. It may seem rather naïve that a man should take
pleasure in being mentioned in a *sermo* of this kind, but we should
remember that later on the emperor himself was not too proud to
ask for a similar favour.[53]

Maecenas and his friends knew very well that this was their
poem. Not only were they the object of the pest's endeavours,
but without them the whole episode would have been incon-

ceivable. As they listened to Horace's account of the fellow's
efforts to ingratiate himself their amusement must have been
spiced with a dash of self-congratulation. Secure in their own
eminence they could smile on the antics of the social climber and
enjoy that 'sudden glory' which Hobbes saw as the very essence
of laughter. No one is pained by flattery when it is offered with
such tact, and it may be assumed that Horace's friends liked him
all the more for inviting them to admire themselves.

A lack of self-knowledge produces comic as well as tragic
figures. Part of the fun in this satire comes from the pest's failure
to recognize his own absurdity. An especially neat touch occurs
in vv. 23–5, where he boasts of his facility in versification and of
his prowess as a singer and dancer—arts which his listener happened
to despise. Notice too the way in which Horace turns the pest's
mistakes to his own advantage. It was impudent of the fellow to
imagine that by accosting Horace in the street and forcing his
company on him he could obtain even a casual acquaintance. So
much is made clear in the first twenty lines. It follows that for
such a man to covet the esteem enjoyed by Viscus and Varius
was nothing short of grotesque. By implication, therefore,
Horace arrays himself alongside his friends, and in doing so affirms
the solidarity and exclusiveness of the group. It is clear throughout
that the pest's attentions are inspired not by a genuine liking and
respect, but by *invidia*.[54] Such *invidia*, however, is an index of
Horace's success. The point is still plainer if we think in terms of
ambitio. In vv. 56–60 the pest shows his mettle:

> haud mihi dero:
> muneribus servos corrumpam; non, hodie si
> exclusus fuero, desistam; tempora quaeram;
> occurram in triviis; deducam. nil sine magno
> vita labore dedit mortalibus.

I shan't be found wanting. I'll bribe his servants; and if the door is
shut in my face to-day I shan't give up. I'll bide my time, contrive
meetings in the streets, escort him home. If at first you don't succeed, try, try again.

Such an attitude sharpens the contrast between the two men; for Horace did not approach Maecenas directly, and when he was introduced he gave a simple account of his background, leaving it to others to praise his abilities.

The satire, therefore, contains a note of pride, which Horace would have cheerfully acknowledged. We can call it complacency if we like, but then we have to ask why no one finds it offensive. The answer, it seems to me, lies in the oblique, ironic approach which we have been studying. As David Daiches has observed: 'Irony and paradox are important because they are devices for including or at least taking account of all attitudes which threaten the one assumed by the poet in the poem.'[55] Horace's pride in his social success is threatened by the accusation of pretentiousness. He counters this by laughing at himself, appearing in turn as the harassed soldier, the dejected prisoner, and the helpless victim. Though proud and content in being a member of Maecenas' circle, he does not claim a position of absolute equality:

> nil mi officit, inquam,
> ditior hic aut est quia doctior; est locus uni
> cuique suus. (50–2)

It does me no harm, I assure you, that this man is richer or more learned than I; each has his own place.

So too in the final episode, although we are reminded of the poet's special status as the favourite of Apollo, we cannot grudge him his release, for by now he is a broken man. After v. 71 he no longer tries to control the course of events, and he appears to be just as surprised as we are at his miraculous escape.

This ironical technique clearly allows a greater tightness and economy. Whereas in 1. 6 Horace's ambiguous position had to be defined by carefully worded assertions and denials, in 1. 9 the qualifications are, as it were, built into the statement, and so a multiple effect is obtained. In the end, however, it is wrong to speak wholly in terms of 'devices' and 'techniques', for while there was no doubt an element of calculation in the writing of the poem, such an effort would have been quite futile had not the tact and wit been spontaneous projections of the poet's nature. So when we have finished our scrutiny, we should in fairness to Horace remove the poem from under the microscope and read it straight through from beginning to end. That, after all, was how Maecenas heard it.

CHAPTER IV

HORACE AND LUCILIUS

1. 4, 1. 10, 2. 1

In the hands of Ennius, its first known exponent, literary *satura* was an informal medley in which the author moralized in various metres on various aspects of life and society. The tradition was carried on by Ennius' nephew Pacuvius, and was then taken over and transformed by Gaius Lucilius, a wealthy knight from Suessa Aurunca on the borders of Campania and Latium. Lucilius began his satires about 133 B.C. after returning from the Spanish wars, and he continued to write until his death in Naples in 102. He started off like Ennius by using iambic and trochaic metres as well as the dactylic hexameter, but after a few years' experimentation he settled on the hexameter as being the most suitable vehicle for his purpose. This was an important decision for the future of the form.

But if he narrowed the metrical range of Ennius' miscellany Lucilius enlarged its scope in keeping with his personality. Meagre as they are, the thirteen hundred fragments bear witness to his multifarious experience and insatiable curiosity. Sailing and horsemanship, phonetics and orthography, medicine, cookery, politics, and sex—everything came within his province. Artistically he was often careless, but he compensated for this fault by an immense gusto of the kind which a modern reader associates with Rabelais. This wide-ranging energy, however, was very much an individual trait. Lucilius' main contribution to the development of *satura* lay in a more specialized area, namely that of censure and ridicule. Taking advantage of his position as a friend of Scipio Aemilianus he gave free rein to his pugnacious temperament, attacking Scipio's political enemies, his own literary opponents, and anyone he happened to dislike. We cannot tell how large a

86

proportion of his writing was devoted to polemic; it is certain that later authors like Persius and Juvenal give a false picture by concentrating exclusively on this aspect of his work. Nevertheless, the vigorous criticism which he employed was regarded by his successors as an essential feature of the genre. In this personal sense it was Lucilius who made *satura* satirical.

After his death interest in Lucilius continued. His two friends Laelius Archelaus and Vettius Philocomus lectured on his satires, and their pupils included men like Pompeius Lenaeus and Valerius Cato.[1] Lenaeus, as his first name shows, was a freedman of Pompey, and when Pompey was attacked by Sallust after his death Lenaeus hit back in defence of his patron, calling Sallust 'a lecher, a glutton, a wastrel, and a boozer'.[2] Cato also put his Lucilian studies to good use in a short pamphlet entitled *Indignatio*, which affirmed the freedom of his birth and gave a spirited reply to his detractors.[3] The more academic side of Cato's work is attested by the eight lines prefixed to Horace's tenth satire, in which Cato is said to be preparing an edition of Lucilius' poems. Other work on Lucilius was done by Curtius Nicias, who like Lenaeus was a client of Pompey;[4] and it seems that one commentator specialized in Lucilius' fishes—traces of his monograph appear in Varro's *De Lingua Latina*.[5] Varro also speaks of Lucius Abuccius, a highly educated man whose books were written 'in the Lucilian style' (*Luciliano charactere*).[6] We do not know how closely Varro himself followed Lucilius in his four books of *Satires*, but Lucilian influence was certainly apparent in the lampoon written by Cicero's friend Trebonius against Mark Antony (*Fam.* 12. 16. 3) and presumably also in the poems by Varro of Atax mentioned by Horace in 1. 10. 46.

To Horace, who may well have read him at school, Lucilius ranked as the *inventor* of satire (1. 10. 48). It is hard to say how fair this was to Ennius. If we had more material the differences between the two poets indicated above might stand out more strongly; or possibly Horace saw the differences as greater than they really were. In any case the fact remains that Horace never

87

mentions Ennius as a satirist. He also ignores Varro, who in addition to his four books of *Satires* had written 150 books of *Menippean Satires*—a form which contained a mixture of prose and verse. As far as we can judge from his fragments, Varro had only a very minor influence on Horace's work.

By taking up the Lucilian tradition Horace put himself in an awkward situation. In 39 B.C. as a pardoned Republican and a man of no social consequence he could not afford to give indiscriminate offence, and even if he toned down the inventor's polemic there would always be people who disapproved of satire on principle. In spite of this he wrote the diatribe on adultery (1. 2)—a work of courage as well as craftsmanship. It was read by people for whom it was not primarily intended and, predictably, complaints were made.[7] Horace therefore resolved to write another poem, justifying his activity as a satirist and setting out the main features of the genre as he saw it. This involved a further hazard, for any modification of satire whether in style or content would necessitate some criticism of Lucilius, and there were men in Rome (some of them quite influential in the world of letters) who would not relish criticism of this kind. Horace knew who they were and was undeterred by the prospect of their displeasure. The satire in question (1. 4) opens with these words:

The poets Eupolis, Cratinus, and Aristophanes, and the other men who constitute the Old Comedy, used to brand with great freedom anyone who deserved to be portrayed as a blackguard and a thief, a lecher or a cut-throat, or as notorious in any other way. Lucilius derives entirely from them, having followed them in every respect except rhythm and metre. He was witty and keen-scented, but harsh in his versification. This was where his fault lay. As a *tour de force* he would often dictate two hundred lines an hour standing on his head. He was a muddy river from which you would wish certain things removed. A man of many words, he was reluctant to take the trouble of writing —writing properly, that is; as for quantity, I care nothing for that.

Lucilius and Aristophanes are associated here in three general respects. First, and most important, both were quick to detect vice (*emunctae naris*—'keen-scented'—in v. 8 corresponds to the critical vigour of Old Comedy); secondly, both were amusing

(*facetus*—'witty'—in v. 7 recalls *comoedia* in v. 2); thirdly, both
wrote poetry (*versus* in v. 8 harks back to *poetae* in v. 1). Within
the last category we have a contrast, for Lucilius abandoned the
metres of Old Comedy and he was also harsher in his composition. But in spite of his inferior craftsmanship and polish we are
still meant to think of Lucilius as a poet.[8] So far as general influence
is concerned, we may be pretty sure that, although there is nothing
in the fragments to prove it, Lucilius had read the old comic
poets.[9] In that case he must have admired their courage and wit.
The dramatic techniques which he himself employed in the *Council
of the Gods* (W. 5 ff.) may well have owed something to Old
Comedy, and would not the *Frogs* have fascinated the man who, as
Pliny says (*NH* Praef. 7), was the first Roman with a nose for style?

The problem here is not that Lucilius is compared to Aristophanes and the rest, or even that some general influence is discerned, but rather that he is said to 'derive entirely from' Old
Comedy (*omnis pendet...mutatis tantum pedibus numerisque*). This,
of course, is an absurd over-simplification, ignoring as it does not
only the various Hellenistic influences on Lucilius' work but also
its characteristically Roman flavour. To account for this some
scholars have suggested that Horace did not know the facts—an
incredible idea.[10] Others, like Leo, have thought he was paying a
discreet compliment to Varro,[11] who is supposed (with some
reason) to have held theories of this kind.[12] But even if Leo's
view were correct it would not explain the function of the passage
within the satire as a whole. The only satisfactory answer is to
regard the lines as a piece of special pleading in which Horace
exaggerates the dependence of Lucilius on Old Comedy in order
to claim that Aristophanes, Lucilius, and himself are all links in
the same illustrious tradition. This should warn us against taking
the rest of the poem as a dispassionate, carefully balanced essay in
literary theory.

In justifying his satire against the charge of malice Horace makes
the following points: Old Comedy and Lucilius branded criminals
(1–7); unlike Crispinus I write very little (17–18); unlike Fannius

I do not seek publicity (21-3); the innocent have nothing to fear (67-8); I do not intend my poems to be sold, nor do I give public recitations (71-4); real malice is something quite different—it means backbiting one's friends and spreading scandal (81-103); I was taught to notice wicked behaviour by my father; he used individuals simply as examples of different vices (103-31); I am really quite a good-humoured fellow (91-2, 103-4); my observations are for my own improvement (137-8); and my writings are just an amusing pastime (138-9). He then concludes the piece with a disarming smile (140-3).

It is clear from this summary that Horace at no time denies that his poems may have an aggressive tone; nor does he give any guarantee for the future. His evasive tactics can be seen in the opening passage quoted above. After hearing of Lucilius' wit and his keen nose, we expect Horace to clarify his own position in regard to personal attack. Instead he swerves aside to discuss the question of style. The same thing happens later on (33 ff.). Because people in general are prone to wickedness 'they dread verses and detest poets' (*metuunt versus, odere poetas*). To them the poet is a savage creature. 'Whatever he has smeared on his pages he will be eager to tell to all the people as they come home from the bakehouse and water-tank—servants and old women alike.' 'Well now,' says Horace, 'listen to a few words in reply. First of all, I shall exclude myself from those whom I would count as poets.' (In other words 'you may hate poets, but you shouldn't hate me; for I'm no poet'.) He then goes on to contrast the plain style of satire with the 'true poetry' of epic, thus evading the charge of malice by a quibble. The question is raised again in vv. 64-5: 'Are you right to regard this genre with suspicion?' In answer Horace says that the innocent are quite safe from the attacks of the soap-box orators Caprius and Sulcius. He then quickly adds 'Even if you are like the highwaymen Caelius and Birrius, I would not be like Caprius and Sulcius'. And where is the difference? 'No shop or stall would ever have my books exposed to the sweaty hands of Hermogenes Tigellius and the rest of the mob.' But what happens if some of the poems find their way outside Horace's own circle? We are not told. Nor does Horace give any firm undertaking that he will abstain from forthright censure. Rather the reverse. 'If I am a little outspoken in the future...remember that I got the habit from my father' (103–5). That may be an excuse; it is certainly not a promise.

Another point often overlooked is that 1. 4 carries no condemnation of Lucilius' spirit. In the opening lines we are told that the types of criminal portrayed by Old Comedy (and Lucilius) *deserved* to be shown up. There is no suggestion of disapproval until *durus componere versus* (8). This is made clear by the *nam* in v. 9, which explains the abrupt transition from praise to blame, and also by the emphatic *hoc*—'it was here that his fault lay'. Finally there is the statement in 1. 10. 3–4 that Lucilius had been *praised* in this earlier passage 'for scouring the city with plenty of wit'. It is sometimes maintained that in the reference to Caprius and Sulcius (65 ff.) Horace is criticizing Lucilius.[13] But there is no need to bring Lucilius into that passage at all. Caprius and Sulcius represent the most vulgar type of pamphleteer; and in any case even they cause no anxiety to the innocent. In vv. 86–90 Horace complains that the sort of person who calls him malicious is often prepared to traduce his own friends and to laugh at the jokes of the drunken parasite. Here too some scholars think that in the parasite, who makes insulting remarks about the guests and even about the host himself, we are intended to see a picture of Lucilius.[14] This I am unwilling to believe. In v. 90, immediately after the description of the parasite, we read:

> hic tibi comis et urbanus liberque videtur.

> That's the kind of man *you* regard as genial, witty, and frank.

Since 'you' refers to Horace's opponent, it follows that in Horace's opinion the parasite is *not* witty and frank; but according to the opening lines Lucilius *is*. If Horace has already justified himself by appealing to the example of Lucilius, he would hardly allude to him in the same poem as a malicious buffoon.

Why, then, is Horace not more explicit? It seems that he wanted to leave himself free to develop various lines of defence. If he identified himself too warmly with the censorious ridicule of Old Comedy and Lucilius he could not pose as a timid spirit anxious to avoid offence (17–18), and the influence of his father (103–29) would become a factor of minor importance. On the other hand he could not simply disavow the Lucilian spirit, partly because 1. 2 (and perhaps other pieces) had shown its influence, partly because he wanted to reserve the right to make personal attacks if he saw fit, and above all because he was writing satire— and satire without ridicule was like comedy without humour. For these reasons he declined to elaborate the distinctions which really did exist between Lucilius' outlook and his own.[15]

The problem of style was more straightforward. Although in certain quarters Lucilius was still regarded as the prince of satirists, Horace could see no reason why the genre should be associated with slapdash writing, and so in vindicating his own approach he says quite frankly that Lucilius was harsh and careless in his composition and that he wrote too much (8–13). Later on (39 ff.) he indicates the place which satire should occupy in the hierarchy of poetic kinds. If you claim, he says, that my satire is not great poetry I quite agree with you. The same is true of Lucilius. His verses, like mine, are more in the nature of metrical prose. In this respect, as well as in its subject-matter, satire has affinities with comedy. Even in its angry scenes the diction of comedy (and here we are to think of New Comedy) stays close to everyday speech, it does not rise to the heights of true poetry, whereas the sonorous and elevated language of Ennius would remain poetic even if his metre were destroyed.

As Horace no doubt foresaw, these remarks annoyed the champions of Lucilius. Rallying to the defence of their favourite, they stressed the colour and vigour of his style and affirmed that he had a genial and sophisticated wit. Since Lucilius had now been brought to the forefront of the controversy, Horace felt obliged to amplify and, where necessary, modify his earlier statements.

And so he composed the second of the 'literary' satires, namely
1. 10. The poem begins as follows:

> nempe incomposito dixi pede currere versus
> Lucili. quis tam Lucili fautor inepte est
> ut non hoc fateatur? at idem, quod sale multo
> urbem defricuit, charta laudatur eadem.
> nec tamen hoc tribuens dederim quoque cetera: nam sic
> et Laberi mimos ut pulchra poemata mirer.
> ergo non satis est risu diducere rictum
> auditoris: et est quaedam tamen hic quoque virtus:
> est brevitate opus, ut currat sententia, neu se
> 10   impediat verbis lassas onerantibus auris;
> et sermone opus est modo tristi, saepe iocoso,
> defendente vicem modo rhetoris atque poetae,
> interdum urbani, parcentis viribus atque
> extenuantis eas consulto. ridiculum acri
> fortius et melius magnas plerumque secat res.
> illi scripta quibus comoedia prisca viris est
> hoc stabant, hoc sunt imitandi: quos neque pulcher
> Hermogenes umquam legit, neque simius iste
> nil praeter Calvum et doctus cantare Catullum.

True enough, I did say that Lucilius' verses lurched awkwardly
along. Who is so perverse an admirer of Lucilius as not to admit
this? But he is also praised on the very same page for scouring the
city with plenty of caustic wit. While allowing him this quality,
however, I would not grant him the others as well; for then I should
have to admire the mimes of Laberius as beautiful poems. So it is not
enough to make your listener bare his teeth in a grin—though there
is some virtue even in that. You need terseness, so that the thought
may run freely on and not become tangled in a mass of verbiage which
will weigh heavily on the listener's ear. You also need a style which is
sometimes severe, sometimes gay, taking the role now of an orator
and poet, now of a clever talker who keeps his strength in reserve and
carefully rations it out. Great issues are usually resolved more forcefully and more effectively by wit than by castigation. This was the
mainstay of the men who wrote Old Comedy; this is what makes
them worth imitating—men who have never been read by the pretty
Hermogenes or by that ape whose only artistic accomplishment is to
croon Calvus and Catullus.

Horace therefore stands by his criticisms of Lucilius' style, but modifies what he said about his tone. While granting that Lucilius was witty, he now maintains that his wit was too often harsh and vulgar. This is a less favourable estimate than that given in I. 4, where Lucilius was called frank and witty. But as we can see from the usage of Cicero the terms *liber* and *facetus* had considerable flexibility;[16] and so Horace could argue that his two judgements were quite consistent. 'I said Aristophanes and Lucilius both used *libertas*. So they did. But the *libertas* of Lucilius was apt to degenerate into abuse. I also said Aristophanes and Lucilius were both *faceti*. So they were. But the *facetiae* of Lucilius tended too often to be crude and hurtful. Admittedly Aristophanes and the others were not wholly free from these defects, but their lapses were less frequent and should certainly not be imitated.' The tenth satire, which contains the fullest exposition of Horace's literary theory so far, shows that he no longer needs the protection of Lucilius. He can stand on his own feet.

The rest of the poem is about style. In v. 20 an opponent commends Lucilius for producing an agreeable blend of Latin and Greek. That, replies Horace, was no great achievement; Pitholeon of Rhodes did as much. When men use language for a serious purpose, as in the law-courts, they invariably speak pure Latin. The same should apply to satire:

> scilicet oblitus patriaeque patrisque Latini,
> cum Pedius causas exsudet Publicola atque
> Corvinus, patriis intermiscere petita
> verba foris malis, Canusini more bilinguis?　(27–30)

Whereas Pedius Publicola and Messalla Corvinus sweat out their cases, you I suppose would forget about your fatherland and father Latinus and would sooner interlard your fathers' speech with foreign importations like a two-tongued Canusian?

Horace himself had once tried his hand at Greek verses, but had been deterred by Romulus, who (he says) appeared in a dream and warned him of his folly. Now he writes only Latin. Unlike the swollen Alpman (*turgidus Alpinus*) he prefers a modest style, and his pieces are not intended for recitation in any public contest (36–9).

When Horace began his career as a poet the main genres were capably represented: Virgil was writing pastoral, Fundanius comedy, and so on. Satire appeared to be the only area in which development was possible. This did not mean that Horace ranked himself above Lucilius. As a pioneer the latter had a place of special distinction, but stylistically he left much to be desired, whether because of his nature or his material.[17] Certainly, whatever his merits, he would have written more carefully had he been born a hundred years later:

> fuerit Lucilius, inquam,
> comis et urbanus, fuerit limatior idem
> quam rudis et Graecis intacti carminis auctor,
> quamque poetarum seniorum turba: sed ille,
> si foret hoc nostrum fato dilatus in aevum,
> detereret sibi multa, recideret omne quod ultra
> perfectum traheretur, et in versu faciendo
> saepe caput scaberet, vivos et roderet unguis.   (64–71)

Suppose, I say, Lucilius was genial and witty, suppose too that he was more polished than the author of a rough verse untouched by the Greeks[18] and than the crowd of older poets; nevertheless if destiny had postponed his birth until our own day he would now file his work down drastically, he would cut back everything that rambled beyond the limits of true art, and in composing his verses he would often tear his hair and bite his nails to the quick.

After expressing his contempt for those who aim at a large audience and whose works are used as school texts, Horace goes on to name some of his detractors—Hermogenes, Demetrius, and Fannius. By their vindictive gossip these men are trying to belittle his achievement; well, let them do their worst; if he can please patrons like Maecenas, Pollio, and Messalla, and poets like Virgil and Varius, he will be more than content. With one last gibe at Demetrius and Hermogenes ('Go and sing to your female students!') Horace rounds off the poem and the book.

To trace the genesis and growth of these literary theories would be far too complicated a task and would in any case have only an indirect bearing on our subject.[19] Part of the background, however, can be sketched in by summarizing two passages of Cicero. Describing the so-called Attic style of oratory Cicero says it is plain and unpretentious with a deceptive appearance of simplicity; the structure is loose but not rambling; the language scrupulously correct. The Attic orator is restrained in his use of metaphors, archaisms, and new words; his wit is revealed in the elegance of his narrative and in his use of ridicule. Buffoonery, obscenity and cruelty are all to be avoided (*Orat.* 75–90). The same concern for propriety is seen in the description of *sermo* in *De Officiis* I. 134–7. This conversational style, in which the Socratic writers excelled, should be lively but at the same time relaxed and free from dogmatism. It will be grave or gay according to the subject in hand; and except when reproof is called for it will avoid any display of anger. In remonstrating with a friend the speaker may be stern but never insulting.

Clearly Cicero had a strong and direct influence on Horace's view of satire. But Cicero was an eclectic with few claims to originality. The Attic style, which he regarded as only a part of the complete orator's equipment, was studied and practised by several of his contemporaries, who modelled themselves on Lysias, the fourth-century Greek. In the passage of the *De Officiis*, which was based on Panaetius' περὶ τοῦ καθήκοντος, we are told that the best exponents of *sermo* are the Socratics, i.e. writers like Plato and Xenophon. And the concept of refined wit had already been formulated by Aristotle.[20] Horace, moreover, drew on many sources besides Cicero. His preference for a minor genre, which would express his personal views in a careful and polished manner, doubtless owed something to Callimachus, and his reading of Philodemus must have contributed to his choice of a straightforward style which would suit the middle-brow reader.[21] So, too, when Horace calls for an easy alternation between severity and humour (*modo tristi, saepe iocoso*), he is affirming a widely acknowledged tradition. In Aristophanes' *Frogs* (391–2) the Chorus hopes to speak 'many funny *and* many serious things'— πολλὰ μὲν γέλοιά μ' εἰπεῖν, πολλὰ δὲ σπουδαῖα. The Cynic Diogenes would sometimes wag his tail and sometimes bite (D.L. 6. 60), and the Stoic Panaetius, as represented in *De Officiis* I. 134, varied his mood according to his topic. Other writers used both manners simultaneously. Monimus, the pupil of Diogenes, wrote 'amusements blended with disguised earnestness', παίγνια σπουδῇ λεληθυίᾳ μεμιγμένα (D.L. 6. 83); Menippus, as described by Lucian (*Bis Accusatus* 33), 'used to bite as he grinned', γελῶν ἅμα ἔδακνεν, and the Epicureans were told by the master to 'laugh and philosophize at the same time', γελᾶν ἅμα δεῖ καὶ φιλοσοφεῖν (*Sent. Vat.* 41). All these passages imply a mixture of earnestness and gaiety, though of course the content of the earnestness and the type of gaiety varied enormously.

To see more clearly how these theories affected the development of satire we shall now examine Horace's criticisms of Lucilius in the light of the fragments themselves.

(1) Lucilius was too coarse and abusive (1. 10. 5–8, 14–17). This charge is not hard to substantiate. One satire apparently took a brothel for its title and subject (*Fornix* after W. 909); others portrayed scenes of violent farce, e.g. in W. 937–47 some characters attempt to smash in a door, while another threatens to throw a pot down on their heads. The same level of humour is found in fragments which refer to men feeding (W. 70), belching (W. 130), scratching (W. 356) and bellowing with laughter (W. 131); sometimes people are jeered at for their physical appearance (W. 37, 354–5), and often this effect is enhanced by some animal simile in the manner of Chaucer; thus one fellow has a jaw and tooth like a rhinoceros (W. 109–10), another resembles a huge butcher's dog (W. 1175), and another has one eye and two feet like half a pig's carcass (W. 112–13). It is also clear from a glance at the fragments that a good deal of Lucilius' humour is based on the bed-rock of sex and excretion. This element, which was recognized in Lucilius' work by Porphyrion,[22]

appears much more rarely in Horace. Apart from the early poem on adultery (1. 2), it is found only in scattered lines and words; a late example is the passage on fornication spoken by the slave Davus in 2. 7. 47–52.

Coarse humour was only one weapon in Lucilius' armoury. Direct abuse was another. Unfortunately a full appreciation of his invective is impossible, because we often cannot tell who the victims were and whether or not the insults were uttered by Lucilius himself. Who, for example, was the 'witless old sophist' (*senium atque insulse sophista*) in W. 1210, or the 'jailbird hardly good enough for the cage' (*carcer vix carcere dignus*) in W. 1176? And who was the speaker in W. 1181?

> vicimus o socii et magnam pugnavimus pugnam!
>
> Allies, we have prevailed and fought a good fight!

According to Donatus' note on Terence, *Eun.* 899, this refers to an act of debauchery, and the line may well be a parody of Ennius. Whether it is comedy or satire depends wholly on the context.

Nevertheless, the fragments which do preserve the victim's name are still numerous enough to bear out what Horace says. Other writers also refer to Lucilius' pugnacity. Persius (1. 114) says 'he lashed the city' (*secuit Lucilius urbem*), and Juvenal (1. 165) describes him as 'raging with drawn sword' (*ense velut stricto*). There were protests against Lucilius in his own day, if we can judge from certain fragments in Book 30, especially W. 1075:

> nunc, Gai, quoniam incilans nos laedis, vicissim...
>
> Now, Gaius, since you castigate us with your censure, in return...

We also know from *Auct. ad Herennium* 2. 19 that on one occasion an actor was bold enough to criticize him from the stage. Lucilius thought this such an outrage that he took the man to court. The case was dismissed.

(2) Lucilius was muddy and prolix (1. 4. 9–12; 1. 10. 50–1, 67–71). This can be illustrated by the longest fragment extant:

virtus, Albine, est pretium persolvere verum
quis in versamur, quis vivimus rebus potesse,
virtus est homini scire id quod quaeque habeat res,
virtus scire homini rectum, utile quid sit, honestum,
5   quae bona, quae mala item, quid inutile, turpe, inhonestum;
virtus quaerendae finem re scire modumque,
virtus divitiis pretium persolvere posse,
virtus id dare quod re ipsa debetur honori;
hostem esse atque inimicum hominum morumque malorum,
10 contra defensorem hominum morumque bonorum,
hos magni facere, his bene velle, his vivere amicum;
commoda praeterea patriai prima putare,
deinde parentum, tertia iam postremaque nostra.

(W. 1196–1208)

Virtue, Albinus, is the ability to pay what is actually due in our business dealings and in our social life. Virtue is the knowledge of what each issue involves for a man. Virtue is the knowledge of what is right, advantageous, and honourable for a man, what is good and likewise what is bad, what is disadvantageous, wrong, and dishonourable. Virtue is knowing the boundary and limit for acquiring riches. Virtue is the ability to pay wealth its due. Virtue is giving what is in fact owed to honour, being an enemy and an opponent of bad men and habits, a champion on the other hand of good men and habits, prizing the latter highly, wishing them well, and living on friendly terms with them; it means, furthermore, putting the interests of one's country first, then one's parents', then, thirdly and lastly, one's own.

Here we have Lucilius in his Sunday best. The language is pure Latin, the arrangement of the various triads and antitheses shows deliberate artifice, and the moral content is admirable, in its hard-headed Roman way. One can almost see the poem hanging on a boy's bedroom wall like some ancient precursor of Kipling's *If*. And yet how un-Horatian it is. The Augustan would never have dealt those hammer-blows of *virtus...virtus...virtus*; he would have branded the fifth and tenth lines as otiose; and he would have barred all those monotonous effects of rhyme and alliteration from a piece which claimed to be serious poetry.

99

Describing an early stage in his journey to Sicily Lucilius writes:

> verum haec ludus ibi, susque omnia deque fuerunt,
> susque haec deque fuere inquam omnia ludus iocusque;
> illud opus durum, ut Setinum accessimus finem,
> αἰγίλιπες montes, Aetnae omnes, asperi Athones.

(W. 102–5)

But at that point all this was child's play and everything was free and easy; this was all, I say, free and easy and mere child's play and fun. But when we reached the outskirts of Setia, that was a tough haul—goat-forsaken mountains, each one an Etna and a rugged Athos.

This lively passage has several features which Horace would have avoided. Here we shall note simply that the second line is a good example of the older poet's *garrulitas*, and that in Horace 1. 5. 79 Lucilius' painful exertions have dwindled to the single word *erepsemus*; so too the passage on *virtus* has just the faintest echo in *Epist.* 1. 1. 41 *virtus est vitium fugere*—'Virtue is the avoidance of vice'.

An opportunity for a more direct comparison is supplied by some verses from the legend of the fox and the lion. Lucilius has:

> quid sibi vult, qua re fit ut introvorsus et ad te
> spectent atque ferant vestigia se omnia prorsus?

(W. 1119–20)

What does it mean, how does it come about that the tracks face inwards and towards you and all move forwards?

In *Epist.* 1. 1. 74–5 Horace writes:

> quia me vestigia terrent
> omnia te adversum spectantia, nulla retrorsum.

Because those tracks frighten me; they all face towards you, none the other way.

In Horace's shorter version the duplication of *quid sibi vult* and *qua re fit* has disappeared; and the thrice repeated notion of *introvorsus...ad te...prorsus* with its clumsy rhyme has been replaced by a new design which puts *vestigia* first and then observes the

tracks from two aspects. The last two words of Horace show that
a gain in neatness does not invariably entail a loss of strength.

It is rather surprising, however, when we come to Lucilius with
Horace's criticisms in mind, to discover occasional fragments like
these, which are admirably swift and concise:

> adsequitur nec opinantem, in caput insilit, ipsum
> conmanducatur totum conplexa comestque. (W. 157–8)

> She takes him by surprise from behind, jumps on his head, envelops
> him, and then chews him all up and devours him.

> aurum vis hominemne? habeas. 'hominem? quid ad aurum?'
> (W. 588)

> Do you want the money or the man? Take your pick. 'The man?
> What's he in comparison with the money?'

One recalls that Cicero often praised Lucilius for his elegance.
Quintilian in a later age took Horace to task for calling him muddy
(10. 1. 94), and Lactantius seems to have regarded the *virtus*
passage as a miracle of compression (*Inst.* 6. 5. 2). Such contradictions will become familiar in the next few pages, and presently
an attempt will be made to reconcile them. Meanwhile the
following example might be of interest: Lucilius uses certain
traditional devices for keeping his readers' attention—'to make a
long story short', 'here's what I'm getting at' and so on. At one
point he says:

> summatim tamen experiar rescribere paucis.
> (W. 1063)

> Nevertheless I shall try to write a short reply in a few words.

So even his promise of brevity contains a pleonasm. In a roughly
similar situation Horace writes *pauca accipe contra* (1. 4. 38)—
'Hear a few words in reply'.

(3) Lucilius was eager for publicity. This criticism seems to
arise from the remarks on Lucilius' style; for no direct accusation
is made. In 1. 4 the charge is laid against Fannius, Caprius and
Sulcius; in 1. 10 against those who wrote for the theatre and
competition hall. One has the impression that Horace was mainly

concerned to justify his own position as a poet of the *élite*. However, the innuendo against Lucilius cannot be ignored and it seems to gain support from fragments like:

gaudes cum de me ista foris sermonibus differs.

(W. 1085)

You enjoy spreading abroad those bad reports about me in your satires.

et sua perciperet retro rellicta iacere. (W. 1090)

And saw that his own poems were being left behind in neglect.

et sola ex multis nunc nostra poemata ferri.

(W. 1091)

And that out of many poems only mine were now in circulation.

The first records a complaint about the publication of scandalous material; in the other two cases Lucilius seems to be boasting of his own popularity. But before we think of Lucilius' satires as a kind of *News of the Ancient World*, we should take account of the information preserved by Cicero (*De Orat.* 2. 25):

C. Lucilius...used to say that he wished to be read neither by the very ignorant nor by the very learned, since the former understood nothing and the latter perhaps more than himself. In this connexion he also wrote 'I don't want Persius to read me' (*Persium non curo legere*)—Persius, as we know, was about the most learned of our countrymen—'I do want Laelius Decumus to do so' (*Laelium Decumum volo*). The latter was a worthy man and by no means uneducated, but he was nothing compared to Persius.

Another piece of evidence is contained in *De Fin.* 1. 7 where Lucilius is quoted as saying that he feared the opinion of Scipio and Rutilius and was writing for the people of Tarentum, Consentia, and Sicily. This was clearly ironical. The places in question spoke very little Latin, as Lucilius who had estates in those areas knew quite well. The quotation does show, however, that Lucilius was sometimes wryly aware of his failure to meet Scipio's standards. As for the total size of Lucilius' work, we cannot form any reliable opinion about it. The average satire may have been longer than its Horatian counterpart, but an output of thirty books in thirty years need not have been excessive.

(4) Lucilius was rough in his language and versification.

Language. No special complaint is made on this score, but since diction played such a large part in the notion of correct writing (*scribendi recte*, 1. 4. 13) a few comments are in order. Purity of diction was based on *Latinitas*—a concept which had more than one aspect. Politically it meant restrictions on foreign words, socially the avoidance of provincialisms and vulgarisms (whether in vocabulary, grammar, idiom, or pronunciation), and historically it implied fairly close limitations on the use of archaisms and new words. In short, it represented the more formal type of urban upper-class speech. In what ways, then, could Lucilius have infringed these rules in the eyes of a critic like Horace writing in 35 B.C.? First of all his satires contained a large number of imported words. The great majority were Greek and will be discussed separately, but others came from Gaul, e.g. *bulga*, 'bag', *bracae*, 'trousers'; others were Oscan like *pipas*, 'you cheep', *sollo*, 'whole'; others Syrian (*mamphula*, 'loaf'); Etruscan (*mantisa*, 'makeweight'); Umbrian (*gumiae* 'gluttons'); and possibly Sardinian (*musimo* 'wild sheep'). These licences were not due to ignorance. Lucilius was quite alive to the effect of provincialisms, as may be seen from Quintilian 1. 5. 56, where he is said to have censured a certain Vettius for using Tuscan, Sabine, and Praenestine words, and from W. 232 where Caecilius is mocked for his rural manner of speech. Other fragments testify to the satirist's interest in grammar, etymology, and euphony. So it looks as if he claimed certain priviliges for his *sermones* which he denied to other forms of speech and writing.

The same expansive view of the genre is reflected in Lucilius' coinages, of which Marx notes some thirty examples.[23] Here are a few specimens:

> depoclassere aliqua sperans me ac deargentassere
> decalauticare, eburno speculo despeculassere.

(W. 640–1)

A woman hoping to decup, deplate and destole me and to demirror me of an ivory mirror.

huncin ego umquam Hyancintho hominem cortinipotentis
deliciis contendi?   (W. 311–12)

Did I ever compare this fellow to Hyacinthus, the darling of the Lord
of the three-legged cooking-pot [i.e. Apollo]?

viginti an triginta domi vel centum cibicidas alas
                                                          (W. 760)

(I do not care) whether in your house you feed twenty, thirty, or
a hundred food-murderers.

This is Lucilius the heir of Plautus. They did not talk like that in
the Scipionic circle.

The fragments contain a number of words which had become
obsolete by Horace's day, e.g. *incilo*, *peniculamentum*, *petilus*. A
few, like *pigror* and *zonatim*, are found only in Lucilius. Other
words are used in senses later abandoned, e.g. *prodo*, 'I defer',
delico, 'I make clear'. But the largest number of cases are simply
forms which were no longer current in 35 B.C. Thus Lucilius did
not object to using, say, *viai* for *viae*, *mani* as an ablative from *mane*,
and *fluvium* as a genitive plural; we find *guttur* and *collus* in the
masculine, *gladium* in the neuter, and *gracila* as a first declension
adjective. Occasionally *simitu* is used for *simul*, *indu* and *endo* for
in, *noenu* for *non*. Verbs may be ante-classical in form (*siem* and
potissem for *sim* and *possem*), in the case they govern (*fungor* with
the accusative), or in voice (*manducor* deponent, *partio* active). Not
all these usages were serious. *Endo*, for example, occurs only in
W. 1024:

omnia tum endo muco videas fervente micare

Then you could see everything shimmering within the seething
depths of the house

—a line which was almost certainly mock-heroic. Therefore, in a
sense Lucilius does not take direct responsibility for the word.
More will be said about this type of case in section (5) below. As
for the rest, Horace did not find fault with such features simply
because they were out of date. A man as sensitive as he was to

organic changes in language would never have made such a vulgar error. What did annoy him was the prejudice of those who either overlooked such features altogether or else used them as a means of extolling the dead at the expense of the living.

The situation is less clear-cut in regard to what might be called comic vulgarisms. If we take nouns of abuse, we find that Horace does not by any means exclude them—he has *agaso, popino, furcifer, vappa*, and others; but Lucilius has nearly three times as many. Again, Lucilius uses nearly twenty words metaphorically in connexion with the human body and its functions, e.g. *rostrum* ('snout') for face, *bulga* ('bag') for womb. Horace has about half a dozen instances—mostly confined to 1. 2. Another feature of popular speech was a frequent use of diminutives. Lucilius has more than twice as many as Horace, and it must be remembered that we are comparing twelve hundred lines of Lucilius, half of which are incomplete, with two thousand lines of Horace. Apart from categories of this kind, a reading of the fragments gives an impression of racy colloquial speech which is not easily reduced to statistics. I have in mind expressions like *nummos inuncat*, 'he gets his hooks on the cash', *me exenterat*, 'he's tearing my guts out', *depilati omnes sumus*, 'we've all been fleeced', *decumana ova*, 'king-size eggs'. Such effects do occur in Horace, but much less often.[24]

Versification. Here Horace's complaints are frequent and direct (1. 4. 8 ff., 10. 1–2, 9–10, 56–73). Unfortunately in this area above all others comparison is hindered by the state of Lucilius' text; so we shall have to confine ourselves to the general features which Horace had in mind. One of these, no doubt, was the treatment of final -s. In Lucilius' day a final -s after a short vowel was weakly pronounced and had no prosodic function, e.g. W. 4 ends *plăniŭs dīcĭt*. This practice was continued by Lucretius, but it sounded 'rather countrified' (*subrusticum*) to Cicero (*Orat.* 161) and was abandoned by Catullus and the Neoterics.

Since Horace calls Lucilius *durus*, it might be thought that Lucilius had a noticeably higher proportion of spondees; yet this does not seem to be the case. According to the calculations of D. Bo,[25] Horace's favourite combination in the first four feet consists of a dactyl followed by three spondees (DSSS); after that comes SDSS; the sequence ssss is three times as common as DDDD. As for the fifth foot, it is true that whereas Horace never allows a spondee in this position Lucilius does so on three occasions. But two of these cases involve proper names, the third is defensible as a special effect, and anyhow the figure is too small to have much significance. Rather more important, perhaps, is the fact that Lucilius was much freer in his use of pentasyllabic endings. I have counted twenty instances in four hundred lines, i.e. 1 in 20; in Horace's first book there is 1 in 74, and in his second 1 in 217.

Horace's main complaint, however, was directed at the frequency of Lucilius' elisions. Horace occasionally permitted himself three in a line (there are eleven such lines in Book 1) and very exceptionally four (1. 3. 20; 2. 3. 86), whereas in four hundred fragments of Lucilius I counted twenty-three lines with three elisions, nine with four, and two with five. The overall frequency, according to Siedow, is 84·8 in a hundred lines of Lucilius as opposed to 40·1 in the case of Horace.[26] Of the vowels elided by Lucilius 27 per cent are long; for Horace's first book the figure is 18 per cent.[27] Apart from this there does not appear to be any notable difference in the kinds of elision practised or in the places where they occur.[28] The offensive feature about Lucilius' elisions was their sheer number. It was this that gave the impression that his only concern was 'to jam something into six feet' (1. 10. 59–60).

It would be wrong to conclude, however, that Horace's versification was in every way stricter than that of Lucilius. In certain respects he felt (at least when he was writing the first book) that his forerunner had been unnecessarily rigid. In the use of monosyllabic endings, for example, Horace allowed himself much greater freedom. In his first four satires, which contain 540 verses, there are 79 final monosyllables, omitting cases of elision; that gives a proportion of about one in seven.[29] The figure for four hundred hexameter-endings in Lucilius is twenty-six, i.e. less than one in fifteen. Horace also obtained greater smoothness by letting the sense flow on from one line to the next. Of his final monosyllables only a third mark the end of a clause; the figure for Lucilius is apparently nearer to a half. Closely related to this is the fact that Horace was willing to make a strong pause in sense within the last two feet, e.g. *relinquendis. age, quaeso* (1. 10. 51), *turba: sed ille* (1. 10. 67), *concurritur: horae* (1. 1. 7) and even *levius valeat: nam* (2. 7. 78). Such effects are scarcely ever found in Lucilius' fragments, though this is no doubt partly due to the circumstances of their preservation. In some respects, then, Lucilius took too many liberties; in others he did not take enough. It was all a question of relating the movement of the verse to the rhythms of educated conversation; and in deciding this question Horace could appeal to only one authority—the authority of his own ear.

(5) Lucilius was too rhetorical and poetic. This is implied in 1. 10. 12, where Horace states that the satirist should *occasionally* rise to the level of the orator and poet—*modo rhetoris atque poetae*. Lucilius' tendency to abandon the conversational manner is also mirrored by Crispinus (1. 4. 19–21), who resembles the bellows in a blast-furnace, and by Cassius (1. 10. 61–4), who is like a boiling torrent.

This contention can only be valid within a rather limited field. Horace maintains elsewhere (1. 4. 41, 56–62) that Lucilius was essentially an exponent of the plain style, and Varro (see note 6) chose him as an example of slenderness (*gracilitas*). The names which Lucilius used for his verse, such as *sermo* (causerie), *schedium* (impromptu), and *ludus* (amusement), indicate the modesty of his pretensions. There are, moreover, a few fragments which suggest that when Lucilius had the opportunity to write epic he declined to do so. In W. 713 and 714 we have:

hunc laborem sumas, laudem qui tibi ac fructum ferat.
percrepa pugnam Popili, facta Corneli cane.

You should undertake this task which will bring you distinction and profit; tell of Popilius' battle, sing of the deeds of Cornelius.

These lines look very much like the promptings of Trebatius in
Horace 2. 1. 10–12:

> aude
> Caesaris invicti res dicere, multa laborum
> praemia laturus.

Dare to tell of invincible Caesar's exploits; you will win many
rewards for your pains.

And the words:

> ego si qui sum et quo folliculo nunc sum indutus, non queo...
> (W. 691)

If I, because of who I am and the little frame in which I am now
enclosed, cannot...

may well reflect a refusal like that of Horace in 2. 1. 12–13:

> cupidum, pater optime, vires
> deficiunt.

I am eager, sir, but my powers are insufficient.

(It is noticeable that both the metaphor and the diminutive are
missing in Horace.)[30]

Finally, the ridicule which Lucilius directed at writers of epic
and tragedy makes it impossible to believe that he himself aspired
to the grand style. Homer seems to have come off more lightly
than the others. He could be faulted on points of detail—'a line,
a word, a thought, or a passage' (W. 410), and some of his fantasies, like the monster Polyphemus with his walking stick the
size of a ship's mast (W. 522–3), appeared rather naïve to a sophisticated rationalist, but his greatness was unchallenged and the
allusions to his work are made in a spirit of good-humoured
parody. Ennius, though still respected, was treated less gently.
According to Horace (1. 10. 54) Lucilius made fun of certain lines
which he thought undignified. One such line was:

> sparsis hastis longis campus splendet et horret.

Dotted with long spears the plain gleams and shivers.

Horret was too much for Lucilius. Hinting that the line was
frigidus, i.e. flat or tasteless, he said that Ennius should have written
horret et alget—'shivers and freezes' (W.413).[31] Another line
of Ennius, this time from his tragedy *Thyestes*, ran as follows
(Thyestes is cursing his brother Atreus):

latere pendens saxa spargens tabo sanie et sanguine atro.
(W. 885)

May he hang by his flank, spattering the rocks with putrid gore and
black blood.

We do not know how Lucilius used the line, but in view of the
violent imagery it can hardly have been quoted with approval.
Cicero, who preserves the fragment, points out that, since Thyestes
has already prayed for Atreus to be drowned, the victim would
never feel these agonies and so the line was mere empty bombast.[32]

Pacuvius fared no better. Apart from a reference to his involved
prologues (W. 879), several fragments survive from parodies of
the *Antiopa* (W. 727-30), the *Chryses* (W. 665-9, 880), and the
Armorum Iudicium (W. 731-4). There is less evidence in the case of
Accius, but Horace (1. 10. 53) says that Lucilius found fault with
a number of individual passages; and this criticism is attested by
both Gellius[33] and Porphyrion.[34]

If Lucilius was so suspicious of great writing, what substance
can there have been in Horace's charge? First of all, though
Lucilius attacked the epic and tragic writers for their fantastic
subjects and high-flown style, both of which were remote from
the realities of life, he could not suppress his admiration for their
grandeur and power. As with Aristophanes, this admiration
revealed itself in frequent and expert parody. When Lucilius
called Apollo *cortinipotens* 'Lord of the three-legged cooking-
pot' (i.e. of the Delphic tripod) he was glancing at compounds like
bellipotens and *armipotens* which occurred in Ennius and Accius.
When he talked of *pecus Nerei rostrique repandum* (W. 235),
'the herd of Nereus with upturned snout', he was mocking
the Pacuvian description of dolphins as *Nerei repandirostrum*

incurvicervicum pecus (W. 352), 'the upturnedsnouted neckin-curved herd of Nereus'. But however effective this may have been as parody it did involve a departure from the plain style. One cannot travesty a very tall man without using stilts.

Even when he was not satirizing tragedy, Lucilius' energy would carry him beyond the range of cultured conversation. This is obvious in the comic passages, which abound in colourful metaphors and verbal high jinks; it can also be seen in effects which are not so much funny as lively—in, for example, the alliteration of *porro procedere porcent* (W. 260), the accumulated rhymes of *surgamus, eamus, agamus* (W. 1007), and in the self-conscious cleverness of the lines on insatiability (W. 208–9):

> nam si quod satis est homini id satis esse potisset
> hoc sat erat.

> For if what is enough for a man could be enough, that would be enough.

It was probably in his invective, however, that Lucilius came closest to the style of the orator and poet. Rhetoricians of all periods gave an important place to the censure of vice (*vituperatio*), and it was recognized that this function called for a highly emotional style which would rouse the listener's indignation and carry him along with the speaker. In describing this type of orator Cicero (*Orat.* 99) calls him 'weighty, vehement, and fiery'—*gravis, acer, ardens*. Two of these terms are significant for us, because Lucilius is called an *acer et violentus poeta* by Macrobius (3. 16. 17) and he is called *ardens* by Juvenal (1. 165). The force and sweep of the grand style are described by Cicero (*Orat.* 97) in terms appropriate to a mighty river; the analogy with invective can be seen in Horace 1. 7. 26–7 where Persius in his abuse of Rex 'rushed on like a wintry river in a place where the axe seldom falls'. So too Juvenal's picture of 'the great son of Aurunca driving his team across the plain' (1. 20) may be compared to Cicero's description of the grand style in *Orator* 128–9, where he seems to have in mind a charging steed.

In making this last point, however, we must again beware of over-simplifying the picture. In W. 269 there is a fair specimen of the orotund style:

> nequitia occupat hos petulantia prodigitasque.
>
> They fall into the grip of wantonness, wastefulness, and irresponsibility.

We have good reason to believe that these words were delivered by a demagogue for whom Lucilius had nothing but contempt.[35]

(6) Lucilius was too fond of Greek importations (1. 10. 20–30). In his index to Lucilius Marx lists over 180 Greek words, ignoring those like *oleum* and *poena* which had become naturalized by the poet's day. This figure, which gives an average of one case in eight lines, remains remarkable even when one bears in mind that many of the fragments owe their survival to some linguistic oddity.

Greek words entered Latin at various levels. Starting at the bottom we find in Lucilius some half-dozen words of common abuse, like *mastigias* and *cinaedus*, which also occur in Plautus; other words were introduced by Lucilius for purposes of insult (*androgyni, moechocinaedi*) or fantasy (*cercopithecos, elephantocamellos*). All such words were avoided by Horace, not just because they were Greek but because he considered them vulgar or silly. At a rather higher level come nautical terms, like *carchesia* and *catapirates*, and military terms, like *ballista* and *catapulta*. The absence of such words from Horace is again due to his narrower social range rather than to his national outlook. On the few occasions when Horace does employ plebeian Hellenisms he usually has a satirical purpose; for example, *hybrida*, 'mongrel', describes Persius (1. 7. 2), and *pharmacopolae*, 'druggists', are among the mourners at Tigellius' funeral (1. 2. 1).[36] This effect is, of course, also found in Lucilius, as when he speaks of a *propola*, 'a huckster', and a *pistrix empleuros*, 'a massive bakeress'. Of the seven words used by Lucilius in connexion with sports and games[37] Horace has only *trigon*—the ball game mentioned in 1. 6. 126—but one should perhaps add *phimus*, the dice-box of the gambler Volanerius in

2. 7. 17. So too, whereas Lucilius uses *diallaxon, psolocopumai* and *eugium* in erotic contexts, Horace has only the hybrid *depugis*, and that in his earliest satire.

At the highest cultural level three types of usage can be distinguished. First, in keeping with his broad interests, Lucilius had no hesitation in using the vocabulary of rhetoric and philosophy in quite a straightforward way, simply to express his meaning. Of the two dozen rhetorical terms half are of this kind, and of these only two (*poema* and *epistula*) are found in Horace. As with *rhetor* itself (1. 5. 2), both these terms had lost their foreign character. An example will illustrate the divergence in the poets' practice. In W. 253 Lucilius speaks of a slaves' holiday 'which you obviously can't name in a hexameter line' (*hexametro versu*).[38] In the Journey to Brundisium (87) Horace refers to a town 'which can't be named in verse' (*quod versu dicere non est*); later, in 1. 10. 59, he speaks of hexameter verse as 'closing up something in six feet' (*pedibus senis*). In each case Horace has avoided the Hellenism.

At a symposium (W. 815 ff.) Lucilius mentions the images and atoms of Epicurus—*eidola atque atomus*; he also uses the word *scole*, softening the alien effect by an explanatory *quam vocant*. Half-a-dozen other philosophical terms are used with varying shades of irony and therefore fall outside this category. Horace, however, does not employ such terms for any purpose, serious or ironic; instead he uses a Latin translation, as with the Epicurean *inane* and *soldum* (1. 2. 113), a fact which reminds us once again that Horace is separated from Lucilius by Lucretius and Cicero.[39]

Secondly, Lucilius often uses Greek to achieve an effect of stylishness, e.g. W. 491–2:

> non paucis malle ac sapientibus esse probatum
> ἢ πᾶσιν νεκύεσσι καταφθιμένοισιν ἀνάσσειν.

> Not to prefer the esteem of the few and the wise rather than to reign over all the spirits of the dead.

Flourishes of this kind must have been as familiar in the conversation of the Scipionic circle as they are in Cicero's letters. When produced at the right moment they gave that feeling of being at once witty, exclusive, and highly civilized which comes to the elderly public school man who has hit on an appropriate Latin tag.[40]

The use of Greek as a status symbol shades off into our third category, which is that of parody and satire. Here there is considerable variation, depending on the nature of the attack. Take, for example, τὸν δ' ἐξήρπαξεν Ἀπόλλων (W. 267)—'but Apollo snatched him away'. As we saw on p. 79, the original is Homer, *Iliad* 20. 443. If Lucilius used the phrase in connexion with some lucky escape, then obviously it represents a mild form of parody. Horace used the same idea (1. 9. 78), but in keeping with his principles he rendered it into Latin as *sic me servavit Apollo*, thus diluting both sense and wit.

A more trenchant example from Lucilius is the passage deriding the ideal of perfect womanhood:

num censes calliplocamon callisphyron ullam
non licitum esse uterum atque etiam inguina tangere mammis,
conpernem aut varam fuisse Amphitryonis acoetin
Alcmenam atque alias, Helenam ipsam denique—nolo
dicere; tute vide atque disyllabon elige quodvis—
κούρην eupatereiam, aliquam rem insignem habuisse,
verrucam naevum punctum dentem eminulum unum?

(W. 567–73)

> Surely you don't think it impossible that any woman with 'lovely tresses' and 'lovely ankles' could have touched her womb and even her crotch with her breasts, that Alcmena 'the wife of Amphitryon's bosom' could have been knock-kneed or bandy, and that others too, even Helen herself, that—(I won't say—think of it yourself and pick any two-syllable word you like)—that 'daughter of a noble sire', could have had some obvious blemish, a wart, a mole, a pock-mark, or one buck tooth?[41]

Here Homer is both a victim and an instrument of satire, but as far as one can tell the ridicule has no serious moral content. For this we must go to the fragments which attack high living. In his recent monograph Mariotti attempts to distinguish between the cheaper and the more expensive fish mentioned by Lucilius.[42] It is perhaps significant that three of the cheaper sort (*muraena, ostrea, peloris*) are found in Horace, but none of the more exotic (*amia, acarna, helops, sargus*). As for drink, χρυσίζον (golden) and Χῖός τε δυνάστης (Chian lord) both refer to high-quality wine, though we cannot be sure how far they represent an attack on the consumers. There is less doubt in the case of the coverings mentioned in W. 13:

> psilae atque amphitapoe villis ingentibus molles.
>
> Soft coverlets with deep pile on one or both sides.

These are condemned as decadent. The following are also mentioned with disapproval (W. 60):

> chirodyti aurati, ricae, toracia, mitrae.
>
> Long-sleeved tunics interwoven with gold, veils, bodices, and hair-bands.

According to Cichorius (p. 240), whose theory has been accepted by subsequent commentators, Scaevola was accused by Albucius of stealing these items for his mistress.

Finally, we have cases where Lucilius uses Greek as a weapon against itself. In the council of the gods we hear of someone who was so phil-Hellenic that he called a water-jug a *pot à eau*— '*arutaenae'que, inquit, 'aquales*' (W. 14); it had become fashionable to call the legs of a couch *pieds de lit* and lamps *chandeliers* (W. 15–16).[43] The craze was typfied by Albucius, whom Scaevola ridiculed by exclaiming *quam lepide lexis compostae* (W. 84)—'How exquisitely are his *mots* fitted together!' Scaevola took the joke further by greeting Albucius in Athens with the Greek word *chaere!* and instructing his attendants to chime in (W. 92–3). These last examples are important, for they show that Lucilius did set some limits to the use of Greek, though in this as in other respects he was far less strict than Horace.

On this rather hurried survey a few general comments suggest themselves. First, in defence of his coarseness Lucilius could point out that he was a quasi-dramatic author writing in a genre akin to comedy; he therefore had to make his characters convincing. 'If common people use vulgar language, that's not my fault.' Horace would have answered that there was a place for broad humour (*est quaedam hic quoque virtus*), but some restraint was necessary, otherwise the more important functions of satire would be obscured. The satirist himself was a man of society with certain standards of decency to maintain; he should not give too much prominence to scenes from low life.

In defending his invective Lucilius could, and apparently did, contend that evil ought to be exposed and that the innocent had nothing to fear from an honest watchdog like himself.[44] Horace granted that the argument had some force; in fact he used it himself. But he knew that it provided so wide an umbrella that the libeller and pornographer could take shelter along with the genuine reformer. And so he insisted that Lucilius' moral purpose could be served just as effectively, and indeed more so, by less drastic means (*ridiculum acri | fortius et melius magnas plerumque secat res*).

But perhaps when viewed in a wider perspective Horace's criticisms were misconceived; perhaps the humour and polemic of Lucilius, though distasteful to a purist of the late Republic, were quite appropriate in an earlier and more robust generation. Horace was aware of this viewpoint, but one has the impression that although he did not actually contradict it he was reluctant to agree. What he does is to concede the point provisionally, for the sake of argument: 'Suppose Lucilius *was* genial and witty (*comis et urbanus*), suppose too that he *was* relatively polished (*limatior*), nevertheless if he were alive today he would have to write more carefully.' And writing more carefully would imply less coarseness and abuse, for the social and artistic aspects of decorum were complementary. Horace, therefore, cannot be accused of lacking historical sense. It is true that as a contemporary of Virgil he believed that the standards of his own age were superior to those

of a century before, and in making this confident assumption he
may well have overlooked the merits of some earlier writers—
his remark on Plautus, for example, in *Epist*. 2. 1. 175–6 is notably
unfair. Nevertheless, Horace had a case, and it would be unwise
for us with our vague catholicity of taste and our confusion about
aesthetic values to patronize a man who believed that in art as in
life the civilized virtues were the best.

When weighing the apparently conflicting evidence about
Lucilius' quest for publicity one has to keep in mind the great
variety of his work. Some pieces, like the letter in W. 186–93,
were meant primarily for the recipient; others, like the essay on
orthography in Book 9, would have interested only the intelligentsia. No doubt Lucilius hoped that most of what he
wrote would win the approval of his friends, but he must have
known quite well that much of it had sensational qualities which
would appeal to a far wider audience. The ridicule of Scipio's
enemies was certainly not intended as coterie verse, and we may
be sure that the more farcical and erotic satires were enjoyed by
large sections of the general public.

It has already been suggested that the difference between
Lucilius and Horace was in part a difference of theory. Lucilius
saw no harm in using a grandiose rhetoric to attack the faults of
the epic and tragic style. Fantastic themes, far-fetched images,
phrases which boomed because of their emptiness—these were to
him failings not only of taste but of character, for they sprang
from pretentiousness and insincerity and fostered the same vices
in the reader. Horace, however, held that rhetoric was still
rhetoric even when used against itself; this kind of effect should
therefore be used sparingly in a genre which was close to
conversation.

The same point can be made in connexion with Greek words.
As we saw, these were often used by Lucilius in a sarcastic way to
attack the more corrupting effects of Hellenic influence, one of
which was the adulteration of Latin. While Lucilius was much
more tolerant than Horace towards the use of conversational

Greek, he did recognize some limits. When a man's speech became so affected that he was unable to describe ordinary objects in his own tongue, and when every other sentence was decorated with a flourish of Greek, then Lucilius reached for his pen and struck. The impact must have been considerable, but the form of his attack was Greek, and to the purist this was like using Satan to cast out Satan. Horace's own practice is expounded in the *Ars Poetica* (48–53): if the poet wishes to use ideas for which there is no Latin name, he may go to the Greek, but this licence must be used with discretion (*dabiturque licentia sumpta pudenter*). Moreover, the foreign word should be taken into the language and given a proper Latin form. Here, as so often, it is hard to tell where nationalism ends and imperialism begins.

Even if Lucilius and Horace had shared the same theories their temperaments would have led to different results. When Lucilius saw the chance to exploit a comic situation his Rabelaisian spirit took control; and when his anger was roused he would hunt down his victims with volleys of invective, forgetting about Panaetius and his rules of taste. It must also be said that he had a far more scholarly mind than Horace. His disquisitions on orthography, etymology, euphony, and other branches of language were probably quite beyond the range of his successor, and the same is true of his interest in the technical details of various skills and trades. In dealing with these matters his chief concern was to convey information or to argue a case; the artistic shape of the verse was of secondary importance. This was never true of Horace, who felt that if a subject could not be subdued to an elegant form it was better handled in prose.

In comparing the two poets it must be agreed that Horace was the superior artist, just as Virgil was superior to Ennius. But while reading the fragments one is aware at times that in the attainment of this greater perfection some qualities were lost—qualities of freshness, spontaneity and rough vigour. And this is enough to cause regret at the decision of the ancients to let Lucilius fall into obscurity. He was a man of letters who participated heartily in life and wrote direct from his experience. In the substantial remains of Roman literature he is a type all too poorly represented.

In discussing the relation of Horace to Lucilius we have considered only two points of a triangular controversy. The third point was occupied by Horace's critics. Who were these people and what did they represent? At the beginning of 2. 1 Horace divided them into two classes:

> sunt quibus in satura videar nimis acer et ultra
> legem tendere opus; sine nervis altera quidquid
> composui pars esse putat, similisque meorum
> mille die versus deduci posse.

Some people think I am too harsh in my satire and push the genre beyond legitimate limits; others maintain that my compositions have no muscle and that a thousand verses like mine could be turned out in a day.

Nothing can be said about the first group. They probably had little in common except the conviction that brawling in public was vulgar and undignified. In the second group we must include the pro-Lucilian critics who had been in opposition to Horace ever since the appearance of 1. 4 and perhaps earlier.

At first glance it might seem that the best label for the Lucilians would be 'archaists', but it soon becomes clear that some at least were archaists of a rather special kind. From the eight lines preceding 1. 10 (which although probably spurious may be held to contain genuine information) we learn that one of Lucilius' champions was the scholar Valerius Cato.[45] As well as being a scholar Cato was also a poet in the Neoteric manner; that is, he drew his inspiration from Callimachus and the Alexandrians. Hermogenes and 'the ape', who had taken Lucilius' side against Horace, also had Neoteric leanings, for Horace says that the ape's only artistic accomplishment is 'singing Calvus and Catullus'— nil praeter Calvum et doctus cantare Catullum (1. 10. 19). The musical interests of Hermogenes and his friends (1. 10. 90–1), along with the adjectives *pulcher*—'pretty', and *doctus*—'artistic' or perhaps 'intellectual', are in keeping with aesthetic tastes of an Alexandrian kind. A similar hint may perhaps be found in 1. 10. 23–4, where a defender of Lucilius says that a style which mingles Greek and Latin is *suavior* 'smoother', as when a Falernian wine is blended with Chian. This reminds us that we are dealing with a controversy rather than straight literary theory; for it is unlikely that Lucilius would have given *suavitas* as a reason for using Greek, whereas a Neoteric might well have done so.[46]

Why, we wonder, should a Neoteric poet like Valerius Cato have been interested enough in Lucilius to edit his work? One suggestion, made by R. P. Robinson, is that Cato's Lucilian studies were 'for professional purposes, to supply material for the instruction of his students'.[47] Perhaps so, but this is not enough to explain why he is called a *defensor* or 'advocate' of the satirist (v. 2 of the disputed lines); and a cold utilitarian attitude of this sort would not account for his part in the quarrel. A more personal theory is advanced by Bardon, who thinks that Cato's editorial work was due to the influence of his old master Vettius Philocomus, who had been a friend of Lucilius. Again, there is some truth in this, but Bardon adds 'je doute fort qu'il ait apprécié le style de Lucilius', and later 'le style en semblait vicieux'.[48] But if Cato was one of those who took exception to Horace's remarks in 1. 4, he must have found *something* to admire in Lucilius' style.

A much wider historical approach was taken by Tenney Frank, who maintained that the Neoterics shared a common hatred of Julius Caesar and therefore the survivors of the school formed a group which was politically antagonistic to Horace and the Augustan establishment:

Some of them, notably Catullus, Calvus, and Memmius, were silenced by Caesar before the civil war, but their published works still contained the bitter lampoons which the Augustan circle found so difficult to forgive. Horace's fling at the *collegium poetarum* and its chief critic Tarpa in *Sat.* 10. 38 should be connected with the fact that Pompey had chosen Tarpa to select and stage official plays during his consulship. Apparently Pompey had been a patron of the *collegium* which Horace scorns. We also remember that Cornificius...died in defence of the Republican cause, and that Cinna, perhaps not wholly by mistake as Plutarch thought, was killed by the mob at Caesar's bier. Of the men criticized in *Sat.* 10 Pitholaus the Rhodian had written a eulogy of Pompey and lampooned Caesar; Fannius had sent his portrait to the poets' club; Furius Bibaculus had ridiculed Augustus as well as Caesar; Valerius Cato...seems to have had a high position in the *collegium poetarum*, and Lucilius...was of course a favorite of Pompey's circle because of his kinship. [Pompey was a descendant of Lucilius on his mother's side.]⁴⁹

The Neoterics, however, were less homogeneous than Frank implies. Some, like Memmius, Calvus, Catullus, and Cinna, had been reconciled to Caesar by the mid fifties. Cinna was in fact a Tribune of the People at the time of Caesar's death, and there is nothing to suggest that he had any sympathy with the conspirators. Others had supported Caesar from the beginning. Cornificius, for instance, gave excellent service in Illyricum and the East. He later sided with the senate against Antony, and died while resisting the take-over of his province; but that does not make him an enemy of Caesar.⁵⁰ If his poems reflected any political feeling, which is unlikely, it was certainly not enthusiasm for Pompey. The writings of Varro of Atax, Gallus, and the young Virgil also disturb the tidiness of Frank's thesis.

As for the others mentioned in *Sat.* 1. 10, Frank is right about Tarpa, probably right about Pitholaus—if we accept the usual identification of Pitholeon (22) with Pitholaus,⁵¹ and just possibly right about Fannius and the poets' club (1. 4. 21-2). Except for Fannius, however, who is associated with Hermogenes in 1. 10. 80, we do not know how far these men were interested in Neoteric poetry, if at all.

The case of Furius Bibaculus is not relevant to our present point; for if he is identical with the Alpman of 1. 10. 36 and the Furius of 2. 5. 40 he is not attacked as a Neoteric.⁵² We are therefore left with Valerius Cato. His political affiliations are uncertain. Marx believed that, like the other Lucilian scholars mentioned earlier, Cato was a follower of Pompey. This view was favoured by Frank, and has recently been presented with as much detail as the evidence allows by W. S. Anderson.[53] If it is true (and it well may be), we now have professional, personal, and political reasons for Cato's interest in Lucilius. I still prefer to think, however, that literary reasons were the most important. One observes that in the case of Hermogenes and the ape (who, unlike Cato, are actually mentioned in the poem) we have no political evidence at all. We know only that they were teachers of music and poetry who supported Lucilius while at the same time admiring Calvus and Catullus.

What elements, then, can be found in Lucilius which would appeal to a devotee of Calvus and Catullus and not to Horace? This last restriction is important if we are to understand the controversy. It means that Lucilius' habit of self-portrayal, his avoidance of the major genres, and the more refined aspects of his wit must all be left out of account.[54] First, a Neoteric might well have admired Lucilius' metrical versatility—not just in the dramatic metres of Books 26–30 but in the elegies of Books 22–5, which dealt with members of his household. One couplet (W. 624–5) shows that the fierce lampooner had a tenderer side:

> servus nec infidus domino neque inutilis quaquam
> Lucili columella hic situs Metrophanes.

> Here lies a servant who was faithful to his master and a help in every way, Lucilius' little pillar Metrophanes.

We have already noted Lucilius' readiness to use a spondee in the fifth foot of a hexameter. In the ending *pedicis mens inretita est* (W. 1107)—'His mind was entangled by chains'—*inretita* foreshadows a favourite effect of the Neoterics; though Catullus would have used a pyrrhic ($\cup\cup$) rather than the long monosyllable *mens*.

Secondly, the satires included love-poems on at least two different girls. Commenting on Horace, *Carm.* 1. 22. 10, Porphyrion says that one of Lucilius' books was entitled *Collyra* because it was written about a mistress of that name—*quod de Collyra amica scriptus sit.* A second mistress is mentioned by Varro (*LL* 6. 69): 'Lucilius writes about Cretaea that when she came to sleep with him she was persuaded of her own free will to remove her tunic and the rest.' Another girl, Hymnis, occurs in five of the fragments, and it may be that she too was a mistress of the poet, though there is not enough evidence to prove it. One other fragment deserves mention because, apart from its tantalizing content, it preserves two of the names which Lucilius applied to his satires (W. 1039–40):

> cuius vultu ac facie ludo ac sermonibus nostris
> virginis hoc pretium atque hunc reddebamus honorem.

> With my light conversation-pieces I gave the girl this recognition
> and reward for her pretty face and looks.

Although there is nothing in any of these pieces to suggest the passionate intensity of the Lesbia poems, and although the tone was probably more hearty than that adopted by the Neoterics, it is still a fair guess that his frank subjective treatment of *amor* was one of the features which commended Lucilius to followers of Calvus and Catullus.[55]

Another was his aggressiveness. Coming to Lucilius from the *nugae* of Catullus one finds the same ebullience, the same trenchant wit, the same dislike of subterfuge and evasion. In moments of anger neither would pause to ask whether their victim was a public figure or whether he might be dangerous to offend; their only concern was to brand him with ridicule.[56] This independent spirit was probably engendered by social as well as temperamental factors, for Calvus and Catullus, like Lucilius, were well off and moved in fashionable circles. In any case it gave rise to various similarities of style. In Catullus we meet the same easy unself-conscious use of everyday language, which included provincialisms, Greek importations, and numerous diminutives, and which sometimes sank to the grossest vulgarity. Occasionally he burlesqued the diction of Ennius or invented a comic compound for himself, and he loved devices like alliteration, assonance, rhymes, and puns. It is true, of course, that even within the *nugae* these features often produced quite un-Lucilian effects; Catullus, for example, was cleverer in his obscenity, and more subtle and versatile in his use of diminutives. In the longer poems it is mainly the contrasts that impress us. When Lucilius borrows the Ennian compound *caelicolae* ('Heaven-dwellers') in W. 21, the setting is a parody of a divine council; whereas in Catullus 64. 386 the word is used in a spirit of wistful reverence. So too, *anceps ferrum* ('double-headed iron'), which sounds like a noble Ennian periphrasis for 'axe', is used by a blustering clown in W. 942; in Catullus 64. 369 it is part of the song of the Fates. Nor is there anything comic or sarcastic in Catullan coinages like *erifuga*, *falsiparens*, and *silvicultrix*. As for the admission of Greek words, it is hard to imagine Lucilius using Greek for pretty, sentimental, or melodious effects, and he never shared Catullus' enthusiasm for romantic proper names. Nevertheless, Lucilius and Catullus were at one in their attempt to win new territory for poetic language. Horace, though lively and vigorous in his own way, was more concerned with entrenchment and organization. And that is why his verse might well have seemed 'lacking in muscle' to survivors of the other tradition.[57]

To sum up. The literary basis of the feud between Horace and his critics was the fact that they each admired Lucilius for different reasons. Hermogenes and Demetrius valued his metrical variety; Horace was glad that he eventually fixed on the hexameter. They saw his amatory verse as in some way clearing the ground for elegy; Horace, who was always reticent about his love-life, could find no room for such writing in his conception of satire. They relished the exuberance of Lucilius' language; Horace felt that it needed pruning. Above all, while they enjoyed the sharply personal element in Lucilius' invective, Horace was more interested in its moral content. To him Lucilius was essentially the good-humoured raconteur, the forceful preacher who in his exposure of vice had shown how the diatribe might be developed as an artistic verse-form.

These differences of theory were exacerbated by other factors. Hermogenes and Demetrius were professionals who made their living by teaching and study. No doubt they resented Horace's subsidized leisure and the kudos he enjoyed as a friend of Messalla, Pollio, and Maecenas. If, moreover, they were politically hostile to Octavian, it must have been galling to see a turn-coat received and acclaimed at enemy headquarters. Their resentment was answered from the other side by contempt. Horace openly scorned the type of criticism practised in the schools and the sort of poetry which it fostered:

> an tua demens
> vilibus in ludis dictari carmina malis?
> non ego. (i. 10. 74–6)

> Would you be mad enough to prefer your poems to be dictated in cheap schools? Not me.

A similar disdain appears in a letter of Messalla's (Suet. *De Gramm.* 4), which says that 'he has nothing to do with Furius Bibaculus or even with Ticidas or Cato the elementary school teacher' (*litteratore*). It was acrimony of this kind which sharpened Horace's critique of Lucilius. No doubt objective truth suffered in the process, and a sober assessment was made more difficult. However, it was not all loss; sober assessments can be so very dull.

2. 1

This is a deceptive poem. Though intended as a prologue to Book 2, it has certain links with the earlier collection which give it a transitional character. In time, moreover, it is the latest of all the satires and so (to risk an Irish bull) it looks forward to what is already written. The relevance of this fact will become apparent as we study the rather strange sequence of argument. In form the satire is a consultation. Horace, who affects to be troubled at the reception given to his previous book, asks the advice of C. Trebatius Testa, the most famous jurist of the day and a man twenty years his senior.[58] The dialogue opens with a passage which may be paraphrased as follows:

Some people think my satire goes beyond legitimate limits (*ultra legem*); others find it insipid. Tell me what to do, Trebatius.

Take a rest (*quiescas*).

Stop writing verses altogether, you mean?

Yes.

Well, no doubt that would be the best thing. But I can't sleep.

Those in need of sound sleep shall swim the Tiber three times (*ter...transnanto*) and before retiring have their system well soaked with wine. Or, if you have this compulsion to write, try recounting the exploits of Caesar.

I would gladly do so, Sir, but my powers are unequal to the task.

Well, at least you could write in praise of Caesar's character, as Lucilius did with Scipio.

I shan't be found wanting when the time is right. Only at a suitable moment will Floppy's words (*Flacci verba*) enter Caesar's pricked-up ear (*attentam aurem*). Rub him the wrong way and he'll lash out with his hooves in all directions.

A eulogy of that kind would be far wiser than writing savage lines about Pantolabus the parasite and the wastrel Nomentanus; invective only causes fear and resentment.

I'm sorry; I can't help it. Milonius dances, when wine brings heat to his head and plurality to the lights; Castor rejoices in steeds; the issue of the same egg rejoices in fists. Everyone follows his own pursuit.

The implication surely is 'Similarly I have to vent my indignation by writing satire'. And that is the inference drawn by many commentators. They compare Persius 1. 12, 'I'm sorry; I can't help it...I have to guffaw'. L. R. Shero says 'The poet makes it perfectly clear that his temperament forces him not merely to write, but to write satire in the manner of Lucilius'.[59] That is certainly what we expect—especially in view of the gibe at Milonius. But it is not what we get. Instead Horace says 'I have to put words into metrical form' (28). So apparently what keeps him awake is not hatred or anger, but simply problems of scansion. Juvenal's Roman had better reasons for his insomnia.[60]

But what of the phrase *Lucili ritu* which follows? Since this means 'in Lucilius' manner', perhaps Horace has in mind his censorious spirit as well as his metrical form. But no. The phrase leads on to something quite different, namely Lucilius' *confessional* manner:

ille velut fidis arcana sodalibus olim
credebat libris, neque si male cesserat usquam
decurrens alio neque si bene; quo fit ut omnis
votiva pateat veluti descripta tabella
vita senis.

In days gone by he used to confide his secrets to his books as if they
were trusted friends. He never turned to any other quarter in failure
or success; as a result the old fellow's entire life lies before us as if
painted on a votive tablet.

Horace now continues with *sequor hunc* (34). Perhaps now we
shall hear something of the Lucilian spirit. Not yet. 'It is uncertain', he says, 'whether I'm a Lucanian or an Apulian; for
Venusia, my birthplace, is adjacent to both.' So that's it. Horace
comes from a long line of fighting men; there's pugnacity in his
blood.[61] But at once a qualification appears: 'This steely point
(*stilus*) will not attack any living person and it will protect me like
a sword in a scabbard' (39–40). Does this mean that after all his
fine talk Horace has formally renounced the idea of personal
attack and that, like Juvenal, he will assail only the dead? Not
quite. We have forgotten the little word *ultro*. 'I shall not attack
anyone *unless provoked*.' It is safe to say that since the time of
Romulus no Roman ever confessed to an act of unprovoked
aggression.

There follows a fervent prayer. 'O Jupiter, Father and King,
let my sheathed weapon decay with rust' (42–3). The effect, however, is rather spoilt by the next line, 'And let no man offend me,
desirous as I am of peace!' People had better treat this peaceable
man with caution. 'Anyone who annoys me ("Better keep
away!" I cry) will be sorry, and his name will become a byword
throughout the city.' The sword is now rattling noisily.

The next section opens on the same minatory note:

Cervius threatens his enemies with litigation; Canidia is dreaded for her poison;
Turius for his savage sentences. Everyone uses the weapon which suits him
best. It's the same in the world of nature. The wolf has his fangs, the bull his
horns; each acts from an inner instinct. Give the wastrel Scaeva ('Lefthand')

charge of his aged mother, and his filial right hand (*dextera*) will commit no crime. Of course not! A wolf doesn't kick or a bull bite. The old girl will be got rid of by a dose of hemlock. (47–56)

We now expect something like 'As for me, I fight with my pen'. And that is what Orelli supplies (*opprobriis dignos libere insectabor*).[62] But after this flamboyant approach Horace shies away into something wholly non-committal: 'Whether a quiet old age awaits me or death hovers round with sable wing, rich or poor, in Rome or, if chance so decree, in exile—whatever the complexion of my life, I shall continue to write' (57–60).

Trebatius, however, behaves as if Horace had threatened to write lampoons. 'I'm afraid, my boy, you won't last long; one of your influential friends will cut you dead.' To which Horace replies (and again I am paraphrasing):

What? Have you forgotten Lucilius the great pioneer of satire? He stripped off everyone's disguise. He wounded Metellus, buried Lupus in a shower of invective, and castigated the people tribe by tribe. So far from being offended by his wit Laelius and Scipio were his closest friends. They used to let their hair down (*discincti*) and romp around with him while the vegetables were cooking. (62–74)

We infer that Horace can be as censorious as he wishes without losing the friendship of Maecenas and Octavian. Orelli's comment is *tales autem nebulones ubi perstrinxero nunquam profecto timebo ne potentes amicos a me abalienem* (introduction to 2. 1). But again, that is not what Horace says:

Whatever I am, although inferior to Lucilius in wealth and ability, Envy will have to admit that I have lived with the great, and if she thinks I am brittle she will find me a tough nut to crack. But perhaps, my learned friend, you hold a dissenting view? (74–9)

This is so discreet as to be almost meaningless. The implication seems to be that if Horace is attacked he can rely on the support of Maecenas. There is certainly no statement about any satirical attacks of his own.

Yet Trebatius replies as if Horace had expressed his determination to write abusive verse:

Well, I can't break the force of your argument (*diffindere*), but I must warn you in case your ignorance of the majesty of the law gets you into trouble. If a party compose foul verses against another party a hearing and a trial ensue.   (79-83)

Horace once again steps neatly aside:

That is true in the case of *foul* verses, but what if a party compose *fine* verses and in Caesar's judgement win commendation?...
The charge will be laughed out of court and you will get off scot free. (83-6)

So ends the most brilliant piece of shadow-boxing in Roman literature. What are we to make of it? Perhaps, as hinted above, the position of the poem may give us a clue. The links with Book I are obvious. The very first line recalls the criticisms which had greeted the previous collection. Lucilius occupies the foreground as if he were still regarded as the model for satiric writing. In the use of proper names Horace continues his earlier practice, and there are numerous echoes of the former literary controversy.[63] And yet things are not quite the same. Horace is now eight years older than when he wrote the fourth satire, and therefore eight years steadier and more responsible (or eight years duller and more complacent, depending on one's point of view). His position in the social and literary world is well established; his enemies realize that any attempt to dislodge him will only injure themselves, and so they accept him, however grudgingly, as a celebrity.

Some scholars would maintain that there was also a risk of legal proceedings.[64] As far as we know there had been no alteration in the law of libel within the previous decade, though it is possible that with the return of order after Actium the existing law (presumably Sulla's *Lex Cornelia de iniuriis*) might be more strictly enforced. It is doubtful, however, if 2.1 reflects any real anxiety. Horace, after all, had the other seven poems before him and he knew quite well that they contained little in the way of defamatory material. Why this was so is another question, which will be touched on in the next chapter. But so far as the present poem is concerned it seems best to attribute the threat of prosecution, like the other legal elements, to the poet's wit rather than to the hazards of contemporary life.

As Horace wrote 2.1 he was about to publish a collection of hexameter verses which ridiculed the follies and vices of his fellow-citizens. To this extent the poems could claim to be a refined version of Lucilian satire, but they lacked the personal abuse which had come to be regarded as a distinguishing feature of the genre. In Horace's first book this had already been greatly modified, but there were several remarks which could have given offence and also touches of coarseness which suggested Lucilius' influence. In the new collection this element had been further diminished; and so in introducing the book Horace could not promise his readers a rich feast of scandal and gossip. Indeed as he looked through the poems he must have realized how far his satire had moved away from the scathing denunciations of his predecessor. Yet he did not wish to disparage the old tradition, even though he was now on the point of abandoning it. There were many aspects of it which he valued, and his admiration for the *inventor* remained unaltered.

The result of these stresses was the poem which we have been discussing. The links with Book 1 give the appearance of continuity. Horace's pose is the one he had previously adopted in his more bellicose moods. He has taken guard once again in the ring where Lucilius had battered so many opponents. But there is one big difference. Behind the pugilist's gloves we can detect a mischievous grin, and it gradually becomes apparent that in spite of the threatening stance and the elaborate feinting and ducking Horace does not really intend to come to blows. To use a word from an early article of Fraenkel's, it is all *Scheinpolemik*. He has disposed of his problem by a joke.

In this poem we are struck again and again by a playfulness almost amounting to farce. We catch glimpses of Milonius glassy-eyed and unsteady, poor Lupus smothered in a shower of Lucilian invective, Scipio and Laelius freed from the trammels of *gravitas* enjoying a bit of horseplay while the greens are cooking. The satire's vividness is matched by its verbal dexterity. One recalls the play on *stilus* (pen and dagger), the juxtaposition of Scaeva and *dextera*, and that amazing metaphor which begins with a pun on Horace's name (Flaccus) and ends with a comparison of the emperor to a nervous horse. In the resounding line *Panto-labum scurram Nomentanumque nepotem* everything is impressive except the content. And what of that superb periphrasis in v. 26 *ovo prognatus eodem* ('born from the same egg')? Pollux is at once exalted by *prognatus* and diminished by *ovo*, and the final *eodem* reaches back along the line to disturb the dignity of Castor. The myth of Leda was never touched more lightly. At the end of the satire the principles of aesthetics are cleverly confused with the law of libel, and this brings us back to the opening phrase *ultra legem* ('beyond legitimate limits'), which refers to the definition of satire as well as to illegal pasquinades.

The fiction of a consultation is maintained partly by Horace's respectful attitude (*pater optime, docte*), partly by his quasi-technical words (*praescribe, dissentis*), but mainly by the language of Treba-tius, who preserves not only the sententious brevity of a jurist (*quiescas, aio*) but also a correctly legal turn of phrase. The solem-nity of this phrasing, however, is always compromised. I doubt if the verb *transnanto*, though impeccable in form, ever appeared in a Roman statute. The technical precision of *diffindere* is marred by the fact that it echoes *fragili quaerens illidere dentem* and there-fore evokes a picture of the great lawyer trying to crack a nut with his teeth.[65] The libel law is cited in language reminiscent of the Twelve Tables, only to be turned upside down. Even the tablets of the indictment are dissolved in laughter.

As a piece of drama the satire is much more fully realized than the introductory poems of Persius and Juvenal, both of which are descended from it.[66] As we have seen, Horace keeps the pro-fessional setting before our minds, and in Trebatius he gives us a real person who is quite unlike the lay figures of Persius and Juvenal. The older man is anxious to restrain Horace from rashness and at the same time to enhance his material prospects (*multa laborum / praemia laturus*). He is not portrayed as a fool—far from it; but in his advice he recommends two pastimes which we know from Cicero to have been especially congenial to him, namely swimming and drinking.[67] His recipe for sound sleep can in fact be summed up in Heinze's comment: 'Nass äusserlich und innerlich appliziert.' Horace knew he would enjoy the joke, and indeed this whole poem is a confirmation of the very attractive picture which emerges from the correspondence of Cicero.[68]

Such, then, is the last of Horace's satires. It is designed as a bridge leading from the cultivated but open ground of Book 1 to the walled garden of Book 2. From a distance the structure appears strong enough, but at close quarters it is seen to be largely ornamental and incapable of bearing much weight.

CHAPTER V

THE NAMES

There is, perhaps, a natural tendency to assume that the best information about Horace's characters is to be found in the ancient commentators. Though Porphyrion's notes date from about the third century and the pseudo-Acron's may be as late as the fifth, both men had access to a lot of earlier material which has since been lost, including monographs on Horatian prosopography.[1] As a result they occasionally preserve fragments of a genuine tradition. But if we ask them for reliable detailed information they will let us down. Sometimes their notes conflict, as in the Fannius passage (1. 4. 21–2): *beatus Fannius ultro / delatis capsis et imagine*—'Fannius is happy after the presentation of a case of books and a bust of himself as an unsolicited gift'. Here we are told that Fannius presented book-cases to the senate, that the senate presented book-cases to him, that his heirs presented his books to public libraries, and (splendidly) that at the hour of death Fannius begged to be cremated on a pile of his own books.[2] Sometimes the scholiasts misinterpreted what was in front of them. At 1. 2. 64, for example, some of them missed the irony of *Villius...Sullae gener*—'Villius the "husband" of Sulla's daughter'—and stated that Villius (who was not, in fact, the husband) was a metrical substitute for Annius (who was). Often, as in the case of Trebatius the famous jurist, they tell us much less than we can learn from other sources. And often they are simply guessing. Recently I asked a group of students to comment on the name Mucius in Juvenal's line *quid refert dictis ignoscat Mucius an non?* (1. 154). The inventions of those who didn't know the answer sounded remarkably like the pseudo-Acron. On the whole, then, the scholiasts are not of much assistance, except where they provide corroborative evidence. In their treatment of Horace's names they usually assumed that they were dealing with real individuals. As we shall see, this, like other simple theories, is far from adequate.

For the sake of convenience I have classified the material as (*a*) the names of living people, (*b*) the names of dead people, (*c*) the names of Lucilian characters, (*d*) significant names, (*e*) the names of other type characters, and (*f*) pseudonyms. Not all the categories are self-contained—(*b*) and (*c*), for example, obviously overlap. And there are several figures who cannot be assigned with confidence to any one group. In such cases the most we can do is to assess probabilities. We shall not be dealing with all the names mentioned. Only *satirical* references need be considered. And even here there is room for selection, for some of the figures are so obscure that nothing useful can be said about them.[3]

(*a*) *Living people.* The first ones we meet are the hot gospellers Crispinus and Fabius.[4] The bearded, 'bleary-eyed' Crispinus was an obvious target. Like Stertinius, who appears in a later satire, he denounced many habits which Horace himself found objectionable, but his doctrinaire idealism ('all sins are equally culpable'), his lack of social graces, and his eccentric pose disqualified him from serious consideration. Also, from an aesthetic standpoint his sermons were deplorable, being long-winded, over-heated affairs with as little art as his own doggerel verses. The 'gas-bag' Fabius represents the same type. He was one of those speakers who hit the nail on the head with such relentless persistency that the wood eventually splits. As well as being a pedantic bore he has also been put down as an adulterer, but that is unfair. In 1. 2. 134, after listing the dangers of adultery, Horace concludes *deprendi miserum est; Fabio vel iudice vincam*, 'To be caught is a horrid experience—I could prove that even before Fabius'. This has been taken to imply that Fabius had once paid the penalty himself, but a more natural interpretation is that even a Stoic like Fabius would find the consequences painful. So we may take it that Fabius was not an adulterer, but simply a man who had argued himself into believing that the true philosopher was immune to pain, or (to use the old paradox) that the good man could be happy on the rack. Horace would certainly have applauded the student who remarked that it would have to be a very good man and a very bad rack. On the trip to Brundisium (1. 5) three more characters make their appearance. One is Aufidius Luscus the mayor of Fundi, who receives the travellers with such amusing ceremony; the others are Sarmentus (a satellite of Maecenas)[5] and a local stalwart called Messius Cicirrus, both of whom kept the company amused by their bucolic repartee. Back in the city we come across the unfortunate Nasica (2. 5. 57), who married his daughter to a rich old fogey in the hope of a legacy and then discovered too late that his aged son-in-law had outwitted him. Two money-lenders also catch our attention. One is the younger Novius (1. 6. 121) who has his table beneath Marsyas' statue and whose face, we are told, accounts for the statue's gesture of abhorrence. The other is Ruso (1. 3. 86), an amateur historian whose readings are always well attended—debtors find his invitations so hard to refuse. A third member of the profession is the 'mongrel' Persius (1. 7. 2), but we do not meet him in Rome since the scene of his operations is Asia Minor. Finally, mention should be made of Turbo, the fierce but diminutive gladiator in 2. 3. 310. So far, then, we have two cranks, a petty official, a legacy-hunter, three money-lenders, a gladiator, and a couple of buffoons. Not an impressive collection. They may all be dismissed as harmless nonentities, provided we remember that a nonentity may be guilty of a very unpleasant vice and that nonentities also have feelings.

A more worthy target was presented by Tillius, a stingy and unpopular magistrate who had risen from lowly origins. At some time Tillius had lost the senatorial stripe but had regained it and become a tribune (1. 6. 24 f.). In 1. 6. 108 he is even referred to as a praetor. We do not know who this man was. It has been suggested that he was a brother of Tillius Cimber the conspirator, whose origins are also obscure. It seems unlikely that a brother of one of the conspirators would have been acceptable to the

Triumvirs. Yet it is not impossible. Casca, who was himself a conspirator, held the tribunate in 43 B.C. Tillius might have done the same. And he could even have been one of the sixty-seven praetors who were appointed in 38 B.C. (Dio 48. 43). At any rate, in view of his official position Horace's Tillius was clearly in a different category from the people already mentioned.

In 1. 2. 48 a certain Sallustius is said to be just as mad on freed-women as an adulterer is on married ladies. Since the name is not common and the man concerned must have been fairly well known, it is usually supposed that Horace is referring either to the historian or to his adoptive son. If it was the son he must have made his reputation at an early age, for the satire was written about 39 or 38 B.C. and he did not die until A.D. 20. Moreover, since the younger man was in fact Sallust's grand-nephew, he can hardly have been born much before 55 B.C., for Sallust himself was born in 86. It is also quite possible, as Syme has pointed out,[6] that the heir did not acquire the name Sallust until the historian's death in 35 B.C. If this is so, then Horace would seem to be speaking of the older man. The trouble here is that while Sallust certainly had a reputation for sexual adventure it was adventure of the wrong kind. Varro, as reported by Gellius (17. 18), and Asconius, as reported by the pseudo-Acron on *Sat.* 1. 2. 41, record the story that Sallust was caught in adultery with Fausta, Sulla's daughter, and was given a sound thrashing. But Horace's Sallust prides himself on his *avoidance* of married ladies—*matronam nullam ego tango* (54). One solution is to reject the allegation of adultery. Varro, as a Pompeian, was biased against Sallust, and Asconius may simply have taken the story from Varro without necessarily believing it. This on the whole is the answer favoured by Syme. Another answer, suggested by the pseudo-Acron in his note on 1. 2. 49, is that Sallust was charged with adultery in the senate and defended himself by saying that he pursued freedwomen, not married ladies. This, however, looks like a forlorn attempt to reconcile Varro with Horace. Whatever the truth may be, it does seem that Horace was glancing at a man who, if not politically influential, was at least prominent in society. It may be pointed out quite rightly that none of these people *inspired* Horace's satires; they did not interest him enough to arouse his anger; and their main function was to provide his essays with coloured illustrations. But the victims might not have been mollified by such a delicate distinction.

From these rather detached and incidental allusions we turn to a few expressions of genuine dislike. They are to be found for the most part in 1. 10, where they centre on characters like Hermogenes, Demetrius, Pantilius, and Fannius. Of these gentlemen one, we are told, is a pansy, another is an ape, a third is a louse, a fourth a fool, and they are all a crowd of malicious backbiters. As we have already seen, the names belong not to any monsters of crime or vice but to men whose taste in poetry happened to differ from Horace's own. The only victim of this kind in Book 2 is Furius the writer of epic poetry. Horace first of all 'places' Furius by telling us that he is 'bloated with greasy tripe', *pingui tentus omaso* (2. 5. 40); a sample of the tripe is then displayed in the following line, which (except for the substitution of Furius for Jupiter) is taken from Furius himself:

Furius hibernas cana nive conspuet Alpis.

Furius bespews the wintry Alps with hoary snow.

Quite different in spirit from any of these passages is the treatment of Trebatius in 2. 1. As we have seen, the tone throughout is one of light-hearted banter, and this is one of the factors which give the poem a unique place in Horace's *Satires*.

Up to now we have been discussing people who were certainly or most probably living when the *Satires* were written. More doubt exists in the case of Fausta (1. 2. 64), Alfenus (1. 3. 130), the son of Albius (1. 4. 109), Damasippus (2. 3. 16), Labeo (1. 3. 82), the son of Aesopus (2. 3. 239), and the sons of Arrius (2. 3. 243). Fausta, that lady of high birth and low morals, was born in 86 B.C. She was certainly living in 51 B.C.,[7] and when the second satire was written she could not have been more than

forty-seven years old. Her lovers Villius and Longarenus could
also have been alive. Alfenus, if identical with Alfenus Varus the
celebrated jurist,[8] was definitely alive; if not, there is no firm
evidence either way. He was a man who had risen in the social
scale, and it was naughty of Horace to recall his associations with
trade. (See the translation in chapter I.) To judge from the context, the son of Albius was a young spendthrift at the time of
Horace's boyhood.[9] If we allow a difference of ten to twenty
years in age, the former could easily have been alive in 35 B.C.
when the satire was published. But we know no more about him
than we know about Baius, Scetanus and Trebonius—the other
examples of wickedness mentioned in I. 4. 110–14. Damasippus
the wealthy art dealer is shown by Cicero's correspondence to
have been alive in 45 B.C.[10] In Horace he appears as a man driven
out of his wits by financial losses and only saved from suicide by
the timely intervention of Stertinius, who persuades him that he
is really no madder than anyone else. The other names all belong
to men who had achieved fame through some act of conspicuous
lunacy. Labeo cannot be identified with certainty and should
perhaps be put in another category,[11] but the son of Aesopus is
mentioned by Cicero (*Att.* 11. 15. 3). He was a young man in
47 B.C.—about fourteen years before the poem in question was
written. His mistress Caecilia Metella (2. 3. 239) may quite
well have been alive too. Her divorce from Lentulus Spinther in
45 B.C. is the last we hear of her (*Att.* 13. 7. 1). Arrius, who is
also mentioned by Cicero, must have died about 50 B.C.[12] His
sons could well have survived to see the publication of Book 2 in
30 B.C. If they did, they must have been disconcerted to find
themselves described as 'a famous pair of brothers, twins in
depravity and silliness and in their love of evil'.

Certain other figures are mentioned as though they were contemporary, but it is often hard to tell whether they are real or
fictitious. Those who appear to be fictitious will be discussed
presently. In the case of the others one can point out that Cerin-
thus the pretty boy (1. 2. 81) is directly addressed in the most

personal of all Horace's satires, that the reference to Rufillus and
Gargonius and their contrasting odours (1. 2. 27) is repeated in
1. 4. 92 in such a way as to imply that it had given offence, that
'dirty Natta' (1. 6. 124) does not sound like a type name, and
that the phase *fragilis Pediatia*—'dainty Miss Pediatius'—in 1. 8.
39 seems too carefully pointed to be without a target. But none
of these arguments would impress a tough-minded sceptic.

(*b*) *Dead people.* A number of Horace's gibes, though perhaps
not quite so many as one often assumes, are aimed at persons
whom we know to have been dead. Some of these characters
may be classified by their attitude to money. Thus while
Staberius and Ummidius worshipped it with the devotion of
true misers, Aristippus was senselessly indifferent to it; so was
Marsaeus who ruined himself for the sake of an actress.[13] Fufidius the miser (1. 2. 12) may also belong to this group. One
thinks first of the Quintus Fufidius mentioned by Cicero in
Pis. 86, *QF* 3. 1. 3, *Att.* 11. 13. 3, 14. 3, 15. 2 (P–W, no. 1).
If this is the man in question he must represent a type, because
although dead he is spoken of in the present tense. Alternatively
Horace might have had in mind a living person. We know of a
Fufidius who was alive in 46 B.C.,[14] but there is no evidence that
he was a miser.

Passing quickly over Sisyphus (Antony's dwarf, 1. 3. 47), the
blustering poet Cassius Etruscus (1. 10. 61 f.), the black sheep
Laevinus (1. 6. 12), and Volanerius the obsessive gambler (2. 7.
15), we come to Priscus (2. 7. 9) the senator whose life was a
jumble of absurd contradictions. On reading Horace's description
of him one is reminded of the French diplomat's comment on
one of his English counterparts: 'Quel homme étrange! Son
centre n'est pas au milieu.' Or perhaps we should say that Priscus had no centre at all. The problem of consistency, which in
morals involves the integration of the personality and in art the
achievement of unity amid variety, held a special interest for
Horace. So it is no accident that whereas most Horatian characters are presented with a few strokes here and a touch of colour

there, Priscus should be honoured with a seven-line verbal cameo. But even Priscus is eclipsed by another of his kind—I refer to that splendid bohemian Tigellius, who occupies the opening section of 1. 3. Tigellius was a musician from Sardinia who had been quite a well-known figure in Roman society a few years before. He was on familiar terms with Julius Caesar and Octavian; he knew Cicero well enough to quarrel with him; and he had the distinction of being lampooned by Calvus.[15] In 1. 2, written shortly after his death, he is depicted as one who spent money freely in rather raffish company. And the description in 1. 3 suggests a man who lived not according to this or that philosophy but simply for dramatic effect. Had someone reminded him of the old Delphic maxim 'Know thyself' he would have answered with a sigh 'Ah, but which one?' Flamboyant and unstable, amusing and insincere, Tigellius represented the antithesis of the ideal Roman type. The empire called for sound purposeful men with a strong sense of duty and not too much imagination; and Stoicism, when suitably adapted, provided the necessary in-tellectual framework—rather like public school Christianity. So in commending the man who is 'all of a piece' Horace is affirming a national ethical tradition. Yet the amount of time spent in deriding Tigellius reminds us that Horace himself was not always a model of *aequabilitas*. We all tend to be harsh to-wards our own vices, when they occur in other people.

Before leaving this group one should say a word about Cervius the informer, Turius the crooked judge, and Scaeva the poisoner, who all appear in 2. 1. 47–56. The charges against them are grave ones, but they are made in a poem which, because of its late date, is unlikely to contain any real aggressiveness; moreover, they come immediately after Horace's promise that he will not attack any live person unless provoked. Therefore it is best to assume that the characters in question were not living. This leaves two possibilities; they may be fictions, in which case we can hardly hope to guess why these particular names should have been chosen,[16] or they may be real people whose sinister reputation was still fresh. The second suggestion, which is that adopted by the scholiasts, would be well in line with the satire's jocular tone, for we all know how a criminal who has captured the popular imagination becomes on his death a kind of mythological hero-villain. Rasputin periodically makes his appearance in the Sunday newspapers, and Dr Crippen is still with us, enshrined by an affectionate public within the chamber of horrors.

(c) *Lucilian characters.* The most straightforward case is that of Gallonius (2. 2. 46–8):

> haud ita pridem
> Galloni praeconis erat acipensere mensa
> infamis.

Not so long ago the table of Gallonius the auctioneer became notorious on account of a sturgeon.

This is a clear reference to the gluttonous auctioneer attacked by Lucilius (W. 203):

> 'o Publi, o gurges Galloni, es homo miser' inquit.

'O Publius, O Gallonius of the maw, you are a wretched fellow', he says.

We can also feel fairly confident about Maenius. His extravagance is mentioned in *Epist.* 1. 15. 26–41, and also by Porphyrion on *Sat.* 1. 3. 21, who tells us that when Maenius was forced to sell his house in the Forum he reserved one column to enable him to watch the gladiatorial shows—a column which Lucilius referred to in the fragment *Maenius columnam dum peteret.*[17] So the Horatian and the Lucilian Maenius are probably the same person. There is an equal degree of probability in the case of Pacideianus, who according to Lucilius was 'far and away the best gladiator the world has ever seen' (W. 174–5). A Pacideianus also appears in *Sat.* 2. 7. 97 and it is most likely that the two men are identical, though Heinze thinks that the name had been adopted by a fighter of Horace's own day—a practice which was not unknown.[18] The Albucius of Horace 2. 1. 48, who succumbed to Canidia's poisons, has no apparent connexion with his Lucilian namesake. But the situation is rather different in the case of the other Albucius, who, we are told, was unnecessarily harsh in assigning work to his slaves (2. 2. 66–8). Now although we do not hear of any cruelty on the part of Lucilius' Albucius, we know from W. 87–93 that he was devoted to the Greek style of life. Cicero (*Brut.* 131) calls him 'a complete Epicurean' (*perfectus Epicureus*), but his Epicureanism seems to have been of a non-ascetic kind, if we may judge from Varro (B. 127), who speaks of 'matrices from Albucius' sows' (*volvae de Albuci subus*). If, then, Albucius was something of a gourmet, this would provide a link with Horace's character, for the latter shows his harshness in the context of a dinner-party.[19]

From now on more serious problems arise. Take the rich skin-flint Opimius (2. 3. 142 ff.). There is also an Opimius in the Lucilian fragments, in fact there are two. One is Quintus Opimius, consul in 154 B.C., who as a boy had a reputation for sexual depravity; the other is his son Lucius Opimius who held the consulship in 121 B.C. and was later exiled for accepting bribes from Jugurtha.[20] Obviously neither has anything to do with the Horatian figure, who owes his name to the oxymoron *pauper Opimius*—'Poor Mr Richly'. In *Sat.* 1. 4. 69 Caelius is a brigand. What was the Caelius in fragment 1008 of Lucilius? Wickham, very conveniently, thinks he was a brigand. Others have seen in him a poet, a historian, a judge, a ball-player, and a friend of the satirist's. The most likely guess is that of Lucian Müller, namely that he was an officer celebrated by Ennius for his deeds in the Istrian war.[21]

> quid mi igitur suades? ut vivam Naevius aut sic
> ut Nomentanus?

> Well, what do you want me to do? Live like Naevius or Nomen-
> tanus?

These exasperated words come from the miser in 1. 1. 101. Porphyrion comments: *Naevius autem fuit in tantum parcus ut sordidus merito haberetur Lucilio auctore.*[22] So Naevius appeared as a miser in Lucilius. That is very interesting, if true. But he is not a miser in Horace; in fact he is the very opposite. Porphyrion must have misread the lines. A further complication is introduced by 2. 2. 68–9 where Naevius is a careless host who gives his guests greasy water to wash in. This is certainly not the action of a spend-thrift, nor does it quite suggest a miser. It is rather a sign of slackness. The *simplex* Naevius carries informality too far.

Last of all there is Nomentanus.[23] He is so widely accepted as a Lucilian character that one is apt to forget that he owes his place in the fragments to the good offices of Scaliger and Stephanus. At W. 80–1 Scaliger proposed *Nomentani quae* for the MSS. *nomen iamque*. This conjecture is endorsed by Müller, Cichorius and Warmington,[24] and it is called 'uncertain, but neat and plausible' by Housman;[25] it is rejected by Baehrens, Marx and Terzaghi. The admission of Nomentanus to W. 82 is likewise disputed. Donatus on Terence, *Phormio* I. 2. 73 gives *qui te mon-tane malum*. By his correction *Momentane* Stephanus opened the way for *Nomentane*. In his text of Donatus Wessner prints *Nomentane*, but in the Appendix he apparently accepts *qui di te, montane, malum* with Marx.[26] Suppose, however, that Nomen-tanus should be restored in both passages, then the Lucilian character would appear to have been L. Atilius Nomentanus, an associate of Scaevola's. This suggestion is advanced by Cichorius (pp. 244 ff.), and notice what he adds: 'Eine Beziehung freilich auf den bei Horaz mehrfach vorkommenden Verschwender Nomen-tanus, der nach Porphyrio zu Horaz *Sat.* I. I. 102 L. Cassius Nomentanus hiess, muss ganz ausser dem Spiele bleiben.' This statement may be a little over-confident, because Porphyrion could have been wrong. It is also fallacious to argue, as Cartault does,[27] that since Nomentanus was present at Nasidienus' dinner-party he cannot have been the man mentioned by Lucilius. But at least we *can* say that no certain connexion has been established between the Horatian and the Lucilian Nomentanus.[28]

Under this heading, therefore, we have found three characters (Gallonius, Maenius, and Pacideianus) and perhaps a fourth

(Albucius) who may be said with confidence to have been drawn from Lucilian satire. There may be others, but we cannot be sure.[29]

(d) *Significant names*. Let us start with names which were certainly or probably chosen solely on account of their derivations. Opimius (2. 3. 142) has already been mentioned. Apart from the oxymoron involving his name, the context is that of a fable which could well have begun with 'once upon a time'. Then we have Maltinus (1. 2. 25). According to Nonius 37. 6 *malta* meant an effeminate fop,[30] and that is just what Maltinus was. The coincidence is too great and the name too uncommon to permit the possibility of a personal reference. Moreover the opposite extreme, namely that of virile exhibitionism, is represented by the colourless *est qui* (25). Cupiennius the adulterer (1. 2. 36) is a similar case. Again the aptness of name to context is too good to be true, and again the antithesis is supplied by an anonymous phrase *quidam notus homo* (31). Porcius (Hog) also belongs to this group. He is projected by his situation and we see him just long enough to catch his party piece, which was to polish off a whole cake in a single mouthful (2. 8. 24). He is linked with Nomentanus, who, whatever his origins, had now become a type figure. The same goes for Nomentanus' other comrade, the *scurra* Pantolabus (1. 8. 11 and 2. 1. 22).

If the five names just quoted are clear cases, another five can be cited which do not allow the same degree of confidence. In 2. 6. 72 the dancer Lepos no doubt epitomizes the subjects of fashionable gossip, but Lepos is also just the kind of name which a real dancer might have had. Heinze reminds us of an actor called Favor (he omits the reference, which is Suet. *Vesp.* 19), and Stein in P–W, 6. 2078 assures us that this was not an isolated instance. The mean Avidienus (2. 2. 55) looks like a type figure until we find that he possesses a nickname—*Canis* 'The Dog' (56). This is inconclusive, since *Canis* may recall simply the general notion of Cynic asceticism, but the pun in v. 64—*hac urget lupus hac canis*—is slightly improved if one assumes that Horace had not invented the nickname. Or consider Ofellus

(2. 2. 2). At first sight it seems a suspiciously neat paradox that the virtues of frugality should be expounded by a man called Mr Titbit (*ofella*), but when Horace steps forward in v. 112 with the words:

puer hunc ego parvus Ofellum
integris opibus novi non latius usum
quam nunc accisis

> When I was a small boy I remember this Ofellus living at the same
> level when his property was intact as he does now when it has been
> reduced,

and when we hear that Ofellus' farm has now been assigned to a veteran with the very specific name of Umbrenus, we begin to believe that we are dealing with a real person after all. There is also something more than word-play behind 'that louse Pantilius' (πᾶν τίλλειν = 'to nip everything') in 1. 10. 78. The name is found in *C.I.L.* x. 5925 (Dess. 6260), and it occurs here in a context full of personalities. The least we should assume is that Pantilius was a nickname for some carping critic of the day. Finally, let us take an instance where the balance appears evenly poised. In 1. 6. 40 the upstart Novius seems a perfect example of a significant name. What then are we to say of the younger Novius in 121 who, as we argued above, is almost certainly an individual? Perhaps the least difficult solution here is to break the balance in half and to say that the two figures are unrelated.[31]

A significant name, though in theory quite general, may be limited in some way by its context. Thus while Porcius on his own would represent The Glutton, his frame of reference is narrowed by his appearing at table in the company of Fundanius, Viscus, Varius and Maecenas. So that readers would tend to see him not just as The Glutton but rather as the sort of glutton that Horace knew.

This leads on to a further point. In English literature we are all familiar with My Lord Plausible, Sir John Brute, Lady Fanciful, and the other types which bow and sidle through the drawing-rooms of Restoration Comedy. Now in spite of the dramatist's assurance that no personal references were intended the audience would persist in using its imagination. This practice can be illustrated by the epilogue to *The Way of the World*:

> Others there are whose malice we'd prevent
> Such as watch plays with scurrilous intent
> To mark out who by characters are meant.
> And though no perfect likeness they can trace
> Yet each pretends to know the copied face.
> These with false glosses feed their own ill nature
> And turn to libel what was meant a satire.

Something of the same kind must have happened to Horace. Granted his readers were as a whole less idle, less sophisticated, and less malicious than the patrons of the London playhouses; on the other hand his names, unlike those of the Restoration Comedy, were in actual use at the time. The truth is that the Roman system of *cognomina* made it difficult to employ significant names *without* appearing personal. One need only recall the dramatic role played in republican politics by gentlemen called Pea, Bald, Dull and Soak—names which an Englishman would not expect to encounter outside a Shakespearian romance. Or think of that occasion in 59 B.C. when the actor Diphilus raised a storm of applause by declaiming the innocuous line *nostra miseria tu es magnus*—all because of Pompey's *cognomen*.[32] In much the same way when Horace's *Satires* first appeared they caused a certain amount of enjoyable if misguided speculation. Several of the names clearly belonged to individuals; as for the rest, a little stretching here, a little padding there, and the cap could usually be made to fit someone. Cupiennius, for instance, was linked by one tradition with C. Cupiennius Libo of Cumae, an acquaintance of Augustus, and some scholars still find this credible.

Apart altogether from readers' fantasies, there are several places where a definite person is named, and where the derivation, however apposite, can be of only secondary importance, e.g. Stertinius (*stertere*), Furius (*furere*), and Philodemus (φιλεῖν + δῆμος).[33] The last is of special interest, for Palmer (p. xvi) took Philodemus as a

type name symbolizing 'the man of low tastes'. When Philodemus
of Gadara joked about his name suiting his nature:

αὐταί που Μοῖραί με κατωνόμασαν Φιλόδημον
ὡς ἀεὶ Δημοῦς θερμὸς ἔχει με πόθος[34]

It must have been the Fates themselves who named me Philodemus,
for I am always an ardent Demophile [i.e. a lover of Demo],

he little thought that a similar coincidence would some day be
used to argue him out of his place in a Roman diatribe. One other
case may be mentioned here, since it is usually passed over. In
1. 2. 64–5 we have:

Villius in Fausta Sullae gener, hoc miser uno
nomine deceptus.

Villius, who in connexion with Fausta was Sulla's son-in-law, was
deceived to his sorrow solely by this name.

A Roman reader would have known that Sulla was Sulla the
Happy (Felix) and that his daughter was called Joy. So language
conspires with love to deceive the wretched Villius.

Etymology therefore, if used with restraint, does help us to
appreciate the *Satires*. But when we are asked to note the significance of Luscus ('One-Eye'), Nasidienus ('The Nose'), and
Arellius ('Dry Old Croesus'), and when we are urged to alter
Gargonius to Gorgonius and Scetanus to Sectanus, then it is time
to call a halt.[35]

(e) *Names of Other Type Characters.* Under this miscellaneous
heading we may include mythological figures such as Tantalus,
Sisyphus, Agave, Orestes, Atrides, Ulysses, Ajax, Tiresias, Penelope and Helen;[36] the slave types Dama and Davus;[37] and also
probably Apella the superstitious Jew.[38] Apella was a common
name among freedmen, and most of the Jewish community in
Rome belonged to that class. This would not rule out the further
possibility that Horace was punning on the custom of circumci-
sion. Such was the view of the scholiasts (the pseudo-Acron, for
example, comments *finxit nomen quasi sine pelle*), and this would

link up with the phrase *curtis Iudaeis*—'the circumcised Jews'—in
1. 9. 70.

Lastly, we should include the figures mentioned in 2. 3. 69 ff.
Nerius suggests a man of wisdom and prophetic insight. Cicuta
('Hemlock') is the keen financier. In spite of their astuteness, we
learn that both can be tricked by Proteus, that archetype of
slippery customers. Since in the context Proteus cannot be a nickname, it is unlikely that Nerius and Cicuta are nicknames either.
Moreover, in v. 175 Cicuta is associated with the type figure of
Nomentanus. Therefore it is best to take Nerius and Cicuta as
standing for 'Something in the City'. This leaves us with Perel-
lius in v. 75. As it is not taken from legend and as it is neither a
significant name nor a nickname, one concludes that it belonged
either to the man who had been foolish enough to lend Damasippus money or else to one who had become well enough known
to represent a type.

(*f*) *Pseudonyms.* It is well known how love poets like Catullus
and Propertius used to conceal their girl-friends' identity under
false names. Perhaps 'conceal' is hardly the right word, for since
the pseudonyms were metrically equivalent to the real names
(Lesbia = Clodia, Cynthia = Hostia), and since tongues wagged
as busily in the Forum as they do in Mayfair or Park Avenue, the
disguise tended to be about as effective as Coan silk. What we
should like to know is whether Horace used the same device in
the *Satires*. Certainly the scholiasts thought he did, and there is
no *a priori* reason why he should not have done so. Nevertheless,
not one case has been proved, and the guesses vary greatly in
plausibility. The most widely accepted case is that of the poet
Alpinus (Alpman) in 1. 10. 36 whose real name was Furius. The
nickname may be due to his place of origin, his subject matter,
or his notorious metaphor about the Alpine snows. Another
probable case is Pitholeon (1. 10. 22) whom Bentley identified
with the Pitholaus mentioned in Suetonius, *Jul.* 75. Tenney Frank
may also be right in his theory that Heliodorus (1. 5. 2) is the
scholar Apollodorus.[39] But these last two instances are somewhat

exceptional in that the alteration would have been made for metrical reasons, not for the sake of concealment. One of the ancient rumours which have come down to us alleges that Maltinus (1. 2. 25) is a mask for Maecenas. The latter certainly dressed in an effeminate style,[40] and the satire in question was written before Horace met him. But if this was a genuine allusion it is hard to explain how Horace could have published the poem unchanged after enjoying Maecenas' patronage for over three years. As for other proposals, while it is interesting to toy with the idea that Catius (2. 4. 1) is a skit on the gourmet C. Matius or that Nasidienus Rufus (2. 8. 1) is based on memories of Salvidienus Rufus,[41] one may pass quickly over attempts to link Baius (1. 4. 110) with Bavius and the son of Aesopus (2. 3. 239) with Ticidas.[42]

The most tantalizing name is, of course, Canidia. In addition to other brief appearances she plays a major role in *Sat.* 1. 8 and *Epodes* 5 and 17. Porphyrion on *Epod.* 3. 8 says her real name was Gratidia and that she was a cosmetician from Naples. The first detail may be an invention, and the second a combination of Neapolis (*Epod.* 5. 43) with *nardo perunctum* (*Epod.* 5. 59). On the other hand, it must be conceded that no other fictitious character crops up so persistently, and a detail like *cum Sagana maiore* (*Sat.* 1. 8. 25) makes one pause before saying anything too dogmatic. The problem is largely a matter of degree. No one believes that Canidia is either a personified idea or a recognizable portrait, but between these limits there is room for argument. Three intermediate types of creation may be distinguished: (1) a figure constructed imaginatively on the basis of a group, (2) a figure constructed imaginatively on the basis of a group but with overtones hinting at a real individual, (3) a figure constructed imaginatively on the basis of an individual. If Canidia belongs to type (1) we can say that Horace created her from his knowledge of contemporary witchcraft, intending her, perhaps, to serve as a fictitious substitute for Archilochus' Neobule. If we are dealing with a case of the second type then the individual, whoever she may have been, will remain a shadow in the background and can never be identified. If Canidia falls under the third heading the witches will cease to have much importance, and Canidia herself will emerge as a travesty of one of Horace's acquaintances. Some supporters of the last view have even been bold enough to hazard an identification.[43] My own feeling is that the second possibility is the most likely. On points like this Roman opinion was probably as divided as our own. Not everyone would have accepted Canidia and the rest as composite figures, and Horace's lack of precision may well have increased rather than checked the flow of rumour and conjecture. Martial gives us an example of this ageless curiosity in 9. 95 b:

> nomen Athenagorae quaeris, Callistrate, verum.
> si scio, disperean, qui sit Athenagoras.

You want to know Athenagoras' real name, Callistratus. Blow me if I know who Athenagoras is.

An earlier instance occurs in 2. 23:

> non dicam, licet usque me rogetis,
> qui sit Postumus in meo libello.

Though you ask me again and again, I will not tell you who is the Postumus in my little book.

The foregoing analysis shows that Horace's use of names was far from uniform. Such a conclusion is neither new nor surprising, but this variety has to be constantly reaffirmed if we are to avoid the generalizations which so often appear in editions and literary histories. Clearly the scholiasts and modern critics of similar leanings such as Cartault and Courbaud[44] cannot be right in maintaining that Horace usually had real people in mind. But there is an opposite way of thinking which can also mislead and which is more frequently encountered. Put crudely it goes like this: Lucilius, a man of high social standing protected by the powerful Scipio family, could afford to attack contemporary statesmen (so far so good); 'the conditions under which Horace wrote were altogether different', 'the political situation between 42 and 31 B.C. would not have borne rough handling and the softening of manners had put a check on personalities'. 'Personality is the essence of satire and Horace dared not be personal.' He had to beware of infringing the law of libel—'there is a touch of serious anxiety beneath the jest upon the *mala* and the *bona carmina* with which *Sat.* 2. 1 closes'. Horace's *Satires* are therefore 'free from vehemence', 'they are directed against types rather than individuals'. 'Horace is the dragon-fly of satire, ornamental but stingless', and one can hardly doubt that 'he was acting wisely...in avoiding personal attacks on living men'. In brief Horace 'stood to Lucilius in much the same relation as Menander to Aristophanes'.[45]

There is much truth in these statements, but they are so over-simplified as to be misleading. It is, of course, a fact, and a significant fact, that Horace did not attack men of real importance—least of all prominent politicians. Something more will be said about this below; here I would simply point out that the political and the personal are not coextensive. The absence of Marcus Antonius does not make Crispinus fictitious. Moreover, even where no living individual is involved it is hardly enough to say 'so-and-so is a type figure', for, as we have seen, type figures can be of several kinds.

In drawing attention to the diversity of Horace's names I have also tried to bear in mind the effect which the *Satires* were likely to produce when they first appeared. This point should not be overstressed, and I have only given it this much prominence because it is usually ignored altogether. It would be absurd to suggest that the first book of *Satires* caused anything in the nature of a public outcry or even widespread resentment; but it does seem that in certain quarters Horace was regarded with suspicion. True, the names were mostly employed as a means to some ethical or aesthetic end. (An indication of this is the fact that with Horace, as opposed to many of the eighteenth-century satirists, our ignorance concerning a name rarely if ever makes a passage unintelligible.) But people do not like being used to point a moral or adorn a tale, especially when the tale is one of vice and stupidity.

As for the dead, they were beyond taking offence, but their relatives were not, and in the Roman family relatives mattered. We may therefore assume that 2. 1. 23:

cum sibi quisque timet, quamquam est intactus, et odit

When everyone is afraid on his own behalf and hates you, though untouched,

for all its ironic exaggeration, contains a core of truth, and that the opening words of Book 2 *sunt quibus in satura videar nimis acer* ('Some people think I am too sharp in my satire') do reflect an authentic situation. The critics were naïve in their judgement and too remote from the poet to appreciate his real intentions, yet occasionally they were right, and sometimes their mistakes were excusable.

So much for Book 1 and its reception. In Book 2, which is over fifty lines longer, the total number of names drops by 20 per cent. Much more significant is the fact that in 1083 verses there are scarcely ten satirical references to living people. One notices, on the other hand, that most of the type characters in group (e) above are drawn from the second book. We can guess at some of the factors behind the change. For one thing, unlike its predecessor, Book 2 must have been written with the prospect of publication in mind, and so it is possible that by cutting down the number of personal references Horace wished to forestall the kind of half-informed criticism mentioned above. Moreover, the poet now enjoyed a position of esteem and security such as he had never known before, and as the gliding years carried him into his middle thirties he began to take a more detached view of his material. I do not mean that he became less sensitive to moral evil, but rather that he saw it in less personal terms. This tendency towards greater detachment can also be seen in the form of the poems; for instead of being delivered by Horace himself the sermons are in most cases put into the mouths of intermediate characters like Ofellus and Stertinius. The increase in dialogue is part of the same process.

It may be asked how far the change was due to political developments. The chief development in the years 34–31 B.C. was the widening of the rift between Octavian and Antony. While this was taking place, the friendship between Horace and Maecenas was growing steadily stronger, as is shown by the gift of the Sabine farm. It is therefore true, no doubt, that Horace would have found it very difficult to deride any important member of the pro-Octavian faction. On the other hand, if he had really wanted to attack public figures, he could surely have chosen some Antonian sympathizers as examples of vice and folly. Antony himself was a favourite target for lampoons at this period. As we have seen, however, Horace *reduced* the personal element in his second book, and when his security was finally guaranteed by Octavian's victory at Actium he abandoned satire altogether. So it looks as if fear was not a significant factor in Horace's change of policy.

To conclude this survey I should like to consider a more general question of interpretation which is closely connected with Horace's use of names. I have in mind what might be called the evolutionary approach to the *Satires*. This approach, which regards Horatian satire as a kind of living organism passing through the phases of growth, maturity, and decay, is associated in particular with the distinguished name of Eduard Fraenkel, who presents it in some detail in 'Das Reifen der horazischen Satire',[46] and again, more briefly, in his *Horace*.[47] The facts underlying this analysis are as follows. In 1. 2, which is by common consent one of the earliest of the *Satires*, numerous people are mentioned by name and the poet himself remains out of sight; in 1. 6 the names occur in the first half only, and the rest is autobiographical; names play a much smaller part in Book 2 as a whole, and in 2. 6, one of the latest pieces, they have almost disappeared, leaving the entire stage to Horace himself; finally the *Epistles* may be said to abandon personal censure still more completely in favour of a genial moral discourse centred on the poet and his friends.

Abstracted in this way the scheme is certainly impressive, but we have to see how the pattern is affected when all the other satires are included. The biological analogy when applied to art has two aspects, both of which cause trouble in the present case. The first aspect is chronological. If 1. 3 comes immediately after 1. 2 we can argue, as Fraenkel does, that it shows signs of growth, since names are fewer and vv. 63–5 (which allude to the poet's friendship with Maecenas) give the first hint of self-portraiture. But it may well be that 1. 4, which lacks any reference to Maecenas, is earlier than 1. 3. If so, then 1. 3 marks a retrogression, for its autobiographical content cannot be compared with the account of Horace's upbringing in 1. 4. 105 ff. Again, 1. 1 is probably later than both these pieces, yet it contains no self-portraiture at all. If, however, it is earlier, why are there so few names? Finally, why should 1. 10, the latest poem in the book, be so sharply personal in tone?

The problem is not confined to Book 1. A poem like 2. 3 proves on these grounds to be a less developed specimen of Horatian satire than 1. 6; yet it can hardly represent a decline, since it was written two years before his crowning achievement (2. 6). Fraenkel does point out that 'the evolution of the style of a poet . . . does not, as a rule, proceed in an unbroken straight line'.[48] But once this is admitted the comparison with nature is weakened, since no fruit or vegetable periodically recedes in the course of its growth.

The other aspect of the analogy is evaluative, as may be seen from terms like 'ripeness' and 'maturity'. This means that Fraenkel's approach involves some rather severe judgements. The first part of 1. 6, for instance, is a 'parade of dreary characters' and both writer and reader are relieved 'to get out of the Lucilian masquerade'.[49] This implies that using names was a rather regrettable mannerism which Horace had to grow out of.[50] To Fraenkel 2. 6 represents the acme of Horace's career as a satirist—the poet is the centre of interest and there is an absence of personal ridicule. Accepting this for the moment we ask how the rest of the book fares when measured by the same standards. All the poems, it appears, except one are found wanting. The third 'looks like a prolonged *tour de force*', the fifth is 'full of vigour and brilliant wit, but acid and cynical throughout', and when Tiresias returns to Hades 'we are not sorry to see him go'. All six indicate that 'the stage of over-ripeness has now arrived', and in some of them Horace has 'betrayed his noble ideal of *satura*'.[51]

These verdicts prompt us to ask whether the criteria adopted are really satisfactory. If maturity in Horatian satire is marked by self-portraiture and an absence of names, then a poem like 2. 5, which on other grounds would be considered excellent (and which is just as late as 2. 6), must be classed as inferior. Also is it not strange that the *Satires* should reach their highest point of perfection in a poem which, to quote Courbaud, 'est déjà une véritable épître'?[52] One cannot help feeling that the *Satires* are being assessed as so many imperfect attempts at writing epistles, and that the τέλος of the form has been placed outside the form itself.

Against these criticisms it may be urged that since the *Satires* and *Epistles* both belong to the same genus the latter must represent a more mature conception of what the genus should be like. The biological method might then be justified in this larger perspective. There is something to be said for this objection and it demands careful consideration.

Ancient writers, including Horace himself, had no uniform method of referring to the hexameters. If we let A stand for the *Satires* and B for the *Epistles* we get the following scheme:

(1) Horace: A   *satura* (generic) (*Sat.* 2. 1. 1)
          saturae (*Sat.* 2. 6. 17)
          sermones (*Epist.* 1. 4. 1 and *Epist.* 2. 2. 60?)

$\left.\begin{array}{l} A \\ B \end{array}\right\}$ *sermones* (*Epist.* 2. 1. 250)

In *Epist.* 2. 2. 60 Horace speaks of his *Bioneis sermonibus et sale nigro*—'Bionean talks and their caustic wit'. The great majority of modern commentators take this as referring only to the *Satires*, on the ground that the *Epistles* are not characterized by caustic wit. Hendrickson, however, argues that Horace has the

Epistles in mind too, and that *sal niger* is merely a conventional phrase.[53] No certain conclusion is possible. What we can say is that Horace himself never uses *satura* in reference to the *Epistles*.

(2) Persius (1. 114–19) justifies his satire by appealing to the precedent of Lucilius and Horace:

> secuit Lucilius urbem,
> te Lupe, te Muci, et genuinum fregit in illis.
> omne vafer vitium ridenti Flaccus amico
> tangit et admissus circum praecordia ludit,
> callidus excusso populum suspendere naso.
> me muttire nefas?

Lucilius cut the city to pieces—you Lupus, and you Mucius—and smashed his tooth on them. Horace cunningly puts his finger on all the faults of his laughing friend, and after gaining access plays about his heart, clever as he is at hanging the public on the end of his critical nose. May I not even mutter?

Our analysis of the names has shown that friendly, personal banter is not a feature of the *Satires*. Trebatius is the only instance, unless we include the hot-headed Bolanus of 1. 9. 11. Some scholars, therefore, like Conington and Némethy, maintain that Persius is referring more particularly to the *Epistles*. Perhaps so, though I can find no more than half a dozen instances of such banter even in the *Epistles*. In that case Persius has attempted to combine the *Epistles*, as described in vv. 116–17, with the *Satires*, as described in v. 118, and the effect is clumsy to say the least. I prefer to think, however, that it is *through* his satirical criticism of the public in general that Horace twits his friends. They laugh at his wit, and at the same time (or perhaps a little later) they realize that their own faults are being discussed.[54] 'Change the name,' says Horace in 1. 1. 69–70, 'and the story is about you'—*mutato nomine de te / fabula narratur*. If this is correct, Persius is referring primarily to the *Satires*, though one cannot prove that the *Epistles* are excluded. It should be noted, however, that in general Persius draws quite freely on Horace's *Epistles* and actually includes an epistle among his own *Satires* (viz. no. 6). Lucilius had done the same (W. 186 ff.).

(3) Quintilian: A ⎫
            B?⎬ *satura* (generic)

In discussing the tradition of *satura* represented by Lucilius, Persius, and Horace, Quintilian (10. 1. 93–4) praises Lucilius for his learning, his frankness, his pungency, and his wit. Horace is commended for his terseness and the purity of his style. Persius is said, quite generally, to have won distinction. Did Quintilian consciously include Horace's *Epistles* or was he thinking only of the *Satires*? Again, certainty is impossible.

(4) Statius: A   *satura* (singular for plural)
           B   *epistula* (singular for plural)

With Horace's *œuvre* in mind Statius writes in *Silvae* I. 3. 102–4 to his friend:

>   sive
> liventem satiram nigra rubigine turbes,
> seu tua non alia splendescat epistula cura.

Whether you stir up (?) dark satires with black blight or whether your letters sparkle with just the same polish.[55]

Statius therefore regarded the *Satires* and *Epistles* as similar in style but distinguishable in spirit and in name.

(5) Suetonius: A ⎫
            B?⎬ *saturae*

In his *Life of Horace* Suetonius says 'He was short (*brevis*) and fat (*obesus*) as described by himself in the satires (*in saturis*) and by Augustus in a letter'. Now there is quite a long passage about Horace's shortness in *Sat.* 2. 3. 308 ff. and a brief reference (*corporis exigui*) in the self-portrait at the end of *Epist.* I. 20. His fatness is mentioned in *Epist.* I. 4. 15–16—*pinguem* and *Epicuri de grege porcum*. If, then, Suetonius was being precise, he must have regarded the *Epistles* as *saturae*. It could be argued that he was referring only to the *Satires* and that he thought of Horace's obesity as being included in *Sat.* 2. 3. 308 ff. This is not impossible, for in that passage Horace is compared to a frog which inflates itself in a vain attempt to rival a calf. Or he might have thought in a moment of error that the phrase *Epicuri de grege porcum* occurred in the *Satires*. Or perhaps he was just being vague. The weight of probability, however, favours the view that Suetonius classified the *Epistles* as *saturae*.

(6) Horace, according to the scholiasts:

$$\left.\begin{array}{l} \text{A} \quad \textit{sermones} \\ \text{B} \quad \textit{epistulae} \end{array}\right\} \textit{satura} \text{ (generic)}$$

In the introduction to Book 1 the scholiasts say:

quamvis igitur hoc opus satyram esse Horatius ipse profiteatur cum ait 'sunt quibus in satyra videar nimis acer...' tamen proprios titulos voluit ei accommodare, hos priores duos libros Sermonum, posteriores Epistularum inscribens.

> So although Horace himself asserts that this work is *satura* when he says 'Some people think I am too sharp in my satire', nevertheless he wished to give specific titles to it; so he inscribed these first two books as *Sermones* (Talks) and the later ones as *Epistulae* (Letters).

This shows that the scholiasts thought of the *Epistles* as *satura*; but their reason for doing so is unsound. For they have taken the word *satura* from *Sat.* 2. 1. 1 and extended it to the *Epistles*.

(7) Sidonius: A *sermones*

B *epistulae—saturae*

With direct reference to Horace's works Sidonius (9. 221-2) speaks of the *saturas epistularum sermonumque sales*—'The medleys of the *Epistles* and the wit of the *Sermones*' (i.e. the *Satires*). He therefore believed that the *Epistles* could be termed *saturae*, though he used *satura* in the early sense of medley rather than in the sense given to it by Diomedes, i.e. 'an abusive poem written to attack men's vices in the manner of Old Comedy'.

The picture, therefore, is not as clear as one could wish. 1 and 4 indicate that *satura* should be confined to the *Satires*; 7, probably 5, and (on false reasoning) 6 suggest that it can include the *Epistles*, and this is supported by Persius, *Sat.* 6; 2 and 3 are inconclusive. If we forget labels for the moment and consider only the facts, we find that the *Satires* and *Epistles* are broadly similar in metre, in stylistic level, and in subject-matter (that is, both are concerned with the behaviour of men in society). But they present important differences in form and manner. In the *Epistles* dialogue gives way to letter, and the lively direct speech which was such a prominent feature of the *Satires* is greatly reduced. A recent writer has described the change by saying that 'the conversationalist...absorbs the dramatist'.[56] This is a good way of putting it, though one should perhaps substitute 'talker' for 'conversationalist'. More important is the change of manner. The emphasis moves from censure to affirmation. Moral defects are still observed, but instead of exposing them to ridicule the poet is more concerned to reform them by exhortation and advice. Adapting the remark quoted above, we might say that 'the moralist absorbs the satirist'. Names occur less frequently than in *Sat.* 2, and the old practice of ὀνομαστὶ κωμῳδεῖν (ridicule by name) is abandoned. It is significant that *Epist.* 1. 19, which is an angry poem, does not name a single adversary—a remarkable contrast with *Sat.* 1. 10. In short, Lucilius has been left behind.

In the present book I have indicated these differences by using the separate titles of *Satires* and *Epistles*, reserving the term *sermones* for the hexameter poems in general. This is a very common procedure, and in adopting it I can appeal to the authority of Professor Fraenkel himself, who says of Horace's later work 'He returned to the writing of *sermones*...but not as satires' (p. 153) and 'The potentialities of the Horatian *satira* were exhausted, the potentialities of the Horatian *sermo* were not' (p. 309). If one prefers to call the *Epistles* satires too (and in view of the evidence presented above this may well be correct), it is still fair to uphold the distinction between the Lucilian, or quasi-Lucilian, satire of the first two books and the non-Lucilian satire of the rest. And within this framework the evolutionary approach would break down again.

Reverting to the *Satires*, one feels that these poems are not a very suitable field for the biological method, partly because they were all written within the space of eight or nine years and therefore belong to the same period of the poet's career, partly because within that period so few of the pieces can be dated with certainty, but mainly because, being *saturae*, they show a considerable variety of subject and treatment. Is 2. 8 more 'evolved' than 1. 1? Or is 2. 2 more 'developed' than 1. 6? Such questions are hardly to the point.

The discussion may be summed up by saying that while there are fewer names in Book 2 than in Book 1 the decrease is not a regular process, nor does it either enhance or diminish the satires' literary merit. As for self-portraiture, this forms an element in several of the finest pieces, but it appears as often in Book 1 as in Book 2, and as we shall see in the next chapter it is probably more straightforward in the first collection. Moreover, self-portraiture is not the only element, nor even the most essential. Throughout Horace's *Satires* it is ridicule and criticism (however impersonal and however mild) that remain predominant. When these activities cease to be Horace's main concern he abandons satire and turns to other forms of poetic creation.

CHAPTER VI

THE DIATRIBES OF BOOK 2

2. 2, 2. 3, 2. 7

Before moving on to the poems of Book 2 it may be well to say something about the arrangement of the *Satires* as a whole. Like Virgil's *Eclogues*, Book 1 contains ten pieces.[1] Of these the first three go closely together in form and subject, and the same is true of the literary satires—numbers 4 and 10. Apart from this, however, there is scarcely any discernible pattern. It is true that 6 recalls 1 by its theme of contentment as well as by its opening address to Maecenas, and this might lead the reader to expect some kind of balance between numbers 1–5 and 6–10. In fact there is none. Some scholars would arrange the satires in three groups of three, taking 1, 2 and 3 as diatribes, 4, 5 and 6 as poems about Horace himself, and 7, 8 and 9 as short anecdotes. They then leave 10 aside as a concluding piece.[2] But 10 is also about Horace himself and it is closely related to 4, whereas 5 and 6 are not. Nor does 9 bear any significant resemblance to 7 or 8. If, however, we bracket 4 with 10 and 5 with 9 (the latter pair being concerned with Horace's relation to Maecenas' circle), we are then left with the ill-assorted 6 and 8 enclosing the trivial 7.

With Book 2 the situation is rather different. There is a clear thematic connexion between 4 and 8, which are both concerned with the follies of gastronomy. Numbers 3 and 7 have a Saturnalian setting and each contains a sermon on one of the Stoic paradoxes. F. Boll, who pointed out these correspondences over fifty years ago,[3] went on to connect 2 with 6 on the grounds that both satires were written in praise of rural simplicity. He then balanced the consultation of Trebatius in 1 with the consultation of Tiresias in 5. The parallels, of course, are by no means exact. Numbers 1 and 5 have no similarity of content; 4 and 8

are quite different in form, as are 2 and 6. Yet the correspondences are close enough to establish that this was Horace's
principle of arrangement. And when we contrast such symmetry,
limited though it is, with the rather miscellaneous character of
Book 1, it is hard not to believe that one or two of the poems
were written to fit the scheme. Nevertheless, any precise and
detailed theory is threatened by the fact that 1 and 5, which are
probably the latest pair, have less in common than any of the
other pieces. No doubt we shall never know how the book
came into being, but at least we can say that the present sequence
gives the maximum amount of variety within a fairly regular
plan. The plan itself, however, has no symbolic significance;
it confers no extra meaning on any individual poem; and as far
as I can discover it involves no mathematical secrets.

2. 2

'Dis-moi ce que tu manges, je te dirai ce que tu es'—such was the
boast of M. Brillat-Savarin, that dedicated gourmet who worshipped Gastéréa as the tenth muse. If he ever thought of the
ordinary Roman, as distinct from kindred spirits like Lucullus,
the great savant must have shaken his head, for the plebeian diet
had little to excite him. In order to visualize its content we have
to set aside even such common items of our own experience as
potatoes, butter, sugar, tomatoes, oranges, bananas, chocolate,
coffee, tea and beer. Fresh meat was a rarity available only at
religious celebrations. Cattle, bred for draught purposes, provided tough and inferior beef; sheep were reared for wool rather
than mutton, and goats were kept for milk. The commonest
meat was pork, which could be dried, smoked or salted for winter
consumption. But even pork was beyond the means of the very
poor. Salt fish was more familiar, but the fresh variety cost
nearly five times as much and was therefore a luxury. The staple
food consisted of the cereal grains—often in the form of porridge
rather than bread—and a few vegetables like beans, peas, lentils,

turnips, and cabbage. To this might be added chestnuts, occasionally eggs, and fruit such as figs, dates, apples and grapes. The usual drink would be cheap local wine from the Alban hills.[4]

In the early centuries such a diet was almost universal, and throughout Rome's history most of the population never knew anything better. But as her armies marched over Greece and Asia Minor they encountered a new world of luxury and refinement. Clothes, furniture and jewellery, food and wine, statues, paintings and books—never had they seen such magnificence, and they at once resolved to seize as much as could be transported. No doubt the bulk of this plunder found its way into the villas of the aristocracy, but once the demand for such goods had been created the new mercantile class made sure that the supply was maintained and in so doing enriched itself.

Describing the effect of the new affluence Livy (39. 6) says:

> Female lute-players and harpists and other kinds of festive entertainment became a feature of banquets; and from now on greater care and expense were bestowed on the banquets themselves. The cook, who in earlier times was regarded and treated as the cheapest kind of slave, began to be valued more highly, and what had once been a menial occupation came to be viewed as an art.

The excesses which resulted from this concentration of wealth led historians to connect Rome's moral decline with the rise of her imperial power. In the passage from which I have just quoted Livy attributes the beginning of corruption to the army's return from Asia in 187 B.C. For Polybius the significant date was 168 B.C.—the year of Pydna; Piso the annalist chose 154. But after Sallust the turning point was usually placed in 146 B.C., when Carthage and Corinth were overthrown.[5] As Pliny the Elder said: 'The year that saw the birth of luxury also witnessed the downfall of Carthage; and so by a fateful coincidence the desire and the opportunity for embracing vice occurred simultaneously' (NH 33. 150). Whatever its date of origin, this complex process continued through the first century, assisted by the victories of Sulla and Pompey. And Tacitus shows that it did not stop at Actium (Ann. 3. 55).

Concern was expressed in many ways. The commonest, and not necessarily the shallowest, reaction was to say: 'Our parents did not bring us up to admire luxury. Rome's greatness was won by toughness, discipline and hard work. And apart altogether from our training and history we have always believed that laziness and self-indulgence are, quite simply, wicked.' Some, more politically-minded, would say: 'Extravagance calls attention to the gulf between rich and poor. It encourages the disruptive emotions of envy and contempt and so endangers the stability of the state.'[6] Others, arguing on an individualistic basis, would contend that the spendthrift was ruining his health and reputation as well as his fortune. And a few might add that by purchasing vast quantities of foreign goods he was leading indirectly to the impoverishment of Italy.[7]

As a result of such feelings repeated efforts were made to curb extravagance, especially in the matter of food.[8] In 181 B.C. the *Lex Orchia* placed a limit on the number of guests allowed at dinner. Twenty years later the *Lex Fannia* decreed that on ordinary days a dinner should cost no more than ten asses. On ten days of every month the host could spend thirty asses, and on special occasions like the *Ludi Romani* and the *Saturnalia* a hundred.[9] Towards the end of the century the *Lex Licinia* raised the ordinary daily figure to thirty asses. It placed no limit on the amount of bread, wine, fruit and vegetables, but fixed a certain weight per day for dried meat and salted fish. In Sulla's time the terms of the law had to be revised again. The maximum cost on ordinary days was now fixed at thirty sesterces. Later we find Augustus trying to hold the line at two hundred. Admittedly these figures are less dramatic than they look, for allowance has to be made for rises in price and alterations in currency. But I am assured by Professor F. M. Heichelheim that when these factors have been taken into account the sums mentioned still indicate an impressive change in the standard of living.

They also indicate the futility of sumptuary legislation. The trouble was, of course, that those who supported the laws did so in the belief that such measures would be highly salutary for other people. Senators agreed that the ostentation of businessmen really ought to be curtailed, but insisted that they themselves had to maintain a style appropriate to their rank; and such feelings were, in fact, recognized by Julius Caesar.[10] Again, it was admitted that office-holders might be open to certain temptations, and accordingly Antius Restio had a law passed about 70 B.C. forbidding magistrates and candidates to dine out, except with certain specified people. But if you were, shall we say, an aedile, and you knew that a contractor or a merchant or a fellow-politician was relying on you to do him a favour—in the public interest of course—it would surely have seemed rather churlish to refuse the man's hospitality.

We are not surprised, therefore, to find that in practice these well-intentioned laws were defied or evaded. In response to the *Lex Fannia* men like Tubero, Rutilius and Mucius bought game and fish from their servants well below market price. Athenaeus, who gives this information, adds approvingly that they did not make such arrangements only for themselves; they gave presents to others as well—especially to their friends, 'for they adhered to the teachings of the Stoa'.[11] A character in Lucilius speaks contemptuously of 'Fannius' miserable little hundred'[12]—a hundred asses being the *maximum* allowed for any occasion. Outside the city the Fannian law was apparently disregarded, for eighteen years later Didius had it extended to the whole of Italy. We are told by Macrobius (*Sat.* 3. 17. 13) that after the enactment of the *Lex Antia* poor Antius dined at home for the rest of his life because he couldn't bear to see his own law flouted. Julius Caesar's regulations were also unpopular. And no wonder, for under his régime not only did inspectors snoop around the markets in search of illegal delicatessen, but according to Suetonius (*Jul.* 43) policemen would suddenly descend on a man's dining room like harpies in uniform and carry off any titbits which had escaped the inspector's eye. One scarcely needs the words of Cicero (*Att.* 13. 7) to establish that even Caesar's laws were ignored when the great man was away.

The truth is that luxury could only have been quelled by a national crisis like that which followed Cannae, or else by a much more ruthless and efficient dictatorship than Rome ever possessed. The most that could be done (and this was little enough) was to influence the attitude of the wealthy classes in a general way. According to Tacitus (*Ann.* 3. 54), the disenchanted Tiberius once said *reliquis intra animum medendum est: nos pudor, pauperes necessitas, divites satias in melius mutet*—'The other ills must be healed within the heart. Let us all learn to behave better—the senators through self-respect, the poor through necessity, and the rich through surfeit'. It was one of Horace's aims to arouse men's self-respect, but he was not so cynical as to believe that *pudor* was a prerogative of the senatorial order. In fact the diatribe which we are about to discuss is based on the conversation of a peasant. Its thought may be paraphrased as follows:

Introduction (1–7). Here are the virtues of simple living. (This talk is not my own but represents the teachings of the peasant Ofellus, a sage unattached to any school, a man of sturdy common sense.) Consider the matter now, before lunch—not amid the splendour of a banquet when the eye is dazzled by senseless glitter and the mind inclines in favour of the sham, rejecting what is better.

Section 1A (8–22). A corrupt judge does not weigh the truth properly. Do some hard riding or hunting, or (if you prefer the softer exercises of the Greeks) play a game of ball or throw a discus. Then, when the exertion has knocked the finickiness out of you, see if you can resist plain food. The butler is out, the stormy sea protects the fish—well, bread and salt will appease your yelping stomach. How so? Because the chief pleasure does not reside in the rich savoury smell but in yourself. Get your sauce by sweat. The man who is pale and bloated from excess will not enjoy oysters, trout, or grouse.

After establishing his principle Horace turns to those who reject it in practice, and the satirical tone now emerges more strongly.

1B (23–38). In spite of this fact you can hardly be prevented from choosing a peacock in preference to a pullet. You are led astray by empty appearances; for the peacock costs gold and its coloured tail is a pretty sight. But do you eat the tail? Does it look so magnificent when cooked? Although there is no difference in the meat, you try to obtain this bird rather than that, deceived as you are by their difference in looks. Well, suppose you *can* distinguish their flavours, how do you tell whether this bass was caught in the Tiber or in the sea, between the bridges or at the river mouth? You praise a three-pound mullet, you silly fool, though you have to cut it into separate helpings. You are attracted solely by its appearance. Why then dislike long bass? Presumably because the bass is large by nature and the mullet small. It's not often that a hungry stomach spurns everyday food.

1 C (39-52). 'I'd like to see something huge stretched out on a huge dish', says a gullet which in its voracity would do credit to the Harpies. Oh ye warm south winds, come and 'cook' the delicacies of these fellows! And yet their fresh boar and turbot are *already* rotten, because their stomachs are sick of gorging and prefer radishes and pickles.

This folly is relatively recent. The poor man's food has not yet been wholly banished from the tables of the rich—eggs and black olives still have a place. It is not so long since Gallonius won notoriety by serving a sturgeon.[13] Why is that? Did the sea feed fewer turbots in those days? The turbot was safe and the stork safe in its nest until the authority of a praetor taught you the new fashion. Nowadays if someone issued an edict proclaiming the deliciousness of roast seagull the youth of Rome would obey him, amenable as they are to everything perverse.

Before concluding the first half, Horace now redresses the balance, as in 1. 1. 101 ff., by asserting that the opposite extreme is just as vicious.

1 D (53-69). According to Ofellus a simple style of living is quite different from stingy squalor. The latter is no less a vice than extravagance. Avidienus eats olives five years old and cornels from the forest. He hates to open his wine till it's sour; and the smell of his oil is unbearable. On festive occasions he does make an effort. He dons a white toga and pours out the oil drop by drop with his own hand. He is lavish with his vinegary wine.[14] That's *his* idea of a celebration. The wise man will avoid both extremes. He will not be over-particular, like Albucius, in superintending dinner, nor will he be so slack as to tolerate dirtiness, like Naevius.

So far, then, the main themes have been: hunger is the best sauce; the craving for exotic food has really nothing to do with flavour but is simply a matter of appearances based on fashion; the right kind of diet represents a mean between extravagance and stinginess.

The thread connecting 1 A, 1 B, and 1 C is provided by the idea of corruption—a corruption which cannot distinguish the genuine from the fake. Thus in the introduction the mind is said to be misled by the glitter of a banquet (*stupet acies...acclinis falsis animus*). This notion of a judgement unbalanced by corruption is taken up in 1 A, *male verum examinat omnis / corruptus iudex* (8–9), and it reappears at the end of the paragraph in connexion with the man whose enjoyment has been ruined by excess. In 1 B the gourmet is said to be corrupted or led astray by irrelevancies (*corruptus vanis rerum*), deceived by appearances (*formis deceptum*), and attracted solely by looks (*ducit te species*). And in this search for the unusual there is more than a touch of the perverse. This last observation leads into 1 C, which opens with the cravings of an unnatural appetite. In the end, says Horace, such morbid desire is self-defeating, for when the huge meal comes the jaded stomach is unable to accept it.

In v. 44 Horace turns rather abruptly to the vagaries of fashion. Every new vogue must have a leader. Of the two examples given Gallonius the rich auctioneer was a contemporary of Lucilius, but there is less certainty about the unnamed praetor who introduced a craze for storks.[15] Porphyrion says he was called Rufus and quotes an epigram to the effect that he suffered an ignominious defeat at the polls—a defeat which was supposed to represent the people's vengeance for the death of the storks. At any rate the fame of such men implied the existence of a public waiting to be pampered and exploited. This leads Horace back to the theme of corruption—the youth of Rome will follow any leader, provided he is blatantly frivolous.

All this does not mean, of course, that Horace had no palate. He enjoyed good food as much as anyone and he respected the character of an old Falernian. He did sincerely feel, however, that the gluttony which flourished around him was wasteful and foolish and that a great deal of his contemporaries' connoisseurship was no more than snobbish affectation.

Section 2A (70–93). These are the benefits of simple living. First, good health. Remember how fit you were when you ate plain food. A mixture of delicacies will cause the stomach to revolt. The body, sluggish from yesterday's excesses, weighs down the soul and nails to the earth a particle of the divine spirit. The man who eats sparingly falls asleep at once and rises fresh to his daily business.

And yet he can enjoy a treat from time to time—when a holiday comes along, when he's run down, or when he's getting old. The glutton, however, has no pleasure to fall back on. How different from the men of old, who instead of devouring all their meat when it was fresh, would keep it in case of a guest's arrival, even though in the end it might be rather high. What giants they were in those days!

2B (*94–111*). Secondly, restraint earns a good reputation. Huge turbots and dishes bring notoriety and ruin. And when you are destitute you won't be able to afford a rope to hang yourself. 'You can talk like that to Trausius,' says the listener, 'but my fortune is large enough to support this kind of luxury.' Well, is there nothing better to spend it on? Why should any good man starve when you are rich? Why are the temples in decay? Why not give some of your vast wealth to the country of your birth? I suppose you of all man-kind are bound to stay rich for ever. What glee there will be at your fall! Who, then, is better trained to meet misfortune—the man accustomed to every kind of excess or the man content with little?

2C (*112–36*). Ofellus lived his philosophy. Before his eviction, in the days when he owned his property, his life was just as simple as it is now. You can see him today, working with his cattle and sons on the farm which now be-longs to someone else. This is what he has to say: 'On a working day I usually ate no more than a shank of smoked ham and greens. But when I had a visitor I celebrated with a pullet or a kid, and for dessert we had nuts, raisins and figs. Then we would enjoy a pleasant evening's drinking. Whatever troubles lie ahead, this style of living cannot be greatly reduced, and indeed it has remained much the same even though a new occupant is now in residence.

'I say "occupant", for actual ownership of the land is not granted to him or me or anyone else. He turned us out, and he will be turned out by his own worthlessness or his ignorance of the tricks of the law, or finally by the heir who outlives him. This land is now in the name of Umbrenus; once it was called Ofellus'. No one will ever own it, but the use of it will pass now to me now to someone else. So be brave and confront adversity with brave hearts.'

In 2A we have a fresh beginning which corresponds closely with the opening lines. Compare *quae quantaque* with *quae et quanta*, *victus tenuis* with *vivere parvo*, and *accipe* with *discite*. Also the contrast between good and bad health has much in common with Section 1A, the main difference being that the benefits of a simple diet which were implied in the earlier passage are now made explicit. Half way through 2A (at v. 82) a second argument appears, namely that a simple diet leaves room for an occasional treat. This is not a new theme; it occurred previously in connexion with the miserly Avidienus (59–62). But the effect is one of ironic contrast rather than repetition, for Avidienus' idea of a celebration was painfully restricted—in spite of his white toga. A further contrast comes in vv. 89 ff. The men of old, who preferred to eat their pork high so that they could share it with a guest, are the very reverse of the jaded sensualists in 1 C to whom even a fresh boar tasted unpleasant.

Except for the big turbots and the big dishes (95), which recall v. 39 and vv. 49 ff., 2 B is unconnected with anything in Section 1. To the medical and aesthetic arguments which have gone before it adds considerations of ethics, finance, and common prudence. The ethical argument appeals to the regard which a man has for the opinions of society (*fama*), of his neighbours (*vicinos*), and of his family (*patruum*); but it rests ultimately on his own self-respect (*te tibi iniquum*). The financial argument cannot be divorced from this, though of course it also includes the element of material self-interest. The concluding argument, on the precariousness of fortune, is drawn from the deepest wells of ancient thought and religion. Such an awareness provides material for every kind of utterance from the most elaborate and sophisticated odes of Greek tragedy to the tritest clichés of popular wisdom. At an intermediate level the idea received its most memorable form in the words:

> sperat infestis metuit secundis
> alteram sortem bene praeparatum
> pectus.   (*Carm.* 2. 10. 13–15)

The heart which is well prepared hopes for a change of fortune in adversity, is on guard against it in prosperity.

The mutability of fortune leads smoothly into the last section (2 C), which describes the altered circumstances of Ofellus and his reaction to them. In Horace's boyhood Ofellus owned a small farm near Venusia. Like many another, he was evicted after Philippi (42 B.C.) to make room for one of Octavian's ex-servicemen (Appian, *BC* 4. 3). The new owner, however, allowed Ofellus to work the farm, in return, presumably, for a regular payment in kind. In his closing speech Ofellus begins by dealing with his experience wholly in terms of food and drink, and so continues the satire's main theme. In particular, the idea of a special celebration looks back to Avidienus (59–62) and to the healthy man (82–8). But towards the end we are taken on to quite a different level, from which the glutton and all his concerns fade into insignificance. In Lucretius' famous words, *vitaque mancipio nulli datur, omnibus usu* (*DRN* 3. 971)—'And life is granted to none on freehold, to all on lease'—a line which, like many in Shakespeare's sonnets, transmutes the dry terminology of law into memorable poetry.

A closer look at the opening verses will reveal some of the sophisticated art which makes the poem what it is. In *boni* (1)—'Gentlemen'—Horace has chosen a mode of address directly parallel to the Greek ὠγαθοί—a trivial point until we read *nec meus hic sermo est* (2). As the editors say, this is an echo of Plato's οὐ γὰρ ἐμὸς ὁ μῦθος—'The tale is not mine'. It may be just a happy accident that the quotation comes from the *Symposium* (177A) and is spoken there by the doctor Eryximachus; but it is a kind of accident to which Horace is markedly prone. The lines on Greek games, introduced by the slightly pejorative *graecari* (11), contain three Greek importations (*austerum, aera, disco*). The gnomic injunction *tu pulmentaria quaere / sudando* ('Get your sauce by sweat') goes back to a remark of Socrates who, when asked why he was walking so long, replied ὄψον συνάγω πρὸς τὸ δεῖπνον—'I'm getting my sauce for dinner'.[16] Finally, the reader who knew his Homer by heart would remember on seeing *latrantem stomachum* (18)—'yelping stomach'—that Odysseus had said οὐ γάρ τι στυγερῇ ἐπὶ γαστέρι κύντερον ἄλλο (*Od.* 7. 216)—'There is nothing more cur-like than the belly in its hateful persistence'.

With this allusiveness go a continual variation of long and short sentences and a lively mixture of statement, question, and command. There is even one notorious passage where the speaker loses for a moment the thread of his construction and has to pick it up again in the next line.[17] The flow of spontaneous discourse is also assisted by the metre. If we except the anacoluthon just mentioned, there is not a single end-stopped line between vv. 8 and 22. When we add to all this the kind of thematic development already described, it is clear that the passage represents a very subtle and very unusual type of verse. Anyone who tends to believe that the *Satires* are *really* little more than metrical prose would do well to read Cicero's treatment of the same subject in *Tusc. Disp.* 5. 97 ff.

In one general respect, however, 2. 2 is less satisfying than other satires in the book. There is a lack of clarity in the setting which reflects a larger uncertainty about the relationship of Horace to Ofellus. In v. 7 the speaker says 'Discuss the matter here (*hic*) with me before lunch'. Palmer is convinced that *hic* refers to 'some spot on Ofellus' farm'. This involves the view that *quae* (2) means 'the words which' and hence that 'Ofellus is reported *verbatim*'. Now it is true that the last twenty lines or so do purport to be Ofellus' actual words; and there is nothing in the ideas to prevent us from accepting the fiction. But for the greater part of the poem such acceptance is impossible. Even granting that Ofellus owned the farm before his eviction, it is hard to imagine a Venusian peasant being so familiar with the high life of the capital. He knows about the best mead and the choicest fish and game; he has heard of connoisseurs who can tell whether a bass has fed in the estuary or in the city centre; and he is concerned about the state of Rome's temples. Odder still, he is conversant not only with jokes from Plautus and Terence but with topics from Lucilius.[18] Even this is not too much for Lejay, who tells us (p. 313) that Ofellus could have had some rolls of Lucilius in his house. Presumably he also had works of Stoic or Pythagorean philosophy, for in v. 79 he speaks of bodily indulgence as nailing the soul to the earth.[19]

If, however, one believes (as I do) that the setting is Rome and that Horace is transmitting the teachings but not the words of Ofellus, then the old farmer becomes rather a feeble device. Clearly he is supposed to have some kind of independent existence which will prevent the reader from ascribing all the sentiments in the poem to Horace himself. But for the most part Ofellus is too vague and shadowy a figure to perform this function, and so dramatically 2. 2 is weaker than several of the other pieces.

Editors like Morris may well be right in interpreting this technical uncertainty as a sign of early composition. But even if the satire was written in 34 B.C. it still contains two passages which provide interesting hints of Horace's later career as a lyric poet. In v. 100 the glutton claims that he can well afford his extravagance: 'I have a large income and a fortune big enough for three kings.' Horace answers 'Well, is there nothing better for you to spend your money on? Why does any good man stand in need when you are rich? How is it that the ancient temples of the gods are in decay? You worthless wretch! Why don't you give a portion of that great pile to the country of your birth?' This passage is unique in the *Satires*. In several other places we hear that the happy life consists in living on good terms with one's family, friends, and neighbours, and this implies a certain degree of kindliness and hospitality. (The miser in 1. 1 is an example of one who has failed to reach this standard.) But there is nothing elsewhere to suggest that a man has any responsibility to the state. Temples and public works did not come within the field of private morality, and that is what the *Satires* are about.

In addition to civic virtue there is another element missing from the *Satires*' ethical scheme. That is, the relation of an individual to the universe as a whole. A genre whose laws were developed to deal with the follies and vices of social behaviour was not equipped to move in the vaster areas of human experience. The age of the earth, the transience of human life, and the absolute dominion of death—these are not satiric themes, and so the reflexions of Ofellus in vv. 129 f. have a rather unusual sombreness:

> nam propriae telluris erum natura neque illum
> nec me nec quemquam statuit.

For nature has appointed neither him nor me nor anyone else as master and owner of the land.

A similar mood appeared for a moment at the end of 1. 1 and was hastily laughed off; it recurs in 2. 6 in the philosophy of the city mouse, but thanks to the atmosphere of the fable and the character of the mouse himself it is easily contained within the limits of satire. Here there is no irony to diminish the effect, and as a result the satire looks as if it is going to end on a note of solemnity far removed from its main subject. Horace realized this himself, but there was no going back, and so he took one step further, *exaggerating* a little so as to lighten the air of gravity and to finish, as it were, in a major key:

> quocirca vivite fortes,
> fortiaque adversis opponite pectora rebus.

So take your stand bravely and confront adversity with brave hearts.

2.3

In this, by far the longest of the *Satires*, time and setting are cleverly supplied in the first few lines, which, amusingly enough, are part of a severe scolding administered to Horace by Damasippus. In paraphrase, the introduction begins as follows:

1–16. 'You write so little that you scarcely finish four poems a year; instead you unravel everything you've written. You are angry with yourself because in spite of generous amounts of wine and sleep you produce nothing worth talking of. You say you've taken refuge out here during the Saturnalia. Very well, if you're so abstemious, give voice to something worthy of your promises. Go on, begin...There is nothing forthcoming. It's no use blaming your pen or cursing and beating at the wall. Yet you had a purposeful air which promised great things as soon as you had time and could get away to your warm country house. What point was there in packing Plato, Archilochus, and the comic poets? Do you think you can reduce your unpopularity by deserting the cause of virtue? You will win only contempt, you poor creature. You must either keep away from that brazen Siren Sloth or else bid farewell to whatever you've achieved in better days.'

We are to imagine, I take it, that Damasippus is visiting Horace at the Sabine farm during the Saturnalia (17–19 December), and has seized the opportunity to give the poet a good lecture. Horace replies equably:

16–38. 'In return for your sound advice, Damasippus, may heaven reward you—with a barber! But how do you know me so well?'

173

'I've been minding other people's business ever since my own crashed on the Stock Exchange. Once I enjoyed asking what bronze basin Sisyphus had washed his feet in; I valued such and such a statue expertly at five thousand pounds; no one else got such bargains in real estate. And so the crowds at the auctions used to call me "The Man of Mercury".'

'Yes, I know, and I'm amazed that you've been relieved of that ailment. Yet the amazing thing is that a new ailment has driven out the old, as happens with physical complaints when, say, a headache passes into the stomach or when a torpid patient suddenly becomes a boxer and attacks the doctor. Provided nothing like that happens, have it your own way.'[20]

'My dear fellow, don't deceive yourself. You are just as mad, and so are all fools, if there is anything in Stertinius' spiel. It was he who taught me this lesson. After consoling me he urged me to cultivate the beard of wisdom and to go home from the Fabrician bridge leaving my sadness behind. For when my business collapsed I intended to cover my head and jump in the river. But providentially he appeared beside me and said...'

The subsequent speech, which comprises the main part of the satire (38–299), expounds the Stoic paradox that all fools are mad.

This introductory section is characteristically gay. 'That brazen Siren Sloth' comes well from a proselytizing Stoic. Such men could see no value in the *Odyssey* until they had turned it into a moral allegory. Sisyphus' footbath is also a nice touch. Corinthian bronzes fetched high prices, and as Sisyphus was the founder of Corinth a very early piece like his footbath would have caused quite a stir at the Roman Sotheby's. It was, in fact, a famous antique even in the fifth century. In a fragment of Aeschylus' *Sisyphus*, which was one of his satyr plays, the king calls imperiously for water:

καὶ νίπτρα δὴ χρὴ θεοφόρων ποδῶν φέρειν·
λεοντοβάμων ποῦ σκάφη χαλκήλατος;[21]

Water must be brought for the feet that bear a god. Where is the bronze bowl with the lion base?

And yet there are one or two disappointing features. The first concerns Damasippus as a character. His opening tirade, his beard, his salvation by the Stoic Stertinius, his habit of quoting Chrysippus—all these suggest the zealous convert, earnest and confident in his new-found faith. Such a character would make an excellent foil for the ironical Horace. But unfortunately the picture becomes blurred at a number of points. Damasippus' remark about minding other people's business after wrecking his own (*aliena negotia curo,* / *excussus propriis*) might be just inadvertence, but he ought not to use the disrespectful 'spiel' (*crepat*) in connexion with his teacher's sermon,[22] and he ought not to refer so flippantly to his own beard, which was the symbol of his belief.[23] All these are Horace's jokes and should not be put in Damasippus' mouth. Moreover, Damasippus remains oddly ambiguous about his present condition. Is he insane or not? Clearly we are meant to suppose that after his conversion he is in some sense wiser than before. Yet when Horace begs him not to become violent his only reply is 'You too are insane' (32). Later, after recounting Stertinius' teaching he says 'These were the weapons which Stertinius gave me, so that I could hit back if anyone called me names. Whoever says I am mad will be told as much in reply' (296–8). This seems to imply a lack of certainty in Damasippus' own mind and it weakens the effect of the final gibe in which he is addressed as *insane* (326). In this respect Catius in 2. 4 is a more convincing figure, for he never doubts his wisdom for a moment.

The other difficulty is one which we have met before, especially in 1. 6. It is the absence of any firm link between the introduction and the main theme. Damasippus upbraids Horace for his idleness; the poet, it seems, has been so lazy that when he does try to write he is unable to do so. This, however, has really nothing to do with the gospel which Damasippus learned from Stertinius, namely that all fools are mad. Horace is apparently aware of this, for in v. 301, when the sermon is over, he asks what particular form of madness he is suffering from. He is told that by building extensions to his farm he is attempting to emulate Maecenas—a ridiculous ambition. Then, warming to his theme, Damasippus says:

> adde poemata nunc, hoc est, oleum adde camino,
> quae si quis sanus fecit, sanus facis et tu.

> Now throw in your poems, that is, throw oil on the furnace; if any
> sane man ever wrote poetry then you are sane too.

All this fooling, amusing as it is, cannot alter the fact that the very activity which Damasippus enjoined at the beginning now turns out to be a form of madness.

More will be said about the overall structure of the poem when we go on to consider the homily of Stertinius. Before this, however, we should note a few points in the closing dialogue between Damasippus and Horace. After citing Horace's poetry as a proof of his insanity Damasippus continues with a time-honoured trick of rhetoric: *non dico horrendam rabiem*—'I say nothing of your appalling temper'.[24] At the mention of his temper Horace, who has been admirably cool so far, gives himself away. 'Now that's enough!' he cries. Damasippus ploughs on 'Your living beyond your means'. 'Mind your own business, Damasippus!' shouts the poet. But, as we know, that is the one thing Damasippus cannot do. 'Your infatuation with thousands of girls and boys.' In desperation Horace cries out 'O have mercy, please! You are indeed my superior—in madness'—*o maior tandem parcas, insane, minori!*

The largest element in the concluding dialogue is the fable of the calf and the frog:

> absentis ranae pullis vituli pede pressis
> unus ubi effugit, matri denarrat, ut ingens
> belua cognatos eliserit. illa rogare
> quantane, num tantum, sufflans se, magna fuisset.
> 'maior dimidio.' 'num tantum?' cum magis atque
> se magis inflaret, 'non, si te ruperis' inquit,
> 'par eris.'

When a mother frog was away her young were crushed under the hoof of a calf. One escaped and told his mother how a huge beast had trampled on his brothers. She asked how big it had been—had it been this big?[25]—puffing herself out. 'Half as big again.' 'This big?'[26] As she inflated herself more and more, he said 'Not if you burst yourself will you equal it'.

In the Greek version of Babrius (28) an ox who was drinking trampled on a young toad. When the mother returned she asked the toad's brothers where he was. They said:

τέθνηκε, μῆτερ· ἄρτι γάρ, πρὸ τῆς ὥρης,
ἦλθεν πάχιστον τετράπουν, ὑφ' οὗ κεῖται
χηλῇ μαλαχθέν.

He is dead, mother. For just an hour ago there came a huge four-footed creature and he was crushed to pulp under its hoof.

This little scene is more poignant than Horace's in its detail, and the 'huge four-footed creature' gives a more convincing toad's-eye view of the accident. Horace's account, however, is more economical. With his compressed hypotactic style he takes only two and a half lines to reach this point as compared with Babrius' five and a half. Moreover, whereas Babrius set out to make a well-rounded story, Horace was primarily concerned with the second part, and here he is much superior. Babrius gives no increase in tension. The toad only inflates herself once, and the final warning is less forceful.

In Phaedrus' version (1. 24), which is followed by La Fontaine (1. 3), the frog sees the ox in a field and in envy of its size blows herself up until she bursts. This is a rather cruder treatment, not only because the tragedy of the young frogs is abandoned but because the mother, instead of being amusingly absurd, is made into a complete fool. In Horace's account she doesn't know what she is competing with; her performance is designed for the benefit of her son, but the little fellow knows the truth and remains unimpressed. In Phaedrus, however, she is motivated solely by envy; and the violent conclusion is also less subtle.

Analysing the history of the Graeco-Roman fable, Perry distinguishes three stages of development.[27] Down to the end of the fourth century the fable was used incidentally to illustrate some point in a larger context; in the Alexandrian age fables were gathered into collections for the use of writers and speakers; about the time of Phaedrus (i.e. the first century A.D.) the compiler turned his collection into verse and presented it as literature in its own right. The third period saw the emergence of the *epimythium*, that is, the appended moral which gave the fable a general application. It is clear, therefore, that Horace's version represents the fable in its earliest form. By this I mean that he uses it as a literary tool with a specific purpose; the moral refers directly to the situation described:

haec a te non multum abludit imago. (320)

This picture fits you pretty well.

La Fontaine's version, representing the third stage, adds a general moral, which begins as follows:

Le monde est plein de gens qui ne sont pas plus sages:
Tout bourgeois veut bâtir comme les grands seigneurs.

We know where he found the bourgeois builder.

We turn now to the main body of the poem, in which Stertinius preaches to Damasippus on the Stoic text 'All fools are mad'. The reasoning may be summarized as follows:

You, with your misplaced sense of guilt, are afraid that people will think you mad; but these people are mad themselves. I shall begin by asking what madness is. According to Chrysippus and his flock a madman is one impelled by folly and ignorance. That accounts for everyone except the sage. Now I want to tell you why those who call you mad are just as mad themselves. They think that because you've gone astray in one respect they are perfectly sound, failing to realize that they've gone off the rails in other ways. One type of fool is absurdly timid, another is incurably rash. Damasippus is mad on collecting old statues; but what of the man who lends him money? If the fellow asks no security he is virtually giving the money away; if he asks for a whole series of written guarantees he is equally foolish, for the guarantees of a rascal are worthless.

This part is almost the same length as the introduction (38 lines). The next is much longer. Making a fresh beginning at v. 77, and no longer confining his remarks to Damasippus, Stertinius undertakes to prove that everyone who suffers from greed, ambition, self-indulgence, or superstition is mad. The section on greed (82–157) is much the longest, being equal in length to the introduction and the first part put together— i.e. 76 verses. It begins with the tale of Staberius:

Staberius' one purpose in life was to save money. When he came to write his will he was so proud of his thrift that he ordered the sum of his estates to be inscribed on his tombstone. Now a non-musician who kept buying harps or a non-cobbler who collected knives and lasts or a non-sailor who amassed quantities of sail-cloth would be considered mad. So why not Staberius? Take the sort of man who lies awake with a club in his hand, watching over a huge supply of grain, and yet refuses to eat anything except bitter leaves; one who drinks vinegar though he owns a well-stocked cellar and who lies on straw when he has a chest full of soft coverlets. No doubt few would judge him mad, because most men suffer from the same disease. Yet he must be out of his mind, for his behaviour is utterly senseless.

If you threw stones at people in the street or at slaves who had cost you money, all the boys and girls would mock you as a lunatic. Strangle your wife and poison your mother—and you are perfectly sane! How is that? Presumably because you do not perform this deed at Argos, nor do you kill your mother with a sword like the mad Orestes. Or perhaps you think that Orestes was only mad *after* killing his mother? That is not true. He was driven mad before the murder; afterwards he did nothing unusual.

The attitude attacked by Stertinius in this last paragraph was something like this: 'Throwing stones at people is a recognized sign of madness[28]—especially if you injure a slave who has cost you money. But my wife and mother didn't cost me anything, so there's nothing absurd about killing them. Moreover, Argos is the place where men butcher their mothers in a fit of madness. This is Rome; here we do it quite sensibly and unobtrusively with poison or a length of rope.' Stertinius' own attitude is: 'You are thought mad if you throw stones at strangers or slaves; how much madder must you be to kill your mother, who is so much more precious?'

After speaking of another miser, Opimius (whose story will be translated below), Horace reminds us that avarice is not the only form of madness. Extravagance is just as senseless, especially when combined with ambition. Then, concentrating on the lust for power and glory, Horace presents a scene in which Agamemnon is cross-examined by a Stoic in the guise of a Greek soldier (187 ff.). The subject is Ajax who, after attempting to kill the Greek leaders in a fit of madness, had committed suicide on recovering his wits. He now lies unburied on the orders of Agamemnon. In opposing this decision the Stoic tries

179

to get Agamemnon to admit that he himself was guilty of a far madder act in murdering his daughter Iphigenia. Ajax in his frenzy had only killed some sheep; Agamemnon had slaughtered his own kith and kin. If anyone treated a lamb as his daughter he would be judged insane by law. For the sake of his own glory Agamemnon treated his daughter as a sacrificial lamb; how is he any saner?

Self-indulgence (*luxuria*) is handled under the headings of extravagance and infatuation (224–80). First we have a short dramatic sketch in which a young rake who has just inherited a fortune summons all the ministers of his pleasure—fishmonger, fruit-merchant, perfumer, etc. A pander speaks on their behalf, promising that the young man's orders will receive prompt attention. But instead of placing orders the prodigal cries 'You deserve the money far more than I do!' and immediately gives it all away. The section ends with a couple of short anecdotes— one about the son of Aesopus who swallowed a pearl dissolved in vinegar,[29] the other about the sons of Arrius who lunched on nightingales.

If, continues Stertinius, a man built dolls' houses and rode on a rocking horse, he would obviously be mad. The behaviour of a lover, with his stockings and scarves and garlands, is no more sensible. Like a perverse child who refuses an apple when you offer it and clamours for one when you don't, the lover cannot decide what he really wants. He moans when he is shut out, but refuses to return when invited. He plays little games with apple pips in the hope of a good omen and goes in for silly baby-talk. More seriously, the lover may be driven to an act of violence —as in the case of Marius, who killed his beloved Hellas and then jumped to his death.

The sermon ends with a short passage on superstition (281–95). A certain freedman would fast and wash and then implore the gods to grant him immortality. A mother prays for the life of her son who is in a high fever; if the gods spare him she will make him stand naked in the Tiber as a sign of gratitude. The boy recovers 'thanks to luck or to the doctor', and thereupon the mother kills him by plunging him in the cold river.

Most of the forms of lunacy already mentioned are referred to again in the epilogue. Horace, says Damasippus, is ambitious in his building programme; he has a terrible temper (the word used is *rabiem*); he lives recklessly beyond his means; and he is wildly promiscuous. One is given the impression that, if Horace had not interrupted, Damasippus would have completed the list with superstition. But superstition, like greed, was so out of character that Horace could not allow himself to be accused of it, even as a joke.

Roman lawyers never discussed the question of what constitutes insanity.[30] When in a specific case a man was adjudged insane (*furiosus*), the *praetor urbanus* deprived him by an *interdictum* of the control of his property and handed him over to the care of his *agnati*, i.e. those who were related to him through the male line.[31] If there were no *agnati* the duty devolved upon his *gentiles* or clansmen. In a passage of the *Tusculan Disputations* (3. 11) Cicero distinguishes *furor*, which involved an incapacitating frenzy or delusion (and which might be only temporary), from the much vaguer *insania*, which meant a general lack of sense. But he did not always observe his own distinction,[32] and Horace uses the two terms interchangeably.

Such imprecision did not matter in ordinary discourse, but a reading of Celsus—a prominent physician of the first century A.D.—shows that even within the medical profession the classification of mental illnesses was rudimentary. The treatment was correspondingly haphazard. Some of the methods were sensible enough—the patient was soothed with sleeping-draughts or rocking or massage, or cheered up with stories or games; but raving madmen were restrained by starvation, fetters, and beatings. Blood-letting was a common procedure, and so was the administration of emetics and purges.[33]

The best-known of these was hellebore, of which there were two

types—one black and one white. Both were used in the treatment of insanity and were regarded with considerable awe.
Pliny (*NH* 25. 56) says the white variety was much more terrible
than the black. But the black must have been quite bad enough,
for according to a modern authority 'in overdose it produces
inflammation of the gastric and intestinal mucous membrane,
with violent vomiting, hypercatharsis, vertigo, cramp, and con-
vulsions which sometimes end in death'.[34] All these treatments
were derived from the Greek theory that one's health depended
on a correct mixture of the four humours—blood (αἷμα), phlegm
(φλέγμα), yellow bile (χολὴ ξανθή), and black bile (χολὴ μέλαινα).
Disease was a sign that one of the humours had become excessive.
It was the doctor's task to reduce it and restore a proper harmony.
In the case of madness the harmful humour was usually thought
to be black bile.[35]

Horace takes it for granted that the reader of 2. 3 will be as
familiar with these legal and medical affairs as he is with the pranks
and pastimes of children. And this sense of actuality is further
enhanced by stories of peasant life, society gossip, and several
references to banking, marketing, real estate, politics and the
theatre. The literary background is equally broad and miscellaneous. One short scene (259-71) is transferred almost literally
from the opening of Terence's *Eunuchus*, another (187-213) is
based on Roman tragedy,[36] and the description of madness probably owes something to Lucilius, who according to Porphyrion
demonstrated what madness is (after W. 1247). No doubt
Horace had also read Varro's *Eumenides*. In this work a man sets
off to find a cure for his madness. After approaching various
religions and philosophies without success he concludes that
'no invalid could dream anything so unspeakable that some
philosopher would not affirm it'. He then meets white Truth
(*cana Veritas*) who presents a catalogue of human follies and so
convinces him that he is no madder than anybody else.[37] The
resemblance to Horace, however, does not go very deep. Apart
from obvious differences of language and metre Horace is much

simpler in the structure of his narrative. He discards Varro's vision of the Furies harassing mankind, he assigns no part in the action to allegorical figures like *Veritas* and *Existimatio*, and he is not interested in the vagaries of rival schools.

Through Varro, Terence, and Roman tragedy Horace is, of course, indebted to Greek literature, but he also draws on it more directly in proverb, fable and myth,[38] as well as in stories from popular philosophy. Furthermore, although the satire as a whole centres on a Stoic paradox, several of the arguments are based on the commonplaces of Hellenistic morality. Thus in the long section on avarice Horace insists on the folly of not enjoying what you have—*nescius uti / compositis* (109–10), *numquam utare paratis* (167). The idea is found, as usual, in Plato and Aristotle,[39] but was especially important to the Epicureans. 'We regard self-sufficiency as a great good,' says the Master (*Menoec.* 130), 'not that we may always enjoy just a few things, but rather that if we do not possess many things we may enjoy the few we have....' A character in Menander voices the same sentiment: 'I have never envied a very rich man who gets no good out of what he has' (ἀπολαύοντα μηδὲν ὧν ἔχει).[40] The failure of such a man, says Teles (37), is a sign that his possessions are κτήματα rather than χρήματα, for the latter term implies use. Senseless hoarding is also attacked by Phoenix of Colophon, and the theme recurs in such diverse writers as Lucilius, Cato, Plutarch, and Epictetus.[41]

The organization of all this material called for considerable skill. In the main part of Stertinius' sermon (77–295) monotony is avoided by a clever variation in the placement of key words.[42] Sometimes the word occurs in the first line of its section, as in *danda est ellebori multo pars maxima avaris* (82)—'Much the biggest dose of hellebore should be given to misers'—and in *nunc age, luxuriam et Nomentanum arripe mecum* (224)—'Come now and arraign with me self-indulgence and Nomentanus'. In vv. 247–80, however, the key word *amare* is withheld until the fourth line, and so we are kept guessing about the type of folly in question. In the closing section (281–95), although we know what the folly

is, we are not given its proper name until the very last line—
timore deorum ('superstition').

Ambition is named more than once, e.g. *gloria* (179), *vitrea
fama* (222), but the topic is introduced in a somewhat loose and
uncertain way. In the course of a rather obvious demonstration
that not all fools are misers (158–63), Horace says in effect 'Although a man may not be given to lying and meanness he may
be ambitious and rash'. Lying has previously been associated
with avarice (127) and rashness may conceivably look forward to
the action of Agamemnon, but here they have no immediate
function in the argument. What we do expect, in view of the promise in vv. 78–9, is some comment on ambition. Rather surpri-
singly, however, Horace continues by saying 'For what difference
does it make whether you consign all you have to a pit or never
use your savings?' With these words ambition seems to disappear,
and we are back with the old antithesis of prodigality and avarice.
Now comes the story of Servius Oppidius who had two sons, one
a spendthrift and the other a miser. On his death-bed he forbade
the former to reduce and the latter to increase the fortune he left
him. At this point, when we have almost forgotten about ambition, Oppidius goes on to say 'Moreover, to protect you from
the itch for glory I shall make you both swear that whoever
becomes aedile or praetor shall be an accursed outcast'. This does
get us back to the theme of ambition, but it is clumsily managed,
for the miserly son will not in fact be open to that temptation—
public life is far too expensive, as Horace shows in the following
lines. And so one is left with the impression that instead of being
set cleanly side by side or welded smoothly together the vices of
greed and ambition have been rather awkwardly interlocked.

A much firmer control is evident in the section on infatuation
(247 ff.). This begins by mentioning a number of children's
games, such as building toy houses and riding on reeds. The
lover's behaviour is then woven into these pastimes (*amare...
trimus...amore*) and so put in a ridiculous light.[43] After the reference to Polemon (253 ff.) Horace reverts to the child analogy,

comparing the lover's games and baby-talk to the child with his toy house (272–5).

The first part of the section on avarice ends with the words *metuensque velut contingere sacrum* (110). This reminded Horace of *tamquam parcere sacris*—a phrase he had used in 1. 1. 71 in connexion with a miser lying on a heap of money-bags. And so he now goes on to describe a miser lying beside a heap of corn (111 ff.). In most of Horace's discussions about greed there is no clear distinction between the acquisitive and the hoarding instincts.[44] It is assumed that the greedy man will indulge both. Thus the frantic pursuit of gain in 1. 1. 38–40 is followed at once by the burial of the proceeds. Here, after the squalor of the miser's life (111–26), we get a glimpse of the way he makes his money—it is by lying, stealing, and plunder. This goes some way towards preparing us for the violence of the next paragraph in which we are told that even murder is condoned when it involves no waste of money. The sardonic, almost Juvenalian wit of this passage is followed immediately by the comic tale of Opimius which pushes the argument to its final absurdity: some people are so stingy that they'd sooner die than pay for medicine.

The folly of avarice, then, can lead to death. As the sermon proceeds we learn that the same is true of ambition, for Agamemnon slew his daughter; the same is true of infatuation, for Marius killed Hellas and then took his own life; and the same is true of superstition, for a mother killed her son in fulfilling an idiotic vow.

One of the minor techniques of style is the introduction of an anonymous listener. I say 'listener' rather than adversary, for in 2. 3, unlike 1. 1, the figure does not answer back. The most he does is to ask Stertinius for further information (97, 160). Yet at times he acquires an identity, becoming a mean old man (123), or a besotted lover (252, 273); and once he joins a group of fellow-invalids (81). Another device is to adopt the style of a Stoic disquisition. This comes in with rather implausible suddenness in v. 41, where Stertinius, after restraining Damasippus from suicide, launches forth with 'First of all I shall inquire what madness is'.

Then, with a dutiful reference to Chrysippus, he goes on to define a madman as 'anyone who is driven blindly on by accursed folly and by ignorance of the truth'. After this definition or *formula* he says 'Now I shall proceed to tell you how it is that those who call you mad are just as mad themselves'. As further examples of Stoic methodology Lejay (pp. 357 ff.) would add the enumeration of cases, the frequent appeals to common opinion, and the habit of putting the point in the form of a question. But one doubts whether in Horace's day these were thought of as primarily Stoic techniques. They belonged rather to the general tradition of the diatribe.

More could be said about the brilliance of individual passages and the deftness of the poet's joinery, but it is time to give some estimate of the satire as a whole, and one has to admit that it is not among Horace's best. This is due in some degree to the lack of proportion in its parts. One does not ask for symmetry, but by writing seventy-six lines on avarice and only fifteen on superstition Horace has produced a disturbingly lop-sided effect. Lejay remarks (p. 357) 'Le prédicateur populaire n'a ni prévu son discours ni calculé son effort. Il s'essouffle en parlant et finit court.' No doubt this is true, but we cannot exonerate Horace from his failures by attributing them to Damasippus or Stertinius. If Horace intended to parody the faults of a Stoic sermon it was his business to do so without reproducing the same faults himself. Furthermore, by choosing to deal with a number of different vices Horace ruled out any possibility of a continuous development. All he could do was to strike out in one direction after another, always returning to his central theme of insanity. Given his virtuosity even this might have come off—it has been noted, for example, that he uses nearly thirty different expressions for madness. But unfortunately the paradox itself has no real profundity, and so the axle on which the poem revolves is not strong enough to support it.

The germ of the paradox is found in Xenophon's *Memorabilia* (3. 9. 6) where Socrates is said to have maintained that madness

(μανία) was the opposite of wisdom (σοφία). Socrates went on
to assert, however, that a man was usually considered mad only if
he went wrong on matters which most people knew about. He
did not contend, as the Stoics did, that the majority were themselves mad. In the pseudo-Platonic *Alcibiades 2* (139 C) it looks
at first as if the writer is arguing that all people without sense
(ἄφρονες) are mad. But this is recognized to be a mistake; for, as
wise men are few, the majority would then be mad and the rest
would be subjected to knocks and blows and similar violence.
The conclusion therefore is that not all unwise men are mad
(140 C). Some of them are, namely those who are *most* lacking
in sense. Others are called 'simple-minded', 'stupid' and so on.
This is perfectly straightforward, because madness is used in its
regular sense and the speaker recognizes degrees of imbecility.
Neither of these rules was observed by the Stoics.

The paradox is perhaps most clearly presented by Cicero.
In the *Tusculan Disputations* (3. 7 ff.) the leader of the discussion
says that perturbations or commotions, such as fear, lust and anger,
are signs of an unsound *animus* or *mens*, and the name for un-
soundness of mind is *insania*. What worries us about this is not so
much the failure to distinguish mental from moral (a distinction
which has become blurred in our own time), as the absence of any
sense of proportion. Fear, suspicion, anger and lust are not signs
of insanity unless they are experienced with abnormal frequency,
in abnormal circumstances, and in an abnormal degree. Admittedly the Stoics did not insist that fools always behaved in-
sanely; but the tendency, they said, was there and would be
revealed in certain conditions. Mud does not always give off a
nasty smell, but stir it and you will find it stinks. Stir up an
irascible man and you will see him raging (*Tusc. Disp.* 4. 54).
But this does not remove the difficulty; for non-Stoics, then as
now, did not count an angry man mad unless he constantly
became enraged at things which would leave a normal person
unmoved. Another interpretation of the paradox is recorded by
Athenaeus (11. 464D), who says that according to Chrysippus

μανία (madness) is commonly applied to very many things, e.g. to men who are 'woman-mad', 'fame-mad' and so on. But this reduces the paradox to the status of a vulgar idiom.

It has to be admitted, then, that the satire's central idea is rather weak—at least in the form presented by Stertinius. Yet architectural unity is not the only virtue. When the impression of the poem as a whole has faded, we may still recall stories like this (142–57):

Mr Richly, a poor man in spite of all the silver and gold which he had stored away, used to drink cheap Veientine wine from a cheap Campanian mug. That was on holidays; on working days he drank fermented must. Once he was sunk in so deep a coma that his heir was already running round the chests and keys in triumphant joy. The doctor, who was a loyal fellow with really quick reactions, roused him by this method: he had a table brought; then he ordered some bags of coins to be poured out and several people to step forward and count them. After bringing the patient to in this way he added 'If you don't watch your money, your greedy heir will make off with it at any moment'. 'Over my dead body!' 'All right then, wake up and stay alive. Here.' 'What's this?' 'Your pulse is dangerously low. Your system is running down. It needs food and a really strong tonic. What are you waiting for? Come on, take a sip of this rice gruel.' 'How much was it?' 'Oh, not much.' 'Well *how* much then?' 'A bob.' 'Ah dear me! What difference does it make whether I die from illness or from theft and pillage?'

2. 7

Here, as in 2. 3, the scene is set by the opening speaker. This time it is Davus, one of Horace's slaves. He has been listening at the door, eager but afraid to address his master. Horace calls him in and, because it is the Saturnalia, invites him to speak his mind. Davus at once launches into a diatribe, which I paraphrase throughout:

Some men are loyal to their vices, but most are not. They vacillate weakly between good and evil. Priscus, for instance, would change his clothes and insignia every hour; he would emerge from a mansion to go slumming; and after living the life of an adulterer in Rome he would depart to the scholarly seclusion of Athens. Volanerius was quite different. Gambling was so important to him that when he became crippled by arthritis he employed a man to replace the dice in the box. Because of this single-mindedness Volanerius was the happier man.　　　　　　　　　　　　　　　　　　　　　　　　　　　(6–20)

Here we have a neat symmetrical introduction: steadiness (*constanter*) and vacillation (*modo...interdum*), vacillation (Priscus) and steadiness (Volanerius), steadiness (*constantior*) and vacillation (*iam...iam*). As in the diatribes of Book 1, there follows a line in which the listener demands to know where all this drivel is pointing—*non dices hodie quorsum haec tam putida tendant, | furcifer?* Davus replies 'At you'. And he then proceeds to lecture Horace on his inconsistencies (22–43):

You praise the habits and conditions of the good old days, but if a god suddenly offered to take you back you'd refuse to go—either because you're a hypocrite or because you're weak-willed. At Rome you long for the country, in the country you praise city life. When no one has asked you to dinner you say 'Thank God!'—as if dining out were a form of servitude. Then comes a late invitation from Maecenas, and you shout and bellow in your impatience to be off. The hangers-on who came to dine with you are turned away cursing. You can imagine Mulvius, one of their number, saying 'Granted I'm easily led by food and drink. But as you're no better how can you have the face to preach at me and to wrap up your own vices in euphemisms?' Why, you may even be a bigger fool than I, whom you bought so cheaply.

We think first, perhaps, of 1. 1 with its theme of μεμψιμοιρία and the god who offers to grant wishes. But the earlier poem was concerned only with occupations, not with time or locality. Moreover, the third example of Horace's inconstancy mentioned here—i.e. his dining habits—is not a case of μεμψιμοιρία at all. Rather the reverse, for Horace claims he *enjoys* eating at home. The connexion with 1. 3 is somewhat closer. Horace (foreshadowed by Priscus) takes the place of Tigellius, and the treatment of *aequabilitas* is much the same. In 1. 3 we found that the introductory passage on inconstancy was related to the main theme of fairness through the common idea of balance. Here there is also a connexion, for the lack of steadiness described in the long introduction leads naturally enough to the lack of control which is the satire's main topic. The control in question, however, is that which ought to be exercised by the reason over irrational desires. When such control is wanting, the unruly desires gain the upper hand and the true self becomes enslaved. This, says Davus, is what has happened to Horace. Therefore, except for his legal status, the master is in no way superior to the slave. The Stoics contended that as the slave was free if he was a wise man, so the free man was a slave if he was a fool. This belief was expressed in the paradoxes μόνος ὁ σοφὸς ἐλεύθερος ('Only the sage is free') and πᾶς ἄφρων δοῦλος ('Every fool is a slave').⁴⁵

Apart from the underlying notion of firmness, the relation of the opening passage to the main theme of slavery is indicated in two ways. The first is by introducing the antithesis of freedom and servitude at various points in vv. 1–43. Thus Davus, a slave, takes advantage of the freedom provided by the Saturnalia (4); Priscus' behaviour was sometimes hardly worthy of a freedman (12); the inconsistent man struggles with the rope which is now tight, now loose (20); Horace, though he sees the good, is unable to drag his foot from the mire (27); he pretends that dining out is a dreadful 'bind' (31); but he is away like a shot when summoned by Maecenas (32 ff.); Mulvius, the *scurra* or hanger-on, is led by his stomach (38). The second way is by contriving a smooth transition between the two parts. This begins with Mulvius, who confesses that he is *levis* ('easily swayed'). The same has been said of the inconstant man in v. 19 (*levius*) and of Horace himself in v. 29 (*levis*). But Mulvius' *levitas* is restricted to the area of food and drink—a sign that the general idea of inconstancy is being abandoned. The rest of Mulvius' words show that in the matter of gluttony Horace is no better than his own *scurra*, that he is, in fact, a *scurra* himself. The final step is for Davus to assert that Horace is no better than his own slave. The notion of *inconstantia* has now receded; for whether Davus is inconsistent or not is irrelevant. And the idea of slavery has come to the fore.

As this part of the lecture ends Horace glares at the speaker and raises his fist. But Davus restrains him and proceeds to his main theme, which he has picked up from another eavesdropper, viz. the janitor of Crispinus (46–115):

You are captivated by another man's wife, Davus by a tart. Which of us commits the worse sin? When I sleep with a girl, everything's straightforward and above board. I incur no social disgrace and I don't care if a richer or more handsome rival enjoys the same favours.[46] You remove all the badges of your rank and throw a cloak over your perfumed head, disguising yourself as a slave. But isn't that just what you are? You are let in, torn between lust and terror. When you leave you may be handed over to be whipped or cut to pieces; or you may be smuggled out in a chest with your head stuffed between your knees. In either case you've made yourself a slave. The husband of the lady who sins has the right to punish both, more particularly the seducer. She, however (unlike the seducer), does not change her clothes or her station, nor does she *inflict* the sin. When the woman is reluctant and suspicious will you deliberately humiliate yourself like a slave and put your whole estate and life and reputation at the mercy of a raging master? (46–67)

In tone and subject this takes us back to 1. 2, in which adultery, with all its dangers and indignities, is contrasted with a casual liaison. The writing here is just as vivid, and a greater unity is obtained through the technique of theme and variations. The theme, of course, is servitude, and the first variation is found in *capit* (46), which denotes sexual captivity. Then, in v. 47, Davus asks 'Who sins more deservingly of the cross (*cruce dignius*)?'— the cross being a punishment inflicted on slaves. The adulterer in disguise is on the same level as Dama, a typical slave. When detected he may be *auctoratus*, i.e. be 'delivered up' like a gladiator to be beaten and killed; or, to escape capture, he may be enclosed in a chest—another form of confinement. The adulterer falls into the husband's power (*potestas*). He puts himself under the fork (*furca*)—another servile punishment, in which the wrists were bound to a beam resting on the neck; and he surrenders everything to his *dominus*.[47] One other point deserves mention. The frankness of Davus' transaction is symbolized by the bright lamp (*lucerna*) in v. 48; the furtive guilt of the adulterer by the concealing cloak (*lacerna*) in v. 55. So the all-important difference depends on a single vowel. The effect may be unintentional, but who can say it was an accident?

Davus goes on to speak of the compulsive nature of the adulterer's vice (68–82):

You've escaped. I suppose you'll be careful in future. Not a bit of it. You'll seek another opportunity for terror and ruin—slave that you are. What animal after escaping gives itself up again to its chains? 'I'm not an adulterer', you say. No! Nor am I a thief when I carefully leave the silver untouched. But take away the danger! Then, when the snaffle is removed, nature will leap forward. Are you my master—you who are under the control of so many things and people, and who, though manumitted again and again, are still the slave of fear? Better call me your under-slave or fellow-slave; for you are not a master. You serve someone else and have no more independence than a wooden puppet.

Here Davus continues to ring the changes on slavery, but at v. 72 the argument takes a new turn. So far the case against adultery has rested entirely on prudence—the adulterer is a fool to take such risks. But in v. 72 Horace is supposed to say *non sum moechus* ('I'm not an adulterer'), a simple statement which deprives Davus of a target and ought to leave him speechless. But after shooting wide, Davus, like an ancient Dr Johnson, proceeds to knock his adversary down with the bow. 'Take away the danger!' he cries, as if the danger had not been the foundation of his case, 'And then your nature will be seen in its true colours.' However clumsily made, this point takes the argument to another, more purely Stoic, level. For while the Cynics and Epicureans condemned adultery because of its risks, the Stoics concentrated on the unhealthy state of the offender's soul. Even if there were no risks, they said, the virtuous man would abstain because of his inner discipline. This helps to prepare us for the noble description of the truly free man (83–8):

Who, then, is free? The wise man, who is master of himself, who is undaunted by poverty, death, or bonds, who bravely defies his passions and despises positions of power, who is complete in himself, smooth and round, so that no foreign element can adhere to his polished surface, and who always causes Fortune to lame herself when she attacks him.

Davus now mentions four respects in which Horace fails miserably when measured by this standard (88–115):

A woman asks you for a couple of thousand, bullies you, shuts you out and drenches you with cold water. Then she invites you back. Shake the yoke off your neck! Say you are free! You can't. For a harsh master turns you round and goads you back against your will.

You stand entranced by one of Pausias' pictures. Am I any worse when with my legs rooted to the spot I admire a charcoal poster of a gladiatorial fight? Yet I am a good-for-nothing dawdler while you are called a fine and expert critic.

If I follow the whiff of a cake I'm a worthless wretch. But can you say no to a rich dinner? Why does it do more harm for *me* to be the servant of my belly? Because, you say, I am beaten as a punishment. But you suffer just as much when you go in quest of expensive food. Your endless banquets turn sour, and your legs can no longer support your bloated body. A slave steals a scraper and sells it for a bunch of grapes. But is there nothing servile about one who sells whole estates at the behest of his gullet?

Moreover, you can't stand your own company or manage your leisure properly. Like a runaway slave you try to escape from yourself and to beguile your *Angst*—all to no purpose, for that black companion follows hard on your heels.

After failing to uncover any illicit relationship between Horace and a married woman Davus here accuses him of subservience to a *meretrix*—a sequence which can be paralleled from 1. 2. 57–9. The treatment, however, is in the style of comedy. One thinks immediately of the Terentian scene in 2. 3. 259–64, but the absurdly high price and the bucket of cold water are more in the Plautine manner. The peculiarly Horatian contribution lies in the blending of this comic situation with a strong didactic tone. The picture of lust as a charioteer is in the grand style.

As McGann has pointed out,[48] there is a clever connexion between the passage on art and that which goes before, in that Pausias (a fourth-century painter of the Sicyonian school) was distinguished not only for his subtle technique but also for the gay wantonness of his subjects. There is one other point here which has not, I believe, been properly understood. Davus says he gazes at a drawing of two gladiators *contento poplite* (97). From the time of the scholiasts this phrase has been taken either with *miror* or with the gladiators. I believe it goes with the colourless *miror*, thus balancing the vivid *torpes* of v. 95. Yet neither 'on tip-toe' nor 'with legs straddled' gives the proper sense. Surely, as *torpes* implies physical immobility, so *contento poplite* means that Davus is rooted to the spot. He cannot tear himself away, and *that* is why he is a dawdler (*cessator*). This means that the theme of constraint or servitude is present here as well as in the preceding and following lines, and so Heinze's note on v. 95 should be modified.[49]

The verses on gluttony, along with vv. 29–42, bracket the passages on sex. They also recall the diatribe of Ofellus (2. 2) in both language and subject. Finally, the ending of the poem, with its allusion to the crazy poet, is very similar to that of 2. 3. As Davus takes a breath Horace suddenly breaks in:

'Someone give me a stone!' 'What for?' 'Or arrows!' 'The man's raving or else composing verses.' 'If you don't get out of here mighty quick you'll make drudge number nine on my Sabine farm!'

From what has been said above it is clear that 2. 7 is the most inclusive of all the diatribes. It contains the discontent of 1. 1, the adultery of 1. 2, the inconstancy of 1. 3, the subservience of 1. 6, and the gluttony of 2. 2. The most important comparison, however, is offered by 2. 3. Both poems have a Saturnalian setting. They open with a dialogue in which the poet is in a good humour, proceed to a central section in which a Stoic paradox is expounded at second or third hand, and end with an exchange in which Horace shouts the speaker down. The weaknesses which we noticed in 2. 3, however, have now been remedied. The sprawling length has been cut to a third, and the masses of argumentation have been better distributed. Thus, allowing for some blurring at transitions, we have a prologue (5 verses) followed by four large units (15, 25, 22, 15). Then, after the picture of the free man (6 verses), we have four shorter units (6, 7, 10, 4) followed by the concluding dialogue (3). Moreover, the gap which we noted in 2. 3 between introduction and main theme has here been closed; for a lack of constancy is closely akin to a lack of rational control.

As well as being more appropriate to the Saturnalian scene Davus is a clearer character than Damasippus. He stays before us more constantly through the poem; he knows himself better; and he is more independent in adapting his borrowed material.

By using the second person throughout Davus keeps a single target in view. Thus whereas Damasippus drew his specimens of madness from every quarter, Davus employs just the one figure—that of Horace or 'the master'—to illustrate the various types of servitude. And this brings a gain in tightness.

Last of all, the paradox 'all fools are slaves' appears to be more substantial than 'all fools are mad'. I am not sure why this is so, for both formulae rest on the same principle, namely that irrational desires are not a part of the true self. Perhaps the first suggests something of more positive significance whereas the second looks rather like the proposition 'all grays are black'. Or perhaps it is because freedom, with its social, political and religious implications, has a wider interest than sanity, which seems largely a matter of the individual's psychology. At any rate the idea of freedom contained in 'all fools are slaves' and in its corollary 'only the sage is free' has played an immense role in the history of religion and philosophy, and in one form or another it is still a force in modern thought.

Among the features which we noted as common to the diatribes of Book I was the fact that the poet spoke *in propria persona* and took direct responsibility for what he said. In the diatribes of Book 2 this is no longer the case. The critique of table luxury in 2. 2 is supposed to be based on the teachings of Ofellus; the substance of 2. 3 is ascribed to Stertinius and communicated by Damasippus; and in 2. 7 the source of wisdom is even more remote, for Davus heard the sermon from a janitor who heard it from Crispinus. Accordingly the nature of the impact is different. The first method is undoubtedly more incisive, but it is the method of one who, if not an outsider, is still not a member of the establishment. By 33 B.C., however, Horace was a more familiar figure in society and had numerous friends among the rich and powerful. As a result he seems to have felt unable to preach with his former directness. Perhaps we find this regrettable, and it may well be that in the end Horace's career as a satirist was destroyed by social success. But the later and subtler method should not be dismissed too quickly. Horace may have had reason to believe that he could get his message across *more* effectively in this way. It is as if he were saying:

Now I don't presume to lay down the law to an audience like this. Of course not. Old Ofellus may praise the virtues of peasant life, but I'm not Ofellus, gentlemen, and neither are any of you. Damasippus and Stertinius are rather absurd; Crispinus, as we all know, is a figure of fun; and certainly I'm not so doctrinaire as to take those Stoic paradoxes literally. So you won't imagine, will you, that I'm *lecturing* you on your moral failings? But as you leave, you might consider whether there's anything in what these odd people have been saying. Truth, after all, is found in some unlikely quarters.

So instead of a sermon the preacher has presented a sort of comic morality-play. But the message is still there.

By now a general picture of Horace's thought should have emerged, but perhaps a few comments may be added on those aspects which are less congenial to us. In regard to 1. 2 there is no point in pretending that the discussion is conducted on a decent moral level. The arguments against adultery are almost entirely selfish, and the recommendation of the 'call-girl' takes it for granted that she will be used simply as an instrument of gratification. But before applying the censor's mark too gleefully we should remember that to a young man in his twenties, who was watching his country tearing itself to pieces and who scarcely dared to think of the future, independence seemed essential for survival. Friends were safe enough; but it was folly to think of a wife and children; and even a romantic affair might bring dangerous emotional entanglements. Sex therefore was to be treated as a recurrent need which might be satisfied with zest and gaiety so long as it involved no commitment to another person or to society at large. If this outlook seems unduly cynical it is worth recalling that in our own time, when sexual mores are in a state of ferment, many competent observers have maintained that *some* of the trouble arises from over-romantic and over-sentimental notions of what sex is about. Such notions have not always been

current. On 11 December 1762 Boswell records the observations
of Mr Macpherson:

He told me that he was very susceptible of tormenting love. But that London
was the best place in the world to cure it. 'In the country,' said he, 'we see a
beautiful woman; we conceive an idea that it would be heaven to be in her
arms. We think that impossible almost for us to attain. We sigh. We are
dejected. Whereas here we behold as fine women as ever were created. Are
we fond of one of them? For a guinea we get full enjoyment of her, and when
that is over we find that it is not so amazing a matter as we fancied. Indeed,
after a moderate share of the pleasures of London, a man has a much better
chance to make a rational unprejudiced marriage.'

Mr Macpherson's sentiments would have sounded quite normal to
Horace, though as it turned out the poet was never to make a
marriage—even of a rational unprejudiced kind.

If 1. 2 strikes us as cynical, 1. 1 may seem reactionary. It is
certainly conservative in tone—that was almost ensured by the
combination of Roman temperament, Hellenistic philosophy,
and the state of the country at the time. But we should be clear
on what the poet does and does not say. First, he is concerned with
certain misguided attitudes to money rather than with the amount
of money a man should have. He never says that poverty is a
virtue and wealth a vice, nor does he decry the ordinary business
of earning a living. What he does say (amongst other things) is
that if you spend all your time and energy *making* money, you'll
never enjoy it, and that resentment is not a good recipe for
happiness. Later, in 2. 2, he adds that if you have a large fortune
there are more useful and satisfying ways of spending it than on
food and drink. To see how inoffensive Horace really is in his
treatment of μεμψιμοιρία one may compare 1. 1 with Swift's
sermon *On The Poor Man's Contentment*. There Swift sets out to
show that the poor have many temporal blessings not enjoyed by
the rich and the rich have many temporal evils not enjoyed by
the poor. As a preliminary he excludes beggars, drunkards, and
debtors, for they mostly deserve their condition, and also the
honest destitute, for they are few in number. Taking 'the honest
industrious artificer, the meaner sort of tradesman, and the

labouring man', Swift goes on to assert that such men are healthier, sleep better, and are more assisted by their children; they incur no general hatred or envy, are untroubled by ambition, and are unworried by party squabbles. Whereas the rich are plagued by gout, dropsy, stone and cholic; they have no appetite; they cannot sleep because of their fear and vexation; and worst of all, their idleness exposes them to sin. As they stood in St Patrick's listening to the great man preach, the Dublin poor must surely have marvelled at their own good fortune.

The idea of freedom as expounded in 2. 7 also calls for comment. Epictetus, who holds the same theory, begins his essay on the subject (4. 1) with the deceptive words ἐλεύθερός ἐστιν ὁ ζῶν ὡς βούλεται[50]—'He is free who lives as he wishes'. In spite of having the air of a truism this masks a serious confusion between wishes and constraints. Suppose you have the opportunity of going on a world tour (i.e. you are not prevented by lack of money, leisure, or the necessary documents), yet you do not wish to take advantage of it, then you are *free* to go, although to you the freedom will be of little importance. If you have neither the opportunity nor the wish, you will *not* be free to go, though you will not feel any distress in consequence. In the last type of case the Stoics argued as if they had removed the constraint by removing the wish. Thus if a man was debarred from a political career on the orders of a dictator, he might in their view still be free if he eliminated his ambition.

In answer to this criticism a Stoic might say that the freedom to tour the world or campaign for office was not a *real* freedom. If you pointed out that in his ordinary speech he still *called* it a freedom, he might then assert that it was an *unimportant* freedom. This would be quite defensible, one supposes, on an individual basis. Such freedoms would not matter to one who had voluntarily restricted his wishes in those respects. But they might well matter to others, and it is here, in the broader social and political field, that the dangers of the view become apparent. Anyone who insists that certain freedoms, which other people value, are insignificant or unworthy is encouraging their suppression. And when they have been suppressed the same kind of talk will hinder their revival. From holding that freedom of the reason is the *only* freedom it is all too easy a step to say that people must be *made* free by having their undesirable impulses restrained. And so the rational freedom of the philosopher passes into the tyranny of a party, institution, or church.[51]

Yet one would still wish to maintain that rational or moral freedom was one of the most important freedoms. And that is probably all that Horace, as distinct from Crispinus, would have cared to say. He would certainly not have denied the importance of those freedoms which were guaranteed by law, and however much he may have valued character above birth he would never have claimed that the social distinctions between slave and free were trivial or unreal.

If we concede that, in spite of the more objective and dramatic form employed in Book 2, Horace's opinions are still discoverable, and that the poet is not, like Joyce's perfect artist, 'invisible, refined out of existence, indifferent, paring his fingernails', we are then faced with the question of his consistency. Luckily the problem is not too complex in our area of concern. If we were studying Horace's work as a whole we should have to ask how the inspired *vates* of the Augustan renaissance was related to the cultivated wit who shunned politics and wrote bitter-sweet lyrics on wine, friendship, and death. But in the *Satires* it will be sufficient to consider, very briefly, two or three main points.

First, Horace had a genuine respect for men of homogeneous character. He recognized their potential heroism, and could formulate the ideal in memorable terms. Thus the description of the truly free man in 2. 7 anticipates the *iustum et tenacem propositi virum* of *Carm.* 3. 3 and the famous portrait of Regulus in *Carm.* 3. 5. But he evinces no affection for such men, and it is clear that he himself was made of quite different stuff. He was a man of changing moods, sensitive to the feelings and behaviour of others, and responding quickly to the events of his world. The equilibrium which he attained came not so much from a placid temperament as from wisdom and experience, and even in his later years that equilibrium was not always stable.

As an example we may take 2. 6, a poem in which Horace thanks Maecenas for the Sabine farm, and celebrates the joys of the country by contrasting them with city life: Rome is a place of sickness and noise and frenetic bustle; there is no rest, no privacy, and one lives amid the hum of malicious gossip. The poem concludes with the story of a country mouse who was lured to Rome by his city friend and was frightened out of his life when he got there. All this suggests that Horace will never willingly set foot in the capital again. In fact, of course, he will return quite regularly; for Rome is more than smoke and corruption. As queen of cities it represents some of man's greatest achievements, and to the poet it offers fame, fellowship, and gaiety. And so one motif in Horace's life is the fruitful alternation between town and country. Sometimes, to be sure, the spiritual gyroscope breaks down, and then he becomes restless and depressed as in *Epist*. I. 8. 12:

Romae Tibur amem ventosus, Tibure Romam.

Changeable as the wind I long for Tibur when in Rome and for Rome when in Tibur.

But abnormal phases of this kind reveal the regular pattern all the more clearly.

Finally there is the matter of diet. Here we find the same kind of alternation. Its limits can be inferred from the habits of Ofellus in 2. 2 and of Catius the epicure in 2. 4, and I say 'inferred' because Horace's own habits cannot be equated with either. More will be said about Catius in the next chapter. Here I would only suggest that the satire on his 'foodmanship' reveals a lively interest and appreciation on the part of the poet. There is nothing surprising in this; for Maecenas, with whom Horace must have dined fairly often, was not renowned for his frugality. And there are several indications elsewhere that the poet could do justice to a well-cooked meal. Nevertheless, Horace's interest in food stopped well short of the obsession revealed by Catius, and, whatever he may have eaten at Maecenas' table, his normal fare, both in Rome and in the country, was of a much plainer kind.[52] We need not imagine, however, that it was quite so Spartan as the diet of Ofellus. The function of the old peasant is to show that even at that degree of simplicity it is possible to live not only a healthy life but also in some measure a pleasant one. For Ofellus is not an ascetic. He enjoys his food and is glad to allow himself extra when entertaining a guest. In these respects he is contrasted with Avidienus, who represents the extreme of joyless parsimony.

The essence of Horace's life, as of his style, will therefore be found in the idea of controlled variety. Because the limits are relatively narrow and the movement normally *is* controlled, the poet is in a position to mock the wild oscillations of Priscus and Tigellius. But he does not pretend that the control is infallible. He admits that, sometimes at least, there is a gap between his principles and his performance. And it is this faculty of wry self-criticism that makes him the most likeable of Roman moralists.

CHAPTER VII

FOOD AND DRINK

2. 4

Prometheus has always been a hero of mankind, and for a very good reason. Without his gift of fire cookery would never have been discovered, and this, after all, is what raises us above the beasts. The role of cooking in the ascent of man was well understood by the Greeks, as may be seen from the chef's remarks to his assistant in the *Samothracians* of Athenion:

C.   Do you not realise that piety
      owes most of what it is to cookery?
A.   Really?
C.   Of course, you poor barbarian!
      It turned a lawless animal into man,
      brought order, stopped our cannibalistic strife,
      and dressed us in our present mode of life.

Like all great inventions, cooking was something of a happy accident. But if we are to believe the dramatist, the first barbecue was not quite so fortuitous a discovery as Lamb's roast pig:

  When man ate man and human life was cheap,
  a clever lad once sacrificed a sheep
  and cooked the flesh; men found it more delicious
  than human chops, and ceased to relish dishes
  consisting of their kin. Liking the treat
  they henceforth roasted sacrificial meat,
  and pressing onward from that simple start
  enlarged the realm of culinary art.

As one researcher discovered sausages, and another stew, and another mincemeat, the old life began to lose its attractions:

  Because of such delights men grew soft hearted
  and disinclined to eat the dear departed.
  They said 'Let's live together!' Crowds collected
  and, thanks to cooking, cities were erected.[1]

In addition to its historic importance in effecting a gourmet's social contract, cookery had also a high place on the epistemological scale. According to Sosipater and Nicomachus it entailed a knowledge of astronomy (for how else could one tell when a dish was in season?), architecture (for kitchens had to be scientifically designed), medicine (for obvious reasons), and even strategy.[2] The strategic side of cookery brings out the connexion between culinary and verbal art. As Cicero's orator marshals his material and advances his arguments, so the chef knows exactly how the various dishes should be arranged and brought in. As Horace's dramatic poet can see the right style for a character to employ at a critical moment so the chef will size up the morale and capabilities of each guest and serve him accordingly. The same Horatian *decorum* is also an asset to the diner. In Hoffman's words: 'Avant de vous faire initier aux mystères de la gueule, consultez bien vos forces et vos dispositions naturelles, examinez sans présomption *quid valeat stomachus, quid ferre recuset.*'[3]

The technical virtuosity of these comic chefs has a sound scholarly foundation. They are acquainted with the work of their predecessors and are proudly aware of their own contributions to the great tradition. Thus a young cook in Anaxippus says:

> The chief Ionian authority
> is Sophon; he, you know Sir, tutored me.
> I am an expert too; my highest aim
> is that a standard work shall bear my name.[4]

So, too, a cook in Alexis gives a detailed recipe for one of his original creations.[5] And Euphron has a professional chef who boasts about his pupils in the accepted common-room style.[6]

This interest in gastronomy, which at times amounted to an obsession and for which I have never seen a satisfactory explanation, was not continued to anything like the same extent by Plautus and Terence. So in this case Horace's affinities to the New Comedy are largely confined to the Greek originals. As usual, however, there is no single source for his work. In trying to define the

tradition behind 2. 4 we must also take account of Archestratus
and his Roman imitators. About 330 B.C. Archestratus, a Sicilian
from Gela, wrote a poem called *Hedypatheia* or 'Gracious Living',
which described and criticized the various dishes he encountered
on a gastronomic voyage of discovery. Although it lacks the conventional invocation, it is, as Athenaeus realized,[7] essentially a
didactic poem in the manner of Hesiod and Theognis. Early on, the
writer announces his topic and the name of the recipient:

πρῶτα μὲν οὖν δώρων μεμνήσομαι ἠυκόμοιο
Δήμητρος, φίλε Μόσχε· σὺ δ'ἐν φρεσὶ βάλλεο σῇσιν.[8]

> First then, dear Moschus, will I tell the gifts
> of lovely-haired Demeter; listen carefully.

In the 350-odd lines preserved by Athenaeus we meet the various
types of recommendation and assertion that are characteristic of
the genre. Yet this is a didactic poem with a difference; for in
spite of his extensive researches the author does not take himself too seriously. He parodies his more earnest predecessors
and gives his subject a comic elevation by frequent Homeric
allusions, e.g.

> At Rhodes demand the fox-shark (that's the one
> the Syracusans call 'fat dog'), and if
> they will not sell, then seize it for yourself.
> This may mean death—who cares? Enjoy the fish,
> then brave whatever Fate may hold in store.[9]

> If you are in Ambracia's happy land
> and see a boar-fish, buy it; never fail,
> e'en though it cost its weight in gold; for else
> the terrible wrath of heaven may strike you down.[10]

Determined to put eating on a scientific basis Archestratus makes no
concessions to individual taste. His manner throughout is one
of magisterial authority. It is true that at one point, after condemn-
ing the cod of Anthedon for its unpleasant sponginess, he adds:

> And yet it holds a place of high esteem
> with some—for one likes this, another that.[11]

But we suspect that if anyone had dared to challenge him on the principle of *de gustibus* he would have retorted in the style of Morris Bishop's friend:

'Twas long ago in Boston, Mass., I knew a wise old person.
(He was an advertising man named Edward K. McPherson.)
Esthetic problems he'd resolve in words I've not forgotten.
'It's all a question of taste,' he'd say, 'and your taste
is rotten.'[12]

In Archestratus, then, we have a cheerful sensualist with an extremely erudite palate. The one thing we do not expect from him is moral criticism; after all, tirades against the cult of the belly do not come well from Michelin inspectors. But when this genre was taken over by the Romans it was inevitable that sooner or later the note of censure would be heard. We cannot be sure about Ennius' *Hedyphagetica* ('Delicatessen'), which was a translation, or imitation, of Archestratus; for Apuleius, who implies that it was a work of pure science, is not concerned to give a full account of it.[13] But when we come to Varro's περὶ ἐδεσμάτων ('On Eatables') the testimony is very much clearer. According to Aulus Gellius it contained a clever description in senarii of the eatables 'which those gormandizers (*helluones isti*) procure from land and sea'.[14] Later Gellius speaks of the foods 'which insatiable greed (*profunda ingluvies*) has tracked down and which Varro has described with disapproval (*opprobrans exsecutus est*)'. The passage ends with a few lines of the work quoted from memory.[15] The only other fragment of the περὶ ἐδεσμάτων is in prose:

si quantum operae sumpsisti ut tuus pistor bonum faceret panem, eius duodecimam philosophiae dedisses, ipse bonus iam pridem esses factus. nunc illum qui norunt, volunt emere milibus centum, te qui novit, nemo centussis.

If you had spent on philosophy a twelfth of the trouble which you have taken to ensure that your baker makes good bread, you yourself would long ago have become a good man. But now those who know your baker would gladly buy him for 100,000, while no one who knows you would give sixpence for you.[16]

This shows that Varro's work contained a dialogue between a gourmet and a moralist, and it may well be that the former, like a Roman Archestratus, recited a long list of exotic foods while the latter arraigned him in the manner of a Cynic or Stoic preacher.[17]

The Ofellus satire has already shown what Horace could do in this line. The present poem, however, is a very much subtler piece of work. The preacher gives way to the ironist, and the merits of rustic simplicity are left behind. The disquisition on eating and drinking, which is delivered second-hand by Catius, follows the order of a Roman *cena*. So one might perhaps have expected the speaker to begin by recommending a good aperitif. According to the Elder Pliny, however, this outlandish habit did not develop until the time of Tiberius; its introduction was, like many other evils, 'due to foreign ways and to the doctors' policy of continually advertising themselves by some new-fangled idea' (*NH* 14. 143). And so Catius begins with the *hors-d'œuvres* (*gustum* or *gustatio*), consisting of eggs, cabbage, various kinds of shellfish, mushrooms, and a fowl. He then unexpectedly shifts to lunch, saying that it is advisable to round off the midday meal with black mulberries, a fruit which Celsus mentions as a laxative (2. 29. 11). The digression may be due to the fact that the items just named in the *hors-d'œuvres* often figured on the luncheon menu as well. At any rate Catius immediately returns to the *gustatio*, or rather to the drink which followed it. This consisted of dry wine, or sometimes must, mixed with honey. It was called *mulsum*; hence the term *promulsis*, which was yet a third name for this part of the meal.

As possibilities for the *mensae primae*, or main course, Catius mentions boar, venison, hare and fowl. Then, giving a few tips on the preparation of Massic and Surrentine wine, he proceeds to the *mensae secundae*, which includes prawns, snails, sausages and other savouries intended for the flagging drinker. Two recipes, one simple, the other more complicated, are suggested for sauces to accompany the prawns and snails. Then the section ends with a brief discussion of apples and grapes. At this point (73) Catius mentions a couple of minor innovations for which his teacher is responsible. One is the practice of serving a certain type of raisin along with the apples; the other is the provision of *faex* and *allec* on small dishes. *Faex* is wine-lees which have been dried, roasted, and ground to powder. *Allec* can best be described in conjunction with *garum*—a delicacy which added zest to the banquet of Nasidienus (2. 8. 46). According to one recipe *garum* was made as follows: take the entrails of a tunny, along with its gills, juice and blood. Add sufficient salt. Leave it in a jar for two months at the most. Then knock a hole in the jar. What trickles out is the type of *garum* called 'blood-garum'.[18] What is left behind is *allec*.

If this recipe makes the reader uneasy, let me assure him that this was the very best *garum*. Many other grades were available, and there was even a recognized technique for freshening up stale *garum*. In any case it seems rather parochial to entertain doubts over other men's meat. The two ladies who a few years ago edited and translated Apicius' cookery book actually made some *garum*, and they insisted that 'even considerable quantities could be used without leaving an unpleasant taste'.[19] So too Pierre Grimal tells us that *garum* is still manufactured in Turkey, that it is virtually identical with the Indo-Chinese delicacy known as *nuoc-mam*, and that when you get used to it it smells no worse than Camembert.[20] In view of its popularity in Indo-China, one may predict that *nuoc-mam* or *garum* will eventually reach America, where they will probably spread it on a strawberry sundae.

After going through the dinner *ab ovo ad mala* Catius finishes with a few remarks on service. The ware should be of ample size and scrupulously clean. 'It really turns the stomach if the waiter has been handling the cup with fingers which are greasy from nibbling at stolen pickings.' And how little it costs to keep a dining-room decently tidy!

This is all straightforward enough. The critic's problem is to decide about the satire's tone. How are we supposed to take this gastronomical lecture, and what are we to think of Catius and his anonymous professor? The obvious place to start our investigation is the prologue. Horace's opening words *unde et quo Catius?* are a conventional greeting and in themselves have no special significance. But when Catius answers that he has just come from a lecture which beat anything by Pythagoras, Socrates, or Plato, then Horace's audience would almost certainly have caught the allusion to Plato's dialogues, several of which begin with a similar encounter.[21] The academic background is also conveyed by the fact that Catius is about to write notes on what the professor has been saying. Thus, as Fiske points out,[22] what follows can be classified both as ὑπομνήματα (notes to aid a student's memory) and as ἀπομνημονεύματα (recollections of what a notable personality has said). But if all this is meant to prepare us for a piece of heavenly wisdom, something has gone badly wrong; for Catius' haste (*non est mihi tempus*, etc.) is more in keeping with the comic stage than the philosophical school, and his ecstatic claims for the teacher's *praecepta* warn us of irony ahead. So we are not wholly surprised when, in response to Horace's elaborately polite request, Catius reveals this as the first of his doctrines:

> longa quibus facies ovis erit, illa memento,
> ut suci melioris et ut magis alba rotundis,
> ponere; namque marem cohibent callosa vitellum.
>
> (12–14)

Remember to serve eggs which are long in shape, for they are superior in flavour to the round, and their whites are whiter—the reason being that their shells are harder and contain a male yolk.

In the epilogue Horace resumes his tone of ironic deference, addressing Catius as *doctus* and complimenting him once again on his amazing memory. But however admirable a spokesman Catius may be, Horace is eager to hear the master in person:

> at mihi cura
> non mediocris inest, fontis ut adire remotos
> atque haurire queam vitae praecepta beatae.   (93–5)

I long for the chance to approach those secluded springs and to draw therefrom the rules for a life of blessedness.

The Lucretian parody is more complicated than in 1. 5. 101–3. First of all Horace has altered the context. In Lucretius 1. 927 ff. the *integri fontes* and the *novi flores* symbolize a new poetic theme; to render Epicureanism into poetry is a formidable task, but well worth undertaking; success will be a sign of the Muses' favour. In Horace, however, it is Catius' teacher who is the *fons*, and what issues from him is not poetry but wisdom. In other words Lucretius' poetic springs and his philosophical teacher (Epicurus) have been combined into a single metaphor. Secondly, the irony is subtler than in 1. 5, because instead of using Lucretius directly to attack a wrong-headed attitude he makes his point by pretending that Catius, Lucretius and himself are all fellow-converts.

By now it is obvious that Catius is a figure of fun. Engrossed in his new learning he seems to be quite unaware of what is happening to him. In this respect he is closer to the pest than to Trebatius; for the old lawyer has his wits about him, and in the verbal fencing of 2.1 he gives as good as he gets. But if Catius is ridiculous it does not follow that his instructions are absurd in principle or that where they are amusing they are all amusing in the same way. In particular we must beware of assuming that because a proposal sounds silly to us it must have sounded silly to a Roman. Our own certainties are irrelevant, even when true. So although we may be inclined to dismiss as nonsense what Catius says about the sex of eggs, we should bear in mind that this was a matter of genuine controversy amongst the ancients. Aristotle believed that round eggs were male and long eggs female. In this he was opposed by Antigonus of Carystus and (after Horace) by Columella and Pliny.[23] What, then, is Horace's point? Is it not that the attempt to discriminate between the male and female flavours is carrying connoisseurship a little too far, and that to enunciate this distinction as a gastronomic principle is mere pompous foolery? Again, it is quite common to kill a fowl by stifling it or wringing its neck. To drown it in wine, as Catius prescribes, is a little recondite. I am told that in modern Normandy ducks are drowned in wine and subsequently appear on the tables of certain Parisian

restaurants as *le canard au sang*. But even today the refinement is
not widely known.

In his *Natural History* Pliny says with a notable lack of dogmatism 'It seems that the best way of treating the finest Campanian
wines is to place them in the open air and to let sun, moon, rain
and wind beat upon them' (14. 136). Catius is much more precise:
'To remove the coarseness from Massic wine you should put it out
of doors *in the night air, when the weather is clear*' (51–2). This
practice, he says, will also get rid of the aroma, which is bad for the
sinews. Pliny often mentions the effect of wine on the sinews,
but he never goes so far as to suggest that the aroma by itself is
deleterious.[24] Furthermore, is it not rather odd of Catius to dis-
trust the wine's aroma, when in the next sentence he deplores the
common process of straining on the grounds that it weakens the
natural flavour?

The section ends with a hint for clearing a Surrentine which
has been fortified with Falernian lees. There is nothing abnormal
in the idea itself. Surrentine was by all accounts a thinnish, rather
dry wine, suitable for convalescents. Tiberius and Caligula both
had to take it as medicine. The former called it *generosum acetum*,
'high-quality vinegar', and the latter *nobilis vappa* (*vappa* was wine
which had gone flat).[25] Galen, as reported by Athenaeus, calls it
ἀλιπής and ψαφαρός—words usually interpreted as 'thin' and
'dry'.[26] Warner Allen takes ψαφαρός in the sense of 'powdery'
and infers that it threw a heavy sediment. He then has to believe
that Catius would make Surrentine 'even thicker with a blend
of Falernian lees'. But this seems unlikely, and even Allen admits
that 'a very old Surrentine...might seem rather flat and thin
compared to the full-bodied Falernian'.[27] In any case the satiric
point lies not in the practice of clearing but in the method which
Catius lays down. The sediment, he says, should be collected by
means of pigeons' eggs; 'for the yolk will sink to the bottom
carrying the foreign matter with it'. Most people realized that the
sediment actually clung to the white. The originality of Catius'
teacher lay in stressing the role of the yolk (which was important

only for its weight) and in specifying pigeons' eggs. Finally, the man who treats Surrentine in this way is said to be *vafer* (55)— a word which, like *sapiens* in v. 44, implies the knowing wink of a connoisseur. Many of Catius' rules reflect a pedantic fussiness which fastens on some minor detail as if it were crucial. After recommending a laxative of shellfish and sorrel, he adds that it must be taken with white Coan wine (29); in making a sauce one must use only the brine which comes from Byzantium (66). In fact Catius' head is so full of brand-names that he often sounds like a second-rate ad-man—or perhaps the hero of Mr Fleming's thrillers.

In other cases the advice seems quite balanced and straight-forward. 'Aufidius used to mix honey with strong Falernian— mistakenly, for when the veins are empty nothing which is not mild should be introduced into them.' It was a common belief that wine passed directly into the veins, and Falernian was thought to have a particularly violent effect—*nullo aeque venae excitantur*, says Pliny.[28] What we are supposed to note is how the teacher enhances his prestige by bluntly contradicting a rival authority. Again, Catius is quite sensible in his remarks about mushrooms— more sensible than Pliny.[29] But the gnomic brevity of his advice and his quasi-technical language give an impression of pedantry and conceit. This impression is strengthened by didactic clichés like *doctus eris*, *decet* and *nec satis est*, which sometimes assume a more ceremonious note, as in *memento* ('forget not') and *est operae pretium* ("'tis worth one's while'). The same effect is produced by the teacher's confident assertions about local speciali-ties (32–43,[30] 70–2), by claims which he makes for his art (it demands a mastery of detail, a wide general view, and a har-monious blend of intellect and taste), and finally by his unabashed boasting, e.g. 'The right age and the natural properties of fish and fowl were never disclosed to any researcher's palate before mine' (45–6). In this last passage it would be wrong to imagine that Horace had lost sight of the distinction between Catius and his teacher. The truth is that Catius has memorized his master's words

so thoroughly that he does not think of changing the pronouns. He
has ceased to exist as a separate person. The acolyte has surrendered
his identity.

What we have been saying about Catius and his teacher runs
counter to Lejay's interpretation at several important points.
The French scholar sees no parody in any of Catius' remarks.
To him Catius is an Italian countryman like Ofellus, with no
interest in foreign delicacies; he is opposed to wealth and extravagance, unimpressed by novelties, and genuinely concerned for
people's health. 'Malgré ses prétentions, Catius reste l'homme
simple et sans pédantisme imaginé par Horace.'[31] I have already
indicated what I regard as parody and pedantry. As for foreign
foods, they are not, admittedly, given much prominence, and
the satire is in a large measure *un éloge de l'Italie* (p. 451); but one
cannot simply brush aside Catius' insistence on Coan wine (29),
African snails (58), Byzantine brine (66) and Corycian saffron
(68). To say that Catius is unimpressed by novelties is to overlook his original discoveries. And while Catius may not be
addressing millionaires, he does take for granted a comfortable
prosperity. Let us consider the passages cited by Lejay. It is not
enough, says Catius, to buy expensive fish if you cannot prepare
a decent sauce (37–9), nor should one spend a large sum on fish
and then serve them in a dish that is too small (76–7). Brushes,
napkins and sawdust are cheap; to forget them is a disgrace (81–2).
It is inexcusable to sweep a mosaic (*lapides varios*) with a dirty
broom and to put soiled covers on Tyrian cushions. These things
require relatively little trouble and expense (83–6). This, surely,
is not a plea for the simple life but for decent standards of tidiness.
A man who urges his readers to keep clean covers on the up-
holstery of their Rovers and Pontiacs can hardly be called an
apostle of austerity.

If our view of Catius and his teacher is sound, what then is the
satirical point of vv. 76–87? Horace is certainly not indifferent to
cleanliness—if proof is wanted we need only turn to *Epist.*
I. 5. 21–4. What Catius says on this score is quite acceptable in

principle. But surely there is something a little excessive in his language. A man who calls a small dish an *immane vitium* ('an atrocious offence') and a soiled cover a *flagitium ingens* ('an absolute scandal') will have no words left for things that really matter. *Adsit regula*—let's have a scale of values.

I would contend, therefore, that Catius is ridiculous because he is the mouthpiece of someone else's ideas and because the ideas themselves are those of a pompous and over-fastidious gourmet whose obsession with food and drink is from the moralist's viewpoint basically frivolous. I do not think we are justified in going further and arguing that by making fun of Catius in this way Horace is really attacking luxury. The points made about large (silver) plates and Tyrian cushions are not strong enough to assume this kind of prominence. And the various dishes are mentioned with the zest of one who appreciated a well-cooked dinner as much as the next man. Consequently, whereas the diatribe of Ofellus shows how far Horace would go towards the asceticism of Diogenes, this satire implies (perhaps unwittingly) a limit in the direction of Aristippus.

2.8

About twelve years before this satire was written Cicero sent a letter to his friend Paetus urging him not to give up the habit of dining out.

There is nothing more appropriate to life, nothing more conducive to happy living. I am not thinking of the sensual pleasure involved but of the life and living in common and of the mental relaxation which comes above all from friendly talk. This kind of talk is at its most pleasant on convivial occasions. Here our countrymen have been wiser than the Greeks, for the Greeks call such occasions συμπόσια or σύνδειπνα, that is 'drinkings together' or 'dinings together', but we call them 'livings together' (*convivia*), because then we most truly share a common life.[32]

Since the dinner-party was virtually the sole method of private entertaining in the ancient world, it provided a background for many kinds of social activity. Guests might expect to hear singers and musicians, to watch exhibitions of dancing and acrobatics, and to enjoy the jokes of professional comedians. All these features, however, were secondary to the food and conversation. And so when, from the fourth century on, banquets became an independent literary topic, writers tended to fall into two categories—those who, like Plato and Xenophon, concentrated on what was said, and those who, like the poet Matron and the historians Hippolochus and Lynceus, concerned themselves primarily with the food and drink.[33] Although comparatively little is extant from the period before Christ, it is clear that a great deal of material existed. We know, for instance, that symposia were written by representatives of all the philosophical schools; and one later specimen by Heracleides of Tarentum was virtually a medical treatise in disguise.[34] Anyone wishing to follow the matter further may consult Hug's outline in Pauly-Wissowa, or if his stamina is equal to the task he can tackle Josef Martin's huge survey, *Symposion*.[35] The point to be made here is that none of the pre-Horatian material bears much resemblance to the dinner of Nasidienus, and certainly nothing should be regarded simply as its 'model'.

The Ἀττικὸν δεῖπνον by Matron of Pitane begins thus:

δεῖπνά μοι ἔννεπε, Μοῦσα, πολύτροφα καὶ μάλα πολλά,
ἃ Ξενοκλῆς ῥήτωρ ἐν Ἀθήναις δείπνισεν ἡμᾶς.[36]

Sing, O Muse, of the dinners sumptuous and right many, on which Xenocles the orator dined us in Athens.

The poem continues in the same vein for about 120 lines, describing how the guests encountered and dealt with a succession of dishes, which came before them like figures in a Homeric catalogue. As parody it is quite a clever piece of work, but it has no dialogue and no dramatic form; it has no satirical target, and, except for the parasite Chaerophon who is 'like a ravenous gull, empty, but well versed in dinners provided by others', it makes no attempt at characterization.

Menippus, the third-century satirist, is known to have written a *Symposium*. This fact has led to an argument which runs as follows: Lucian resembles Horace, Lucian could not have imitated Horace, Lucian is known to have imitated Menippus, therefore Horace must have imitated Menippus. If we consider only the first proposition and compare Lucian's *Symposium* (or *Lapiths*) with *Sat.* 2. 8, we shall find that Lucian's work describes a wedding-feast; the food, however, is scarcely mentioned, and the satire is directed not at the host, who behaves throughout like a gentleman, but at philosophers of various schools who squabble over places, exchange crude invective, and finally turn the whole proceedings into a bloody brawl in which the groom has his head split open and a flute girl is nearly raped. The resemblance to Nasidienus' banquet is not obvious.

Only a few fragments of Lucilius' *cenae* need concern us here. We know from Cicero, *Brut.* 160, that at least one of the satires described a dinner-party given for Crassus by the auctioneer Granius in 107 B.C. It is practically certain that the description came in Book 20 and contained the line:

> purpureo tersit tunc latas gausape mensas
>
> Then he wiped the wide tables with a crimson towel

—a line which leads at once to a comparison with *Sat.* 2. 8. 11:

> gausape purpureo mensam pertersit.
>
> He wiped the table well with a crimson towel.

On the strength of this one parallel Fiske (p. 165) refers to Lucilius' poem as 'the original of Horace's *Sat.* 2. 8'. But even if other correspondences existed, we still could not speak of anything more than a superficial likeness, because while Nasidienus, like Catius, is portrayed as a humourless ass, such a treatment would have been impossible in the case of Granius, who was renowned for his agile wit.[37] Shero, who sees this point, goes on to suggest that 'in the *cena Nasidieni* we have a *contaminatio* (i.e. a conflation) of the picture of lavish entertainment at Granius' dinner-party with a picture of meanness and bad taste in connexion with a dinner-party which occurred elsewhere in the satires of Lucilius, perhaps in Book 14'.[38] But the sordid meal described in Book 14, like that in Book 5, would only be relevant to *Sat.* 2. 8 if it could be proved that Nasidienus was guilty of meanness. This, in fact, is a widely held opinion,[39] and since the matter is of basic importance to our view of the poem we had better examine the evidence.

(*a*) Vv. 6–7. The boar, which was served cold as part of the *hors-d'œuvres*, was slightly high. This cannot have been due either to meanness or to bad cooking, for Nasidienus was *proud* of the fact and drew attention to it more than once. In his view the rather strong flavour was an added refinement, and such an idea did not seem unreasonable to Porphyrion. This does not mean, of course, that the meat was rotten. The animal was caught when a *gentle* South wind was blowing. A really strong Auster would have ruined the meat entirely—cf. *praesentes Austri, coquite horum obsonia* (2. 2. 41). Finally, boar's meat was not cheap. According to Diocletian's edict of prices it was the dearest kind of big game.[40]

(*b*) Vv. 10–11. The table was of maple-wood. 'Maple is named by Pliny, *NH* 16. 66, as an inferior material "*citro secundum*". It would seem that what is laughed at is the pretentious care of a second-rate table.' So Wickham, following an opinion which goes back to the commentator Cruquianus. But what Pliny says (in an account which deals with many types of wood and their uses) is *acer...operum elegantia ac subtilitate citro secundum*. That is, as a material for high-quality furniture maple was second *only* to citrus. One type, according to Pliny, was actually superior to citrus, but this was suitable only for small objects (16. 68).

(*c*) Vv. 14–15.
> procedit fuscus Hydaspes
> Caecuba vina ferens, Alcon Chium maris expers.

Dark Hydaspes entered with Caecuban wine, Alcon with Chian unmixed with sea-water.

Our attention centres on *maris expers*. Why was the Chian unmixed with sea-water?[41] Since Greek wines were frequently salted, some scholars have believed that Nasidienus intended to make his Chian less drinkable. But this would be strange behaviour in a man who served his Caecuban 'straight'—for Caecuban too was a wine of first-rate quality. Moreover it has been pointed out that according to Galen, who was writing in the second century A.D., some of the finest wines (including one from Chios) were left without salt.[42] In the first century A.D. Columella states that the best wines require no preservative (12. 19. 2). We may therefore picture Nasidienus as a member of a self-conscious *avant-garde* who preferred to drink their Chian unsalted. Warner Allen observes that the legitimacy of salting has also been debated in modern times.[43]

(*d*) Vv. 16–17. Nasidienus now turns to Maecenas and says 'If you like Alban or Falernian better than what is before you, we have both'. Since Pliny (*NH* 14. 62) rates Alban and Falernian below Caecuban, the host is probably implying something like this: 'I have served what I regard as the very best; but if you prefer Alban or Falernian, which are admittedly respectable, I can provide them also.' If Nasidienus had served all four wines (including Chian), he might have appeared less of a connoisseur; if he had served only two and left it at that, his resources and his knowledge might have seemed less comprehensive. The result was a clumsy compromise, but the chief point has been successfully made—namely that Nasidienus' cellar is equal to all demands. 'You name it, we got it.' Such behaviour is not mean, whatever else it may be.

(*e*) V. 18. Horace greets this account, which is given by his friend Fundanius, with the exclamation *divitias miseras!*—'Ah, the miseries of wealth!' There has been much dispute about this phrase, but it certainly need not imply stinginess on Nasidienus' part. Probably it is just a vague expression referring sarcastically to his foolish ostentation. If, however, we want to examine it more closely, we may start from the remark of Ofellus in 2. 2. 65–6:

> mundus erit qua non offendat sordibus, atque
> in neutram partem cultus miser

> (The wise man) will be stylish enough to avoid giving offence through meanness, and in his way of living he will not be unhappy in either direction (i.e. towards meanness *or* extravagance).

When a man's conduct misses or exceeds the appropriate mean he fails to achieve happiness and becomes to that extent *miser*. He may be unaware of this himself; he may not *feel* unhappy. But the fact that others view him with dislike or contempt is an index of his true condition. 'So-and-so's a miserable character', we say. By a slight extension the adjective can then be applied to the cause of the man's condition, as in *misera ambitione* (1. 4. 26). In Nasidienus' case it is lavish ostentation which makes him an object of ridicule; hence riches are *miserae* 'unhappy'—a striking way to speak of something which is supposed to make a man *beatus*. And one remembers that in the first line Nasidienus *is* called *beatus*.

(*f*) Vv. 25 ff.

If anything happened to escape our notice, Nomentanus was there to point it out with his forefinger; for the uninitiated, that is we ourselves, were dining off fowl, shell-fish, and fish, which contained flavours quite unlike the usual ones. This became clear right at the beginning when Nomentanus passed me the inwards of a plaice and turbot which no one had previously tasted (*ingustata*).

By *ingustata* Fundanius means that during the meal no one had yet tasted this particular preparation; he was the first to discover its surprising flavour. That, at any rate, is how I take the word; the more common view that *ingustata* means 'which I had never tasted in my life' conflicts with the only natural interpretation of *dissimilem noto* (28). But whatever one's opinion on this point, the fact remains that the startling effect of all these creations was intentional. The chef had not bungled the job, as Palmer thinks; he had merely given proof of the talent which had earned him his post—namely his perverse ingenuity.

In reading this passage one thinks of the elaborate artifice encouraged by Trimalchio, but it would perhaps be a mistake to imagine that such tricks were confined to the tables of rich parvenus. Apicius has a recipe for Patina of Anchovy without Anchovy, consisting of minced fish, pepper, rue, liquamen, eggs, oil and jellyfish. 'Serve with ground pepper', he says, adding with a craftsman's pride *ad mensam nemo agnoscet quid manducet*— 'at table no one will recognize what he is eating'.[44] The various sauces had much the same effect. One is reminded of Henry Thrale's remark to Johnson in Paris in 1775: 'The cooking of the French was forced on them by necessity, for they could not eat their meat unless they added some taste to it.' Thackeray held a similar view:

> Dear Lucy, you know what my wish is—
> I hate all your Frenchified fuss:
> Your silly entrées and made dishes
> Were never intended for us.

It is, of course, a perennial British conviction that the French cuisine is a technique of meretricious concealment. That is why, when Horace pleads for some recognition of nature, he is hailed as a genuine beef-eating Englishman.

(*g*) In vv. 35 ff. one of the company, who is anxious to begin some serious drinking, calls for larger cups; whereupon Nasidienus turns pale—a sign which editors at once attribute to his stinginess, ignoring the fact that Fundanius himself gives two quite different explanations. Nasidienus, he says, foresaw an outbreak of ill-mannered abuse or else was apprehensive in case too much strong wine would dull the palate and so stultify his chef's art. Both fears were perfectly reasonable. Why invent others?

(*h*) Vv. 90 ff.

> tum pectore adusto
> vidimus et merulas poni et sine clune palumbes

> Then we saw blackbirds with crisped breasts laid before us and pigeons without their rumps.

According to Palmer the blackbirds were not crisped but burnt—a theory refuted by the very next line:

> suavis res, si non causas narraret eorum et
> naturas dominus.

> These were real delicacies, if only the host had not kept recounting their underlying causes and their natural properties.

As we have seen in the case of Tigellius, Priscus and others, Horace was very much alive to inconsistencies of character. If he had intended Nasidienus to appear both mean and extravagant he would surely have exhibited the contrast in bold colours.

It will be inferred from all this that in his attitude to food and drink Nasidienus stands very close to Catius. The lamprey served in the main course was pregnant when caught; after spawning, its flesh would have been inferior (44). The gourmet eats only the wings of a hare (cf. 2. 4. 44); the crane provided is a male bird, and the goose's liver comes from a female; the pigeons are served without the rump. The last three items all indicate refinements on the usual practice. Nasidienus is also a pedant. His lecture on fish sauce, which occupies the central position in the poem, has much in common with the recipes given by Catius. He is aware of other work done in the field (52) and has made contributions of his own. All these affectations are treated by Horace with grandiose irony. Asking Fundanius to describe the party he says:

> da, si grave non est,
> quae prima iratum ventrem placaverit esca.

> Tell me, if it is not too much trouble, what dish first appeased your raging belly.

The appeasement of wrath is Homeric, the *da* parodies an epic invocation, and *prima* reflects the traditional desire to hear a tale from the start.[45] Later, when all his plans seem about to be wrecked by his guests' intemperance, Nasidienus turns pale in the time-honoured epic manner:

> vertere pallor
> tum parochi faciem.[46]

So too, the host's reappearance in v. 84 is hailed with a solemn apostrophe:

> Nasidiene redis, mutatae frontis

> Nasidienus, thou dost return with altered countenance.

In all these points, as well as in its Platonic preamble, 2. 8 resembles 2. 4. But its dramatic form makes the *cena Nasidieni* a much more interesting poem. Whereas Catius is a mouthpiece and his teacher a disembodied voice, Nasidienus emerges from the background of the *cena* as a distinct personality. The fact that the dinner began at noon instead of at three o'clock already tells us something about him; so does the fact that his waiters were dressed like chorus-girls and were trained to move like priests in a procession. We are told that he assigned his own place to his client Nomentanus with instructions to keep Maecenas informed about what he was eating—perhaps a wise precaution, for instead of offering one or two special dishes Nasidienus was determined that every course should be a sensation. Unfortunately, in his anxiety to impress his distinguished guests he overlooked the fact that Maecenas and his friends had other conversational resources besides food and drink, and that they would not appreciate being reduced to what Lucilius had described as so many 'bellies'.[47]

Our picture of Nasidienus is further illuminated by the collapse of the awning. The episode is described with a fine epic simile:

> interea suspensa gravis aulaea ruinas
> in patinam fecere, trahentia pulveris atri
> quantum non Aquilo Campanis excitat agris.
>
> (54–6)

Meanwhile the awning spread above fell with a mighty crash upon the platter, dragging with it more black dust than the North wind raises on Campanian fields.

When the guests lifted their heads they found the feast in ruins and the host sobbing like a bereaved father.[48] The great god Bathos had taken his revenge. At this point Nasidienus' vanity and his utter lack of humour are cruelly exposed. 'What a shame!' cries Balatro. 'To think of all the trouble you took over the bread and the sauce and the waiters' uniforms! And then look what happens. The canopy goes and falls down. But after all, a host is like a general; adversity shows his mettle, success conceals it.' It is all the most patent ridicule, but Nasidienus is too stupid to see it. 'God bless you!' he exclaims. 'You're a fine fellow, and

it's a pleasure to have you as a guest.' With that he calls for his
shoes (another neat touch) and disappears into the kitchen.

Nasidienus is therefore wholly credible as a character. But he is
more than a character. He stands for a type common enough in
Horace's day, a type which always appears when wealth is acquired
without either education or a social conscience. Hence as a piece
of social criticism *Sat.* 2. 8 has a wide field of reference. It might
be urged that with all his silliness Nasidienus deserves sympathy,
and that, like his distant descendant Jay Gatsby, he is basically
pathetic in his quest for recognition and esteem. I doubt, however,
if Horace saw him that way. In this, as in most other matters, we
are more sensitive than the Romans, and we must avoid reading
our own preconceptions into an ancient text. At the end of this
satire Fundanius, Maecenas and the others rush out of the house
leaving the latter part of the meal untouched. Structurally it is the
weakest ending in the book, and (however fictitious in content)
it puts the guests in an exceedingly poor light—to our way of
thinking. But this cannot have been Horace's intention, for the
piece, like 1. 9, was written for the entertainment of these very
people. He must have seen their departure as a dramatic gesture
which paid the host back for his absurd and vulgar display.

If, after this, we wish to remind ourselves of the relative gentle-
ness and good humour of 2. 8 we need only compare it with the
fifth satire of Juvenal. In both poems the scene is recounted by a
guest, but whereas the *cena Nasidieni* is described by a man whom
the host was honoured to entertain, Virro's dinner-parties are
seen through the eyes of a despised client. Granted, there are clients
at Nasidienus' table too, but they are not humiliated as they are in
Juvenal; in fact it is they who make a fool of the host. As for
Nasidienus himself, in spite of his vanity and his naked ambition,
he does try to please his guests and he treats them all, including
Porcius and Nomentanus, with the same consideration. Consequently, when set beside the appalling Virro, he appears quite a
tolerable human being. At every course Virro's clients receive
inferior food, served by ugly and contemptuous waiters. Even

the water is different. And always there is the threat of violence. These indignities are recounted with a bitter resentment and a hyperbolical wit quite alien to Horace's temper. One example must suffice. In 2. 8. 31–3 the apples reveal Nasidienus' astonishing expertise, for according to Nomentanus they owe their rich red glow to the fact that they were picked by the light of a waning moon. In Juvenal the apples illustrate Virro's calculating cruelty; for the host eats apples like those of Phaeacia or the Hesperides, while his clients are given the sort of rotten object that is gnawed by a performing monkey (149–55). The violence of Juvenal's contrast, with its sardonic use of legend and its squalid realism, is wholly characteristic. It is also fair to see a symbolic correspondence between the frightened, miserable monkey and the downtrodden client. Juvenal makes it clear that Virro's behaviour is due solely to malice. His object is to degrade his dependants while enjoying his own sense of power. And there is, says Juvenal, a certain grim justice in it all; for if you can endure such treatment then you don't *deserve* to be free.

CHAPTER VIII

A CONSULTATION

2. 5

Viewed as a social document this satire has something in common
with 1. 6. As the earlier poem reflects the decline of the old caste
system, 2. 5 arises from the disintegration of family life. The old
custom had been that a girl should marry early (twelve was the
minimum age), and that she should then devote her life to manag-
ing the household and bringing up her numerous children. Since
marriage represented an alliance between two houses with the
primary purpose of producing children who would perpetuate
the name, prestige, and property of the family, no one thought
of demanding that there should be a romantic affection between
the two partners. In all likelihood the girl would be betrothed
without her consent; and although consent was supposed to be necessary before the marriage took place, it is clear that in many cases
this amounted to no more than a passive acceptance of the
father's decision.[1]

One cannot easily account for the decay of this highly organized system; but it must have been partly due to factors which
have been operating in our own society during the last hundred
years. While their husbands were away, fighting wars from which
many would never return, the womenfolk had to face greater
responsibilities at home, and these responsibilities helped to en-
gender a spirit of independence. At the same time the proceeds
of empire brought larger and more luxurious houses, with a
ready supply of cheap labour. While a suffragette movement
would have been out of the question, there is evidence that by
the first century B.C. women were wielding an unofficial, but by
no means negligible, influence in political affairs.[2] The social
effects of their growing independence were wider still. The old

manus marriage, which brought the wife and her property under the husband's control, fell into disuse. Most women now contracted free marriages in which they retained ownership of their property and were not legally dependent on their husbands for financial support. Freedom within marriage resulted in a higher divorce rate, and at the same time the birth rate began to fall. The liberalization of divorce was almost certainly easier for the Romans than it has been for us. In our experience it has involved the extension of grounds, the simplification of procedure, and the reduction of costs. Time has also been required for people to modify their religious objections. For the Romans, on the other hand, divorce could be effected by a simple formula based on the wish of either party.

In view of the usual pious moralizing on Rome's falling birth rate, it is refreshing to find Fritz Schulz asserting that 'the true cause of the decline was not debauchery, not a general aversion to marriage, not a mysterious decline in the reproductive capacity of the Roman population, not race-mixture, and least of all the liberal law of marriage. The main cause was Roman *humanitas*. It led to drastic birth-control, i.e. to one- or two-child families, which, owing to the state of medicine and hygiene, was glaringly insufficient for the replacement of the population.'[3] This emphasis on *humanitas*, by which Schulz means the acceptance of a woman as a person in her own right, is wholly welcome, though one wonders what this 'drastic birth-control' may have meant in terms of abortion and infanticide. It may be, however, that the violence and insecurity of these years had as much to do with the falling birth rate as anything else.

Aversion to marriage must also be reckoned as a contributory cause. Celibacy, after all, had many advantages. When combined with wealth, it offered not only the various freedoms which it offers today; it also brought a certain kind of social esteem. As he carried out the ceremonial duties of the day, receiving greetings, appearing in court, witnessing documents, attending recitations, and so on, the rich bachelor could be sure of company. He also knew that this company would become more numerous, more attentive, and more deferential as the years went by. It was generally recognized that personal services merited something in return, and even people whose motives were not wholly mercenary would expect some friendly acknowledgement in the rich man's will. Parting gestures of this kind became so normal that silence was tantamount to insult. And so the will itself came to be regarded both as a final judgement on the deceased's friends and as a mirror of his social life.[4]

In view of all this it might be assumed that the *captator*, or legacy-hunter, would confine his attentions to rich bachelors. But two passages in 2. 5 indicate that this was not always the case. In vv. 45–50 the *captator* is told that if the rich man has a delicate son he should contrive to be named second heir; then, if anything happens to the boy he can step into his place. In vv. 27–31 Tiresias says that in a legal action a childless rascal should always be supported against a man who has at home a son or a fertile wife—which suggests that children, not wives, were the *captator*'s chief enemy. It may now be asked why a rich, childless husband, if wooed by a legacy-hunter, could not exploit the odious creature for all he was worth and then cheat him in the end by leaving everything to his wife. It must be remembered that a wife was not legally part of her husband's family. Her property remained separate, except for her dowry, which could be used by the husband during the marriage but which reverted to her on his death. Now admittedly a man was not obliged to choose an heir from among his own immediate kin. He could appoint someone else, but if he belonged to the 'top income bracket' he was forbidden by the *Lex Voconia* of 169 B.C. to institute his wife *heres*.[5] By *heres* the Romans meant a person who would assume the rights and duties of the deceased, which included settling the dead man's debts and paying the *legata*, or bequests, decreed in the will. In former times this system was open to abuse, because the testator might assign so many *legata* to his friends that little or nothing remained for the heir. But in 40 B.C. (that is, ten years before the writing of 2. 5) the *Lex Falcidia* enacted that if legacies exceeded three-quarters of the total, they should be cut down *pro rata*. Thus the heir, after paying out his various dues, could be sure of at least a quarter of the estate. To the *captator* this meant that even if the wife received a substantial legacy he himself might still hope for a handsome profit.

The seriousness of this whole situation was recognized by Augustus, and eventually, about 18 B.C., he tried to cope with it by legislation.[6] Under the terms of the *Lex Iulia de maritandis ordinibus* (later modified in A.D. 9 by the *Lex Papia Poppaea*) the inheritance rights of *orbi*, that is childless men, were curtailed, and fatherhood was encouraged by certain privileges in public life. Marriage was made easier by limiting the parents' veto and by allowing men outside the senatorial class to marry freedwomen. At the same time, by the *Lex Iulia de adulteriis coercendis*, an effort was made to safeguard the purity of family life. Whatever success they may have had in other respects these laws did little to check the disease of legacy-hunting. In fact, to judge from numerous passages in Tacitus, Seneca, Petronius, Pliny and Martial, the practice actually increased in the century following Horace's satire.[7] The advantages of childlessness became so impressive that 'some men pretended to hate their sons, and disowned them, thus depriving themselves of parenthood'.[8] Other *orbi* avoided the official penalties as follows: 'When elections were drawing near or when provinces were to be assigned, they would acquire sons by fake adoptions; and then, as soon as they had received their praetorships and provinces by lot among the other fathers, they immediately emancipated those whom they had adopted.'[9] These and similar passages are cited in the social histories of Friedländer and Dill.[10]

Here, however, we are concerned with the problem as treated by Horace. The poem opens as follows:

> hoc quoque, Tiresia, praeter narrata petenti
> responde, quibus amissas reparare queam res
> artibus atque modis.

> Answer me this question too, Tiresias, in addition to what you've told me. By what ways and means can I recover my lost wealth?

The reader has come unawares upon a private conversation and remains to eavesdrop. Before the voice stops speaking he knows he is present at a famous Homeric scene which has been familiar to civilized men for over two thousand years. What exactly has gone before? Ulysses, on Circe's instructions, has come to visit Tiresias in the land of the dead to obtain information about his voyage home. Tiresias has warned him that if he harms the cattle of the sun he will face disaster:

I foresee ruin for your ship and your companions; even if you yourself escape, you will return late, on board a foreign ship and in a miserable plight, having lost all your companions. And you will find trouble in your house, for arrogant men are consuming your resources and courting your noble wife with suitors' gifts. (*Od.* ii. 112–17)

After the prophet's speech, which predicts many other things, including Ulysses' death, the hero answers 'No doubt, Tiresias, the gods themselves have spun these threads; but come, tell me this as well, and tell me true...' (139–40). Here, I think, is the point at which Horace takes up the dialogue; for his opening line corresponds closely with this request, and he is not at all concerned with what follows, i.e. with the question of how the spirit of Ulysses' mother can be enabled to recognize her son.

So the scene is a heroic one. But already a disquieting note has entered, because in a Horatian context the acquisition of *res*— even of *res* which have been lost—is something irredeemably squalid. So, too, by even listening to such a request, Tiresias is in danger of compromising himself. At first he is sarcastically non-committal. 'Well well! Is it not enough for the man of many wiles to reach Ithaca and to see the gods of his ancestral hearth?' But soon he accepts his new role. 'Since, not to mince words, poverty is what you're afraid of, here's the way to get rich...' He then proceeds to instruct Ulysses in the art of legacy-hunting. This is what has become of the prophet whom Sophocles called 'the divine man in whom alone truth is implanted' (*OT* 298–9).

After advising Ulysses to concentrate on wheedling a legacy out of some rich old man, Tiresias continues:

qui quamvis periurus erit, sine gente, cruentus
sanguine fraterno, fugitivus, ne tamen illi
tu comes exterior si postulet ire recuses.   (15–17)

He may be a liar and a man of no family, a runaway slave, stained
with his brother's blood; nevertheless, if he asks you to accompany
him, be sure to walk politely on his outside.

Ulysses' reaction is instructive:

utne tegam spurco Damae latus? haud ita Troiae
me gessi certans semper melioribus.

What? Am I to give the position of honour to filthy Dama? I did not
comport myself thus at Troy, where I always strove with my peers.

In other words a liar and a murderer may pass, but to show respect
to a social inferior—that is a different matter. Such humiliations
were never dreamed of 'far on the ringing plains of windy Troy'.
Tiresias shrugs and makes to turn away. 'Very well, in that case
you'll be a pauper.' That is the one unbearable thought. With an
immense effort Ulysses conquers his repugnance. If dancing
attendance on a menial is the price of prosperity, well, then it
must be paid: fortem hoc animum tolerare iubebo;
et quondam maiora tuli.[11]

I shall bid my heart to be brave and endure this. I have borne even
greater ills before today.

After removing this scruple Tiresias proceeds to develop his theme.
    The rhythm of the poem is now clear. It consists of a satiric
interaction between the speaker's Homeric background and the
context in which the poet is writing. After a long passage on the
techniques of legacy-hunting, which is purely Roman in character,
the Homeric background is in danger of being forgotten; so at a
point half way through the poem Horace reaffirms the speaker's
identity in a piece of oracular bombast:

plerumque recoctus
scriba ex quinqueviro corvum deludet hiantem,
captatorque dabit risus Nasica Corano.   (55–7)

More than once will a raven with open beak be outwitted by a civil servant cooked up out of a police official. And Coranus will have the laugh over Nasica the fortune-hunter.

'Are you raving?' asks Ulysses, reasonably enough. 'Or are you deliberately teasing me?' 'Son of Laertes,' comes the answer, 'whatever I say will or will not come to pass, for mighty Apollo has granted me the gift of second sight.' Ulysses is in no mood to notice that this proud boast may easily be an absurd tautology. Instead he presses for information about Nasica and Coranus, and Tiresias' answer (62 ff.) takes us forward again to first-century Rome in the period immediately following Actium.

> tempore quo iuvenis Parthis horrendus, ab alto
> demissum genus Aenea, tellure marique
> magnus erit, forti nubet procera Corano
> filia Nasicae metuentis reddere soldum.

In the day when a young hero, the scourge of the Parthians, born of Aeneas' noble line, shall rule over land and sea, the gallant Coranus shall take in marriage the queenly daughter of Nasica who hates to pay his debts in full.

'In the day when...' This solemn formula, which is derived from the Delphic oracle,[12] puts us in mind of a later parallel:

> cum iam semianimum laceraret Flavius orbem
> ultimus et calvo serviret Roma Neroni.[13]

At the time when the last of the Flavians was tearing at a world already half dead, and Rome was in bondage to a bald Nero.

These two passages, the one humorous but basically respectful, the other acid and resentful, epitomize the contrast between Horace and Juvenal in their attitudes to their respective sovereigns.

But what of the story? Well, Nasica placed great hopes in the marriage of his daughter. His son-in-law Coranus was rich and encouragingly decrepit, while he himself had some very tiresome debts. When the wedding was over, Coranus offered to show him the will. After a few token refusals Nasica took it in his hands and read to his dismay that neither he nor his daughter had been left a penny. That is the prophecy of Tiresias. As a glimpse of the new age it provides an interesting contrast with another vision of Rome from beyond the grave, which was soon to take shape in the mind of the poet's friend.

After a few more verses of purely Roman material we are again reminded of the Homeric setting:

> scortator erit: cave te roget; ultro
> Penelopam facilis potiori trade.   (75–6)

Suppose he is a lecher. Don't wait to be asked; Do the decent thing and hand over Penelope voluntarily to your successful rival.

Ulysses is astounded at the very idea:
>   putasne,
> perduci poterit tam frugi tamque pudica,
> quam nequiere proci recto depellere cursu?[14]

What? Do you think she can be seduced, a lady so proper and so virtuous, whom the suitors have been unable to tempt from the strait and narrow path?

Astounded rather than shocked. As Madame Dacier points out, with feline acumen, 'Ulysse ne marque pas la moindre répugnance, et toute son inquiétude est que sa femme ne se rende trop difficile'.[15] Tiresias disposes of his doubts: The suitors have failed simply because their price was not right; in fact 'they were less interested in sexual conquest than in the palace cooking. That's why Penelope is virtuous.' We are moving towards that beautifully simple view of womanhood which Ovid summed up for all time: casta est quam nemo rogavit.[16] It is a proposition which half the male world would like to be true and the other half actually believes.

In all these manœuvres, however, Tiresias has a nice sense of proportion. He is, after all, a Horatian Tiresias. The captator, he says, must not appear over-eager, or else all may be lost. That is the point of his next story, which is set in his native Thebes:

In Thebes an outrageous old woman was buried as follows in accordance with the terms of her will: her body was thoroughly soaked in oil; then it was carried out on the bare shoulders of her heir. No doubt she hoped to slip out of his clutches after her death—presumably because he had pressed her too hard when she was alive.

Except for the mention of Ulysses' name in v. 100, that is the last Greek reference until the closing words:

> sed me
> imperiosa trahit Proserpina; vive valeque.
>
> But stern Persephone calls me back—*Lebe wohl!*

With these words Tiresias breaks off the interview and returns into the darkness to walk among the lowest of the dead.

The Greek background is, of course, no more than a witty pretence. The poem is firmly rooted in the social life of Rome. Thus Ulysses is returning to his *Penates* (4). To become rich, however, he must pay more respect to his quarry than to his *Lar* (14). He will undertake litigation in the *forum* (27), becoming the rich man's *cognitor* (38). The rich man himself may be called Quintus or Publius (32). The *captator*'s persistence is conveyed by a parody of a Roman poet (41). And so on. The Roman sections have a design of their own. Up to v. 44 (i.e. for about the first half of the poem) the emphasis falls on the *captator*'s persistence and audacity. After this Tiresias is more concerned with the need for subtlety and caution. The two sections are drawn together by the theme of flattery, which runs through the satire like a thread of gilt.[17]

The instruction in *captatio* contains some of the poet's most brilliant writing. Two features may suffice by way of illustration. The first is his use of the central metaphor, which is taken from hunting (whether it be fish, flesh, or fowl). 'If a thrush or some other delicacy is given to you for your own use, let it fly away to the glitter of a great household where the master is aged' (10–12). On its first appearance the metaphor has already been given an ironic twist, because the bird which the old man will receive is in fact only a lure. Such a ruse will suit the *dolosus Ulixes*; for is not *dolosus* connected with δέλεαρ, the Greek for bait?

In 23 ff. the metaphor changes to fishing. 'You must fish cunningly for old men's wills wherever possible. If one or two are clever enough to nibble the bait off the hook and so escape your clutches, don't give up hope, and don't abandon your craft because of an occasional disappointment.' In this, as in other fields, nothing succeeds like success. By being attentive to one or two the *captator* will attract the notice of others. 'More tunnies will come swimming up', and his fish-ponds will grow (44).

Then the metaphor alters again. 'If there is a danger of exposing yourself by paying open respect to a bachelor, find a man who is bringing up a delicate son in affluent circumstances, and then by your constant services creep slowly towards your goal.' The verb *adrepe* and the idea of cover suggest that Horace has in mind the stalking of game. Then in vv. 55–6 birds come to the fore again as Tiresias predicts that 'more than once a raven with open beak will be outwitted by a civil servant cooked up out of a police official'. This is sometimes supposed to refer to the fable of the raven who was flattered by the fox into dropping a piece of cheese. But the parallel is far from clear, and it is wiser with Heinze and others to regard the raven as simply a creature that feeds on carrion.[18] This represents another variation in the metaphor, because now the bird is itself the predator.

The second stylistic feature is the lively use of colloquial expressions. 'Breeding and character without assets are *vilior alga*— more worthless than seaweed.'[19] Tell me, says Ulysses, how I can rake together 'piles of cash'—*aeris acervos*. The *captator* will not allow his prey to be cheated of even a nut-shell, *cassa nuce*, and he advises him to go off home and 'look after his precious skin'— *pelliculam curare*. To have oneself named second heir is 'a gambit that rarely fails'—*perraro haec alea fallit*. Once Penelope gets a taste of cash there'll be no holding her; 'she'll be like a bitch which cannot be kept away from a greasy hide'—*ut canis a corio numquam absterrebitur uncto*.[20] The fawning *captator* is told to 'keep on blowing and inflate the old balloon with windy compliments', at which point the poor dupe has ceased to be even a sentient creature.

The satire's wit, however, defies all simple categories. What of the art whereby *honores* (13) anticipates *venerabilior* in the next line, and *sparge* (103) prepares us for *illacrimare*? What of the secondary meaning in *carum caput* (94)? (One is reminded of the fashionable physician in Cronin's *The Citadel*, who after sounding a rich old lady with his stethoscope turns to his friend and murmurs 'My dear fellow, that's an absolute treasure-chest!') And what of those expressions which resist translation because they embody the unique power of the Latin language, e.g. *ante Larem gustet venerabilior Lare dives* (14), or *laudes, lauderis ut absens* (72)? These are the marks of a master craftsman.

Finally, amid the parodies of Homer, Furius and the Delphic oracle, amid all the legal niceties and the technical rules, notice how a single theme is brought to its conclusion. In v. 18 a horrified Ulysses says 'What? Am I to walk politely on the outside of filthy Dama?' In v. 101 he is to sob 'Ah well well! So my old friend Dama is no more!' That is the lesson to be learned. And it does not end with Dama's death. 'If one of your co-heirs is getting on in years and has a churchyard cough, tell him that if he'd like to buy an estate or a town house which is part of your share, you'll let him have it for a song.' Fishing, after all, like cricket, is a way of life.

Scholars more interested in the history of ideas than in literary appreciation have sometimes suggested that this satire was written as a protest against the early Cynic and Stoic practice of idealizing Ulysses. Antisthenes, writing in the late fifth century, had commended the hero for his endurance, his self-sufficiency and his loyalty to a common cause.[21] A hundred years later the Stoic Zeno read the *Odyssey* as a record of the good man's triumphs over hardship and temptation. Traces of this moralizing approach, which sometimes developed into allegory, may be seen in Horace (*Epist.* I. 2), Plutarch, Seneca, Marcus Aurelius, and various Christian authors.[22] Now there is good evidence that some of the later Cynics reacted against this roseate conception of Ulysses' character. Crates pointed out that the figure so admired by

Antisthenes had no real existence in Homer's work. So far from being the tight-lipped man of adamant, Ulysses had in fact shown himself lazy, sensual, and inconsiderate; to represent him as the father of Cynicism was a grotesque perversion of the truth.[23]

But this philosophical controversy, though interesting in itself, has very little to do with the poem we are studying; because Horace was not seriously concerned with Homer's character at all. The Ulysses of 2. 5 is a comic abstraction, designed as an instrument of social satire. And the target of that satire is legacy-hunting. In the same way (and it is strange how often this is forgotten) the Ulysses who appears in *Epist.* 1. 2 as an example of *virtus* and *sapientia* is an abstraction designed to meet the purpose of a moral epistle. It is needless condescension on our part to imagine that Horace's real view of the Homeric Ulysses differed in any essential feature from our own. And indeed the two abstractions just mentioned, when set side by side, point to a lively awareness of that ambiguity in the hero's character which Stanford has so fruitfully explored.

There are other, more general, reasons against limiting the satire's scope. For centuries men had amused themselves by writing parodies of Homer. One early specimen was *The Battle of Frogs and Mice*, a skit on those bloody and over-numerous engagements in the *Iliad*.[24] Another, of which we have only fragmentary information, was the tale of Margites, a character 'who knew many things but knew them all badly'. One of the things he knew badly may be inferred from the fact that he was afraid to sleep with his wife for fear she would complain about him to her mother.[25]

Homer's characters were no more immune than his language. From early times his gods and heroes were guyed in both comedy and satyr drama, and Ulysses was a favourite target. After surveying the extensive though fragmentary evidence E. D. Phillips remarks 'His cleverness and cunning, his odd adventures, his familiarity with all kinds of people, his ready tongue and many disguises, and the strain of rascality in him which from time to time delights Athena in the *Odyssey*, all contribute to make him by far the most suitable for comedy of the great heroes of epic and legend'.[26] The same kind of irreverence, which is quite compatible with genuine respect, found expression in art. A well-known example, involving Ulysses, is the so-called Dolon crater. This Italian red-figure vase of the late fifth century, now in the British Museum, shows Ulysses and Diomedes about to pounce on Dolon as the spy tip-toes gingerly through the wood. As Pfuhl remarks, the exaggeration is slightly comic but not to the point of caricature.[27] A much coarser type of humour is represented by a Boeotian black-figure vase of the fourth century, now in Oxford. On one side it shows Ulysses being driven across the sea by the blasts of Boreas, and on the other threatening Circe with drawn sword as she proffers him the magic cup.[28]

In Roman literature aspects of the Ulysses theme had been handled long before Horace's time. Lucilius in his seventeenth book showed Penelope in conversation with a servant or a suitor. The latter says:

> nupturum te nupta negas, quod vivere Ulixen
> speras.[29]

Married as you are, you insist that you will not get married because you hope that Ulysses is still alive.

The same poem contained some very plain speaking on the subject of Greek heroines; if the truth were known, all of them had some unfortunate blemish.[30] More recently Varro had written a piece called Sesculixes—'Ulysses and a half'—which, to judge from its title, treated the hero in an ironical vein. A certain amount of calculated silliness may be discerned in the longest fragment extant, in which Ulysses, speaking of the winds, says 'But if they continue any longer to stir up the sea, I am afraid that when I come back home from Troy no one will recognize me except my dog'.[31]

A favourite form of burlesque was a visit to Hades, based sometimes on the eleventh book of the *Odyssey*, sometimes on other descents such as those of Orpheus and Heracles.[32] The most famous example, of course, is the *Frogs* of Aristophanes, in which

Dionysus sets off to fetch Euripides from the underworld in the hope of reviving tragic drama. But while Horace had certainly read Aristophanes, there were other writers whose purpose was closer to his own. Timon of Phlius, a Sceptic writing in the third century, composed three books of *silloi* or lampoons directed against rival philosophers. 'Book one', says Diogenes Laertius, 'is written in the first person. Books two and three are in dialogue form. Timon represents himself as questioning Xenophanes of Colophon about each philosopher in turn, while Xenophanes answers him.'[33] So here we have an interview like *Sat.* 2. 5; an interview, moreover, which is conducted in the underworld and written in the style of a Homeric parody. With Menippus of Gadara (also writing in the third century) we come a step nearer still, for we know that he wrote a *Nekyia*, which probably included, like Timon's, an attack on contemporary philosophers.[34] Four hundred years later Lucian acknowledged his debt to Menippus by making him one of the chief speakers in his *Dialogues of the Dead*, and by using his name to designate two other works—*Icaromenippus*, in which Menippus flies up to consult Zeus, and *Menippus*, in which he descends to Hades to interview Tiresias.[35] Menippus' interest in supernatural fantasy may be further attested by Varro's περὶ ἐξαγωγῆς. This work, which was one of his *Menippeans*, seems to have described a conversation with certain spirits of the dead on the subject of suicide.[36] Varro, it should be remembered, was still alive when Horace published his second book of *Satires*. These few remarks will indicate how certain features of *Sat.* 2. 5 had already occurred in a wide range of comic and satirical writing—not all of it Cynic. Anyone who wishes to explore this area more fully can start from the references in Lejay's introduction to the poem.

In considering the satire's individuality we shall look first of all at a few fragments of Timon:

ὄγκον ἀναστήσας ὠφρυωμένος ἀφροσιβόμβαξ.[37]

An arrogant blusterer who has reared a great structure of bombast.

That was his verdict on Menedemus. Antisthenes he calls παντοφυῆ φλέδονα[38]—'a prolific babbler'. Of Zeno he writes:

καὶ Φοινίσσαν ἴδον λιχνόγραυν σκιερῷ ἐνὶ τύφῳ
πάντων ἱμείρουσαν· ὁ δ᾽ ἔρρει γυργαθὸς αὐτῆς
σμικρὸς ἐών· νοῦν δ᾽ εἶχεν ἐλάσσονα κινδαψοῖο.[39]

And I saw a Phoenician, a greedy old woman in a dark cloud of
arrogance, yearning for everything. But her little fishing-basket
was gone, and she had no more intelligence than a banjo.

That disposes of the founder of Stoicism. What we have, then, is
personal invective of a simple and rather obvious kind. At times
it must have been quite entertaining, but one suspects that in the
course of a long reading the Homeric parody would begin to
wear thin, and that the writer's energy would not be enough in
itself to sustain interest. The contrast with Horace needs no further
elaboration. Nor is anything to be gained by comparing the
satire with Menippus' *Nekyia*, a work which itself has to be
'reconstructed' from the *Menippus* of Lucian. In attempting to
make this comparison Fiske (p. 401) says '(1) the motive for the
visit to the lower world on the part of Menippus in Lucian, and of
Ulysses in Horace, is to question the seer Tiresias as to the best
means of improving their fortunes. (2) Hence both themes
appear to be sarcastic attacks on the teaching of Chrysippus and
the early Stoa that the sage is a χρηματιστικός [i.e. clever at
making money]...(3) Menippus is directed in Lucian to call
himself either Heracles, Odysseus, or Orpheus.' To take these
points in order: (1) Menippus in Lucian has actually quite a different motive. Bewildered by the contradictions and hypocrisy
of philosophers he comes to ask Tiresias 'What is the best life and
the right choice for a man of prudence?' (7). He eventually learns
that 'the life of the ordinary man is the best' (21). (2) Since
Fiske's first point is mistaken, his second cannot follow from it.
Moreover, in Lucian the greed of philosophers is confined to a
single paragraph of a very long essay; Horace, it is true, makes
Ulysses greedy, but there is no reference (as there is in *Sat.* 1. 3. 124
and *Epist.* 1. 1. 106) to the doctrine that the wise man is rich. Any

Stoic who complained that the satire was directed at his philosophy rather than at a contemporary social evil would only have revealed the distortion of his own critical perspective. (3) Lucian chose Heracles, Odysseus and Orpheus because they had all visited Hades in their lifetime. It is possible that Menippus in his own *Nekyia* had disguised himself as Odysseus, but that would simply provide another point of contrast with Horace. As for the works of Lucilius and Varro, the scanty fragments we possess indicate a treatment so different from Horace's that only the vaguest and most general kind of influence can be assumed.

If no one else had ever written anything quite like *Sat*. 2. 5, neither had Horace himself. And in fact the poem is generally recognized as the sharpest of all the satires. Analysis, however, usually ceases at this point, and one is left wondering what it is that produces such an effect. The subject may be partly responsible. For legacy-hunting, as depicted by Horace, seems to involve elements of almost every vice. On the part of the *captator* it is inspired by envy and avarice, and pursued with deceit; while in the quarry it engenders pride, sloth, gluttony and lust. This dual action suggests a further point, namely that whereas other vices often degrade only one person, *captatio* degrades hunter and hunted alike. Thus in Horace's poem the vain and gullible old man is only one degree less contemptible than Ulysses himself. The root of our distaste, however, is probably the fact that legacy-hunting, like no other vice, takes advantage of our defencelessness against death. We are accustomed, of course, to having our mortality exploited by organized business. Yet it has to be admitted that in the end the insurance man, from whatever motives, is interested in one's life (*vive valeque*), whereas the *captator* is not. Martial as usual has packed it all into a poisonous capsule:

> munera qui tibi dat locupleti, Gaure, senique,
> si sapis et sentis, hoc tibi ait 'morere!'[40]

> You are rich and old, Gaurus. If you had any sense you'd realize
> that whoever gives you presents has a message for you—'Drop dead!'

As a result of the subject's nastiness Horace's attitude is exceptionally simple and direct. This may be seen in his portrayal of character. Unlike, say, Damasippus in 2. 3, who although he is turned into a figure of fun does offer some quite sensible advice, Ulysses is an unscrupulous rascal from start to finish. The same is true of Tiresias.

There are also certain features of style, or rather strategy, which, when taken together, distinguish the poem from Horace's other work. First there is the device whereby a tyro receives instruction from some expert authority. This derives its power from the vast difference in level between the two minds—a difference which ensures that the information given will fall with the maximum impact. At the same time the expertise of one character and the naïve ignorance of the other are exploited for ironic effect. Such a device is not, of course, confined to 2. 5; it is already familiar from other poems in the second book. But here it receives a new cogency from its setting. The setting has also its own special function in that the underworld, like the world of animals, provides a novel standpoint for observing human society—a standpoint shared by writers from the time of the first satiric *nekyia* to the hell scene in *Man and Superman*. Finally, except for 1. 8, where the social criticism is merely incidental, this is the only poem from which Horace has completely withdrawn. He is not even present as a listener. And so 2. 5 represents the culmination of those other pieces in which, after setting the scene, the poet stands back and allows his message to be dramatized rather than stated.

On account of its 'un-Horatian' quality 2. 5 is often regarded as an anticipation of Juvenalian satire. 'If Juvenal recognized any affinity between his own invective and the "*Venusina lucerna*," it must have been with the spirit of this satire, and perhaps the second of Book 1, that he found himself in sympathy.'[41] That is the judgement of W. Y. Sellar, and (except for the reference to 1. 2) Fraenkel (p. 145) pronounces it 'perfectly adequate'. What exactly does it mean? 'Spirit' is not something which exists by itself. It is the product of subject-matter, setting, form, language and

other factors. Now the subject of legacy-hunting, perhaps sur-
prisingly, does not bulk large in Juvenal. Apart from brief
references, the longest passage devoted to it is 12. 93–130. So this
does not bear out Sellar's case, which is that 2. 5 exhibits some
feature which is *characteristic* of Juvenal and not of Horace. Nor
does Juvenal provide any comparable setting, since he never wrote
a *nekyia*. As for the form, Juvenal wrote only one complete
satire in dialogue—the ninth, and even there he himself (or, if you
like, his *persona*) remains continuously on the stage. At no time
does he detach himself from his creation as Horace does in 2. 5.
But perhaps Sellar was referring to the poem's irony? Granted,
this type of irony is not very common in Horace; I mean the type
(in which Swift excelled) where a manner of behaviour which
both poet and reader agree to be disreputable is not only spared
from explicit censure but actually commended. Now by itself
2. 5 represents rather less than one-twentieth of Horace's *Satires*;
but it is fair to add the 95 lines of 2. 4, even though the attitude
described is not so much disreputable as absurd. The proportion
then rises to about one-tenth. What is the position with Juvenal?
The only satire where this technique is applied throughout is the
ninth, in which Juvenal commiserates with Naevolus, an un-
employed male prostitute. The passage nearest in spirit to Horace
2. 5 begins at v. 125, where Naevolus asks Juvenal's advice:

'Well, what do you advise me to do, now that all my time has been wasted
and all my hopes have proved dupes? Like a momentary flower our brief
portion of oppressed and sorry life moves swiftly to its close. As we drink our
wine, as we call for garlands, perfumes, and girls, old age steals up behind us
unnoticed.'
    'Courage! So long as these hills stand firm you will never be in need of an
effeminate friend. Those who scratch their heads with one finger will come
flocking in from all parts of the world in carriages and ships. Greater hopes lie
ahead than the ones you have lost. Just crunch up plenty of aphrodisiacs [and
the crowd of pansies which is growing all the time][42] will simply love you.'

The ninth, as we have said, is the only satire which employs this
type of irony throughout. Elsewhere it is rather rare, the best
example being the last fifteen verses of no. 7 which describe the

absurd demands made on the average schoolmaster. A passage like 14. 189–224 does not really count, because it is followed by straightforward preaching in which the ironic mask is doffed. But even if such cases were included, the total fraction would still be small—certainly less than one-fifteenth of Juvenal's work. So it seems that Horace 2. 5 is not Juvenalian in its irony either. Last of all, it is certainly not Juvenalian in language, for the strategy which Horace adopts, with its matter-of-fact acceptance of wickedness, does not permit any violent denunciation.

In the end Sellar's dictum boils down to something like this: 'Sat. 2. 5 has a nasty subject; nasty subjects (though not this one) are commoner in Juvenal than in Horace. Sat. 2. 5 is unusually sarcastic in tone; sarcasm (though not this kind of sarcasm) is common in Juvenal. Hence 2. 5 is Juvenalian in spirit.' So there is perhaps some residue of significance, but not very much.

CHAPTER IX

POET AND PATRON (2)

2. 6

Hoc erat in votis. This is a poem about wishes. It begins with a day-dream—a piece of land, a vegetable garden, a spring, and a few trees. Such a dream, based, perhaps, on childhood memories, must have haunted the poet during those terrible days in 42 B.C. which he mentions with such reserve:

> dura sed emovere loco me tempora grato
> civilisque rudem belli tulit aestus in arma.

But cruel times took me away from that happy place,[1] and the tide of civil war carried me, raw recruit as I was, into arms.

The storm passed and Horace returned to Italy, but in the meantime his father's estate had been confiscated, and so for nearly eight years he had no property in the country. Now at last his dream has come true, and the poet is full of delight and gratitude —though still a little incredulous. As he addresses Mercury the god of luck he says 'I ask no more, O son of Maia, except that thou shouldst make these gifts mine for ever'.[2] One is reminded of the old Irish belief that if you catch a leprechaun he will offer you gold, or a field full of cattle, in return for his freedom. But you must be careful to stipulate that the gift remain with you; otherwise it will disappear as soon as the little man is released.

As usual with Horace, happiness is related to limit. In itself a reverie often gives harmless pleasure, and if it is not fulfilled, well, that is no great loss. If it is, then we should rest content. To be continually pining for what is not ('if only I had that extra bit of ground'), to become obsessed with the vision of some unlikely stroke of luck ('if only I could find a pot of gold')—such yearnings are merely foolish, and unless they are kept in perspective they can poison a man's happiness.

The poet, then, is content. His one prayer is that what he has may thrive:

> si quod adest gratum iuvat, hac prece te oro:
> pingue pecus domino facias et cetera praeter
> ingenium, utque soles, custos mihi maximus adsis.   (13–15)

> If what I have satisfies and delights me, this is the blessing I ask of thee:
> Make fat the flocks I own and all else, except my head; and as ever
> be my chief protector.

The slight inconsistency in the prayer for wealth is muffled by the introductory *si quod adest gratum iuvat*, and is then blown away completely in the joke which follows.[3]

By returning to Horace's wishes these lines round off the opening section, but, as usual, the transition to what follows is contrived with the utmost art:

> ergo ubi me in montis et in arcem ex urbe removi,
> quid prius illustrem saturis Musaque pedestri?

> Well, now that I have retreated from the city to my mountain citadel,
> what should I rather celebrate in the satires of my pedestrian Muse?

The *montis* looks back to the rural happiness of vv. 1–15, while the *urbe* looks forward to the next passage, which begins at v. 20. Moreover, although we were not aware of it, the pun in vv. 14–15 prepared us for the *saturis* of v. 17. Horace's *Satires* are a product of his *ingenium tenue*; that is why his wit must be kept slim. Finally there is the link between *custos* and *arcem*. Mercury's protection follows the poet imperceptibly into his mountain retreat, a lofty spot where we are surprised to encounter the *Musa pedestris*. And yet why not? The satiric Muse is concerned with the tedium of the megalopolis. What more natural than that on reaching his farm Horace should draw a deep breath and say 'My God, it's good to be out of Rome!'?

This thought is developed in two sections. The first (20–39) presents scenes from a morning in Rome, showing how social life conflicts at every point with the poet's private wishes. As he

fights his way through the crowds, a voice cries 'What do you
want?' This is followed by curses (*preces*) and sneers. On reaching
the Esquiline, where Maecenas lived, Horace is plagued by other
people's concerns, which take the form of unwelcome requests:
Roscius orabat...scribae orabant...cura. 'All right,' he says desperately, 'I'll try.' 'You can if you *want* to', comes the reply.
As this section develops, the strain of living in Rome becomes
more and more closely associated with the disadvantages of knowing Maecenas. In v. 40 this theme takes over, and the second of
the two Roman sections (40-59) has begun. 'Ever since Maecenas
befriended me, even though at first he was only prepared (*vellet*)
to exchange small talk in his carriage, I have been the object of
malicious gibes.' The malice is revealed in requests, this time for
information. 'What's happening about Dacia?' 'Whose land is to
be given to the ex-servicemen?' While the poet is being bom-
barded with questions his mind steals away to his farm in the hills,
non sine votis.

This echo of the opening words introduces the second half of
the poem, which consists of a rustic idyll (60-79) corresponding
to the initial prayer of thanks, and a double section on country
and city life (79-100, 100-17) which balances the double section
on Rome. The expression *non sine votis* also introduces a further
complication in the poet's reverie; for it means that Horace, who
is writing in the country, is thinking of himself in Rome thinking
of the country. Moreover, whereas the original dream showed
only the appearance of the farm, vv. 60-79 reveal the kind of life
it stands for—reading and dozing in the afternoon, dining, and
then talking into the night. The conversation does not turn on
properties and incomes or on the trivia of the entertainment
world, but rather on general ethical questions. 'Is it money or
goodness that makes men happy?' 'What is the purpose of friendship—self-interest or the good life?' 'What is the nature of goodness and what is its highest form?' Then, for a little frivolous
relaxation, Horace mentions the old wives' tales of Cervius
(*garrit* and *anilis* both convey gentle ridicule). Yet the tale we are

given is so serious that it sums up a great deal of the satire's message, and though told by a country neighbour it shows the poet at his most urbane.

The subject, again, is wishes. A country mouse is eager to please his city guest (*cupiens*, 86). He fails, and the other says 'Why do you want to live in the backwoods? (*iuvat*, 90). Would you not like to move into town? (*vis*, 92).' The country mouse agrees, and they make eagerly for the city (*aventes*, 99). For a short while, as they sit nibbling at the remains of a banquet, it looks as if luxury and peace of mind are after all compatible (*gaudet...laetum*, 110-11). But this illusion is suddenly destroyed by banging doors and barking dogs. After narrowly escaping with his life the rustic sets off home, a sadder and wiser mouse.

In form the fable is a *cena*, or rather two *cenae*, within a *cena*. Like Horace with his farm and his bit of woodland (*rus*, 60 and *silvae*, 3), the country mouse entertains in rough and ready surroundings (*silva cavusque*, 116 and *praerupti nemoris*, 91). The town mouse, however, lives in a mansion with a dining room of scarlet and ivory (102-3). The country mouse's simple dinner of peas, oats, bacon, and raisins is not unlike that of Horace, who has beans, green vegetables, and bacon. The town mouse, on the other hand, offers many courses, and provides a much more fashionable type of service (107-8). He even tastes each morsel beforehand to make sure it is acceptable.[4] Unfortunately for him Horatian satire is a genre in which no *repas gastronomique* is ever properly finished. The catastrophe, which is splendidly described, provides an ending even better than that of 1. 2 (because it is part of a specific tale) and far superior to the anticlimax which concludes the *cena* of Nasidienus.

The foregoing is a mere sketch-map of the poem. If we wish to indicate a few contours we must start on high ground, for the opening lines, like certain arias of Mozart, radiate a benign tranquillity which can only be called religious, though it is wholly of this world. The point can be illustrated by a comparison with Swift's imitation:

> I've often wished that I had clear
> For life, six hundred pounds a year,
> A handsome house to lodge a friend,
> A river at my garden's end;
> A terrace walk, and half a rood
> Of land, set out to plant a wood.

This is neat and agreeable enough, but the short iambic lines with their rhyming couplets and rows of monosyllables cannot match the power of Horace's hexameters, and the note of joyful thanksgiving has been lost.

A strict agnostic is always slightly embarrassed by good fortune. He knows it is more than he deserves, but he doesn't quite know whom to thank. This is a dilemma which never troubled Horace. True, his sophistication had taken him beyond conventional piety; nor could he ever commit himself to the Stoic view of providence. Nevertheless, the agnostic position as we understand it today, with its scientific rigour and its imaginative poverty, would not have satisfied him either. He felt that in the gift of the Sabine farm certain human factors could be discerned which were neither mechanical nor fortuitous. Among these would be the sacrifices made by his father, Virgil's kindly assistance, and the generosity of Maecenas. Another such factor would be the conscious discipline which contributed to his own achievement as a poet. Therefore, in so far as the gift was explainable it was explainable in spiritual terms. Yet it was clear that a full explanation would be utterly beyond the compass of the human mind. The causes of his good fortune ramified into infinity. And the most important of them—namely his own poetic talent—was itself a perpetual mystery. The Greek imagination, however, had provided a vocabulary for dealing with these superhuman phenomena which so deeply affected the private life, and Horace had no hesitation in using it. He would express his feelings by offering thanks to Mercury. And, after all, what option did he have? Even Lucretius, that ardent foe of traditional belief, could not dispense with *alma Venus*.

This religious mood, for all its light-heartedness, is quite un-characteristic of the *Satires*, and so, while the poem as a whole recalls 1. 6, the opening lines direct us forward to the *Odes*, where we find Mercury, along with Faunus, the Muses, Apollo, and other divine company, once again associated with Horace's deepest feelings on earthly happiness.

In v. 6 the satirist makes his first appearance, and the level begins to drop, but not so steeply as one might expect. For the series of 'if' clauses, which recalls 1. 6. 65 ff., is a form of self-justification. And although the subject is criminal folly the verses remind us by their incantatory sound that they are still part of a prayer:

> si ne*que maiorem* feci ratio*ne mala rem,*
> nec sum facturus vitio culpa*ve minorem*...

> If I have not increased my wealth by dishonest means, and do not intend to decrease it by wickedness or bad behaviour...

Then, still within the prayer, we have a parody of another kind of petition: *o si angulus ille...o si urnam argenti*. Such is the prayer of the fool who is never satisfied. As for the play on *pingue* (14), it conveys that informal intimacy which in a Christian context the northern Protestant finds hard to understand but which the Catholic often shares with a friendly saint.

The ceremonious note is resumed in the soliloquy which fol-lows, for *quid prius illustrem* is a formula associated with stately lyric,[5] but the effect is promptly diminished by *saturis Musaque pedestri*. So too the invocation of Janus has a distinguished Greek ancestry.[6] One notes the alternative forms of address:

> Matutine pater, seu 'Iane' libentius audis

> O Father of the morn, or Janus if thou dost prefer that name

and the appeal to the god to form the prelude of the song—*tu carminis esto | principium*; but respect is rudely dispelled by what Janus actually does—he pulls Horace out of bed and sends him off to pay his calls. The relentless demands of social duty overrule the elements:

sive Aquilo radit terras seu bruma nivalem
interiore diem gyro trahit, ire necesse est.   (25–6)

Whether the north wind is sweeping the earth, or winter draws the
snowy day into a smaller circle, go I must.

It is not the first time that Horace has used the phraseology of
epic as a counterpoint to his own rueful groans.

After all this impressive poetry we now descend to the language
of the streets. What follows is a brilliant performance, revealing
a technique which might well be envied by the radio journalist
with his tape-recorder and scissors. For the scraps of talk not only
indicate what the poet is subjected to, they also provide an audi-
tory cartoon of the speaker. Thus we have the surly resentment of
'What do you want, you idiot, and what do you think you're
doing?' Then comes the deferential functionary: 'Roscius would
like you to be with him at the Wall tomorrow before eight a.m.'
Another, working on the maxim *gaudent praenomine molles
auriculae*,[7] says 'Oh Quintus, the Secretaries would like you to be
sure to come back today. An important piece of civil service
business has just cropped up.' He is followed by a man who has
made his reputation by refusing to take 'no' for an answer: 'Get
Maecenas' signature on these papers.' 'I'll try', says Horace. 'Oh,
you can if you want to', he replies, and continues to badger him.
After this we hear a snatch of conversation from Maecenas'
carriage, recollected from the early days of the friendship. 'What
time do you make it?' 'Is the Thracian Chick a match for the
Arab?'[8] 'These mornings are quite nippy; you've got to be careful.' Then we are back in the streets again: 'Excuse me Sir, but
you must know (for you are so close to the all-powerful)—you
haven't by any chance heard some news about the Dacians?'
These, and the lines which follow, show that inquisitive impertinence was no less annoying then than it is today, though in
Horace's time it had not become a profession.

The second half of the poem opens with a passage of intense
longing: *o rus, quando ego te aspiciam? quandoque licebit...o quando?*

When, when, when? The love of his country estate, which is also reflected in the intimacy of *ego/te*, has been amply explained by the description of life in Rome, and that, in its turn, illuminates the prayer of thanksgiving with which the satire began. Writing about this passage Brower has justly remarked that 'no commentary or translation can quite catch the attitude of laughing reverence for the country, for sweet idleness, good food, good friends, and "heavenly philosophy"'.[9] But if we wish to say anything at all it is perhaps best to concentrate on the 'heavenly philosophy'. The topics discussed at Horace's table are the perennial problems of ancient ethics as propounded by Socrates, Aristotle and the Stoics;[10] and in this philosophical milieu even the beans are Pythagoreans. Nevertheless, the predominant spirit is undoubtedly that of Epicurus:

> ducere sollicitae iucunda oblivia vitae.
>
> To drink sweet forgetfulness of life's troubles.

This mild, lotus-eating existence has been made possible for Horace, periodically at least, by the gift of the Sabine farm. Its desirability is confirmed by the fable of the two mice, with its warning against troublesome wealth (*sollicitas opes*). In this fable it is well to remember that the town mouse is not a true Epicurean, though he may well typify some who used the name. His seductive speech concludes with the words:

> dum licet, in rebus iucundis vive beatus;
> vive memor, quam sis aevi brevis.
>
> Live while you may in the enjoyment of pleasant things; live in constant awareness of how short a time you have.

These exhortations proceed from that melancholy hedonism which occurs in Greek literature of all periods from Mimnermus on, and which represents, in fact, one of mankind's perennial moods. It is the mood of one who is conscious of the spectre moving up behind him and is determined to regale himself before he is beckoned away from the feast. A similar spirit is found, of course, in some of Horace's most famous odes, usually with qualifications which are too often ignored.[11] But that does not make it Epicurean; and indeed to keep the prospect of death before you and to counter it by an urgent sensuality was a practice wholly contrary to the master's teaching.

The country mouse is much closer to Epicurus' ideal. True, he is not an intellectual; neither is Ofellus (2. 2), whom he resembles in several ways. But he lives a wholesome, untroubled life, and enjoys the occasional celebration which Epicurus sanctioned.[12] It is easy to imagine him taking part in the festivities of Lucretius' peasants,[13] and we are told that when a guest arrived he would 'unfasten his tightly-buttoned spirit'. (One notes the collocation *artum/solveret*, an image perhaps unconsciously suggested by *attentus quaesitis*.) The mouse is well content with this 'hard primitivism'[14] until, in a moment of weakness, he is tempted away by the blandishments of the *bon vivant*. The palatial house which they enter has amenities which recall those mentioned by Lucretius (4. 1131–2):

> eximia veste et victu convivia, ludi,
> pocula crebra, unguenta, coronae, serta parantur.

> With splendid coverings and dishes banquets are served; games are provided along with constantly replenished cups, perfumes, wreaths and garlands.

But unlike Lucretius' lover, the country mouse does not learn of their futility through a nagging remorse. His enlightenment comes in a sudden moment of terror, described by Horace with graphic, Disney-like effects. Doors crash open, the house reverberates with deep barking, and the revellers are sent scuttling from their couches half dead with fright. That is enough for the mouse. After a brief and nervous farewell he hurries back to the safety of the woods, where he hopes to regain his peace of mind.

This brings us back to Horace, whose rural retreat is also *tutus ab insidiis*. How closely does the fable apply to what he has been

saying? For three-quarters of the poem Horace has been contrasting the anxiety and physical strain of city life with the peaceful
leisure of the country. Then, by passing from *sollicitae vitae* (62) to
divitiis (74) and from there to the *sollicitas opes* of Arellius (79), he
imperceptibly alters the contrast to one between luxury and
austerity. Now although his life on the farm has been presented
as simple, there has been no indication that his city life is luxurious;
so it looks as if this new contrast has been introduced for the sake
of the fable. Moreover, as the fable develops, it becomes clear
that two other terms, leisure and exertion, have been switched.
For the city mouse can hardly be said to wear himself out, and his
friend in the country certainly does not pass his time 'in sleep and
idle hours'. It might therefore be argued that this tale of mice and
men is less firmly integrated into the structure of the poem than is
sometimes assumed. Yet in the end the fable does endorse Horace's
original point, for it shows that peace of mind (even when accompanied by hard work and austerity) is not to be exchanged for
anxiety (even in the midst of leisure and luxury).

The picture of Horace's carefree life and simple diet recalls the
earlier description in 1. 6. There are even some verbal links like
solabitur (2. 6. 117) and *consolor* (1. 6. 130), *removi* (2. 6. 16) and
remotos (1. 6. 19). But whereas in 1. 6 the sense of being apart is
purely spiritual—for Horace had then no place in the country—
in 2. 6 it is geographical too. The central idea in these two satires
reappears in the story of Volteius Mena in *Epist.* 1. 7. Volteius,
who made a modest living as an auctioneer's crier, was tempted
into becoming a landowner by Philippus, a busy lawyer who
envied him his contentment. In spite of much hard work Volteius'
animals died and his crops failed. Finally he threw the whole
venture up in disgust, returned to Rome, and urged Philippus to
restore him to his former way of life. Here it is farming which
involves the busy pursuit of profits; the city stands for modest
contentment. Within the context of the epistle this constitutes a
reversal of terms, for Horace is writing from the country to
Maecenas, who has, it seems, been pressing him to return and take

up his duties as a client. It is clear, then, that in these αἶνοι Horace allows himself considerable freedom in points of detail. The constant factor is the quest for tranquillity.

The other bond connecting these three poems is the relationship of poet to patron. Now the way Maecenas is treated in 2. 6 is, to say the least, somewhat ambiguous. Horace lets it appear, over a space of thirty lines, that from his point of view the friendship has some very tiresome drawbacks. The complaints, it is true, are presented in a tone of ironic suffering reminiscent of the Journey to Brundisium and the Encounter with the Pest. Nevertheless, if vv. 29–39, which describe the morning scene on the Esquiline, had survived by themselves, or if we had only the harassing questions reported in vv. 51–6, we might well think them ungracious—in spite of the brief admission in v. 32 (*hoc iuvat et melli est*). But of course they have not survived by themselves, and they are transformed by what comes before and after. For the strain of city life is far outweighed by the joy derived from the farm. As Maecenas heard that magnificent opening, in which a human name would have been quite out of place, and as his mind dwelt on the rustic idyll which has a corresponding position in the second half, he must have felt a glow of friendly satisfaction. And knowing Horace as he did, he probably realized that in the years ahead town and country life would each add zest to the other.

As a final comment on the spirit of the satire, and as an example of the profound influence which Horace exerted on the eighteenth century, I should like to recall Dr Johnson's famous letter to Lord Chesterfield, dated 7 February 1755, at the centre of which we find these words: 'Seven years, my Lord, have now passed, since I waited in your outward room, or was repulsed from your door; during which time I have been pushing on my work through difficulties, of which it is useless to complain, and have brought it at last to the verge of publication without one act of assistance, one word of encouragement, or one smile of favour. Such treatment I did not expect, for I never had a patron before.'

By itself that has weight enough, but when one hears underneath it (as the recipient surely would) the rhythms of:

> septimus octavo propior iam fugerit annus
> ex quo Maecenas me coepit habere suorum
> in numero...
> per totum hoc tempus...

> Seven years have now passed—indeed almost eight—since Maecenas
> began to count me as a friend...during all this time...

the effect is overwhelming.

The latest satires of Book 2 contain a few passages which signify the end of Horace's first poetic phase and point forward to his later achievement as a writer of national lyrics. As we saw, Horace's first engagement with politics ended at Philippi. For the next ten years he avoided any declaration of allegiance, and his only comments on national affairs were two impassioned protests of a purely general kind against the madness of civil war.[15] The first step towards recommitment came with his admission to Maecenas' circle, but that was an implication which Horace failed or refused to notice at the time. In fact the poem which records his gratitude most warmly—i.e. 1. 6—also contains his most emphatic rejection of public life. This somewhat anomalous position is reflected in 1. 5, which shows Horace travelling in Maecenas' entourage, but studiously avoids political comment and (except for the oblique *amicos* in v. 29) never mentions Octavian.

During the next six years Horace came to believe for one reason or another that the future welfare of Rome lay with Octavian rather than Antony. Yet in the first epode, written on the eve of the fleet's departure for Actium, Maecenas is still the dominant figure. In *Epod.* 9 Octavian is assuming a more important position, but he does not appear without Maecenas until *Carm.* 1. 37, and there he has to share the limelight with Cleopatra. In the *Satires*, a genre unsuited to encomia, politics are virtually ignored until after Actium, though the reference to Agrippa in 2. 3. 185 (dated 33 B.C.) may be seen as a straw in the wind. Following

Antony's defeat, when Octavian was still out of the country and
Maecenas was in charge at Rome (2. 6. 38), Horace speaks of the
anxiety which people felt about the emperor's plans for settling
ex-servicemen (2. 6. 55–6). But (leaving aside the question
whether this poem preceded 2. 5) the first *compliment* to Octavian
comes at 2. 5. 62–4:

> tempore quo iuvenis Parthis horrendus, ab alto
> demissum genus Aenea, tellure marique
> magnus erit...

In the day when a young hero, the scourge of the Parthians, born
of Aeneas' noble line, shall rule over land and sea...

Many Romans expected that after settling affairs in Egypt
Octavian would march against Parthia to avenge the defeats of
Crassus and Antony and to fulfil the plans of Julius Caesar—hence
Parthis horrendus. In fact he returned home, and the standards
taken from Crassus remained in Parthian hands until 20 B.C.,
when they were recovered by a diplomatic manœuvre. Yet in
Horace's national odes the Parthians figure more prominently
than any other people, perhaps because, apart from any threat
which they may have presented to Rome's frontiers, they stood
for a way of life which the poet found at once fascinating and
repellent.

The other phrase in our quotation (*ab alto | demissum genus
Aenea*) also has a patriotic ring. The connexion of Aeneas with
Latium can be traced back as far as Hellanicus, a Greek historian of
the fifth century B.C. The tradition was developed by other writers,
including the Sicilians Timaeus and Callias, before being adopted
in Rome by Naevius and Fabius Pictor. From them it passed to
Ennius, Cato, Varro, and eventually Virgil.[16] The story had a
special significance for the Julian *gens*, since they claimed descent
from Venus through Iulus the son of Aeneas. Whether or not
Perret is right in dating the origin of this claim to the period between 115 and 95 B.C., it is certain that Julius Caesar was appealing
to a well-established tradition when he asserted at his aunt Julia's

funeral that she was a descendant of Venus.[17] How this genealogy
was then used as an instrument of political power and eventually
became part of the imperial mystique makes a fascinating story,
of which the best account in English is still Miss L. R. Taylor's
The Divinity of the Roman Emperor.[18]

By referring to the military and religious prestige of the emperor
these lines adumbrate some of Horace's greatest odes; yet in their
context they are the prelude to a squalid anecdote; they parody
the portentous style of an oracle and are uttered by a character
who is morally discredited. In other words, they are part of a
satire.

The same situation recurs in 2. 1, which contains the latest
references to Octavian. In chapter IV we noticed the poem's
light-hearted mood. Here we are concerned with its patriotic
implications and with the new relationship which it indicates
between Horace and the emperor.

> aude
>
> Caesaris invicti res dicere, multa laborum
> praemia laturus.   (10–12)

Have the courage to tell of invincible Caesar's exploits. You will
be rewarded handsomely for your pains.

The suggestion is declined, for not everyone can portray the rout
of Gauls and Parthians. 'But', persists Trebatius, 'if you will not
sing of his achievements, you could at least describe his personal
qualities—his justice and his valour—as Lucilius did with Scipio.'
'All in good time', says Horace. 'Not until the right moment will
the words of Floppy penetrate the pricked-up ear of Caesar. Rub
him the wrong way and he will lash out with his hooves, defending
himself on all sides.' Later in the poem Trebatius warns Horace
that foul verses may lead to a libel action. 'No doubt', he answers.
'But what if they are fine verses and win the praise of Caesar?'

Here, then, we have all the materials for a panegyric. Caesar
is just and brave; his enemies have no chance against him. Such
tribute goes beyond anything we have encountered in the *Satires*,
and it foreshadows Horace's new concern for the fortunes of Rome

and her leader. The ship of state which was once a *sollicitum taedium* is now becoming a *desiderium* and a *cura non levis*. Yet the tone is one of jocular banter, and the compliment comes not from Horace but from the slightly comic figure of Trebatius who is the formal counterpart of Tiresias.

As well as hinting at a new political loyalty the poem also points to a direct acquaintance between Horace and Octavian. The *praemia* of v. 12 may not mean much, but Horace would hardly have mentioned them had they been out of the question. So too the possibility of some kind of official encomium is here broached for the first time. As the patriotism is conveyed in an ironic *recusatio*, so the connexion between poet and emperor, which gave a splendid opportunity for snobbery and conceit, is treated with a perky independence almost amounting to cheek.

Nevertheless, the amusing style of the *sermo* cannot conceal the way things are moving. A hundred years of turmoil had come to an end, and in spite of terrible sufferings the fabric of the state had somehow survived. Hope and excitement were beginning to stir; and whether men thought of what was happening as revival or progress they were conscious of taking part in a great historic transition. This feeling had a profound effect on Horace's mind. We can, if we like, say that he was running short of satiric themes and settings, and point to the fact that Book 2 has only eight pieces instead of the usual ten.[19] But this was not a sign of exhaustion. On the contrary, Horace responded to new conditions by contriving new poetic forms. His resources extended beyond the ridicule of vice and folly, and as the Augustan régime took root he began a fresh phase of activity in a field which no Roman had ever entered.

DRYDEN ON HORACE
AND JUVENAL

A full discussion cannot be attempted here, but it does seem desirable by way of an epilogue to make a few general points about Horace's relation to his great successor. As a framework for our discussion we will use the observations made by Dryden in his *Discourse Concerning The Original And Progress Of Satire*[1]—an essay which has had an immense influence in the past and may still provide many students of English with their only information about the two major satirists of antiquity.

At the outset (p. 79) Dryden concedes that Horace was 'the better poet', but he bases this superiority on the *Epodes* and *Odes*, which he then excludes from his discussion of satire. He is of course right to exclude them, but his reasons for doing so are not satisfactory. 'Horace', he says, 'has written many of them satirically, against his private enemies...but (he) had purged himself of this choler before he entered on those discourses which are more properly called the Roman Satire. He has not now to do with a Lyce, a Canidia, a Cassius Severus, or a Menas; but is to correct the vices and the follies of his time.' First of all it is incorrect to suggest that the *Epodes* and *Odes* precede the *Satires*. The first book of satires was published about 35 B.C. and the second about 30. As for the *Odes*, the first collection, comprising Books 1–3, did not appear until 24 or 23 B.C., and there is no proof that any of these poems were written before 30.[2] So we cannot speak of Horace purging himself of his choler before undertaking the *Satires*.

Then there is the question of names. Cassius Severus, in spite of Dryden's statement (p. 90), is not mentioned in the *Epodes*, nor indeed anywhere else in Horace. His presence in the tradition is due to

the imagination of some ancient scribe who prefixed his name to
the anonymous sixth epode, forgetting that the poem did not
suit his character and was in all probability written before he was
born.[3] The same kind of speculation made Sextus Pompeius
Menas the object of *Epode* 4. These are both historical persons,
but the same cannot be said of Canidia, who is probably a composite character, based on someone known to Horace but heavily
overlaid with fiction. Even if she is counted as a private enemy
this will not help Dryden's case, for she also appears in three of the
satires. And she is not without company. If Dryden had re-read
the fourth and tenth satires of Book 1 he would have found that
Pantilius, Demetrius, Fannius and Hermogenes all suffer for their
criticisms of Horace and his poetry. The distinction which Dryden
had in mind would therefore be more clearly stated by saying
that whereas the *Epodes* contain five lampoons, the *Satires* have
none. By 'lampoon' I here mean a poem addressed to a person
named or unnamed with the sole object of abusing him. Thus
Horace's meeting with the pest (*Sat.* 1. 9) and his account of
Nasidienus' dinner-party (*Sat.* 2. 8) would not rank as lampoons.
Nor would the fourth and tenth satires of Book 1, for there
Horace is not really concerned to abuse his critics but rather to
defend his work against the charges of malice and incompetence,
and in doing so to present his conception of the genre.

Lampoons, says Dryden, may occasionally be justified as revenge 'when we have been affronted in the same nature, or have
been any ways notoriously abused, and can make ourselves no
other reparation' (p. 79). Personal attacks of a more general kind
are defensible when the person is a public nuisance. 'All those,
whom Horace in his Satires, and Persius and Juvenal have mentioned in theirs, with a brand of infamy, are wholly such. 'Tis an
action of virtue to make examples of vicious men' (p. 80). By 'brand
of infamy' Dryden means, I take it, charges of a serious nature.
If, then, his point is that the Roman satirists only made serious
charges against people who were a public nuisance, that may indeed be true; but it is not a great compliment to say so, for all it

APPENDIX

means is that the poets were not guilty of libellous invective. But
Dryden has, I suspect, quite a different idea in mind, namely that
the vicious characters attacked by the satirists were all living contemporaries. We have already seen how limited an application
this has to Horatian satire; it does not apply to Persius at all. As
for Juvenal, he himself says that his victims will be 'those whose
ashes lie under the Flaminian and the Latin Road'. The vices he
castigates are for the most part contemporary, but the names are
usually the names of the dead. Using the dead as *exempla* is a very
different thing from making examples of the living.[4]

From the victims of satire Dryden now turns to its general
subjects, developing the view that 'folly was the proper quarry of
Horace, and not vice' (p. 83). Folly, he says, was a more difficult
target, for 'as there are but few notoriously wicked men, in comparison with a shoal of fools and fops, so 'tis a harder thing to make
a man wise than to make him honest; for the will is only to be
reclaimed in the one, but the understanding is to be informed in
the other'. Instead of examining this rather questionable reasoning we shall concentrate on the proposition that Horace's chief
concern was not vice but folly. It sounds attractive, offering as it
does a neat contrast between the aims of the two satirists; for this
reason, it has been accepted by generations of readers and is sometimes found in handbooks today.[5] Unfortunately it does not
happen to be true. Let us glance quickly at the subjects of the
relevant Horatian satires. First book: (1) greed and envy, (2)
adultery, (3) cruelty and intolerance, (4) backbiting and malice,
(6) snobbery and ambition, (8) witchcraft and superstition, (9)
ill-mannered place-seeking. Second book: (2) gluttony and
meanness, (3) avarice, meanness, murder, prodigality, megalo-
mania, erotic obsession, superstition, (4) gluttony, (5) legacy-
hunting, (7) the tyranny of lust and gluttony. One shudders to
contemplate the moral system of a man to whom these are but
'follies'.

One of the factors behind this error may be that passage of
Persius which we discussed above:[6]

secuit Lucilius urbem,
te Lupe, te Muci, et genuinum fregit in illis.
omne vafer vitium ridenti Flaccus amico
tangit et admissus circum praecordia ludit,
callidus excusso populum suspendere naso.

Dryden (p. 83) prints the third and fourth lines only, and then proceeds as follows: 'This was the commendation which Persius
gave [Horace]: where, by *vitium*, he means those little vices which
we call follies, and defects of human understanding, or, at most,
the peccadillos of life, rather than the tragical vices, to which men
are hurried by their unruly passions and exorbitant desires.' This,
as we have already argued, is a misreading of the lines, for
Horace practically never teases his friends about their foibles.

The main reason for this misconception, however, is undoubtedly the attitude and tone of the two satirists. Horace's
basic objection to greed, lust, ambition, and so on, is that they
make the man himself unhappy and bring consequences which
may ruin his life. To the Christian, who is aware that other people
also suffer from the man's vice, and who bears in mind the offence
against God and his commandments, this outlook is bound to
appear superficial. It is easy to feel that a writer who appeals to
our self-interest in this way can hardly be taken seriously as a
moralist. Moreover, since Horace's tone is one of sensible ridicule
('Don't be such a fool, man! Can't you see that you're making
yourself miserable?'), the Christian reader tends to forget that
most of the faults attacked by Horace really are vices. Take,
for example, these lines from the first satire (70–9):

You scrape your money-bags together from every side and fall asleep on top of
them with your mouth still gaping open. You have to keep them inviolate like
sacred objects and only enjoy them as you would a painted tablet. Don't you
know what money is for? What use it offers? You can buy bread, vegetables,
and half a litre of wine, and other things too which human nature cannot conveniently do without. Or perhaps you *enjoy* lying awake half dead with fright,
spending your days and nights in terror of wicked burglars or fires or slaves who
might clean you out and then disappear? I should always hope to be very
badly off in goods of that sort!

Here the miser is undoubtedly vicious by Roman and Christian standards alike, but Horace has presented him as a ludicrous, slightly pathetic, fool.

It should not be inferred from this that Horace's subjects were really the same as Juvenal's. There are a few very notable differences. First, in every period of his work Juvenal is concerned not only with folly and vice, but with crime. He constantly inveighs against forgery, robbery, perjury, adultery, fraud, murder and treason. In Horace such material is less prominent. Secondly, we do not find any Horatian satire devoted to such themes as homosexuality, male prostitution, or cannibalism. Horace drew his subjects from within the domain of nature, whereas Juvenal often used the perverted and the monstrous in his representations of vice. Finally, while Horace's conception of *nugae*, or trifles, can be inferred from pieces like the seventh and eighth satires of Book 1, the only trifle in Juvenal is an account of how a giant turbot was received at the court of Domitian. There is certainly humour here, but it is humour of a grim kind, and an atmosphere of dread hangs over the scene. Juvenal's own comment is this:

> atque utinam his potius nugis tota illa dedisset
> tempora saevitiae, claras quibus abstulit urbi
> illustresque animas impune et vindice nullo. (4. 150–2)

Yes, and what a blessing it would have been if frivolities of this kind had filled all those cruel years in which he robbed the city of its noblest and most distinguished souls, with none to punish or avenge.

Nevertheless, in a number of cases the poets' subjects are broadly similar, and here it is the contrast in treatment which proves instructive. We have already seen the gulf which separates Nasidienus (Horace 2. 8) from Virro (Juvenal 5). Even *Sat.* 11, which is sometimes called the most Horatian of Juvenal's satires, contains several details which distinguish it from the sermon of Ofellus—a poem with which it has something in common. Thus Juvenal spends a dozen lines telling how a gluttonous wastrel

DRYDEN ON HORACE AND JUVENAL

can end up eating gladiators' hash (20), whereas Horace presents
a similar situation in a short comic phrase—the poor fellow will
long for death in vain because 'he won't have a penny for a rope'.
In vv. 56–76 Juvenal describes the simple menu which he has
planned for his guest, Persicus, and compares it with the diet of the
men of old. But watch how he continues: I will not invite the
sort of people who will sneer at my modest circumstances; the
meat will not be carved by a graduate of Trypherus' school for
chefs; there will be no pretty waiters; and you needn't expect to
see a performance by Spanish belly-dancers. That is not Horace's
voice. Concluding his invitation, Juvenal urges Persicus to forget
his business troubles and to enjoy a day's holiday (183–5). Horace
could easily have written that, but he would never have gone on to
say: 'Don't let your wife cause you secret anger because she goes
out at dawn and comes home at night with her fine-spun clothes
damp and suspiciously creased, her hair rumpled, and her face and
ears burning.'

Other poems offer similar contrasts. In 2. 6 Horace tells how
glad he is to get out of Rome, because he enjoys a rest from the
noisy merry-go-round of social life. Juvenal's Umbricius is leaving for ever (*Sat.* 3), because the old virtues have disappeared and
Rome has passed into the hands of charlatans, pimps, and gangsters.
In Juvenal's eyes an adulterous *matrona* typifies the avarice, dis-
honesty, and utter rottenness of Roman womanhood (*Sat.* 6);
she is a monster, a creature of abhorrence. To Horace (1. 2) she
is simply a hazard which can easily be avoided with a little common sense. In 1. 6 Horace delivers a sermon on ambition and in
doing so gives a memorable account of his upbringing and his
present way of life. In Juvenal (*Sat.* 8) the informal personal note
is missing, and instead the theme of ambition develops into a
long tirade against the aristocracy, who in the recent past have
sunk so low as to make a spectacle of themselves in public.

The difference in treatment implies a different attitude on the
part of the satirist. Like the Epicureans (and all sensible men)
Horace recognized various degrees of folly. Stealing a cabbage is

not the same as robbing a temple. Each case must be judged on its merits. Juvenal's attitude, however, is more like that of the doctrinaire Stoic who regards all sins as equally culpable. The suggestion of philosophical rigour is perhaps misleading, but it is true that in the main Juvenal does not invite us to make distinctions. In the third satire, as Umbricius leaves Rome for good he says 'Let those fellows stay behind who can turn black into white, who don't mind accepting contracts for temples, rivers or harbours, for cleaning drains or carrying corpses to the pyre' (30-2). Here our indignation at fraud and perjury spills over into the following lines, so that the men who make their living from those essential services appear not merely unattractive but actually criminal. Later in the same satire (58-112) we are asked to believe that the clothes, the complaisance, and the lechery of the immigrant Greek are all equally repulsive. Again, in his most elaborate poem—the invective against Roman women—we find the following sequence (6. 379 ff.): If your wife is musical she will plan adultery with professional singers; but let her be musical (with all it entails) rather than a chatterbox in male company; no less insufferable is the woman who gives her plebeian neighbour a brutal beating; worse still is the bluestocking who holds the floor on literature, history, and philosophy, and corrects her husband's grammar. In synopsis this sounds merely funny, but it must be emphasized that in the full version of the passage, which runs for nearly eighty lines, there is no suggestion of anticlimax.

In 8. 211 ff. Juvenal contrasts Nero with Orestes: both killed their mothers, but Orestes was avenging his father's death, and Orestes never murdered his sister or wife, never sang on the stage, never composed an epic on Troy. Juvenal knows we will naturally tend to take this as satiric bathos, so he immediately seeks to cancel this effect by insisting that Nero's artistic performances were as damnable as anything he ever did. In 3. 7-9 no attempt is made to reverse our normal reaction and we are left with an anticlimax: What could be worse, says Juvenal, than living in fear of fires, falling houses, and the thousand and one dangers of this savage city, and poets reciting in the month of August (*Augusto recitantes mense poetas*)? Like many famous quotations, however, this is quite untypical of the author; in fact it would be hard to find a parallel in the *Satires*. For although Juvenal often contrives an anticlimax in order to belittle the person he is speaking of—as in the lines on Hannibal (10. 166–7)—in this case he has undermined the force of his own words, for the reader begins to suspect that Umbricius is not so appalled by the other dangers as he pretends. Nevertheless, if we allow for this and perhaps one or two other exceptions, it still remains true that whereas Horace permits some discrimination, which is an exercise of the reason, Juvenal often overpowers the reason altogether.

This brings us back to Dryden's ill-judged remark about the informing of the understanding being harder than the reclaiming of the will. Ill-judged, because apart from its dubious validity it is largely irrelevant to Juvenal. As a rule Juvenal is not in the least concerned with reclaiming the will. His object is to provoke the same derision, indignation, and disgust as he feels himself. And his technique exactly suits his purpose, for instead of developing a consecutive argument as Horace usually does, he presents a series of lurid pictures accompanied by emotive noises which are designed to play upon our deepest fears, resentments, and tabus:

When a soft eunuch takes a wife, and Mevia goes in for pig-sticking in the amphitheatre with a spear poised beside her naked breast; when a fellow who made my stiff young beard grate under his razor takes on single-handed the entire aristocracy in the contest of wealth; when a guttersnipe of the Nile like Crispinus—a slave bred in Canopus—hitches a cloak of Tyrian purple on to his shoulder and waves a light gold ring on his sweaty finger (for in summer he can't bear the weight of a larger stone), then it is hard *not* to write satire.

(1. 22–30)

Sexual scorn, male arrogance, social snobbery, xenophobia, jealousy, and physical revulsion—one is piled on the other until the satirist explodes with a shout of fury and contempt. That is why the cause of Juvenal's satire is usually identified as an efficient cause: *facit indignatio versum*. Both he and the reader experience through their savage laughter a kind of emotional release, but there is no constructive purpose, no thought of healing the disease of his time, because for a man who assumes this attitude the state of Roman life is irremediable.

This gloomy spirit is visible even in poems which are not prompted by indignation.[7] The cynical quietism to which the tenth satire leads is a wisdom reserved for the few. The rest of Rome and the rest of mankind will continue their misguided dreams. Satire thirteen, though different from the tenth in tone and strategy, takes the same pessimistic view of human virtue:

> rari quippe boni: numera; vix sunt totidem quot
> Thebarum portae vel divitis ostia Nili.   (26–7)

Good men are scarce. Count them—they are hardly as many as the gates of Thebes or the mouths of the rich Nile.

Turning back to Horace, we recall that the cause of his satire is a final cause: *ridentem dicere verum*—'to tell the truth with a smile'. The smile is important, for as well as being enjoyable in itself it makes the truth more palatable and therefore more easy to ingest. In Horace's own words 'Great difficulties are usually cut away more forcefully and more effectively by laughter than by vituperation' (1. 10. 14–15). This must always be the motto of the reforming satirist. It is basically optimistic in outlook, for it implies that the major cause of human unhappiness is a defect of vision, and that once the satirist has made his diagnosis the remedy is in the patient's hands.

This brings us to the question of style. Dryden takes issue with Casaubon over the alleged vulgarity of Horace's style, maintaining quite rightly that it 'is constantly accommodated to his subject, either high or low' (p. 78). Later, however, he seems to modify this position, asserting that 'the low style of Horace is according to his subject, that is, generally grovelling' (p. 85). This remark suggests that Dryden has overlooked many of those subtle gradations which make Horatian satire such a delight. And when it is taken in conjunction with his praise of Juvenal, whose expressions are 'sonorous and more noble', whose verse is 'more numerous', and whose words are 'suitable to his thoughts, sublime and lofty', then it becomes clear that once again Dryden has distorted the picture in his endeavour to produce a striking contrast. For Juvenal's sonorous and vehement rhetoric is inseparable from another feature of his style, which Dryden has seen fit to ignore, namely his brilliant use of demeaning detail. Indeed Juvenal's most characteristic effects result from the tension set up by these two forces co-existing within the same phrase or sentence, or succeeding one another in violent alternation. Because of this ironic method it is not often that the total effect of any Juvenalian paragraph is one of simple nobility. An exception which comes to mind is that magnificent passage in the fifteenth satire beginning 'When nature gave tears to man she showed that she was giving him a tender heart' (131 ff.). But the extreme rarity of such cases refutes Dryden's point. Far more typical is an example like this, picked at random from the seventh satire:

> frange miser calamum vigilataque proelia dele,
> qui facis in parva sublimia carmina cella,
> ut dignus venias hederis et imagine macra.   (27–9)

> (If you have your eye on any patron other than the emperor) break your pen, you poor fool, and destroy the battles which have kept you awake at night, you who fashion lofty verse in a tiny garret with the hope of earning a crown of ivy and a skinny bust.

For further evidence of this polarity in Juvenal's style one can hardly do better than read the tenth satire along with *The Vanity of Human Wishes*.[8] If, therefore, we have to generalize on the styles of the two poets, it would be safer to say that whereas Horace rises and falls between relatively narrow limits Juvenal shoots up and down at a speed which leaves us breathless, exhilarated, and sometimes slightly sick.

The next point is the matter of wit. Here again we are disconcerted by Dryden's vacillations. It will be recalled that at the outset he chose Horace for his instruction and Juvenal for his delight (pp. 81–2). Then, finding that Horace's instruction consisted of ridiculing men's follies, he asserted that 'the divine wit of

Horace left nothing untouched' (p. 83) and that 'Horace laughs to
shame all follies, and insinuates virtue rather by familiar examples
than by the severity of precepts' (p. 84). By now it looks as if
Dryden has received as much delight as instruction. But no. He
now states that the delight which Horace gives him is 'but
languishing', that the poet's wit (which a page ago was 'divine')
is 'faint' and his salt 'almost insipid'. Juvenal on the other hand
'is of a more vigorous and masculine wit'. 'He gives me', says
Dryden, 'as much pleasure as I can bear; he fully satisfies my
expectation; he treats his subject home; his spleen is raised, and
he raises mine.' As far as it goes this is a fair assessment of Juvenal's
wit. And since preferences in wit are highly subjective we are
quite willing to let Dryden keep his opinion of Horace, an opinion
which after some bewilderment we think we have finally grasped:
Horace's wit is feeble and intermittent. But Dryden has not yet
finished. On p. 92 he takes up Barten Holyday's silly remark that
'a perpetual grin like that of Horace rather angers than amends a
man'. Rallying to Horace's defence he says 'Let the chastisement
of Juvenal be never so necessary for his new kind of satire; let him
declaim as wittily and sharply as he pleases; yet still the nicest and
most delicate touches of satire consist in fine raillery'. There
follows a delightful and justly famous account of what Dryden
means by this 'fine raillery'. It is the ability 'to make a man appear
a fool, a blockhead, or a knave, without using any of those
opprobrious terms'; it is 'the fineness of a stroke that separates the
head from the body and leaves it standing in its place'; or again
it is a method which effects 'a pleasant cure with all the limbs preserved entire'. Has Horace, then, been once more reinstated?
Alas no, because we are now told that fine raillery, as described by
Dryden, represents only Horace's *intention*; his *performance* was
sadly inferior (pp. 94–5). We shall not stop to ask whether Dryden
thinks he has now answered Holyday's objection, or how he
himself can ever have enjoyed the instruction of so feeble a wit.
It is more important to inquire where his analysis has gone wrong.
In the first place, Horace has been credited with a purpose which

he never conceived; for Dryden's fine raillery not only involves an attack on living people but also, to judge from the character of Zimri in *Absalom*,[9] entails a great deal more than the passing thrust which was Horace's favourite technique. Secondly, the two pairs of characters chosen by Dryden as illustrations of Horace's incompetence can scarcely be called satiric at all. Sarmentus and Cicirrus in 1. 5 and Persius and Rex in 1. 7 are not censured as either vicious or foolish; they are merely meant to be funny. It has been contended in chapter III that the humour consists not so much in what they say as in the way they are presented. By overlooking the element of parody Dryden seems to have been misled into equating Horace's humour with that of his characters.

The last point which I wish to take up concerns the historical background of the two poets and its effect on their satire. After asserting that Juvenal was the greater satirist, Dryden goes on to say (pp. 86–7):

His spirit has more of the commonwealth genius; he treats tyranny, and all the vices attending it, as they deserve, with the utmost rigour: and consequently a noble soul is better pleased with a zealous vindicator of Roman liberty, than with a temporising poet, a well mannered court-slave, and a man who is often afraid of laughing in the right place; who is ever decent because he is naturally servile...There was more need of a Brutus in Domitian's days, to redeem or mend, than of a Horace, if he had then been living, to laugh at a flycatcher. This reflection at the same time excuses Horace, but exalts Juvenal.

In fact the reflexion does neither, because it is entirely misconceived. Horace wrote his *Satires* at the end of the republican era, when there was no court; and where there is no court there can be no court slaves. It is true, of course, that after Philippi no writer could snipe at Antony, Octavian, or even Sextus Pompeius from an independent position. Pollio, with all his prestige, declined to swop insults with Octavian—'it is not easy to write against a man who can write you off'.[10] But the question still remains whether Horace's reticence was solely, or even primarily, due to fear. If he had been sure of his personal safety, would he then have castigated his enemies with Lucilian abandon? The question cannot

be answered for the first half of the decade, but at least we can
watch how the poet behaved when conditions altered. As the
thirties wore on and hopes of a permanent settlement between
Antony and Octavian began to fade, the air became thick with
propaganda and personal abuse. Credit for many of the most
scurrilous pamphlets must go to the leaders themselves, but they
did not insist on a monopoly of invective and were quite happy to
enlist the help of friends. Here, surely, was Horace's opportunity.
With the protection of Maecenas, and ultimately that of Octavian,
the risks would have been minimal. Yet he never joined in.[11]
In fact, as we have seen, the more security Horace acquired the
milder and less personal his work became, until finally he abandoned satire altogether. It may be, of course, that when he became
emperor Octavian discouraged such writing in the hope of promoting social unity. But I prefer to think that Horace had more
positive reasons for turning to other forms. The matter may perhaps be summed up by saying that, although Horace was not free
to attack all and sundry, such freedom would have made little
difference.

It remains to inquire whether Dryden's history is any more
accurate in the case of Juvenal. In recent years scholars have done
their utmost to treat Domitian fairly. Most people now accept the
view that he was moderately successful in war, shrewd in financial
affairs, and notably fair in his administration of the provinces.[12]
But as time passed he had to contend with a mounting hatred on
the part of the senate. Various reasons have been suggested, e.g.
his monopoly of certain republican *honores*, his increasing emphasis on his own divinity, his restraint of greedy governors, his
lack of tact, his habit of choosing non-senatorial executives, and in
general his tendency to by-pass the senate as an organ of government. Whatever the causes, this hatred led to conspiracies against
the emperor's life and consequent charges of *maiestas*, or treason.
According to a recent article by Waters,[13] we know of at least
nine executions on this charge, two others probably on this charge,
and six more 'for non-political reasons'. In addition to the execu-

tions several people were sent into exile. In view of these figures, which represent the minimum number of victims, I am not inclined to accept Waters' contention that the terror which is said to have prevailed in the last years of Domitian's reign is simply a myth. For many senatorial families it must have been all too real. A few men, who might be called 'zealous vindicators of Roman liberty', protested—and suffered accordingly, but Juvenal was not one of them. Very sensibly, he waited for the assassin to strike. Tacitus, the only contemporary writer of comparable power, chose the same course.

Nerva became emperor in A.D. 96 and was followed two years later by Trajan. 'Now at last our spirits are reviving', says Tacitus. 'Nerva has harmonized the old discord between the principate and liberty, and every day Trajan is increasing the happiness of our times' (*Agricola* 3). Later he speaks of 'the rare good fortune of this age in which we can feel what we like and say what we feel' (*Hist.* 1. 1). The new spirit is also attested by Dio (68. 6. 4), who stresses Trajan's indifference to slander, and by Pliny, who in his panegyric on the emperor (66. 4) says 'You are urging us to be free, and so we shall be; you are urging us to express our feelings openly, and so we shall'. Such liberty was, of course, a privilege rather than a right, and no doubt it fell far short of anything which we would regard as tolerable. Nevertheless, it did represent some easing of tension, and it meant that the régime of Domitian was no longer immune from criticism. Several years passed, however, before Juvenal published his first book of satires. The precise date cannot be fixed; recent estimates vary from A.D. 110 to 117. The second book came out about the time of Trajan's death (A.D. 117), and the rest appeared in the reign of Hadrian, the last complete satire belonging to about 130. As successive books were published it became clear that Juvenal meant what he said about avoiding Lucilian polemic. The evidence on this point has been weighed by Syme, who assures us that 'Juvenal does not attack any person or category that commands influence in his own time'.[14] This does not justify charges of cowardice or timidity; no such charges are made by Syme, and indeed it would be rather unfair if a poet were expected to commit suicide in order to satisfy a modern critic.[15] Anyhow, even in their present form, the *Satires* can hardly have pleased the emperor or any of his magistrates who felt responsible for the state of the nation. But Syme's point does mean that the *Satires* cannot have had the direct and immediate impact which Dryden imagined. And so in this area too we must reject the sharp antithesis which Dryden has presented between Juvenal and Horace.

Finally, in view of Dryden's remark about Juvenal having 'more of the commonwealth genius' we should perhaps recall that in spite of his invective against Nero and Domitian there is no evidence that Juvenal wanted the principate abolished. Still less did he envisage anything like our own form of democracy. As Highet points out, 'Juvenal does not say that the poor are exploited by the governing class or that the middle class is being crushed out of existence. He does not say that "the system" should be changed to put a different social class on top.'[16] What he does deplore is that as a result of Rome's imperial power the old social order has been upset; unscrupulous blackguards with no breeding (many of them Greeks or Syrians) have acquired money and prestige, while decent Romans like himself have been reduced to poverty and humiliation. Thus his angriest satires proceed from a vague sort of reactionary idealism enforced by feelings of personal injustice.

The type of analysis which we have been conducting is often unsympathetic, and it may be urged in defence of Dryden that he had few of the scholarly resources available to a modern critic. He could not walk into a library and inspect the serried ranks of Pauly–Wissowa; and seventeenth-century commentaries, admirable as they were, had not experienced that long process of scrutiny and sifting which lies behind the works of Heinze and Lejay. Moreover, Dryden was in no way eccentric in holding such views. They were shared not only by his contemporaries but also by his successors in the eighteenth century; and indeed some of them flourish today. But however important these considerations may be (and they are of prime importance for an understanding of Dryden's own approach to satire) they ought not to obscure the fact that, as far as Horace and Juvenal are concerned, Dryden's essay is wrong or misleading on almost every major point. And this is the more unfortunate in that its writer was a man of genius.

NOTES

1   Fraenkel, p. 86: 'What does follow is something totally different.'
2   For the sage as king see H. von Arnim, *Stoicorum Veterum Fragmenta*, I. 53. 10; 3. 81. 31; 3. 150. 17; 3. 158. 35 ff.; 3. 159. 1.
3   For the punishments of adulterers see Mayor on Juvenal 10. 315–17 and Ellis on Catullus 15. 19. For the adultery mime see R. W. Reynolds in *CQ*, XL (1946), 77–84, and cf. *Sat.* 2. 7. 59–61.
4   Cf. Lucilius W. 1240; and Cichorius, p. 348.
5   Fraenkel, p. 78, n. 2.
6   A very full and learned guide to this debate is provided by H. Herter in *Rh. Mus.* XCIV (1951), 1 ff.
7   On the text and interpretation of v. 108 these, I think, are the chief points:
    (1) *Ut avarus* cannot mean that the miser is an instance of contentment. Such an idea would conflict with the whole tenor of the poem. The miser who congratulates himself in vv. 66–7 is the victim of a delusion, as is clear from *iubeas miserum esse, libenter | quatenus id facit* (63–4).
    (2) Nor can the miser be an instance of discontent; for in vv. 30–2 Horace has maintained that greed is the *basis* of discontent. It is against his purpose to suggest that there are any discontented people who are not greedy. Even if we take the *avarus* as referring only to the types presented in vv. 41–100, the theory still does not work. For if *ut avarus* is comparative the miser ought to be an instance of the proposition *nemo | se probet ac potius laudet diversa sequentis*. But at no time does the miser wish to change his occupation.
    Therefore if *ut avarus* is a separate phrase, as I believe it is, it must mean 'inasmuch as he is greedy', which is virtually the equivalent of *ob avaritiam*.
    (3) The objections to the *qui* of the oldest Blandinian MS., which is printed by most modern editors, are:
    (*a*) That the formula *illuc unde abii redeo* cannot be continued by an indirect question. I am not sure that this objection is fatal. Such a formula is sometimes taken up by a phrase in agreement (*Sat.* 1. 6. 45), sometimes by an accusative and infinitive (Cic. *Fam.* 1. 7. 5; 4. 8. 2), and sometimes by a *quod* clause (*Sat.* 1. 3. 38–9). On these points see E. L. Harrison, *Phoenix*, XV (1961), 43–4; C. Becker, *Gnomon*, XXXI (1959), 601; and W. Wimmel, *Zur Form der horazischen Diatribensatire* (Frankfurt, 1962), pp. 74–6.
    (*b*) That if *ut avarus* equals *ob avaritiam* then Horace's question would contain its own answer. This also may be over-strict. For the sequence might be: why is it that no one, in his greed, is content with his own life

and envies those in other occupations? The answer, indicated by the whole poem and especially by the closing lines, would be 'For *no* good reason'.

(*c*) Even allowing for the *-qui-* of *nequit* directly overhead, it is hard to account for the absence of *qui* from the MS. tradition, especially as it would derive some prominence from being a repetition of the opening word. It is more probable that, like many modern conjectures, *qui* was proposed as an easier reading by someone who had failed to make sense of what was before him.

(4) Reading *nemon ut avarus*, Fraenkel renders 'Can it be that no greedy person is content with his own situation?' But such a question would imply the answer 'no', and anyhow there is nothing astonishing in the discontent of greedy men. Mr S. A. Handford has pointed out to me that *nemon ut se probet* could also mean 'Is no one ever to be content?' But, as he observes, *ne ut* cannot go together here, because then *nemo* would have to be taken with *avarus*, and the question 'Is no greedy man ever to be content?' does not give satisfactory sense.

If the reading which I have given is correct, then Horace returns to his opening topic, not to repeat his original question (that has already been answered) but to ask another one in various forms. The repeated interrogatives *probet, laudet, tabescat,* etc., do not indicate the poet's indignation; they rather draw attention to the wearisome futility and the wasted energy of πλεονεξία. As for the subjunctives, they are similar to those mentioned by Handford in section 84 of *The Latin Subjunctive*. It should perhaps be added that although this position was reached independently I do not imagine it to be original. It was probably held by various scholars before the nineteenth century, and others may hold it today. The remarks of Professor G. B. A. Fletcher in the *Durham University Journal*, n.s. XXI (1959), 33, certainly point in the same direction.

8 Cf. Plato, *Rep.* I. 349B–350C.

9 A special study of this technique was made by U. Knoche in *Phil.* XC (1935), 372–90 and 469–82.

10 D.L. 6. 96. For a general account of Crates see D. R. Dudley, *A History of Cynicism* (London, 1937), pp. 42–53.

11 D.L. 4. 46–58. Dudley, *op. cit.* pp. 62–9. See also A. Oltramare, *Les Origines de la diatribe romaine* (Lausanne, 1926), pp. 36–9.

12 For the Scipionic circle see Fiske, ch. 2.

13 For Panaetius see M. van Straaten, *Panaetii Rhodii Fragmenta* (Leiden, 1952).

14 Cf. E. Zeller, *A History of Eclecticism in Greek Philosophy*, Eng. trans. (London, 1883), pp. 87–99.

15 Cf. P. H. DeLacy, *TAPA*, LXXIX (1948), 12–23. Velleius represents Epicureanism in Cic. *De Nat. Deorum*.

16 C. O. Brink, *Horace on Poetry* (Cambridge, 1963), p. 177 and reff.

17 Cf. A. Momigliano, *JRS*, XXXI (1941), 149–57.

NOTES

18 Teubner text (Hobein) 15. 1.
19 Ed. E. Littré (Paris, 1861), IX, 368–70. Cf. Diogenes in D.L. 6. 29.
20 *Axiochus* 368 A.
21 Varro B. 78, Cic. *De Off.* 1. 120 (though Cicero allows for the possibility of a change). A later Stoic instance is Epictetus, Frag. 2.
22 Lucretius, *DRN* 3. 1057 ff. and 1082 ff.
23 Teles, pp. 10–11, 42–3.
24 For love of money as the root of all evil see H. Herter, *Rh. Mus.* XCIV (1951), 19. Varro wrote a treatise called περὶ φιλαργυρίας; cf. also Varro B. 126. The μεμψίμοιρος in Theophrastus' *Characters*, however, shows that discontent was not restricted to questions of money.
25 Teles, p. 11. This, like the last example, was noted by Fraenkel, pp. 92–3.
26 Teles, p. 43. Cf. the excerpt from a Byzantine collection cited by Heinze (Kiessling–Heinze, *Satires*, 6th ed. Berlin, 1957, p. 8) and Lejay (*Satires*, Paris, 1911, p. 8) after Wachsmuth: διὰ φιλαργυρίαν μετὰ πόνων γεωργεῖς etc.
27 J. Souilhé (*Platon* III, 3. 117–36) thinks the author of the *Axiochus* was a member of the Academy living in the first century B.C. and drawing without much insight on various schools.
28 Cf. Democritus D. 202. For Cynic interest in Democritus see Z. Stewart, *Harv. Stud. Class. Phil.* LXIII (1958), 179–91.
29 This seems to be the right interpretation, though the construction is certainly awkward.
30 E.g. *Rep.* 8. 558 D–559 C and 9. 571 ff.
31 E.g. *NE* 7. 1147 B–1150 A.
32 Cf. *KD* 29; Cic. *De Fin.* 1. 45 and *Tusc. Disp.* 5. 93. In view of the ascetic tone of many Epicurean sayings it is well to keep in mind a fragment like *Sent. Vat.* 63: 'Frugality also has its limit, and the man who disregards it is on a par with the man who errs through excess.' The notion of nature's limit also occurs in vv. 49–51, 54–6, and 59–60 of the present satire. Cf. also Democritus D. 102, 211, 233; Aristippus M. 71 a; Lucilius W. 1201, *virtus quaerendae finem re scire modumque*; and Lucretius, *DRN* 5. 1432–3.
33 *NE* 2. 1106 AB and 4 *passim*.
34 E.g. *Rep.* 1. 349 E, 4. 443 D; *Phileb.* 31 C–32 B, 64 D–65 D.
35 For references and discussion see W. K. C. Guthrie, *A History of Greek Philosophy* (Cambridge, 1962), vol. 1, index under *medicine* and *music*.
36 Cf. vv. 74 and 124.
37 In *Menoec.* 130 Epicurus says that 'everything natural is easy to obtain'. He even declares that he cannot envisage the good if he rules out the pleasures of taste, sex, hearing, and sight (Frag. 10). But if a pleasure was good *per se*, it did not follow that it should be *chosen*, for the harm involved might be too serious. Some of the school's uncertainty is reflected in Cicero, *Tusc. Disp.* 5. 94.

38 A. D. Knox, *Herodes, Cercidas, and the Greek Choliambic Poets* (printed with
    the Loeb Theophrastus), p. 204. See also *Oxyrhynchus Papyri* 8. 1082.
    Horace's relation to Cercidas is discussed in three Italian articles: L. de
    Gubernatis, *Bollettino di Filologia classica*, XIX (1912), 52–6; Q. Cataudella,
    La Parola del Passato, V (1950), 18–31; M. Gigante, *Rivista di Filologia*,
    n.s. LXXXIII (1955), 286–93. Philodemus is a likely intermediary. Diogenes,
    extreme in this as in all else, is supposed to have thought even Aphrodite
    of the market-place too much trouble (Dio Chrys. 6. 17; ps.-Diog. *Epist.* 42
    (Hercher, *Epist. Graec.* p. 256)). Bion, according to D.L. 4. 49, said that
    if Socrates desired Alcibiades and refrained he was a fool; if he did not, then
    his conduct was in no way remarkable. This observation refers to the
    incident mentioned in Plato, *Symp.* 218 C ff.

39 In *The Brothers* of Philemon (Edmonds, 3 A, Frag. 4) Solon is supposed to
    have safeguarded Athenian marriage by setting up brothels. The girls
    stand in full view; there is no deception, no prudery, no nonsense; take
    cheap and immediate satisfaction with whatever woman you choose, and
    then let her go hang—she's nothing to you, ἀλλοτρία 'στί σοι—a phrase
    which for its crass, self-deluding egotism rivals Aristippus' ἔχω καὶ οὐκ
    ἔχομαι—'I have and am not had' (M. 57). See also Eubulus, *Nannion* 67
    and *Pannychis* 84 (Edmonds, II).

40 E.g. Lucilius W. 923–4 and 927–8.

41 It is interesting to find Epictetus later attempting, in the manner of some
    modern theologians, to narrow the gap between moral theory and moral
    practice:

    In your sex-life remain chaste as far as you can before marriage, and if you
    indulge take only those liberties which are not forbidden by law. At the
    same time, you should not be objectionable or censorious to those who do
    indulge, and you should not keep harping on the fact that you yourself
    abstain.   (*Enchiridion* 33)

    It is not surprising that the man who wrote these words should have
    provided the noblest reason for respecting marriage: ὁ ἄνθρωπος πρὸς
    πίστιν γέγονεν—'man is born to fidelity' (*Discourses* 2. 4). Anyone who
    undermines good faith is undermining the characteristic quality of man.
    Adultery destroys self-respect, loyalty, neighbourly feeling, friendship, and
    (ultimately) the state itself. All of which is a far cry from the cheerful
    squalors of the second satire.

42 Thuc. 3. 82; cf. Isoc. *Antid.* 284–5 and *Areop.* 20.

43 For a later period cf. Juvenal 6. 195; Martial 10. 68.

44 Plato, *Rep.* 474D, also speaks of lovers' euphemisms, but the topic is
    employed in a way quite different from that of Horace.

45 E.g. *NE* 1166–7.

46 E.g. Panaetius, as represented in Cic. *De Off.* 1. 90 and 111; Laelius as

represented in *De Amic.* 65 and 92. We shall be cautioned from thinking too much in terms of schools if we recall Democritus D. 102: 'In all things τὸ ἴσον (balance or equity) is fair, excess and deficiency are not.'

47 For the contrast in dress, cf. Varro B. 301–2.

48 Migne, *Bibl. Patr. Graec.* CXXXVI, 1083. Cf. Themistius as cited by Gildemeister and Bücheler in *Rh. Mus.* XXVII (1872), 440.

49 For Crates see Julian, *Or.* 6. 200A and 7. 213C; for Aeschrion see Knox, *op. cit.* p. 262; for Theocritus see Theoc. 17. 107.

50 E.g. D.L. 2. 66 (Aristippus), 7. 160 (Ariston); Teles, p. 5 (Bion); Menander K. 165; Cic. *De Off.* 1. 114; Epictetus, *Enchir.* 17.

51 Cf. L. Radermacher, *Wien. Stud.* XLVII (1929), 79–86.

52 *Sat.* 1. 1. 114–16. The simile grows out of *superare* (112). The tradition can be seen in Alexis (Edmonds, II, Frag. 235), Varro B. 288, and Cicero, *De Sen.* 83. Horace's language, like that of Virg. *Georg.* 1. 512 ff., recalls certain lines of Ennius' *Annals*, in particular W. 443–4. The failure to compare oneself with those who are worse off (111) goes back to Democritus D. 191.

53 Cf. Bion (Teles, p. 16), Lucretius, *DRN* 3. 938 and 960, Cic. *Tusc. Disp.* 5. 118, Plutarch, *Cons. ad Apoll.* 120B, Epictetus, *Enchir.* 15.

54 It is possible, however, that Horace had at the back of his mind vv. 147–8, in which Menedemus says:

> decrevi me tantisper minus iniuriae,
> Chremes, meo gnato facere dum fiam miser.

> I have decided, Chremes, that I diminish the wrong done to my son in proportion as I make myself miserable.

The link between Fufidius and Menedemus is supplied by the combination of harshness and unhappiness. The phrase *patribus duris* (17) may have had some influence at the subconscious level.

55 Ennius, *Ann.* W. 471–2. Cf. Varro B. 542.

56 See F. A. Wright, *AJP*, XLII (1921), 168–9.

57 *Greek Anth.* 5. 132. Cf. Ovid, *Amores* 1. 5. 19 ff.

58 A. W. Mair, Callimachus (Loeb), *Epig.* 33.

59 Cf. Lucretius, *DRN* 5. 925 ff.

60 The commonplace is represented by Democritus D. 60, Crates in D.L. 6. 89, Menander K. 710 and K. 631, Anon. 359 (Edmonds, IIIA). See also the commentators on Catullus 22. 21.

CHAPTER II

1 For 'Poet and Patron (2)', see ch. IX.

2 This is not certain but probable. See L. R. Taylor, *AJP*, XLVI (1925), 161–70.

3 This goes back to the notes of Porphyrion and ps.-Acron on vv. 17 and 18. For a modern discussion see F. Klingner, *Phil.* xc (1935), 461–3.

4 In essence the idea goes back to the first part of ps.-Acron's note on v. 17: *quanto nos, inquit, minus ad honores possumus pervenire, qui vulgo ignoti sumus?* For a modern discussion see K. Büchner, *Riv. di Cult. Class. e Med.* v (1963), 82 ff.

5 It is a fine point, but I prefer to take *prava ambitione procul* as backing up *cautum adsumere* rather than as an extension of *dignos.* In vv. 50–5 it is part of Horace's tact to imply his own worthiness by stressing the careful discernment of Maecenas, who stands aloof from people on the make.

6 Büchner's article cited above (n. 4) brought it home to me that in *Phoenix,* xv (1961), 196 ff., I had not properly considered the punctuation of vv. 63–4. It is better grammar to take *non patre praeclaro sed vita et pectore puro* with *placui* rather than with *secernis*; it is also rather better sense, for it makes the *vita* Horace's own life, which is then taken up in 65 ff., and the *pater* Horace's own father, who is brought in in 71 ff. Büchner takes *patre, vita* and *pectore* as ablatives of quality loosely connected with *ego* (62), but I do not find this convincing. As for *turpi* and *honestum* (63) I cannot see that it makes much difference to the sense whether these are masculine or neuter, but again I may perhaps have given too little weight to some of Büchner's arguments.

7 This is the suggestion of Niebuhr, recorded by Fraenkel, p. 2, n. 3.

8 Quint. 2. 2. 14; cf. 1. 2. 2 and 1. 2. 4.

9 Quint. 2. 2. 15; cf. 1. 3. 17; Juv. 10. 224; Plut. *De Lib. Educ.* 4 AB; Petron. 85–6.

10 Cic. *Cael.* 6–11; Pliny, *Ep.* 3. 3; cf. 4. 13 and Juv. 10. 295–8.

11 Note how Tillius occurs in the middle of the first and third sections (24 and 107). The name Novius has a similar function (40 and 121).

12 The commentators cite Lucilius W. 101. No one seems to have associated this Lucilian reference to Tarentum with the similar reference in v. 59. For the gelded mule see W. D. Ashworth and M. Andrewes, *CR,* n.s. vii (1957), 107–8.

13 The phrase 'exquisite still life' and the point itself are due to Fraenkel, p. 104.

14 The most recent work on ancient biography is W. Steidl, 'Sueton und die antike Biographie', *Zetemata,* 1 (1951). G. L. Hendrickson, *AJP,* xxiii (1902), 389, quotes the rhetorical divisions of γένος, τροφή, ἀγωγή, φύσις ψυχῆς καὶ σώματος, ἐπιτηδεύματα, πράξεις.

15 A summary of the characteristics of Roman invective will be found in Appendix 6 of R. G. M. Nisbet's edition of the *In Pisonem* (Oxford, 1961). The exchange of insults between Antony and Octavian is chronicled by K. Scott in *Memoirs of the American Academy in Rome,* xi (1933), 7–49. The *Indignatio* of Valerius Cato (Suet. *De Gramm.* 11) must have been written in a situation not wholly unlike that of Horace.

16 Cic. *Dom.* 95; cf. *Har. Resp.* 17, and Quintilian 11. 1. 18.

17 Cic. *Sull.* 83; cf. *Fam.* 5. 2. 8, and *Att.* 1. 20. 3.

18 Plut. *De Se Ipsum Citra Invid. Laud.* 542–4. Cf. the present writer's article 'Humble Self-Esteem: A Mannerism of the Younger Pliny', *Classical News and Views*, VII (December 1962), 5–8.

19 D.L. 4. 47. A glance at Bion's letter will reveal how far removed it is from the sixth satire. Not only is Bion's tone ruder but his attitude to his father (whom he candidly admits to have cheated the revenue) is quite different. Here as elsewhere scholars in search of Horatian 'imitations' have often been misled.

20 See A. M. Duff, *Freedmen in the Early Roman Empire* (Oxford, 1928), pp. 52–5.

21 See, for example, Suet. *De Gramm.* 10, 12, 14, 15, and esp. 21—Gaius Melissus the friend of Maecenas and Augustus.

22 Dio 42. 51. 5 and 43. 47. 3. For Caesar's senate see R. Syme, *BSR Papers*, XIV (1938), 12–18.

23 Dio 52. 42. 1; Suet. *Aug.* 35. 1.

24 See, for example, Livy 23. 2. 1; Cic. *Flacc.* 16; and later Quint. 3. 8. 48; 11. 1. 37.

25 'Sallust', *Ad Caes. Epist.* 11. 3; cf. Sall. *Jug.* 85. 4.

26 *Op. cit.* (n. 14 above), p. 396.

27 C. L. Stevenson, *Mind*, XLVII (1938), 331.

CHAPTER III

1 Wesseling (*Observ. Var.* II. 15, quoted in Schütz's ed. (Berlin, 1889) p. 63) thought Maecenas was travelling south to prepare for the conference, which never took place, in the spring of 38 B.C., in which case 2. 6. 42–3 could refer to the journey. Schütz himself preferred to think that Maecenas was on his way to Athens in the autumn of 38 B.C. He and Palmer, arguing against the traditional date of spring 37 B.C., have asked why the party should have travelled to Tarentum via Brundisium. To answer this one has to rely on Plutarch (*Ant.* 35), who says that Antony first crossed to Brundisium and then, after failing to gain access, sailed on to Tarentum. Other objections to 37 B.C. are more trivial. Palmer, for instance, states that, since Octavian and Antony met in person, there were no ambassadors present at Tarentum. But he has forgotten Dio 48. 54, in which the leaders are said to have presented their grievances 'first of all through friends, and then personally'. Palmer is also wrong in saying that 'the annoying gnats and noisy frogs; the chilly evenings and the fire of branches with leaves on; the heavy rains: these suit Autumn better than early Spring'. If the time was April or early May the travellers would have heard the chorus of frogs in the Pomptine Marshes, just as Cicero had heard it sixteen years before

(*Fam.* 7. 18. 3, written on 8 April). According to the naturalists consulted by Gow, such a chorus would not be expected after the beginning of May (*CR*, xv, 1901, 117). As for the chilly evenings and the fire, the party was then in hilly country and was being served with a cooked meal. Finally, in reply to Schütz, who uses the Sirocco (78) to support the autumn against the spring date, we can cite the *Encyclopedia Britannica* (1961) which says 'these winds...are most prominent in the Spring, when cyclonic winds are common and the sea is much cooler than the desert' (23. 652). The question, therefore, remains open, but that is not enough to dispose of the satire's historicity. (The references above are to A. Palmer's 5th ed., London, 1896).

2 *CW*, xlviii (1955), 159–62.

3 This is made likely by W. 287–8, 655, and Cic. *De Fin.* 1. 3. 7 (quoted after W. 635). Too much stress, however, has been laid on W. 133–4, where a ploughman called Symmachus is said to be dying of pneumonia. It is surely improbable that a squire like Lucilius would have undertaken such a journey on account of a farmhand's illness.

4 Lucilius' poem was the first of its kind in Latin, and no Greek prototype exists. Horace, however, was doubtless familiar with Caesar's Journey to Spain (Suet. *Jul.* 56), and after Horace the tradition was carried on by Valgius (W. Morel, *Frag. Poet. Lat.* p. 106), Ovid (*Trist.* 1. 10) and Persius (if ὁδοιπορικῶν is the right reading in *Vita Persi* 45). At a much later period the form was still alive, as may be seen from the journey of Lactantius to Nicomedia (St Jerome, *De Viris Illust.* 80), the introduction to Ausonius' *Mosella*, and the *De Reditu Suo* of Rutilius Namatianus (see *Minor Latin Poets*, trans. by J. W. and A. M. Duff in the Loeb series). The texts have been collected by L. Illuminati in *La satura odeporica latina* (Biblioteca della 'Rassegna', 1938), and they are the subject of a dissertation by H. Grupp, *Studien zum antiken Reisegedicht* (Tübingen, 1953).

5 The significance of the fragment is established by Porphyrion (on 1. 6. 22), who connects it with a bed (not with a dining couch), and by the use of *pede*. A Hebrew parallel for this use is given by P. Haupt, *AJP*, xlii (1921), 166.

6 The purity of the Corsican diary is perhaps due to the Corsicans' timely warning. 'They told me that in their country I should be treated with the greatest hospitality; but if I attempted to debauch any of their women, I might expect instant death' (*The Journal of a Tour to Corsica*, ed. S. C. Roberts, Cambridge, 1923, p. 9).

7 For the second *poenas* Lafaye has suggested *pronus*, *Rev. Phil.* xxxv (1911), 27.

8 Cf. *egens benignae Tantalus semper dapis*, *Epod.* 17. 66. W. 136–7 may have been one of the passages in which Lucilius made fun of Accius—see Porph. on 1. 10. 53, and cf. Warmington, *Remains of Old Latin* ii, 610–11, nos. 66–7.

9 T. Frank, *Catullus and Horace* (New York, 1928), pp. 178–9.

10 Gibbon, *Miscell. Works*, ed. John, Lord Sheffield (London, 1837), p. 567.

11 A. Noyes, *Portrait of Horace* (London, 1947), p. 75.

12 V. D'Antò, as reported by W. S. Anderson, *CW*, XLIX (1955), 57–9.

13 J. J. Savage, *TAPA*, XCIII (1962), 413–15.

14 This also offended Gibbon. 'The gross language of a boatman, and the ribaldry of two buffoons, surely belong to the lowest species of comedy. They might divert travellers in a mood to be pleased with everything; but how could a man of taste reflect on them the day after?' Well, well.

15 Fraenkel, p. 109.

16 *Ibid.* p. 110.

17 J. Dorsch, 'Mit Horaz von Rom nach Brindisi', *Jhb. des St Gym.* (Prag, 1904), p. 5. Norman Douglas has some characteristically lively remarks on Horace's view of nature in *Old Calabria* (London, 1923), p. 42.

18 Quoted by A. Bischoff, 'De Itinere Horatii Brundisino Commentatio', *Sollemnia Anniv. in Gym. Landavino* (Landavi Palatinorum, 1880), p. 1.

19 I cannot find any support in either Aelian 3. 41 or Pliny, *NH* 8. 76 for the notion that *equus ferus* meant a unicorn. There is plenty of evidence that it meant a wild horse, e.g. Varro, *RR* 2. 1. 5, Pliny, *NH* 28. 159 and 197; cf. also Apuleius, *Met.* 7. 16. The mention of a horn in v. 58 shows that Sarmentus has now changed to another animal. A bull seems the most likely; to introduce a unicorn even at this second stage is rather fanciful. The circular scar on Messius' forehead, which may have resulted from the removal of a large wart, reminded Sarmentus of the Cyclops' eye.

20 G. Norwood, *CR*, XXIII (1909), 240. All the relevant authorities are cited by Monroe Deutsch, *CP*, XXIII (1928), 394–8.

21 Dryden, *Essays*, ed. W. P. Ker (Oxford, 1926), II, 95.

22 L. P. Wilkinson, *Ovid Recalled* (Cambridge, 1955), p. 68.

23 For the Greek *Priapea* see *Greek Anth.* 16. 236–43, 260–1. The Latin *Priapea* are printed by F. Bücheler in his edition of Petronius (Berlin, 1882). His commentary is in *Rh. Mus.* XVIII (1863), 381 ff. The most recent work on the subject is the monograph by V. Buchheit, *Zetemata*, XXVIII (München, 1962), which argues strongly for unity of authorship. With the opening of Horace's satire compare no. 10. 4–5: *sed lignum rude vilicus dolavit, | et dixit mihi 'tu Priapus esto'*.

24 Hippolytus, *Philosophumena* 237 (Cruice).

25 Lactantius, *Div. Inst.* 1. 20; Arnobius, *Adv. Gentes* 4. 7; Augustine, *Civ. Dei* 7. 24.

26 This information is based partly on R. Payne Knight, *A Discourse on the Worship of Priapus* (London, 1865), and the anonymous essay printed with it, partly on F. Cumont's article in Daremberg–Saglio, IV, 1 partie, 645–7. The chief modern authority is H. Herter, De Priapo (*Religionsgeschichtliche Versuche und Vorarbeiten*, XXIII (1932)). Herter has also written the article on Priapus in P–W.

27 Priapus' connexion with the fig is illustrated by amulets in the Musée Secret at Naples, consisting of two arms joined at the elbow, one ending in a phallus, the other in a closed fist with the thumb tucked between the first and second fingers. 'The Italian called this gesture *fare la fica*...the Spaniard *dar una higa*...and the Frenchman...*faire la figue*' (Payne Knight, *op. cit.* p. 150). It has been widely used as a device for warding off the evil eye and for expressing contempt in general. Hence the English 'I don't care a fig'. Cf. the article on *fascinum* by G. Lafaye in Daremberg–Saglio, II, 2 partie, 983–7. For further demonstration of the fig's connexion with fertility, see H. J. Rose's remarks on the Nonae Caprotinae in *Religion in Greece and Rome* (New York, 1959), pp. 217–18.

28 Diodorus 4. 6. 4.

29 Shrieking derived this power from its resemblance to the cries of tormented souls, cf. Tib. 1. 2. 47 *iam tenet infernas magico stridore catervas*. Other examples are cited by K. F. Smith in his article on Graeco-Roman magic in *Hastings' Encyclopedia*, VIII, 280. He relates this sound to the screeching of the owl (*strix*) and to the wailing of the banshee. Another device to make contact with the dead was gathering their bones—a practice mentioned in v. 22 of Horace's satire. The principle here is that the part can be made to attract the whole.

30 See Frazer on Ovid, *Fast.* 5. 432.

31 No knives or spades were permitted, because iron, being a very late invention in the history of magic, was a dangerous novelty and therefore tabu. See Frazer on Ovid, *Fast.* 5. 441. The purpose of the ceremony is that the spirits should drink the blood and so regain the power of speech—a parody, of course, of the great scene in *Odyss.* 11.

32 See A. S. F. Gow on Theocritus 2. 2.

33 The latter stands in an attitude of supplication, like a slave about to be flogged or tortured to death. No doubt its hands are bound as in the figurines reproduced by Hubert in his article on magic in Daremberg–Saglio, III, 2 partie, 1518. A somewhat similar pair are described in the Great Paris Papyrus (C. Wessely, *Denkschrift Wien. Acad.* 36. 2. 44 ff.). For other spells see e.g. H. I. Bell *et al.*, *Proc. Brit. Acad.* XVII (1931), 237–87. Some modern instances of envoûtement are quoted in Maurice Bouisson, *Magic*, Eng. trans. (London, 1960), pp. 30 ff.

34 Cf. Virg. *Ecl.* 8. 80–1.

35 Wooden statues were apt to split in the hot sunshine, cf. 2. 5. 39–40.

36 Tac. *Ann.* 2. 32. For magical beliefs and ceremonies as they appear in Roman literature see E. Tavenner, 'Studies in Magic from Latin Literature', *Columbia Univ. Stud. Class. Phil.* (New York, 1916), S. Eitrem, *Symb. Osl.* XXI (1941), 56–79, and G. Luck, *Hexen und Zauberei in der römischen Dichtung* (Zürich, 1962).

37 The third act of Jonson's *Poetaster* begins with an adaptation of this satire.

Another interesting treatment will be found in the eighth satire of Régnier.

38 The ἀδολέσχης inflicts himself on strangers, skips from one topic to another, and refuses to leave his victim alone (cf. D.L. 4. 50). He differs from the λάλος in that (a) he is an empty-headed fool, whereas the λάλος may be genuinely well informed, (b) he does not demand one's attention, whereas the λάλος does, (c) with his grasshopper mind he is incapable of pursuing a topic, whereas the λάλος is unable to leave off. The λάλος complacently admits his defects (cf. vv. 14–15 of this satire, where the pest knows he is being a nuisance), he is tenacious, aggressive, and (unlike the pest) a 'know-all'. Earlier stages in this tradition of character-drawing are represented by Plato, *Rep.* 8. 554 and Aristotle, *NE* 1115 A ff. On the Latin side Horace's poem owes much to the cheerful self-revelation of Catullus (especially no. 10) and Lucilius. I am not convinced, however, that there was a 'pest satire' in Lucilius—see *Phoenix*, xv (1961), 90–6.

39 If Propertius was born in 50 B.C. and this satire was written in 36 B.C. we are left with a fourteen-year-old pest. Even if we stretch the termini to 54 and 34 B.C. we still have a young man of twenty, and one feels that if Horace had been cowed by someone ten years his junior he would probably have used this for comic effect. As for the pest's mother, we know from vv. 27–8 that she was dead.

40 Fuscus was the recipient of the light-hearted *Carm.* 1. 22 (*Integer vitae*) and *Epist.* 1. 10 (see R. G. M. Nisbet's note in *CQ*, n.s. IX, 1959, 74–5). Porph. on *Epist.* 1. 10 says he wrote comedies.

41 The words are *est tibi mater, / cognati, quis te salvo est opus?* Some take the query as a veiled threat, but this is inappropriate because Horace is on the defensive throughout; others take it as a hint that the fellow is mad or that so accomplished an artist could not hope to live long, but the question ought to be an attempt to get rid of the man. Nor, in view of *non sum piger* (19), can Horace be stressing the length of the walk. L. J. D. Richardson, who collected various ideas in *Hermathena*, LXVII (1946), 93–6, suggested that *te salvo* was an oblique form of the salutation *salve* or *salvus sis*. His translation was '(Have you a mother or relatives) who are obliged to greet you?' It would be rather better if this could be emended to 'Have you a mother or relatives who are waiting to greet you?' But I am not sure if this can be extracted from the Latin. Palmer thought Horace was about to warn the pest against the danger of catching his friend's illness. This gives tolerable sense, but one does not expect to be referred back to v. 18. The most recent suggestion by R. Bogaert in *Les Études classiques*, XXXI (1963), 159–66, does not, I think, bring us any closer to a solution, though his collection of material is useful.

42 For the legal problems posed by the satire see H. J. Roby, *Journ. Phil.* XIII (1885), 233–41.

43 Cf. the use of *pulchre* in v. 62.

44 Plaut. *Poen.* 770, *Bacch.* 251; Petron. 75. Cf. Lucilius W. 519 and Horace, *Sat.* I. 5. 21 (*cerebrosus*); Petron. 45 and 58 (*caldicerebrius*).

45 See A. A. Deckman, *A Study of the Impersonal Passive of the Ventum Est Type*, Diss. (Philadelphia, 1920).

46 Plaut. *Capt.* 246. Other possible instances are *Most.* 357 and *Mil.* 450.

47 W. 314.

48 Fraenkel, p. 117. Several of the foregoing points are noted by J. Marou-zeau, *Introduction au Latin* (Paris, 1941), pp. 153–64.

49 See W. S. Anderson, *AJP*, LXXVII (1956), 148–66.

50 See Platner and Ashby, *Topog. Dict. Ancient Rome* (London, 1929), pp. 441–2.

51 *Ibid.* p. 72; cf. G. Lugli, *Roma Antica* (Rome, 1946), p. 172.

52 Work began on Apollo Palatinus in 36 B.C. (Platner and Ashby, *op. cit.* p. 16). The Villa Publica was probably restored in 34 B.C. (*ibid.* p. 581). Lejay's topographical notes on *Sat.* I. 9. 13 and I. 6. 42 are not reliable. E. T. Salmon in a paper in *Studies in Honour of Gilbert Norwood* (Toronto, 1952), pp. 184–93, sees the pair as walking down the Vicus Tuscus, through a Jewish area around the Forum Boarium, and finally being separated near the temple of Apollo Medicus. F. Castagnoli (*Bull. Comm. Arch. Com.* LXXIV, 1952, 53) objects, maintaining (*a*) that Horace would have crossed the Aemilian not the Fabrician Bridge to reach Caesar's Gardens, (*b*) that Salmon's theories about the Jewish area and about the temple of Apollo are far from certain, and (*c*) that the end of the episode took place near the tribunals of the Forum, for that was where the pest was seized by his adversary (*rapit in ius*); also the crowds are the crowds of the Forum. Of these objections the third seems to me to be the strongest. I agree with Salmon, however, that the explanation of *sic me servavit Apollo* should be either literary or topographical. If we try to accommodate both, one weakens the other.

53 *Post sermones vero quosdam lectos nullam sui mentionem habitam ita sit questus: irasci me tibi scito quod non in plerisque eiusmodi scriptis mecum potissimum loquaris. an vereris ne apud posteros infame tibi sit quod videaris familiaris nobis esse?* Suet. *Vita Horati.*

54 The pest's *invidia* is obvious enough. One should not, however, attempt to illustrate it by quoting v. 45 *nemo dexterius fortuna est usus*; for those words probably refer to Maecenas, not to Horace. Both v. 44 and v. 45 should then be given to the pest. The main arguments for this are presented by Lejay in his textual note. Cf. also K. Büchner, *Horaz* (Wiesbaden, 1962), pp. 113–24. I must therefore withdraw the remarks I made in *Phoenix*, XV (1961), 89, n. 37.

55 D. Daiches, *Critical Approaches to Literature* (London, 1959), p. 161. Daiches is discussing the theories of Robert Penn Warren.

CHAPTER IV

1   Suet. *De Gramm.* 2.
2   *Ibid.* 15. From Suetonius' words Bücheler conjectured that the original
    line ran *lastaurus lurco nebulo turpisque popino*; see his ed. of Petronius
    (Berlin, 1882), p. 243, n. 1. Cf. E. Fraenkel, *Eranos*, LIII (1955), 78.
3   Suet. *De Gramm.* 11.
4   *Ibid.* 14.
5   See F. Marx, *C. Lucilii Carminum Reliquiae*, 1, lii–liii.
6   Varro, *RR* 3. 2. 17. Although Varro's context implies social criticism we
    cannot tell how censorious Abuccius' *libelli* were. The word *character*
    suggests style, not just tone. When discussing the characters of style
    Varro chose Lucilius as the representative of *gracilitas* (Gellius 6. 14. 6).
7   In *AJP*, LXXVI (1955), 165–75, I argued that *Sat.* 1. 4 was prompted in
    part at least by charges of malice arising from 1. 2. I still think that such
    evidence as there is favours this view and that the burden of proof rests on
    those who believe with Hendrickson that 1. 4 is just 'a criticism of literary
    theory put concretely'. There must be more doubt, however, on the
    question whether at this stage Horace had also been criticized for reasons
    of style. In any case the important point is that the satire belongs to a real
    polemical context.
8   The opposite view, namely that Horace is contrasting the 'true poetry' of
    Old Comedy with the non-poetic satire of Lucilius, is advanced by G. L.
    Hendrickson in *AJP*, XXI (1900), 125–30. For a more detailed argument on
    this point see *CQ*, n.s. V (1955), 154–6.
9   See *Mnem.* s. 4, X (1957), 319–21.
10 See T. Frank, *Catullus and Horace* (New York, 1928), p. 161; A. Y. Camp-
    bell, *Horace. A New Interpretation* (London, 1924), pp. 65–6, 152; J. Wight
    Duff, *Lit. Hist. of Rome* (London, 1960), p. 174.
11 F. Leo, *Hermes*, XXIV (1889), 75 ff. Cf. Heinze's note on *omnis pendet*.
12 Cf. C. O. Brink in Fondation Hardt, *Entretiens*, IX (1962), 175–200.
13 So G. L. Hendrickson, *AJP*, XXI (1900), 131.
14 So T. Frank, *AJP*, XLVI (1925), 72–4.
15 The foregoing arguments are set out more fully in *CQ*, n.s. V (1955),
    142–8. In that article, however, I went too far in saying that 'this
    poem must be studied primarily in terms of contemporary feuds'
    (148).
16 Cf. *Mnem.* s. 4, X (1957), 325–32.
17 In this context *res* refers more naturally to Lucilius' subject-matter than to
    the circumstances of his time. (In 1. 2. 76, the first passage cited by Heinze,
    there is no problem, for *res* cannot be anything *other* than circumstances.
    In Heinze's second passage, Quint. 10. 1. 97, *res* does not occur at all.)
    This view also gives a neater line of argument: 'Whether Lucilius' rough-

ness was due to his nature or to his subjects, he would have to write more
smoothly if he were alive today.'

18 See *Phoenix*, XIV (1960), 36–44.

19 Useful material will be found in Fiske, chh. 2 and 3, and in Mary A. Grant's
monograph on 'Ancient Rhetorical Theories of the Laughable' in *Univ.
Wisconsin Stud. Lang. and Lit.* XXI (1924).

20 Aristotle, *NE* 4. 1128A.

21 For a survey of the theories of Philodemus see now G. M. A. Grube,
The Greek and Roman Critics (London, 1965), ch. 12.

22 Porphyrion on *Epist.* I. 19. 34.

23 See Marx's grammatical index under *compositio verborum*.

24 A useful and up-to-date investigation of Lucilius' language will be found
in I. Mariotti, *Studi Luciliani* (Firenze, 1960); for a recent survey of the
sermo cotidianus in Horace see D. Bo, *Q. Flacci Opera* (Paravia, 1960), III,
335–50. The older study by J. Bourciez, *Le Sermo cotidianus dans les satires
d'Horace* (Paris, 1927), is still of value.

25 D. Bo, *op. cit.* pp. 58–62. Bo's calculations include the *Epistles* and *Ars Poetica*.

26 Siedow's figures are cited by N.-O. Nilsson, *Metrische Stildifferenzen
in den Satiren des Horaz* (Uppsala, 1952), p. 8.

27 Sturtevant–Kent cited by Nilsson, *op. cit.* p. 12.

28 The elision of a long vowel before a short syllable accounts for 4·8 per cent
of Lucilius' elisions, 2·9 per cent of Horace's in Book 1, 4·3 per cent in
Book 2 (Nilsson, *op. cit.* p. 15). On five occasions Lucilius elides the last
vowel of a cretic word before a short syllable, e.g. *asperi Athones* (W. 105);
see Marx's metrical index under *elisio*. There is only one case in Horace's
first book, namely *tantuli eget* (I. 1. 59); see Nilsson, *op. cit.* pp. 26–7.
In *occupo at ille* (I. 9. 6) the -*o* was short. Lucilius elides an opening monosyllable six times in seven hundred hexameters (i.e. 1 in 117), Horace
seven times in 1030 (i.e. 1 in 147). In Book 2 Horace's rate drops to 2 in
1083 (i.e. 1 in about 540). Lucilius used a few types of synizesis usually
avoided by Horace, in particular *ui* as in *fuisse* (5 times) and *eo* as in *eodem*
(3 times). For instances in Horace see Bo, *op. cit.* pp. 81–2. According to
Braum's figures quoted by Nilsson (*op. cit.* pp. 86–7) Lucilius has a monosyllable just before the main caesura in the third foot three times more often
than Horace in Book 1. There seems to be no significant difference in regard
to hiatus or tmesis.

29 There is a slip at this point in Heinze's calculations (p. xlii of his edition).
Heinze's is the best short survey of the metre of the *Satires*; I have omitted
many of the features noted by him, because they did not seem to represent
any significant contrast with the practice of Lucilius. Nilsson (*op. cit.*
pp. 114–15) points out that final monosyllables in Horace drop from 119
cases in Book 1 to 83 in Book 2. I was unable to consult J. Hellegouarc'h,
Le Monosyllabe dans l'hexamètre latin (Paris, 1964).

30 Traces of another *recusatio* have been found in W. 1008–15. See Cichorius, pp. 183–92.
31 L. A. Mackay, *CR*, n.s. XIII (1963), 264–5, maintains that the Ennian line is not a hexameter but an incomplete trochaic septenarius.
32 Cic. *Tusc. Disp.* 1. 107.
33 Gellius 17. 21. 49. Cf. *Vita Persi* 50–5.
34 Porphyrion's note on 1. 10. 53.
35 The demagogue is described in W. 273–4:

> haec, inquam, rudet ex rostris atque heiulitabit
> concursans veluti Ancarius[?] clareque quiritans.

This, I say, he will keep yelling and roaring from the platform, rushing up and down like Ancarius and making loud appeals.

36 Other examples are *drachma* (2. 7. 43), *lasanum* and *oenophorum* (1. 6. 109).
37 *Naumachia, petaurum, trigon, stadium, gymnasium, schema* and (figuratively) *palaestra*.
38 Cf. Archestratus—ἰχθύος..., ὃν ἐν μέτρῳ οὐ θέμις εἰπεῖν—'a fish which cannot be named in metre'—quoted in Athenaeus 7. 284e.
39 In the sphere of medicine Horace has *cardiacus, cheragra, collyrium, helleborus, lethargus,* and *podagra.* Lucilius has *apepsia, arthriticus, gangrena herpestica, icterus, mictyris, panacea, podagrosus.* Half of Horace's terms come from the satire on madness (2. 3). Lucilius may well have had many more than those quoted above; it is also probably due to chance that while Horace has two musical terms (*chorda* and *cithara*) Lucilius has none.
40 'Entremêlé aux mots de la langue nationale, le mot étranger déroute les indiscrets, établit entre les interlocuteurs une sorte de complicité, d'intimité; il réveille les souvenirs de l'adolescence studieuse, des voyages faits autrefois aux terres d'une civilisation plus brillante' (J. Perret, *Information littéraire*, III, 1951, 185).
41 This is the interpretation of N. Terzaghi, *Lucilio* (Torino, 1934), pp. 365–6. The hypothetical disyllable is parallel to *acoetin* and has a social not a physical meaning; therefore it is a word like *moecham*, πόρνην, or (in the figurative sense) *cunnum.* But after inviting us to supply our own word Lucilius unexpectedly and ironically supplies κούρην *eupatereiam.* To introduce Tyro, as some editors do, in the sixth line ruins the climax formed by *Helenam ipsam denique.* Nor does it help to transpose the lines, for then the missing disyllable would have to be something physical (Munro, *Journ. Phil.* VII, 1877, 308, suggests *lippam* and *fuscam*); but after using so many physical terms already why should Lucilius balk at another? The aposiopesis must carry a moral imputation, as in Juv. 8. 275 and Prop. 3. 6. 22. Also the list of blemishes *verrucam, naevum,* etc. should not be moved forward; they should form a climax with *alias* and *Helenam.*
42 I. Mariotti, *op. cit.* pp. 55–7.

NOTES

43 The precise interpretation of these fragments is very difficult. It is likely, as Cichorius (p. 227) maintained, that the speaker was reflecting the old-fashioned Roman hostility to all things Greek. Lucilius himself probably allowed Greek terms in everyday speech in connexion with items of luxury but ridiculed their application to more mundane objects. So Mariotti, *op. cit.* p. 54.

44 See W. 1067–9.

45 G. L. Hendrickson's articles on Horace and Valerius Cato in *CP*, XI and XII (1916 and 1917), are still essential reading, though they contain a good deal of controversial material. For articles on the eight lines prefixed to 1. 10, which Hendrickson wrongly (I think) regarded as genuine, see E. Burck's appendix to Heinze's edition, p. 411.

46 These points all tell against the view (most recently advanced by J. Perret in his book *Horace*, Paris, 1959, p. 59) that *cantare* in 1. 10. 19 means 'to mock'. In 2. 1. 46 the verb (with strong aid from the context) refers to the lampooning of a living person. It never means 'to parody', and there is no parallel for its use in connexion with the dead.

47 R. P. Robinson, *TAPA*, LIV (1923), 109.

48 H. Bardon, *La Littérature latine inconnue* (Paris, 1952), pp. 338–9.

49 T. Frank, *AJP*, XLVI (1925), 74, n. 6.

50 The biographical material on all these men is collected and discussed by C. L. Neudling in *A Prosopography to Catullus* (Oxford, 1955). The monograph is no. 12 of the series *Iowa Stud. in Class. Phil.*

51 I do not know what Frank's source was for Pitholaus' eulogy of Pompey.

52 On the old problem of whether Horace's Furius is the Neoteric poet Furius Bibaculus the following points may be made. (1) The epic on Gaul alluded to in 1. 10. 36–7 and 2. 5. 40–1 was surely a contemporary work. Otherwise Horace's phrasing (*dum...dumque...haec ego ludo*) would be very strange and the gibe exceedingly weak. (2) The scholiasts both identify the author as Bibaculus. (3) We know from Macrobius (W. Morel, *Frag. Poet. Lat.* pp. 81–3) that a certain Furius wrote *Annales*. A Virgilian scholiast (Schol. Veron. *Aen.* 9. 379) speaks of *Annales Belli Gallici* and this could be what ps.-Acron on 2. 5. 41 refers to as *Pragmatia Belli Gallici*—a work which he ascribes to Bibaculus. On the other hand (1) we should not expect a Neoteric to have written an epic of this type, (2) at least two of the lines quoted by Macrobius have a decidedly archaic flavour, viz. *pressatur pede pes, mucro mucrone, viro vir* and *quod genus hoc hominum, Saturno sancte create?* (3) Furius Bibaculus, who is known to have abused Caesar and Augustus (Tac. *Ann.* 4. 34), would hardly have written an epic in Caesar's praise. Of the last three points (1) and (2) are not weakened by the precedent of Varro of Atax, for Varro almost certainly wrote his epic on the *Bellum Sequanicum* before he assumed the Neoteric style—see Else Hofmann, *Wien. Stud.* XLVI (1928), 159–76. Nor

19   289   R S H

is there any parallel in the career of Virgil. So one turns without much confidence to the view that Horace's Furius was contemporary with but distinct from Bibaculus.

53 W. S. Anderson, *Univ. California Publ. Class. Phil.* XIX (1963), 63 ff.

54 In certain respects, e.g. his small output and careful craftsmanship, Horace was closer than Lucilius to Callimachus. All the main points of resemblance are stated with force and economy by F. Wehrli in 'Horaz und Kallimachos', *Museum Helveticum*, 1 (1944), 69–76. Some interesting comparisons are suggested by M. Puelma Piwonka in his large book *Lucilius und Kallimachos* (Frankfurt, 1949). It has to be said, however, that the author is sometimes reckless in his use of the fragments.

55 Lucilius may also have written lines of a homosexual character about the boys Gentius and Macedo, though we cannot be sure of the context. See Apuleius, *Apol.* 10. The fragments containing their names (W. 308–10) are by no means clear. In W. 308–9 Cichorius (p. 288) is probably right in reading *nunc, praetor, tuus est: meus, si discesseris horno, / Gentius.* 'Now, Praetor, Gentius is yours; but he will be mine if you depart this year.' If this is correct, then Donatus, who preserves the fragment in his note on Terence, *And.* 976, presumably meant *nunc...tuus est...Gentius* as a parallel to Terence's *tuus est nunc Chremes.* Warmington, more naturally, sees the parallel in *nunc praetor tuus est.* But this, unfortunately, makes no sense of the fragment. (Two minor points: Warmington was mistaken in attributing *discesserit* to Cichorius; Cichorius himself accidentally omitted the important comma after *praetor* on p. 287.)

56 Diomedes (*Gram. Lat.* 1. 485. 11) mentions Lucilius, Catullus, Horace and Bibaculus as the chief iambic writers. Horace, of course, is included for his *Epodes*, not for his *Satires*.

57 It might perhaps be argued that the scholarly element in Lucilius was a further attraction to men like Cato, Hermogenes and Demetrius. The type of scholarship, however, associated with Neoteric poetry (and in particular with the poetry of Cinna) was rather different from what we find in Lucilius. The satirist showed little interest in obscure myths, remote places, esoteric cults, and elaborate genealogies.

58 See P. Sonnet, P–W, under Trebatius 2252–3.

59 L. R. Shero, *Univ. Wisconsin Stud. Lang. and Lit.* XV (1922), 155.

60 Juv. 1. 77–8:

> quem patitur dormire nurus corruptor avarae,
> quem sponsae turpes et praetextatus adulter?

Who can sleep when his son's greedy wife is being seduced, when brides have no morals, and adolescents practise adultery?

On the subject of Horace's insomnia it is perhaps worth remarking that when he says *at nequeo dormire* he still has Trebatius' *quiescas* in his mind.

61 Heinze points out that Horace's father was not descended from the Roman colonists of Venusia but from some Lucanian or Apulian prisoner of war. No doubt this is historically correct and I accepted it in *Hermathena*, XC (1957), 48, n. 4. But it is better to assume that for dramatic purposes Horace is representing himself as a Venusian colonist protecting Roman territory.

62 Cf. Lejay, introd. to 2. 1, p. 295; Fiske, p. 377; Shero, *op. cit.* p. 157.

63 These points are listed in *AJP*, LXXVI (1955), 174.

64 For the libel law at Rome see R. E. Smith, *CQ*, n.s. 1 (1951), 169–79.

65 The double meaning of *diffindere* is untranslatable. It means to 'break off' or adjourn a meeting as well as to 'break off' something from what has just been said, i.e. to diminish its truth. As for the nut-cracking, I am perhaps over-interpreting. But Horace cannot have meant grit in a piece of bread or a stone in a soft fruit. Envy bites the surface, expecting it to be brittle, but instead finds it hard. Horace may have had in mind the fable of the viper and the file (Phaed. 4. 8), but the file is able to bite back, which is more than *solido* implies. P. H. L. Eggermont, *Mnem.* s. 3, X (1942), 69–76, thinks there is an allusion to the proverb *e nuce nucleum qui esse vult, frangit nucem*—'If you want to eat the kernel crack the shell'.

66 These poems have been compared by L. R. Shero, *op. cit.*, and more recently by E. J. Kenney, *Proc. Camb. Phil. Soc.* n.s. VIII (1962), 34–8.

67 See Cic. *Fam.* 7. 10. 2; 7. 22.

68 See E. Fraenkel, *JRS*, XLVII (1957), 66–70.

CHAPTER V

1 Keller's findings on the scholiasts are summarized in E. C. Wickham's edition (Oxford, 1877), I, xxi–xxiii.

2 See *Hermathena*, LXXXVII (1956), 52–60.

3 Certain aspects of this whole subject have been treated by Fr. Vogel, *Berl. Phil. Woch.* XXXVIII (1918), 404–6; W. Becher, *ibid.* LII (1932), 955–8; N. Terzaghi, *Arcadia*, IX–X (1932), 159–72; J. Marouzeau, *L'Ant. class.* IV (1935), 365 ff. The last general treatment to be published was that of A. Cartault in his *Étude sur les Satires d'Horace* (Paris, 1899). This work is still useful, but in his chapter on the names Cartault was apt to look for real individuals where none existed.

4 Crispinus I. 1. 120, I. 3. 139, I. 4. 14, 2. 7. 45; Fabius I. 1. 14, I. 2. 134.

5 What we know of Sarmentus comes mainly from the scholiast's comment on Juv. 5. 3. It is all set out in Palmer's note on Hor. *Sat.* I. 5. 52.

6 R. Syme, *Sallust* (California, 1964), pp. 281–2.

7 Cic. *Att.* 5. 8. 2. Fausta's twin brother was killed after Thapsus in 46 B.C. Her lover Villius is usually equated with the Sextus Villius mentioned in *Fam.* 2. 6. 1 (53 B.C.). Longarenus is unknown. Another of Fausta's

paramours, Pompeius Macula (Macrobius 2. 2. 9), was probably the man referred to in *Fam.* 6. 19. 1 (45 B.C.).

8   This is the traditional view; see Klebs in P–W, I, 1472, and Frank in *CQ*, XIV (1920), 160–2. Such an eminent contemporary, however, seems rather out of place in this satire.

9   An Albius is also mentioned in 1. 4. 28 as having a compulsive interest in bronzes. If he is identical with the *filius* of v. 109, then we have to believe that a man who nearly beggared himself by extravagance in his youth acquired a fortune large enough to support an expensive hobby. We also have to believe that Horace is referring to two different phases in the man's career. All this seems very unlikely. If the Albius of v. 28 is the father in v. 109, then he was dead; for the son is described as wasting his inheritance.

10 Cic. *Att.* 12. 33. 1; *Fam.* 7. 23. 2 and 3.

11 M. Antistius Labeo, the lawyer, is possible temperamentally but not chronologically, having been born *c.* 50 B.C. His father, who died at Philippi, is of the right age, but there is no evidence of any *insania*. The tribune C. Atinius Labeo committed an act of *insania*, but this took place in 131 B.C. Fraenkel, p. 89, suggestst hat we overcome this chronological difficulty by assuming that the name occurred in Lucilius.

12 He was alive in 52 B.C. (*Pro Mil.* 46), but dead before the *Brutus* was composed—i.e. before 46 B.C. (P–W, II, 1253 (Klebs)).

13 Staberius 2. 3. 84; Ummidius 1. 1. 95; Aristippus 2. 3. 100; Marsaeus 1. 2. 55.

14 Cic. *Fam.* 13. 11. 1, 12. 1 (P–W, no. 7).

15 Cic. *Att.* 13. 49, 50, 51; *Fam.* 7. 24. The evidence is summarized by Wickham in his introduction to *Sat.* 1. 3. I have distinguished the Sardinian Tigellius of 1. 2. 3 and 1. 3. 4 from the Hermogenes (Tigellius) mentioned in 1. 3. 129, 1. 4. 72, 1. 9. 25, 1. 10. 17–18, 80, 90. The two men were regarded as identical by the scholiasts and this opinion has been held in recent times by Münzer (P–W, VI, A1, 943–6), Ullman (*CP*, X, 1915, 270–96) and Fairclough (Loeb, p. 54). But since Kirchner many scholars have recognized two different men. Argument has centred on personal characteristics, on the names employed, on the relationship with Calvus, and on the question whether Hermogenes was alive or dead. Nothing can be proved under the first two headings; the traits and names could belong to one person but need not do so. As regards Calvus, we know that he ridiculed the Sardinian (*Sardi Tigelli putidum caput venit*), but according to 1. 10. 17–19 he was *admired* by Hermogenes and his friend (*nil praeter Calvum et doctus cantare Catullum*). The natural interpretation of this point is in favour of the separatists. Realizing this, Ullman wanted to take *cantare* either ironically or else in the sense of 'satirize' (*op. cit.* pp. 295–6). But, as we argued above (p. 289), *cantare* cannot be given a pejorative sense here. Fairclough, who purports to follow Ullman, translates it by 'dron-

ing', but this does not bring out the opposition required by Ullman, namely Horace–Calvus–Catullus–Atticists versus Lucilius–Tigellius–Asianists. We know that the Sardinian was dead. What about Hermogenes? He certainly appears to be alive, because his actions occur in the present tense, except at 1. 10. 18, and there the verb is always taken as perfect rather than preterite. Again the unitarians have to provide another explanation, and they do not offer the same one. Münzer says that Hermogenes had become a type figure and could therefore be referred to in the present tense. Ullman regards Hermogenes as a very specific individual and would explain the tense in terms of expressions such as 'Horace tells us to enjoy our youth'. Münzer's is the more plausible theory (Ullman's idioms are not strictly analogous), and it must be tested by an examination of each passage. Now in 1.3. 129, 1.4. 72, and 1.9. 25 it is possible to substitute some general phrase for Hermogenes, e.g. 'a Hermogenes', or 'someone like Hermogenes'. But in the other passages this cannot be done so easily. In 1. 10. 18 Hermogenes is associated with a particular ape (*iste*); in 80 he is closely connected with Fannius, and almost as closely with Demetrius and Pantilius. And if they are all banished from reality, the following lines with their references to Maecenas, Virgil, and the rest are gravely weakened. Finally, in 90–1 a general substitution of this kind is virtually impossible.

16 Vogel, *op. cit.*, points to the antithesis *Scaeva*/*dextera*. I should think, however, that *dextera* was put in on account of *Scaeva* rather than vice versa.

17 W. 1136–7. In 180 B.C., when Cato was buying land for the Basilica Porcia, Maenius sold his house, reserving the right to build a balcony on one of the columns of the new Basilica. K. Lehmann-Hartleben in *AJP*, LIX (1938), 280–90, rejects the evidence for an earlier column in honour of C. Maenius.

18 See Friedländer, *Roman Life and Manners*, IV, pp. 257–63 of the Eng. trans. by A. B. Gough (London, 1913). The other two names in the passage do not help us. Fulvius is common enough. Rutuba may be a significant name. Varro used *rutuba* in the sense of *perturbatio* (Non. 167.9); hence Marouzeau, *op. cit.* p. 374, renders Rutuba by *Le Grabuge*. All this proves nothing about the figure's reality. No one who saw 'The Brown Bomber' in action would have mistaken him for an abstract type.

19 This is the theory of Terzaghi, *op. cit.* pp. 165–6. He quotes the following note from the ps.-Acron, claiming that it preserves a genuine tradition:

Albucius, cum convivaretur, servis suis officia distribuebat et antequam aliquis eorum peccaret caedebat eos, dicens vereri se ne, cum parassent [sic], caedere illi non vacaret.

When Albucius was giving a dinner-party he used to assign duties to his slaves, and before any of them did anything wrong he used to beat them, saying he was afraid that when they had made preparations he would have no time to beat them later.

I do not know what authority there is for *parassent*. Hauthal's *peccarent* gives better sense—'when they did something wrong he would have no time etc.'.

20 W. 450–3.

21 See Cichorius, pp. 187 ff.

22 *Lucilio auctore* is a conjecture of Marx (1212 in his edition).

23 1. 1. 102; 1. 8. 11; 2. 1. 22; 2. 3. 175, 224; 2. 8. 23, 25, 60.

24 In W.'s translation, however, 'questioning him' appears to be a slip.

25 Housman, *CQ*, 1 (1907), 59.

26 Donatus, vol. II, P. Wessner (Teubner), p. 536. *Montane* was defended in both places by F. Leo in *Gött. Gel. Anz.* XI (1906), 843–4.

27 A. Cartault, *op. cit.* p. 288.

28 The occurrence of Lucilius in the ps.-Acron's comment on 2. 1. 22 makes no sense and must be a slip.

29 Fraenkel has suggested that Labeo (1. 3. 82) and Barrus the effeminate fop (1. 6. 30) may have figured in Lucilius (*Horace*, p. 89, and *Festschrift Reitzenstein*, 1931, p. 130, n. 1). Lejay thinks that Galba (1. 2. 46) may be connected with the Galba mentioned by Cicero in *De Orat.* 1. 239–40, and that Horace may have found the name in Lucilius. Terzaghi, *op. cit.* pp. 166–8, thinks that the Albius of 1. 4. 28 is the slow-witted man who is referred to by Cicero in *De Orat.* 2. 281 and who probably appeared in Lucilius. But *stupet aere* does not necessarily imply slowness of wit, and the identification is unconvincing on chronological grounds.

30 See W. 744.

31 Caprius and Sulcius (1. 4. 65 f. and 70) also present a problem. Radermacher (*Wien. Stud.* LIII, 1935, 80 ff.) thinks (*a*) that the names suggest figs called *caper* and *sulca*—an inference from *caprificus* and Columella 5. 10. 11; (*b*) that this in turn suggests the Greek συκο-φάντης, an informer (cf. Porph.'s note: *hi acerrimi delatores et causidici fuisse traduntur*); (*c*) that the names also hint at *caper* and *sulcus* (=*cunnus*). (*c*) is scarcely apposite. (*b*) is ingenious but somewhat far-fetched. It also depends on (*a*) which is by no means certain. I have not seen *caper* alone in this sense, and the reading at Columella 5. 10. 11 is doubtful. On the whole it is probably best to take the names as referring to contemporary lampoonists (see Ullman, *TAPA*, XLVIII, 1917, 117–19). This would be still more likely if we followed Fraenkel's suggestion (*Horace*, p. 127, n. 3) and read *Sulgius*.

32 Cic. *Att.* 2. 19. 3. The Roman audience was always on the look-out for a line which could be given a contemporary application. Cf. *Sest.* 57, 120.

33 Stertinius 2. 3. 33; Furius 2. 5. 41; Philodemus 1. 2. 121.

34 *Greek Anth.* 5. 115. Cf. *Epig. ascribed to Martial*, 20. 5–6 (Demophiles).

35 Luscus 1. 5. 34; Nasidienus 2. 8. 1; Arellius 2. 6. 78; Gargonius 1. 2. 27; Scetanus 1. 4. 112. These suggestions are to be found in Palmer, p. xvi, and Marouzeau, *op. cit.*

36 Tantalus 1. 1. 68; Sisyphus 2. 3. 21; Agave 2. 3. 303; Orestes 2. 3. 133; Atrides 2. 3. 187 ff.; Ulysses 2. 5. 100; Ajax 2. 3. 187; Tiresias 2. 5. 1; Penelope 2. 5. 76; Helen 1. 3. 107. Tyndaridae (1. 1. 100) should also be included.

37 Dama 1. 6. 38; 2. 5. 18, 101; 2. 7. 54; Davus 1. 10. 40; 2. 5. 91; 2. 7. 2.

38 Apella 1. 5. 100.

39 *CP*, xv (1920), 393.

40 See Seneca, *Epist.* 114. 4 ff., and Mayor on Juv. 1. 66 and 12. 39.

41 Palmer (*Satires*, 5th ed. London, 1896), pp. 314 and 368.

42 Frank, *Class. Stud. presented to Capps* (Princeton, 1936), pp. 159 ff.

43 *Ibid.*; E. A. Hahn, *TAPA*, lxx (1939), 213 ff.

44 E. Courbaud, *Horace. Sa vie et sa pensée à l'époque des Épîtres* (Paris, 1914), p. 5, n. 2.

45 The quotations are taken respectively from Palmer, p. xii; Morris, p. 15 of the introduction to his edition (New York, 1909); Palmer, p. xii; Fiske, p. 370; Page, in his edition (London, 1901) of the *Odes*, p. xv; Hadas, *Hist. of Lat. Lit.* (New York, 1952), p. 167; Highet on *Satura* in the *Oxford Classical Dictionary*; Wilkins, *Roman Lit.* (London, 1890), p. 95; Palmer, p. xiii.

46 *Fest. Reitz.* pp. 119 ff.

47 See, for example, pp. 87–8, 101, 144, 152.

48 *Ibid.* p. 101, n. 2.

49 *Ibid.* p. 103; cf. *Fest. Reitz.* p. 130.

50 It is a short step from this to the not uncommon idea that what Horace took from Lucilius was not 'his own', and that the early poems did not really indicate his true 'self'. The violence and grossness of certain epodes are often excused by reference to the Greek iambic tradition or the harsh circumstances of the poet's life at that period—circumstances which are supposed to have goaded him into writing poems essentially alien to his nature. The ultimate stage in this approach is reached by Courbaud, *op. cit.* p. 21, according to whom neither epode, nor satire, nor ode provided the natural vehicle for Horace's genius; the epistle, it appears, was the only genre for which 'il fût réellement né'. One can only feel thankful that the poet discovered his proper *métier* before it was too late.

51 The quotations are taken respectively from *Horace*, pp. 144, 145; *Fest. Reitz.* p. 135 (das Stadium der Überreife eingetreten ist); *Horace*, p. 129.

52 Courbaud, *op. cit.* p. 11. Cf. on the same page the remark that 'une telle œuvre...n'est plus du tout une satire'.

53 G. L. Hendrickson, *AJP*, XVIII (1897), 323. It should perhaps be added that *Epist.* 2. 2. 22 is the one place where Horace uses the word *epistula*.

54 That is the way the scholiast understood the lines; see O. Jahn's ed. of Persius (Lipsiae, 1843) p. 275).

55 The *turbes* has been disputed. Certainly the metaphor is far from clear. I take it, however, that *splendescat* is contrasted with *nigra rubigine*. This seems to indicate a difference of spirit. *Non alia cura* would suggest that the same pains had been taken over the style of both.

56 R. A. Brower, *Alexander Pope. The Poetry of Allusion* (Oxford, 1959), p. 184.

CHAPTER VI

1 Other collections containing ten (or a multiple of ten) pieces include Horace, *Epist.* 1, *Carm.* 2 and 3; Tibullus 1; Ovid, *Am.* 2.

2 E.g. Heinze, p. xxii. K. Büchner, who accepts Heinze's division in *Horaz* (Wiesbaden, 1962), p. 123, speaks of a movement from the heavy to the cheerful. This is true to the extent that the second trio contains one piece (5) which is lighter than anything in the first, and the third trio contains two pieces (7 and 8) which are lighter than anything in the second.

3 F. Boll, *Hermes*, XLVIII (1913), 143–5.

4 A useful work of reference is J. André, *L'Alimentation et la cuisine à Rome* (Paris, 1961). For the living conditions of the Roman *plebs* see Z. Yavetz, *Latomus*, XVII (1958), 500–17.

5 Polybius 31. 25. 3 ff.; Pliny, *NH* 17. 244; Sallust, *Cat.* 10. 1, *Jug.* 41. 2. Cf. Velleius 2. 1. 1–2. On this whole question see D. C. Earl, *The Political Thought of Sallust* (Cambridge, 1961), chh. 1 and 4.

6 This view is based on Aristotle, *Pol.* 4. 11. 6–7.

7 See Tacitus, *Ann.* 3. 53 with Furneaux's note, and Suet. *Jul.* 43.

8 See Aulus Gellius 2. 24; Macrobius, *Sat.* 3. 17.

9 For a few more details about the *Lex Fannia* see Athenaeus 6. 274 C.

10 Suetonius, *Jul.* 43. For the sentiment compare Livy 34. 4. 14 and Tacitus, *Ann.* 3. 54 (*splendidissimo cuique exitium*).

11 Athenaeus 6. 274 E.

12 W. 1241, cf. Pliny, *NH* 10. 140. For a similar attitude to the Licinian law, cf. Lucilius W. 599.

13 The sturgeon was valued highly in the time of Gallonius, who was a contemporary of Lucilius. Although there is a favourable reference in Cic. *Tusc.* 3. 43, the fish seems to have become less fashionable towards the end of the Republic, and in the middle of the first century A.D. it had, according to the Elder Pliny (*NH* 9. 60), no reputation. By Martial's time, however, it appears to have recovered its former distinction (13. 91). The fortunes of the sturgeon can be followed in Macrobius, *Sat.* 3. 16—a passage which recent commentators on Horace have tended to ignore. (It may be noted, incidentally, that Macrobius and his source have confused the two Plinys.)

14   Palmer is surely right to take *acetum* as wine—cf. *Sat.* 2. 3. 116–17 and
     Persius 4. 32. This gives the sequence: sour wine (58), oil (59), oil (62),
     sour wine (62).

15   The most likely possibility is that he was C. Sempronius Rufus, for whom
     see P–W, Sempronius no. 79. Palmer is probably right in suggesting that
     the defeat which he suffered was in the elections for the consulship, not, as
     Porphyrion says, for the praetorship. It would surely be a feeble witticism
     to refer to the man anonymously as *praetorius* and to expect that people
     would remember that ten years earlier he had *failed* to become praetor.

16   Athenaeus 4. 157E. Cf. Teles 7–8, Dio Chrys. 6. 12.

17   The syntax of vv. 9–13 is certainly loose, but the following summary,
     based on Wickham, seems adequate: 'After a day's hunting or riding (or,
     if you prefer ball or the discus, play with them), in any case when exertion
     has given you an appetite then see if you can despise plain food.' There is
     a contrast between *fatigat* and *studio fallente laborem*. The man who likes
     Greek games may find the sports of the Roman army wearisome, but when
     he plays ball he forgets about the exertion in his keenness. The phrase *pete
     cedentem aera disco* with its vivid metaphor and its Greek words is far too
     good to lose. Gow (Cambridge, 1896) who, followed by Palmer (p. lxi),
     deletes v. 13 cannot make sense of the contrast between Roman and Greek
     mentioned above; he puts a strain on the tense of *fatigat*; and, as he realized
     himself, he brings *laborem* (12) too close to *labor* (14).

18   With vv. 98–9 cf. Plautus, *Pseud.* 88; with v. 77 cf. Terence, *Phorm.* 342;
     with v. 47 cf. Lucilius W. 203, 211.

19   The closest verbal parallel seems to be Plato (*Phaedo* 83 D), who says that
     every pain and pleasure nails the soul to the body.

20   I have assigned these words to Horace, for it would be too gross an in-
     fringement of character if Damasippus spoke about the incompleteness of
     his cure or called his new missionary zeal an ailment. *Esto ut libet* (31)
     means in effect 'I shan't argue with you about your cure'. This gives the
     impression that Horace himself is perfectly healthy, and so Damasippus
     hastens to disabuse him.

21   A. Nauck, *Trag. Graec. Frag.* (Lipsiae, 1926), Aesch. 225; Loeb, II, no. 121.

22   Cf. the use of *grex* in v. 44.

23   For the importance of the Stoic's beard as a sign of sternness and masculinity
     see A. C. van Geytenbeek, *Musonius Rufus and the Greek Diatribe*, Eng.
     trans. by B. L. Hijmans (Utrecht, 1963), pp. 119 f.

24   This was called antiphrasis (see Lucilius W. 1174).

25   In printing v. 317 question marks are in order but surely quotes are
     not.

26   The reading in v. 318 must be *num tantum*, for we need a more urgent
     repetition of *num tantum* (*magna*) in the previous line. In connexion with
     this fable I have sometimes wondered whether Horace got the idea

(consciously or otherwise) from Maecenas' seal, which represented a frog (Pliny, *NH* 37. 10). The roles, of course, had to be reversed.

27 B. E. Perry, *Studium Generale*, XII (1959), 17 ff. Cf. the same author's previous article in *TAPA*, LXXI (1940), 391–419.

28 Cf. Menander, *Dysc.* 81 ff.; Plautus, *Capt.* 593, 600, 602; Plutarch, *Pomp.* 36; and perhaps Aristophanes, *Vesp.* 1491 (reading βαλλήσεις). The examples are taken from A. O'Brien-Moore, *Madness in Ancient Literature*, Diss. (Princeton, 1924), pp. 58–9.

29 According to B. L. Ullman in *CJ*, LII (1956), 197, it takes over three hours to dissolve a pearl in boiling acetic acid. If the pearl is pulverized, cold acid will dissolve it in ten minutes. Chemically the pearl would act as a rather expensive kind of Alka-Seltzer.

30 F. Schulz, *Classical Roman Law* (Oxford, 1951), p. 197.

31 This was laid down in the Twelve Tables, 5. 7 (Warmington, *Remains of Old Latin*, III, 450–3). For notes on the *cura furiosi* see F. De Zulueta, *The Institutes of Gaius* (Oxford, 1953), part 2, p. 52.

32 See, for example, *De Off.* 3. 95. For an account of *furiosus*, *insanus*, and other such words see the index of D. M. Paschall, 'The Vocabulary of Mental Aberration in Roman Comedy and Petronius', Supplement to *Language*, XV, no. 1 (1939) = Language Dissertation, no. 27.

33 Celsus 3. 18.

34 The U.S. Dispensatory, 25th ed. (1955), p. 1712.

35 See O'Brien-Moore, *op. cit.* pp. 20 ff.

36 In v. 197 Ajax imagines he is killing Ulysses. In Sophocles' version Ajax, believing that he has taken Ulysses prisoner, intends to flog him before killing him. There are extant two verses of a Roman tragedy:

> video video te. vive Ulixes, dum licet.
> oculis postremum lumen radiatum rape.

By suggesting that Ulysses' death is imminent these lines foreshadow Horace's reference and may, indeed, be its source. They are preserved by a combination of Cic. *Acad.* 2. 89 and *De Orat.* 3. 162, and in view of the contexts it seems almost certain that they belong to Ennius' *Ajax*. Yet they are not admitted by Vahlen, and they are attributed to an uncertain poet by Warmington (II, 610) and Klotz (*Scaen. Rom. Frag.* I, 324). Varro, who says that Ajax thought he was killing Ulysses (*Eumenides* B. 125), is also un-Sophoclean, but unlike Horace he makes Ajax cut down trees and pigs instead of sheep.

37 This outline of the *Eumenides* is based on J. Vahlen, *In M. T. Varronis Sat. Menipp. Rel. Coniect.* (Lipsiae, 1858), pp. 168 ff. The fragments are found in B. 117–65.

38 Proverb v. 276 *ignem gladio scrutare*—'poke the fire with a sword'; fable v. 186—cunning fox imitates noble lion. Némethy (*Rh. Mus.* LXI, 1906,

139) refers to Halm, *Fabulae Aesopicae Collectae*, no. 41, but the resemblance is not very close. Myth vv. 71–3—Proteus.

39 Plato, *Euthydemus* 280 B; Aristotle, Frag. 56 (Rose), trans. by W. D. Ross, XII, 57.

40 Menander K. 624. Antiphanes 328 (Edmonds, II), Philemon 99 (Edmonds, III); Terence, *Heaut.* 196.

41 Phoenix, Knox Frag. 3. 7–8; Lucilius W. 583; Cato, ed. Jordan, p. 73; Plutarch, περὶ φιλοπλουτίας 525 (*Moralia*, vol. VII in the Loeb series); Epictetus, Frag. 2. Other references are given by Gerhard, *Phoenix von Kolophon*, pp. 113 ff. In his note on *Agamemnon*, v. 350, and in *Horace*, p. 138, n. 4, Fraenkel has collected a number of passages in which the enjoyment of one's present blessings forms part of a prayer.

42 I owe this and other points to M. J. McGann's B.Litt. Dissertation *Some Structural Devices in the Satires and Epistles of Horace* (Oxford, 1954).

43 One recalls that in the Peripatetic tradition a child did not count as a fully rational being.

44 Similarly no distinction is made between gluttony (γαστριμαργία) and gourmandise (ὀψοφαγία). Or, more precisely, the first includes the second.

45 See Cic. *Paradoxa Stoicorum* 5. This work is translated in the Loeb series after *De Oratore*, Book 3. For a comparison of Horace's treatment with that of Cicero see Lejay, pp. 541–2. In the Cynic–Stoic tradition the idea of the fool as a slave goes back to Diogenes (D.L. 6. 66) and Zeno (D.L. 7. 32–3). For other references see Lejay, pp. 539 ff.

46 One wonders whether the idea of crucifixion in v. 47 led to the metaphorical lashes (*verbera*) in v. 49, and whether the suggestion of driving (*acris...natura intendit*) had anything to do with the riding metaphor in v. 50.

47 The interpretation of vv. 64–7 is controversial. I would put a full stop after *superne* (64), for the *cum* clause is needed by vv. 66–7 if they are not to hang in the air. It is not needed by vv. 63–4, and indeed it is rather awkward to tack *mulier* (65) on to *illa* (63). The paraphrase indicates that I am inclined to follow Schütz in putting a query after *famam* (67), but this is not essential. As for the *furca* and the *dominus furens* in v. 66, I would agree with Lejay in giving them a figurative or psychological sense. For (1) Horace is primarily concerned with the psychological condition of the sinner. In vv. 56–61 the man is in a slavish condition *irrespective* of the mode of punishment or escape, and in v. 71, even though he has escaped, he is still a slave. (2) The same emphasis falls at the end of three other paragraphs, namely in 20, 82 and 94. (3) *Dominus furens* exactly suits lust as an irrational master; indeed we have *dominus* in this very sense in v. 93. The phrase is less suitable for the injured husband.

48 M. J. McGann, *CR*, VI (1956), 99.

49 Heinze on v. 95: 'Davus bleibt nicht im Schema der Argumentation', etc.

50 Cf. Cic. *Parad. Stoic.* 5. 34: *quid est enim libertas? potestas vivendi ut velis.*
51 For a lucid and readable discussion of freedom see M. Cranston, *Freedom. A New Analysis* (London, 1954). Interesting illustrations of the various theories of freedom and their perversions have been collected by Miss D. Fosdick, *What is Liberty?* (New York, 1939).
52 See, for example, *Sat.* 1. 6. 115–18; *Sat.* 2. 6. 63–4; *Carm.* 1. 20. 1–2; *Carm.* 1. 31. 15–16.

CHAPTER VII

1 Excerpts from Athenaeus 14. 660 E; Edmonds, III A, 252–5. My translation is based on Edmonds' at a few points.
2 Sosipater in Ath. 9. 378; Edmonds, III A, 280–5. Nicomachus in Ath. 7. 290 E–291 D; Edmonds, III A, 266–9. Cf. Anaxippus in Ath. 9. 404 C; Edmonds, III A, 158–61. So too, in a later age, Brillat-Savarin was to insist that gastronomy involved natural history, physics, chemistry, cookery, commerce, and political economy (*Physiologie du goût*, Paris, n.d., p. 45). Of the many descriptions of culinary skill perhaps the cleverest comes in a scene from *The Foster-Brothers* of Damoxenus, in which the chef directs his staff like the conductor of an orchestra, blending all his dishes into a delightful harmony. The passage shows a verbal ingenuity which is seldom conceded to New Comedy (see Ath. 3. 102–3; Edmonds, III A, 214–15). The most recent and substantial account of comic cooks is by H. Dohm in *Zetemata*, XXXII (1964).
3 Hoffman's foreword to Brillat-Savarin, p. 2.
4 Ath. 9. 404 B; Edmonds, III A, 158–9.
5 Ath. 12. 516 D; Edmonds, II, 456–9.
6 Ath. 9. 379 D; Edmonds, III A, 270–1.
7 Ath. 7. 310 A.
8 Ath. 3. 111 f.; P. Brandt, *Corpusculum Poesis Epicae Graecae Ludibundae* (Leipzig, 1888), p. 141, no. 4.
9 Ath. 7. 286 A; Brandt, *op. cit.* p. 149, no. 21.
10 Ath. 7. 305 E; Brandt, *op. cit.* p. 147, no. 15.
11 Ath. 7. 316 A; Brandt, *op. cit.* p. 146, no. 14.
12 Morris Bishop, *A Bowl of Bishop* (New York, 1954), p. 1.
13 Apuleius, *Apology*, 39; *Remains of Old Latin* (Loeb), I, 408–11.
14 A. Gellius 6. 16.
15 A. Gellius, *ibid.*
16 A. Gellius 15. 19. 2.
17 For examples of such homilies see O. Hense, *Rh. Mus.* LXI (1906), 1–18.
18 *Geoponica* 20. 46. (The *Geoponica* consist of twenty books of Greek writings on agriculture, dating from various periods. They were collected by Cassianus Bassus of Bithynia in the tenth century A.D.) Another recipe,

from Gargilius Martialis 62, is cited by J. André, *L'Alimentation et la cuisine à Rome* (Paris, 1961), p. 198.

19 B. Flower and E. Rosenbaum, *The Roman Cookery Book* (London, 1958), p. 23. A new Teubner text is being prepared by Miss Mary Milham. It would be hard to imagine a work in which the textual critic had graver responsibilities.

20 P. Grimal and Th. Monod, *Rev. ét. anc.* LIV (1952), 27–38. The chief authority in English on this subject is T. H. Corcoran. See his article in *CJ*, LVIII (1963), 204–10.

21 'At 2. 4. 1 it is not sufficient to compare *Unde et quo Catius?* with phrases used at the beginning of certain Platonic dialogues. The answer of Catius *non est mihi tempus* (1)......*Platona* (3) should make it clear that this whole passage is an elegant transformation of the beginning of the *Phaedrus'* (Fraenkel, p. 136). Anyone who looks up the relevant passage of the *Phaedrus*, which extends over nine sections and has only a few points of similarity with the satire, may feel that Fraenkel is asking rather a lot of Horace's readers. There are similar questions at the beginning of the *Lysis*, the *Ion*, the *Protagoras*, and the *Menexenus*; and in the *Menexenus* Plato, like Horace, uses the third person. Furthermore, in the *Protagoras* Socrates is asked about the man he has just met 'Is he a citizen or a foreigner?' (309 c)—cf. *Sat.* 2. 4. 10 *Romanus an hospes*. In the *Theaetetus* (143 A) Eucleides tells how he took notes (ὑπομνήματα) of Socrates' conversation with Theaetetus and added to them from memory (ἀναμιμνῃσκόμενος)— cf. *Sat.* 2. 4. 2, 6, 8, 11. I should therefore prefer to take the allusion to Plato as a general one.

22 Fiske, p. 158.

23 Aristotle, *Hist. Anim.* 6. 2. 2; Antigonus, *Mirab.* 96; Columella 8. 5. 11; Pliny, *NH* 10. 145. Anyone interested in modern superstitions might inquire why an English housewife prefers brown eggs, while her North American counterpart insists on white.

24 Pliny, *NH* 23. 37, 38, 39, 46. Lucretius (6. 804–5) may testify to a belief that the smell of wine had a violent effect on a man suffering from fever (see Bailey's note). But Catius says nothing about fever.

25 Pliny, *NH* 14. 64.

26 Ath. 1. 26D.

27 H. Warner Allen, *A History of Wine* (London, 1961), pp. 112–13.

28 Pliny, *NH* 23. 35. To the parallels cited by Lejay and Heinze add Servius on *Georg.* 2. 93.

29 In *NH* 22. 92–9 Pliny has quite a lot to say about mushrooms. Realizing that certain types may be dangerous he is careful to prescribe antidotes: 'Fungi are less harmful when cooked with soda—at least if they are well cooked. They are safer when cooked with meat or pearstalks. Pears too are helpful if taken immediately after them. The nature of vinegar is also

opposed to them and combats their effects.' On this cautious and well-intentioned passage Jones (Loeb trans.) comments 'Nearly everything Pliny says about toadstools and poisonous fungi is false, and his advice would lead to fatal results if followed'.

30   W. Clausen in *Phil.* CVI (1962), 205–6, would delete v. 32 as an interpolation.

31   Lejay, p. 453.

32   Cic. *Fam.* 9. 24. 3.

33   For Hippolochus and Lynceus see Athenaeus 3. 126 E and 4. 128–30 D.

34   For Heracleides see Gulick's index to the Loeb Athenaeus, vol. VII.

35   Josef Martin, *Symposion* (Paderborn, 1931).

36   For Matron see Ath. 4. 134 D–137 C; Brandt, *op. cit.* pp. 53–95.

37   See Cic. *Brut.* 160, 172, *De Orat.* 2. 244, 253, 281 f., *Planc.* 33, *Att.* 6. 3. 7, *Fam.* 9. 15. 2.

38   L. R. Shero, *CP*, XVIII (1923), 129–30. Shero (p. 133, n. 2) rightly rejects the theory of Fiske (pp. 384 and 411) that Lucilius wrote a banquet satire about Gallonius.

39   It is held, for example, by Palmer, Wickham, and Lejay.

40   Edict of Prices 4. 43.

41   Housman (*CQ*, VII, 1913, 28) took *maris expers* in the sense of 'emasculated', maintaining that Hydaspes was a negro and Alcon a eunuch. The need for a second adjective to balance *fuscus* is not so great as he makes out; the phrase *maris expers* in this context would surely suggest the Greek ἀθάλαττος, and in Persius 6. 39 it probably means 'insipid'.

42   Galen 10. 833 (Kühn); cf. 12. 839. According to Pliny, *NH* 14. 73 and 75, little or no salt was required in wines from Clazomenae, Lesbos, and Ephesus.

43   Warner Allen, *op. cit.* pp. 70–1.

44   Apicius 4. 2. 12. Apicius sometimes shows an appealing simplicity: 'You can make bad honey good for selling as follows: mix one part of bad honey with two parts of good' (1. 11. 2).

45   Cf. *Il.* 1. 6, *Aen.* 1. 753.

46   Cf. *Od.* 11. 43, *Il.* 7. 479.

47   W. 70.

48   The commentators point out that he was *pater cenae*.

CHAPTER VIII

1   See P. E. Corbett, *The Roman Law of Marriage* (Oxford, 1930), pp. 2–5, 51–7, 239–40; H. J. Roby, *Roman Private Law* (Cambridge, 1902), vol. I, book 2, chh. 4 and 12; H. F. Jolowicz, *Historical Introduction to the Study of Roman Law* (Cambridge, 1939), chh. 8 and 14.

2   See *Cambridge Ancient History*, IX, 781 ff.; and now J. P. V. D. Balsdon, *Roman Women* (London, 1962), ch. 2.

that Maecenas should retire from public life. (b) The fare which Horace offers is not luxurious. He could never put on his invitation card the motto of the city mouse *in rebus iucundis vive beatus*. Food and drink make a relatively minor contribution to his convivial spirit. (c) The awareness of death varies considerably in intensity between, say, *Carm.* 3. 21 and *Carm.* 4. 12. Where this awareness is most intense the *carpe diem* mood is least Epicurean.

See Bailey's note on Lucretius 2. 20–33, and the passages cited there.
Lucretius 2. 29–33; cf. 5. 1392–1404.
The term is taken from A. O. Lovejoy and G. Boas, *Primitivism and Related Ideas* (Baltimore, 1935).
Epodes 7 and 16.
The material is presented very fully by J. Perret in *Les Origines de la légende [tr]oyenne de Rome* (Paris, 1942), but Perret's extreme scepticism does not [c]arry conviction. See the reviews by P. Boyancé in *Rev. ét. anc.* XLV [1]943), 275–90, and A. Momigliano in *JRS*, XXXV (1945), 99–104.
[S]uet. *Jul.* 6.
[P]hilological Monographs of the APA, I (1931).
[Se]e Fraenkel, p. 137.

APPENDIX

[Qu]otations are from W. P. Ker's edition of the Essays (Oxford, 1926),

[Th]e fourth book, which contains the attack on Lyce, was published over [...]een years after the *Satires*. The same historical error is repeated on p. 101, [wh]ere Dryden associates himself with Holyday's view that 'there was never [...]h a fall as from his *Odes* to his *Satires*'. No doubt the mistake is largely [...] to the editors' habit of printing the *Odes* before the *Satires*. Another [...]t of the same kind crops up in connexion with Persius. On p. 70 Dryden [...] that Persius' words 'are not everywhere well chosen, the purity [...]atin being more corrupted than in the time of Juvenal, and consequent- [...] Horace, who writ when the language was in the height of its perfec- [...]'. This seems to imply that Persius came after Juvenal, which is an [...] mistake seeing that Persius died in A.D. 62—a date very close to [...]al's birth. Presumably it is just a slip, for on p. 103 we are told that in [...]ing only one main subject in each satire 'Juvenal...has chosen to [...]w the same method of Persius'.

[...]6 is aimed at a cowardly libeller. Cassius fearlessly denounced men [...]women of high rank (Tac. *Ann.* I. 72). He died about A.D. 34, over [...]years after the poem was written.
[...]J. Kenney, *Proc. Camb. Phil. Soc.* n.s. VIII (1962), 38.
[...]he article on Horace in the *Oxford Classical Dictionary* says 'Horace's [...]ur...is directed against...foibles rather than vices'.

3 F. Schulz, *Classical Roman Law* (Oxford, 1951), p. 107. On the meaning of *humanitas* see the same author's *Principles of Roman Law* (Oxford, 1936), ch. 10. In his discussion of the falling birth rate Schulz also quotes para. 100 of the *Report of the Royal Commission on Population* (1949): 'The number of children tended to be limited also...because the fewer the children in the family the more could be spent on each child, and the better start it might have in life.' This is partly what H. Last had in mind when he spoke of the standard of living rising faster than people's incomes (*Cambridge Ancient History*, X, 437). Such considerations no doubt affected the rising middle class, but their influence on the really wealthy is less clear.

4 See, for example, Cic. *Phil.* 2. 40–1, *Att.* 1. 16. 10; Pliny, *Epist.* 8. 18; Plut. *Sulla* 38 and *Pomp.* 15.

5 F. von Woess, *Das römische Erbrecht und die Erbanwärter* (Berlin, 1911), lists the sources of our knowledge of the *Lex Voconia*.

6 See N. Lewis and M. Reinhold, *Roman Civilisation* (New York, 1955), II, 48–52, and *Cambridge Ancient History*, X, 441–56.

7 Many references are given in the notes of J. E. B. Mayor on Juv. 3. 129, 4. 19, and 12. 123. (A casual reader should be warned not to overlook Mayor's *Addenda*, which are printed in his first volume.)

8 Seneca, *De Consolatione ad Marciam*, 19. 2.

9 Tac. *Ann.* 15. 19.

10 L. Friedländer, *Roman Life and Manners under the Early Empire*, Eng. trans. by L. A. Magnus, I, pp. 213–16; S. Dill, *Roman Society from Nero to Marcus Aurelius* (reprinted by Meridian Library, New York, 1957), see index s.v. *captation*. Cf. *Cambridge Ancient History*, X, 438 f. The fullest treatment of the phenomenon is in the dissertation of D. Schmid, *Der Erbschleicher in der antiken Satire* (Tübingen, 1951).

11 Cf. Hom. *Od.* 20. 18.

12 Cf. such passages as Herodotus 1. 55 and 6. 77.

13 Juv. 4. 37–8. It should, of course, be remembered that Domitian was dead at the time of writing.

14 The emotional power of this rhetorical figure may be seen in *Epod.* 16. 3–10 and Virg. *Aen.* 2. 197–8. Notice also the spluttering plosives.

15 Quoted by Lejay on v. 76.

16 Ovid, *Am.* 1. 8. 43.

17 Horace's *captator* has many points of contact with the flatterer and the parasite as portrayed in Theophrastus and Graeco-Roman comedy. A large amount of comparative material on the flatterer will be found in O. Ribbeck, 'Kolax', *Abh. der Königl. Sächs. Ges. d. Wiss.* (Philologisch-Historische Classe 9 (Leipzig, 1883). See also R. G. Ussher's commentary on the *Characters* of Theophrastus (London, 1960), pp. 43–50. Within Horace's work reference may be made to *Sat.* 1. 9 and to those rather uncomfortable epistles 1. 17 and 1. 18.

18 Cf. Petronius, *Sat.* 116. What exactly is the relevance of the Nasica/Coranus anecdote? Most editors think that its purpose was to instil caution. But if Ulysses was to avoid the fate of Nasica he should have been told where Nasica went wrong. This is not at all clear. Perhaps he should have contrived to see the will before handing over his daughter; but there is no indication of that in the text. Certainly in his reluctance to read the will (67) Nasica complied with one of Tiresias' own maxims (51–2). Or did Tiresias mean to suggest that even the best rules did not always guarantee success? Again there is no hint of this in the text. I suspect that strictly speaking there is no relevance, and that the tale was included simply because it was too piquant and too topical to be omitted. The absence of logical rigour is concealed by the oracular darkness of vv. 55–60.

19 Cf. Virg. *Ecl.* 7. 42; Hor. *Carm.* 3. 17. 10.

20 The proverbial expression is discussed by G. W. Williams in *CR*, n.s. IX (1959), 97–100. Passages concerning the behaviour of the ancient bitch are also collected by M. M. Gillies in the *Annals of Archaeology and Anthropology*, XIV, 51–4.

21 See W. B. Stanford, *The Ulysses Theme* (Oxford, 1954), pp. 96–100, and his references.

22 *Ibid.* pp. 121–7. The distinction between the use of example and the use of allegory is emphasized by J. Tate in *Eranos*, LI (1953), 14–22.

23 R. Hercher, *Epistolographi Graeci* (Paris, 1873), pp. 211–12.

24 A translation by H. G. Evelyn-White is to be found in the Loeb series, printed after the same scholar's rendering of Hesiod and the Homeric Hymns.

25 *Ibid.* pp. 536–9.

26 E. D. Phillips, *Greece and Rome*, n.s. VI (1959), 66.

27 E. Pfuhl, *Malerei und Zeichnung der Griechen*, II, 598. Illustration in III, 358, no. 800; or in *Enciclopedia Dell'Arte Antica*, III, 163.

28 E. Pfuhl, *op. cit.* III, 249, nos. 615 and 616; Jongkees and Verdenius, *Platenatlas Bij Homerus* (Haarlem, 1955), nos. 42 and 43; M. Bieber, *Die Denkmäler zum Theaterwesen im Altertum* (Berlin and Leipzig, 1920), pp. 154–5. Other caricatures of heroes will be found on the Phlyakes vases, reproduced in Bieber, pls. 76–86. See also A. D. Trendall, *Paestan Pottery* (London, 1936), esp. pp. 28–9 and fig. 13.

29 W. 565–6.

30 W. 567–73. For a discussion of this fragment see p. 113 above, and the accompanying note.

31 B. 471.

32 See G. Ettig, 'Acheruntica', *Leipz. St. z. Class. Phil.* XIII (1890), 251–410.

33 D.L. 9. 111. Cf. C. Wachsmuth, *Sillogr. Graec. Rel.* (1885), II, 39–40.

34 D.L. 6. 101. The pitiful remnants of Menippus ar[...] the appendix to his edition of Varro (Leipzig, 18[...]

35 Some of the characteristics of Menippus are m[...] *Double Indictment*, 33.

36 B. 405–10, esp. 407. This interpretation was m[...] by Vahlen in his *Conjectanea* (Leipzig, 1858), ar[...] *op. cit.* p. 476.

37 D.L. 2. 126. The ὄγκον is a conjecture of Diels[...]

38 D.L. 6. 18. Wachsmuth thinks that παντοφυῆ [...]

39 D.L. 7. 15. The words σμικρὸς ἐών are a conje[...]

40 Martial 8. 27; cf. 11. 67 and 12. 40.

41 W. Y. Sellar, *Horace and the Elegiac Poets* (Ox[...]

42 I have translated Housman's supplement.

CHAPTER IX

1 *Epist.* 2. 2. 46–7. The happy place was Athens[...]

2 Permanence is the main idea here: cf. Virg[...] *Carm.* 2. 2. 22, *Epist.* 2. 2. 171–4.

3 Cf. Callimachus, *Aetia* 1. 23–4; Virg. *Ecl.* [...]

4 *Praelambens* is often taken as an extension [...] of 'furtively licking beforehand'. I prefer [...] straightforward continuation of *ipsis fung*[...] gracious host and a polite servant. His dig[...] at this point, otherwise the catastrophe [...] usually adduced, e.g. 1. 3. 81, are inexa[...] are being taken away.

5 Cf. Pindar, Frags. 9 and 80 (Bowra). T[...] by Fraenkel, pp. 140 and 292–3.

6 For parallels see Fraenkel on *Agamemno*[...]

7 *Sat.* 2. 5. 32–3.

8 The Thracian Chick and the Arab we[...]

9 R. A. Brower, *Alexander Pope. The* [...] p. 172.

10 See W. S. Maguinness, *Hermathena*, [...] 27–46.

11 The qualifications which I have in m[...] Horace invites his friends is usually [...] business, and is often limited to a [...] example, *Carm.* 4. 12. 26–8 with th[...] 2. 6. 95–7. In spite of the verbal si[...] *part* of the difference consists in t[...] passage. Or again, an ode like 1. 2[...]

6 P. 155.

7 W. S. Anderson reminds us that not all of Juvenal's satires are prompted by indignation—*CP*, LVII (1962), 145–60. I have made no distinction in this chapter between Juvenal the declaimer (or actor) and Juvenal the man, not because I believe that the two are always identical but because the whole question of the relation between biography and criticism is too difficult and controversial to open here. My opinions, such as they are, will be found in 'The Style and the Man', *Phoenix*, XVIII (1964), 216–31. As for Juvenal's biography, it is a pity that Highet's interesting reconstruction, which was suggested as a hypothesis in *TAPA* (1937), should have hardened into assertion in the course of *Juvenal the Satirist* (1954) and appeared as undoubted fact in *Poets in a Landscape* (1957). It has been accepted as an authentic record by Miss Mary Lascelles in *New Light on Dr Johnson*, ed. F. W. Hillis (Yale, 1959).

8 Cf. H. Gifford, *Rev. Eng. Stud.* VI (1955), 157–65; D. Eichholz, *Greece and Rome*, n.s. III (1956), 61–9; J. Butt and M. Lascelles in their contributions to *New Light on Dr Johnson*, ed. F. W. Hillis (Yale, 1959); and esp. H. A. Mason, in *Critical Essays on Roman Literature. Satire*, ed. J. P. Sullivan (London, 1963), pp. 107–23.

9 Zimri is chosen by Dryden himself as an example of fine raillery.

10 Macrobius 2. 4. 21.

11 *Epod.* 9 and *Carm.* I. 37, which celebrate the defeat of a foreign enemy, fall outside the domain of *satura*.

12 See H. W. Pleket, *Mnem.* s. 4, XIV (1961), 296–315.

13 K. H. Waters, *Phoenix*, XVIII (1964), 76.

14 R. Syme, *Tacitus* (Oxford, 1958), II, 778.

15 E. J. Kenney, *op. cit.*, has some realistic remarks on this. His quotation of Quintilian 9. 2. 68 is particularly apt.

16 G. Highet, *Juvenal the Satirist* (Oxford, 1954), p. 51.

BIBLIOGRAPHICAL NOTE

Surveys of modern Horatian scholarship will be found in

L'Année Philologique.

K. Büchner, *Bursians Jahresberichte*, CCLXVII, 1939.

E. Burck, Bibliographical appendix to Kiessling–Heinze's commentary (Berlin, 1957), 353–413.

W. S. Anderson, *CW*, L (1956), 33–40, and *CW*, LVII (1964), 293–301.

E. Thummer, *Anzeiger für die Altertumswissenschaft*, XV (1962), 129–50.

Works which proved of immediate assistance in preparing this book have been cited in the notes. The authors are mentioned in Index 2.

INDEXES

1. HORATIAN PASSAGES QUOTED OR REFERRED TO

*Figures in bold type indicate the pages on which the
main treatment will be found*

Satires

I. 1 (*whole*) **12–16**; 20–3; **27–30**;
35; 153; 159–60; 172–3; 185;
189; 194; 197
(*lines*) (7), 107; (14), 291; (38–
40), 185; (49–51), 276; (54–
6), 276; (59), 287; (59–60),
276; (68), 295; (69–70), 155;
(70–9), 261; (71), 185; (95),
292; (100), 295; (101), 141;
(101 ff.), 166; (102), 142 and
294; (108), **274–5**; (111), 278;
(112), 278; (114–16), 278;
(120), 291

I. 2 (*whole*) **9–12**; 14–16; 20; 24–5;
27; **30–3**; 35; 66; 88; 92; 98;
105; 139; 152–3; 160; 191;
194; 196–7; 240; 246; 263;
286
(*lines*) (1), 111; (3), 292; (12),
138; (17), 278; (25), 143 and
148; (27), 138 and 295; (31),
143; (36), 143; (41), 135;
(46), 294; (48), 135; (49),
135; (54), 135; (55), 292;
(57–9), 193; (64), 132 and
136; (64–5), 146; (74), 276;
(76), 286; (81), 137; (113),
112; (121), 295; (124), 276;
(134), 133 and 291

I. 3 (*whole*) **1–9**; 12; 14–16; 20;
25–8; **33–5**; 139; 153; 160;
189; 194
(*lines*) (4), 292; (20), 106; (21),
140; (38–9), 274; (47), 138;
(63–5), 153; (81), 305; (82),
136 and 294; (86), 134; (107),
295; (124), 238; (129), 292–3;
(130), 136; (139), 291

I. 4 (*whole*) 47; 49; **88–92**; 94; 101;
118–19; 128; 153; 160; 259;
286

(*lines*) (8 ff.), 105; (9–12), 98;
(13), 103; (14), 291; (19–21),
107; (21–2), 120 and 132;
(26), 218; (28), 292 and 294;
(38), 101; (41), 107; (56–62),
107; (65 f.), 294; (69), 141;
(70), 294; (72), 292–3; (92),
138; (105 ff.), 153; (109), 136
and 292; (110), 148; (110–
14), 137; (112), 295

I. 5 (*whole*) **54–64**; 65; 81; 134;
160; 253; 254; 269; 296
(*lines*) (2), 112 and 147; (21),
285; (34), 295; (52), 291;
(56–7), 282; (79), 100; (87),
112; (100), 295; (101–3), 209

I. 6 (*whole*) 15; 35; **36–53**; 81; 84;
152–3; 159–60; 175; 194;
224; 248; 252; 254; 263; 280
(*lines*) (12), 138; (19), 252; (24),
279; (24 f.), 134; (30), 294;
(38), 295; (40), 144 and 279;
(42), 285; (45), 274; (51–2),
279; (63–4), 279; (65 ff.),
248; (107), 279; (108), 134;
(109), 288; (113–14), 73;
(115–18), 300; (121), 134 and
144; (124), 138; (126), 111;
(130), 252

I. 7 (*whole*) **64–7**; 160; 262; 269;
296
(*lines*) (2), 111 and 134; (26–7),
110

I. 8 (*whole*) **67–74**; 148; 160; 240;
262; 296
(*lines*) (11), 143 and 294; (22),
283; (25), 148; (39), 138

I. 9 (*whole*) **74–85**; 160; 222; 253;
259; 303
(*lines*) (6), 287; (11), 155; (13),
285; (14–15), 284; (18), 284;
(19), 284; (25), 292–3; (26–7),

Satires (cont.)
284; (27–8), 284; (44), 285;
(45), 285; (62), 284; (70),
147; (78), 113
1. 10 (*whole*) 47; 82; 86; **92–5**; 101;
120; 136; 153; 158; 160; 259
(*lines*) (preliminary verses 87;
118–19; 289); (1–2), 105;
(3–4), 91; (5–8), 97; (9–10),
105; (12), 107; (14–15), 115
and 266; (14–17), 97; (17–
18), 292; (17–19), 292; (18),
293; (19), 118 and 289; (20–
30), 111; (22), 120 and 147;
(23–4), 119; (36), 120 and
147; (36–7), 289; (38), 119;
(40), 295; (46), 87; (48), 87;
(50–1), 98; (51), 107; (53),
109 and 288; (54), 108; (56–
73), 105; (57), 286–7; (59),
112; (59–60), 106; (61 f.),
138; (61–4), 107; (67), 107;
(67–71), 98; (74–6), 124;
(78), 144; (80), 120 and 292–
3; (90), 292; (90–1), 119 and
293
2. 1 (*whole*) **124–31**; 136; 150; 160–
1; 209; 256–7
(*lines*) (1), 154 and 157; (1–4),
118; (10–12), 108 and 256–7;
(12–13), 108; (22), 143 and
294; (23), 151; (46), 289;
(47–56), 139; (48), 140; (79),
291
2. 2 (*whole*) 159–61; **161–73**; 194–5;
197; 200; 206; 251; 262–3
(*lines*) (2), 144; (9–13), 297;
(41), 216; (46–8), 140; (47),
297; (55), 143; (56), 143;
(62), 297; (64), 143; (65–6),
217; (66–8), 141; (68–9), 142;
(77), 297; (98–9), 297; (112),
144
2. 3 (*whole*) 20; 153; 160; **173–88**;
194–5; 240; 288
(*lines*) (16), 136; (21), 295; (31),
297; (33), 295; (44), 297;
(69 ff.), 147; (71–3), 299;
(75), 147; (84), 292; (86),
106; (100), 292; (116–17),
297; (133), 295; (142), 143;
(142 ff.), 141; (175), 147 and

294; (185), 254; (186), 298;
(187), 295; (187 ff.), 295;
(197), 298; (224), 294; (239),
136–7 and 148; (243), 136;
(259–64), 193; (276), 298;
(303), 295; (308 ff.), 156;
(310), 134; (317), 297; (318),
297
2. 4 (*whole*) 160; 175; 200; **202–13**;
220; 241
(*lines*) (1), 148 and 301; (2),
301; (3), 301; (6), 301; (8),
301; (10), 301; (11), 301;
(32), 302; (44), 220
2. 5 (*whole*) 20; 154; 160–1; **224–
42**; 255
(*lines*) (1), 295; (18), 295; (32–
3), 305; (32–7), 74; (39–40),
283; (40), 120 and 136; (40–
1), 289; (41), 136 and 295;
(51–2), 304; (55–60), 304;
(57), 134; (62–4), 255–6; (67),
304; (76), 295; (91), 295;
(100), 295; (101), 295
2. 6 (*whole*) 20; 152–4; 160–1; 173;
200; **243–57**; 263
(*lines*) (16), 252; (17), 154; (38),
255; (42–3), 280; (49), 41;
(55–6), 255; (63–4), 300;
(72), 143; (78), 295; (95–7),
305; (108), 305; (109), 305;
(117), 252
2. 7 (*whole*) 160; **188–201**
(*lines*) (2), 295; (9), 138; (15),
138; (17), 112; (20), 299;
(43), 288; (45), 291; (47),
299; (47–52), 98; (49), 299;
(50), 299; (54), 295; (56–61),
299; (59–61), 274; (63–4),
299; (64–7), 299; (71), 299;
(78), 107; (82), 299; (93),
299; (94), 299; (95), 299;
(97), 140
2. 8 (*whole*) 159; 160; **213–23**; 259;
262
(*lines*) (1), 148 and 295; (15),
302; (23), 294; (24), 143;
(25), 294; (46), 207; (60), 294
Epistles
1. 1 (14), 20; (41), 100; (74–5), 100;
(106), 238
1. 2 234–5

1.4   (1), 154; (15–16), 156
1.5   (21–4), 212
1.7   252
1.8   (12), 200
1.10   284
1.15   (26–41), 140
1.17   303
1.18   303
1.19   158
        (34), 287
1.20   156
2.1   (175–6), 116; (250), 154
2.2   (22), 296; (46–7), 305; (60), 18
        and 154; (171–4), 305
Ars Poetica (48–53), 117
Odes
1.20   305
        (1–2), 300
1.22   284
        (10), 121
1.31   (15–16), 300
1.37   254; 307
2.2   (22), 305

2.10   (13–15), 169
2.17   73
3.2   (6), 79
3.3   199
3.5   199
3.17   (10), 304
3.21   306
4.12   306
        (26–8), 305
Epodes
3   (8), 148
4   259
     (17–20), 48
5   148
     (43), 148; (59), 148
6   259; 306
7   306
9   254; 307
16   306
     (3–10), 303
17   148
     (66), 281

2. NAMES AND TOPICS

Bold figures indicate the pages on which the main treatment will be found. Hyphens do not necessarily indicate continuous discussion. Names which occur only in chapter v have been omitted.

Academy, 18–19
Accius, 79, 109, 281
Adultery, **9–12**, 24–5, 31, 190–2, 196
Aeschrion, 29, 278
Aeschylus, 174
Aesopus, son of, 136–7, 180
Agamemnon, 179–80, 184–5; *see also* Atrides
Agrippa, 72, 254
Ajax, 146, 179–80, 295, 298
Albucius, 114, 141, 143, 166, 293–4
Alexis, 203, 278
Alfenus, 4, 136–7, (292)
Allen, W., 210, 217, 301–2
Alpinus, *see* Furius
Ambition, **36–53**, 179–80, 184
Anaxippus, 203, 300
Anderson, W. S., 121, 282, 285, 290, 307
André, J., 296, 300
Andrewes, M., 279
Antigonus, 209
Antiphanes, 299
Antisthenes, 234–5, 238
Antony, 36–7, 54, 87, 120, 150, 152, 254–5, 269–70, 279–80
Apicius, 207, 218–19, 302
Apollo, 23, 76, 79–81, 84, 104, 109, 113, 230, 248, 285
Appian, 36, 54, 169
Apuleius, 205, 282, 290, 300
Archestratus, 204–6, 288
Arellius, 146, 252, 295–6
Aristippus, xi, 18, 138, 213, 276–8, 292
Aristius Fuscus, 75–7, 82, 97, 284
Aristophanes, 17, 88–9, 94, 97, 109, 150, 236–7, 298
Aristotle, 10, 23, 26–7, 96, 183, 209, 250, 284, 287, 296, 299, 301
Arnobius, 69, 282
Arrius, sons of, 136–7, 180
Ashby, T., 285
Ashworth, W. D., 279
Athenaeus, 164, 187, 204, 210, 288, 296–7, 300–2

Athenion, 202
Atrides, 146, 295; *see also* Agamemnon
Augustine, 69, 282
Ausonius, 281
Avidienus, 143, 166, 169–70

Babrius, 176–7
Bacon, F., 65
Baehrens, E., 142
Bailey, C., 301, 306
Balsdon, J. P. V. D., 302
Bardon, H., 119, 289
Barrus, 38, 294
Becher, W., 291
Becker, C., 274
Bell, H. I., 283
Bentley, R., 147
Bieber, M., 304
Bion, **17–18**, 21, 49, 154, 277–8, 280
Birth, **36–53**
Bischoff, A., 282
Bishop, M., 205, 300
Bo, D., 106, 287
Boas, G., 306
Bogaert, R., 284
Bolanus, 76, 155
Boll, F., 160, 296
Bore, *see* Pest
Boswell, J., 55, 197, (281)
Bourciez, J., 287
Boyancé, P., 306
Brandt, P., 300, 302
Brillat-Savarin, 161, 300
Brink, C. O., 275, 286
Brower, R., 250, 296, 305
Buchheit, V., 282
Bücheler, F., xi, 282, 286
Büchner, K., 279, 285, 296
Burck, E., 289
Butt, J., 307

Caesar, Augustus, *see* Octavian
Caesar, Julius, 19, 36, 51, 64–6, 72, 80, 119–20, 139, 164, 255–6, 280–1, 289

Callimachus, 32–3, 96, 118, 278, 290, 305
Calvus, 93, **118–22**, 139, 292–3
Campbell, A. Y., 286
Canidia, 71–2, 126–7, 140, 148–9, 258–9
Caprius, 90–1, 101, 294
Cartault, A., 142, 149, 291, 294
Cassius, a poet, 107, 138
Cassius Severus, 258–9, 306
Castagnoli, F., 285
Cataudella, Q., 277
Catius, 148, 175, 200–1, **202–13**, 215, 220–1, 301
Cato, 11, 31, 183, 255, 293, 299
Cato, Valerius, 87, **118–21**, 124, 279, 289–90
Catullus, 60, 66, 68, 79, 93, 105, **118–23**, 147, 274, 278, 284, 290, 292–3
Celsus, 181, 206, 298
Cercidas, 25, 277
Cervius, 126, 139
Chrysippus, 4, 174, 178, 186–7, 238
Cicero, 19–20, 24, 27–9, 43, 46–7, 49–51, 53, 64–5, 77, 87, 94, 96, 101–2, 105, 109–10, 112, 130–1, 137–9, 141, 164, 171, 181, 187, 203, 213, 215, 274–81, 288, 291–2, 294, 296, 298–300, 302–3
Cichorius, C., xi, 114, 142, 274, 288–90, 294
Cicirrus, see Messius
Cinna, 120, 290
Clausen, W., 302
Columella, 209, 217, 294, 301
Conington, J., 155
Coranus, 229–30, 304
Corbett, P. E., 302
Corcoran, T. H., 301
Courbaud, E., 149, 154, 295
Cranston, M., 300
Crates, 17, 29, 234, 275, 278
Crispinus, 4, 89, 107, 133, 150, 190, 195–6, 199, 291
Cumont, F., 282
Cupiennius, 11, 143, 145
Cynicism, **17–21**, 25, 192, 206, 234, 237

Dacier, Mme, 231
Daiches, D., 84, 285
Dama, 146, 191, 229, 234, 295

Damasippus, 136–7, 147, **173–88**, 194–5, 240, 292, 297
Damoxenus, 300
D'Antò, V., 282
Davus, 98, 146, **188–201**, 295
Deckman, A. A., 285
De Gubernatis, L., 277
De Lacy, P. H., 275
Demetrius, 95, 123–4, 136, 259, 290, 293
Democritus, xi, 22, 276, 278
Deutsch, M., 282
De Zulueta, F., 298
Diels, H., 305
Dill, S., 227, 303
Dio Cassius, 51, 54, 72, 135, 271, 280
Dio Chrysostom, 277, 297
Diodorus, 283
Diogenes, 17–18, 28, 97, 213, 276–7, 299
Diogenes Laertius, xi, 24, 97, 237, 275–8, 280, 284, 299, 305–6
Diomedes, 157, 290
Discontent, **12–14**, 16, 20–2, 189, 193–4
Dohm, H., 300
Donatus, 98, 142, 290, 294
Dorsch, J., 60, 282
Douglas, N., 282
Dryden, J., 65, **258–73**, 282, 306–7
Dudley, D. R., 275
Düntzer, H., 57
Duff, A. M., 280–1

Earl, D. C., 296
Edmonds, J. M., xi, 300
Eggermont, P. H. L., 291
Eichholz, D., 307
Eitrem, S., 283
Ellis, R., 274
Ennius, 31, 86–8, 92, 98, 108–9, 117, 122–3, 141, 205, 255, 278, 298
Epictetus, 183, 198, 276–8, 299
Epicureanism, 7, 17, 19–20, 183, 192, 209, 250–1, 263, 306
Epicurus, 22–5, 97, 112, 183, 209, 250–1, 276
Ettig, G., 304
Eubulus, 25, 277
Euphron, 203
Euripides, 22
Evelyn-White, H. G., 304
Extravagance, 180, 184

Fabius, 10, 133, 291
Fairclough, H. R., 292
Fairness, 6–8
Fannius, 89, 101, 120, 132, 136, 259, 293
Fiske, G. C., xi, 208, 215, 238, 275, 287, 291, 295, 301–2
Fletcher, G. B. A., 275
Flower, B., 301
Fosdick, D., 300
Fraenkel, E., xi, 5, 11, 59–60, 66, 79, 129, 152–3, 158, 240, 274–6, 279, 282, 285–6, 291–2, 294, (295), 299, 301, 305–6
Frank, T., 56, 119–21, 147, 281, 286, 289, 292, 295
Frazer, J., 283
Freedom, 37–8, 42, 44–5, 47, 50–1, **188–201**, 299–300
Friedländer, L., 227, 293, 303
Fritzsche, 60
Fufidius, 9, 30, 138, 278
Fundanius, 95, 144, 217–20, 222
Furius, (95), 120, 136, 145, 147, 234, **289–90**, 295
Furius Bibaculus, 120, 124, 289–90
Furneaux, H., 296
Fuscus, *see* Aristius

Galen, 210, 217, 302
Gallonius, 140, 142, 166–7, 296, 302
Gargonius, 27, 138, 146, 295
Gastronomy, **202–23**, 300–2
Gellius, Aulus, 109, 135, 205, 286, 288, 296, 300
Gentius, 290
Gerhard, G. A., 299
Gibbon, E., 57, 282
Gifford, H., 307
Gigante, M., 277
Gillies, M. M., 304
Gluttony, **161–73**, 296–7
Gow, A. S. F., 283
Gow, J., 281, 297
Grant, M. A., 287
Greed, 12–14, 21–2, 29, 178–9, 183–5
Greek, **111–14**, 116–17, 123
Grimal, P., 207, 301
Grube, G. M. A., 287
Grupp, H., 281
Guthrie, W. K. C., 276

Hadas, M., 295
Hahn, E. A., 295
Halm, K., 299
Hamilton, W., 70
Handford, S. A., 275
Harrison, E. L., 274
Haupt, P., 281
Hauthal, F., 294
Heichelheim, F. M., 163
Heinze, R., 20, 66, 75, 131, 140, 143, 194, 272, 276, 286–7, 291, 296, 299, 301
Helen, 4, 113, 146, 288, 295
Heliodorus, 61, 147
Hendrickson, G. L., 52, 154, 279, 286, 289, 296
Hense, O., xi, 300
Heracleides, 214, 302
Hermogenes, 4, 90, 93, 95, **118–24**, 136, 259, 290, 292–3
Herodotus, 303
Herter, H., 274, 276, 282
Highet, G., 272, 295, 307
Hippolochus, 214, 302
Hoffman, 203, 300
Hofmann, E., 289
Homer, 78–9, 108, 113, 170, 174, 204, 214, 220, 228–9, 231, 234–5, 238, 283, 302–3
Housman, A. E., 142, 294, 302, 305
Hubert, H., 283

Iliad, *see* Homer
Illuminati, L., 281
Inconsistency, 5, 7, 27–8, 189–90
Isocrates, 277

Johnson, S., 192, 253–4, (267)
Jolowicz, H. F., 302
Jones, W. H. S., 302
Jongkees, J. H., 304
Jonson, B., 74, 283
Journey to Brundisium, **54–64**, 280–2
Juvenal, 38, 43, 52, 61, 87, 98, 110, 125–6, 130, 132, 185, 222–3, 230, 240–2, **258–73**, 274, 277, 279, 288, 290–1, 295, 303, 306–7

Keller, O., 291
Kenney, E. J., 291, 306–7
Kent, R., 287
Klebs, E., 292

INDEXES

Klingner, F., 279
Knoche, U., 275

Labeo, 3, 136–7, 292, 294
Lactantius, 69, 101, 281–2
Laevinus, 37, 39, 49, 138
Lafaye, G., 281, 283
La Fontaine, 177–8
Lascelles, M., 307
Last, H., 303
Legacy-hunting, **224–42**, 303–4
Lehmann-Hartleben, K., 293
Lejay, P., 171, 186, 212, 237, 272, 276, 285, 291, 294, 299, 301–3, 305
Leo, F., 89, 286, 294
Lewis, N., 303
Literary criticism, **86–131**, 286–91
Livy, 38, 53, 64, 79, 162, 280, 296
Lovejoy, A. O., 306
Lucian, 73, 97, 215, 237–9, 305
Lucilius xi, 14, 25, 29, 38, 45, 47, 54–6, 60, 66, 73, 76–7, **86–131**, 140–3, 149–50, 153–8, 164, 167, 171, 182–3, 215–16, 221, 236, 239, 256, 261, 269–99, 302
Luck, G., 283
Lucretius, 19–21, 25–6, 28, 33, 62–3, 105, 112, 170, 209, 247, 251, 276, 278, 301, 306
Lugli, G., 285
Lynceus, 214, 302

Macedo, 290
McGann, M. J., 193, 299
Mackay, L. A., 288
Macrobius, 68, 110, 164, 289, 292, 296, 307
Madness, **174–88**, 298
Maecenas, 3, 10, 12–13, **36–53**, 54–61, 66–85, 95, 124, 127, 134, 144, 148, 152–3, 160, 175, 189–90, 200–1, 217, 221–2, **245–55**, 270, 279–80, 293, 298, 306
Maenius, 2, 5, 7, 140, 142, 293
Maguinness, W. S., 305
Maltinus, 27, 143, 148
Margites, 235
Mariotti, I., 114, 287–9
Marouzeau, J., 285, 291, 293, 295
Martial, 68, 149, 227, 239, 277, 295–6, 305
Martin, J., 214, 302

Marx, F., 103, 111, 120, 142, 286–7, 294
Mason, H. A., 307
Matron, 214, 302
Maximus, 20–1
Mayor, J. E. B., 274, 295, 303
Mean, the, 9–12, 23, 27, 31
μεμψιμοιρία, **13–14**, 189, 197; *see also* Discontent
Menander, xi, 17, 29–30, 150, 183, 278, 298–9
Menippus, 97, 214–15, 237–9, 305
Mercury, 243–4, 247–8
Merit, 41–4, **49–51**
Messalla, 82, 94–5, 124
Messius Cicirrus, 57, 63–4, 134, 269, 282
Mice, fable of, 246, 250–2
Momigliano, A., 275, 306
Monod, Th., 301
Morris, E. P., 172, 295
Müller, L., 141–2
Münzer, F., 292–3
Mulvius, 189–90
Munro, H. A. J., 288
Musurillo, H., 54

Naevolus, 241
Namatianus, Rutilius, 281
Names, **132–59**, 291–6
Nasica, 134, 229–30, 304
Nasidienus, 142, 146, 148, 207, **213–23**, 246, 259, 262, 295
Némethy, G., 155, 298
Neoterics, 105, **118–24**, 289–90
Neudling, C. L., 289
New Comedy, 17, 62, 92, 203, 300
Nicomachus, 203, 300
Nilsson, N.-O., 287
Nisbet, R. G. M., 279, 284
Nomentanus, 125, 130, 141–3, 147, 183, 221–3
Nonius, 143
Norwood, G., 282
Novius, 134, 144, 279
Noyes, A., 282

O'Brien-Moore, A., 298
Octavian, 2, 36–7, 54, 61, (82), 108, 124–5, 127–8, (130), 139, 145, 152, 156, 163, 169, 227, 230, 254–7, 269–70, 279–80, 289

315

Odysseus, *see* Ulysses
Odyssey, *see* Homer
Ofellus, 143–4, 151, **165–73**, 194–6, 200–1, 206, 212–13, 217, 251, 262
Old Comedy, 88–93, 157, 286
Oltramare, A., 275
Opimius, 141, 143, 179, 185, 188
Orelli, I. G., 127
Ovid, 66, 68, 231, 278, 281, 283, 296, 303

Pacuvius, 86, 109
Page, T. E., 295
Palmer, A., 145, 171, 218–19, 280, 284, 291, 295, 297, 302
Panaetius, 18–19, 27, 96–7, 117, 275, 277
Pantilius, 136, 144, 259, 293
Pantolabus, 130, 143
Paschall, D. M., 298
Pausias, 193
Payne Knight, R., 282–3
Penelope, 146, 231, 233, 236, 295
Perret, J., 255, 288–9, 306
Perry, B. E., 177, 298
Persius (the mongrel), **64–8**, 110–11, 134, 269
Persius (the poet), 38, 87, 98, 125, 130, 155–7, 259–61, 281, 288, 297, 302, 306
Pest, the, **74–85**, 253, 259, 283–5
Petronius, 77, 227, 279, 285, 304
Pfuhl, E., 236, 304
Phaedrus, 177, 291
φιλαργυρία, **13–14**, 21
Philemon, 25, 277, 299
Phillips, E. D., 235–6, 304
Philodemus, 19, 25, 31–2, 96, 145–6, 277, 287, 295
Phoenix, 183, 299
Pindar, 305
Pitholaus, 120, 147, 289
Pitholeon, 94, 120, 147
Platner, S. B., 285
Plato, 23–9, 96, 170, 173, 183, 208, 214, 220, 275, 277, 284, 297, 299, 301
Plautus, 62, 68, 77, 79, 104, 111, 116, 171, 193, 203, 285, 297–8
Pleket, H. W., 307
πλεονεξία, 14, 21
Pliny the Elder, 41, 72, 89, 162, 182, 206, 209–11, 216–17, 282, 296, 298, 301–2
Pliny the Younger, 43, 227, 271, 279–80, 296, 303
Plutarch, 47, 183, 234, 278–80, 298–9, 303
Pollio, 82, 95, 124, 269
Polybius, 18, 162, 296
Pompeius, Sextus, 37, 54, 57, 269
Pompey, 36, 87, 120–1, 145, 162, 289
Porcius, 143–4, 222
Porphyrion, 97, 109, 121, 132, 140–2, 148, 167, 182, 216, 279, 281, 284, 287–8, 294
Priapus, 67–74, 282–3
Priscus, 138–9, 188–90, 201, 220
Propertius, 74, 147, 284, 288
pseudo-Acron, 31, 132, 135, 146, 279, 289, 293–4
pseudo-Hippocrates, 20–2
pseudo-Plato, 20, 22, 187, 276
Puelma Piwonka, M., 290

Quintilian, 43, 101, 103, 156, 279–80, 286, 307

Radermacher, L., 278, 294
Reinhold, M., 303
Rex, Rupilius, **64–8**, 110, 269
Reynolds, R. W., 274
Ribbeck, O., 303
Richardson, L. J. D., 284
Robinson, R. P., 119, 289
Roby, H. J., 284, 302
Rose, H. J., 283
Rosenbaum, E., 301
Rudd, N. (articles cited, 279–80, 284–7, 291, 307)
Rufillus, 27, 138
Rufus, Sempronius, 167, 297
Ruso, 3, 134

Sallust, 50, 53, 87, 135, 162, 280, 296
'Sallust', 280
Salmon, E. T., 285
Sarmentus, 57, 63, 134, 269, 282, 291
Savage, J. J., 282
Scaeva, 126, 129, 139, 293
Schmid, D., 303

Scholiasts, 132, 147, 157, 292; *see also* Porphyrion and pseudo-Acron
Schütz, H., 280–1, 299
Schulz, F., 225, 298, 303
Scipio Aemilianus, 18, 86, 102, 104, (107), 112, 116, 125, 127, 129, (149), 256, 275
Scott, K., 279
Sellar, W. Y., 240–2, 305
Seneca, 227, 234, 295, 303
Sex, **9–12**, 15, 24–5, 31–3, 180, **190–3**, 196–7
Shero, L. R., 125, 215, 290–1, 302
Sidonius, 157
Siedow, A., 106
Sisyphus, 146, 174, 295
Smith, K. F., 283
Smith, R. E., 291
Socrates, 22, 96, 170, 186–7, 208, 250, 277, 301
Sonnet, P., 290
Sophocles, 228, 298
Sosipater, 203, 300
Souilhé, J., 276
Staberius, 138, 178–9, 292
Stanford, W. B., 235, 304
Statius, 156
Steidl, W., 279
Stertinius, 133, 137, 145, 151, **174–88**, 195–6, 295
Stevenson, C. L., 280
Stewart, Z., 276
Stoicism, 7–9, 17–20, 25, 27, 139, 160, 164, 174, 178–9, 183, 185–7, 190–8, 206, 234, 238–9, 247, 250, 264
Sturtevant, E., 287
Suetonius, 72, 124, 143, 147, 156–7, 164, 279–80, 285–6, 296, 306
Sulcius, 90–1, 101, 294
Sulla, 36, 128, 132, 146, 162–3
Swift, J., 197–8, 241, 246–7
Syme, R., 135, 271–2, 280, 291, 307

Tacitus, 162, 165, 227, 271, 283, 289, 296, 303, 306
Tate, J., 304
Tatler, the, 74
Tavenner, E., 283
Taylor, L. R., 256, 278
Teles, xi, 21, 276, 278, 297
Terence, 30, 77, 98, 142, 171, 182–3, 193, 203, 276, (278), 290, 297, 299

Terzaghi, N., 142, 288, 291, 293–4
Thackeray, W., 219
Themistius, 278
Theocritus, 29, 71, 278
Theophrastus, 18, 74, 276, 303
Thrale, H., 219
Thucydides, 25, 277
Tibullus, 283, 296
Tigellius, 2, 5–6, 9, 15, 28, 111, 139, 189, 201, 220, 292–3
Tillius, 47, 134–5, 279
Timon, 237–8
Tiresias, 146, 154, 160, **226–42**, 257, 295, 304
Trebatius, 108, **124–31**, 132, 136, 155, 160, 209, 256–7, 290
Trendall, A. D., 304
Turius, 126, 139

Ullman, B. L., 292–4, 298
Ulysses, 146, 170, **228–42**, 295, 298, 304
Ummidius, 22, 138, 292
Ussher, R. G., 303

Vahlen, J., 298, 305
Valgius, 281
van Geytenbeek, A. C., 297
van Straaten, M., 275
Varius, 41, 52, 61, 82–3, 95, 144
Varro, xi, 20, 79, 87–9, 107, 122, 135, 141, 182–3, 205–6, 236–9, 255, 276, 278, 282, 286, 293, 298
Varro of Atax, 87, 120, 289
Verdenius, W. J., 304
Virgil, 41, 52, 56, 60–2, 79, 95, 115, 117, 120, 160, 247, 255, 278, 283, 290, 293, 303–5
Virro, 222–3, 262
Viscus, 82–3, 144
Vogel, Fr., 291, 293
Volanerius, 111, 138, 188–9
Von Arnim, H., 274
Von Woess, F., 303

Wachsmuth, C., 276, 304–5
Warmington, E. H., xi, 142, 290, 298
Waters, K., 270–1, 307
Wehrli, F., 290
Wesseling, 280
Wessely, C., 283
Wessner, P., 142, 294

INDEXES

Wickham, E. C., 141, 216, 291–2, 297, 302
Wight Duff, J., 281, 286
Wilkins, A., 295
Wilkinson, L. P., 282
Williams, G. W., 304
Wimmel, W., 274
Witchcraft, **70–4**, 283

Wright, F. A., 278

Xenophon, 96, 186, 214

Yavetz, Z., 296

Zeller, E., 275
Zeno, 234, 238, 299